The Bible in Arabic

Jews, Christians, and Muslims from the Ancient to the Modern World

Edited by Michael Cook, William Chester Jordan, and Peter Schäfer

A list of titles in this series appears at the back of the book.

The Bible in Arabic

THE SCRIPTURES OF THE "PEOPLE OF THE BOOK" IN THE LANGUAGE OF ISLAM

*

Sidney H. Griffith

PRINCETON UNIVERSITY PRESS
PRINCETON AND OXFORD

Published by Princeton University Press, 41 William Street,
Princeton, New Jersey 08540
In the United Kingdom: Princeton University Press, 6 Oxford Street,
Woodstock, Oxfordshire OX20 1TW

press.princeton.edu

Jacket art: Harley Trilingual Psalter, Palermo, Italy, between 1130 and 1154.
Psalm 81(80). BL Harley MS 5786, f.106v. Copyright © The British Library Board

ISBN 978-0-691-15082-6
Library of Congress Cataloging-in-Publication Data
Griffith, Sidney Harrison.
The Bible in Arabic : the Scriptures of the "People of the Book"
in the language of Islam / Sidney H. Griffith.
p. cm. — (Jews, Christians, and Muslims from the ancient to the modern world)
Includes bibliographical references and index.
ISBN 978-0-691-15082-6 (hardcover : alk. paper)
1. Bible. Arabic—Versions—History.
I. Title.
BS315.A69G75 2013
220.4'6—dc23
2012038720

British Library Cataloging-in-Publication Data is available

This book has been composed in ITC New Baskerville Std

Printed on acid-free paper. ∞

Printed in the United States of America

3 5 7 9 10 8 6 4 2

Dedicated to the memory of my brother,
Michael Joseph Griffith

Contents

⁕ Illustrations ⁕

* Preface *

IN THIS ERA of scholarly specialization, one is intensely aware of his limitations and of his debt to scholars better equipped than he to address even so seemingly simple a topic as the Bible in Arabic. For the fact is that in every chapter that follows one must rely on the work of scholars who have made the particular subject of that chapter the focus of their own studies. To venture into such territory not immediately one's own does indeed give one pause. Yet the contribution one hopes to make in undertaking the adventure is twofold: first to call attention to the central role the Bible and biblical lore have played in the unfolding of religious thought in Arabic in Islamic times, from Late Antiquity to the Middle Ages; and secondly to highlight the interreligious dimension of intellectual life in the Arabic-speaking world in the same period, even in biblical studies, albeit that it was often a discourse in counterpoint and nothing like the interreligious dialogue of which one speaks so readily in our times. But the fact is that religious and intellectual culture in the World of Islam in the classical period came together in a polyphony of voices in Arabic and the part of the Bible in that chorus, so often actually carrying the melody, has not received the broad recognition it deserves. It is the purpose of the present survey of the available scholarship to call attention to the historical, religious, and cultural importance of the Bible in Arabic, to encourage its continued study, and to provide some bibliographical guidance for the undertaking.

In writing this short book I have profited immensely from a semester's residence at the Hebrew University of Jerusalem's Institute for Advanced Studies at the invitation of Professor Mordechai Cohen of Yeshiva University and Professor Meir Bar Asher of the Hebrew University. The group they assembled there to study the cross-cultural reading of the Bible in the Middle Ages provided the opportunity for a daily colloquy with a community of scholars for whose counsel and inspiration I am profoundly grateful. Where else in the world could I go just next door to Meir Bar Asher's office with my problems in Arabic, or down the hall to Meira Polliack for guidance in Judaeo-Arabic and the history of Karaite biblical study, or around the corner to James Kugel for advice on interpretive strategies? Other scholars too have readily given me their help and advice. I thank in particular Prof. Alexander Treiger of Dalhousie University for much advice and bibliographical help, Dr. Ronny Vollandt for sharing with me his just finished and very rich doctoral dissertation on the Pentateuch in

Christian Arabic, and Dr. Adam C. McCollum of the Hill Monastic Library in Collegeville, MN, for his very helpful and still growing bibliography of the Bible in Arabic. I give thanks too to the publisher's readers who provided insightful comments on the original proposal for this book. I am grateful to Prof. Christine M. Bochen of Nazareth College of Rochester, New York, who has sustained my work every step of the way. I thank Fred Appel, Sara Lerner, and Sarah David of the Princeton University Press for their constant solicitude and ever-ready kindness to me as I prepared my manuscript for publication and Eva Jaunzems whose superb copyediting has immensely improved the readability of my book. In my own academic home, The Catholic University of America, I am much indebted to the support of my colleagues, Dr. Monica J. Blanchard, the curator of the Semitics/ICOR library, Dr. Janet Timbie, Dr. Shawqi Talia, Dr. Andrew Gross, our chairman Dr. Edward Cook, and Mr. Nathan Gibson, who prepared the bibliography and proofread the footnotes. Finally, I wish to express my gratitude for the support and interest of my family and friends throughout the long time I have been distracted by this project. I owe special thanks to Marlene Debole who supported and encouraged this project.

I have approached the study of the Bible in Arabic from the perspective of a historian of Christianity in the Middle East, particularly in Late Antique and Early Medieval times, and especially as that history is disclosed in texts written in Syriac and Christian Arabic. Working from this perspective involves approaching the Arabic Qur'ān, the career and teaching of Muḥammad, and the birth of Islam from the unusual angle of one who encounters them *a parte ante*, in the course of following the trail of Jews and Christians into the Arabic-speaking world. When on this tack one meets with the newly arising Arabic Qur'ān, the Bible in the Qur'ān, and a conspicuous amount of other Jewish and Christian lore, these phenomena appear in a somewhat different light than they do when viewed from the perspective of a researcher who looks back at the rise of Islam from after the fact, and strives to see it in its historical context, as most historians of early Islam do. For one thing, from my perspective the Arabic Qur'ān looms into view as just about the only document in any language that offers me an insight into the Jewish and Christian presence in the Arabic-speaking milieu in the first third of the seventh century. What is more, what I see there as a historian of Christians, their beliefs, and practices, is a remarkable continuation *mutatis mutandis* of both topics and modes of discourse, albeit that in the Qur'ān they appear in a translated, refracted context not so much of congruence as of critique and interreligious polemic. As for the Bible itself, its pervasive presence in the Qur'ān, notwithstanding the almost total want of quotations, bespeaks a strong oral presence of the Bible in Arabic in the Arabian Ḥijāz in the first third of the seventh century. It would not be long before, in the wake of the codification of the Qur'ān, and the twin processes of the Arabicization and Islamification of life in the territories occupied by the conquering Arabs in the later seventh century, Jews and Christians would begin to produce written translations of biblical books and to circulate them in Arabic. This book aims to call attention to the story of how the Bible came into Arabic at the hands of Jews and Christians, and how it fared among Muslims from early Islamic times into the Middle Ages.

⁕ Introduction ⁕

THE STUDY OF THE BIBLE in Arabic is in its infancy. There are hundreds of extant manuscripts containing portions of the Bible in Arabic translations produced by Jews and Christians in early Islamic times and well into the Middle Ages. But until now, with some notable exceptions, they have been of little interest to either biblical scholars or even to historians of Judaism, Christianity, or Islam. This situation is in contrast to the considerable interest in the largely contemporary Abbasid translation movement centered in medieval Baghdad (c. 750–1050 CE) and its environs, in the course of which principally Greek scientific, philosophical, mathematical, and even literary works were systematically translated from Greek, sometimes via Syriac, into Arabic.[1] Less well known is the fact that in relatively the same time and place, in monasteries and in church and synagogue communities, efforts were also underway to translate the Jewish and Christian scriptures, along with other genres of religious books, from Hebrew, Aramaic, Syriac, and Greek into Arabic. For by the beginning of the Abbasid era in Islamic history, when Arabic had become the language of public life in the Muslim caliphate, the non-Muslim 'People of the Book' or 'Scripture People'[2] living outside of Arabia proper, mostly Jews and Christians in the Levant, had also adopted the language. In the new religious environment that prevailed from the dawn of the ninth century onward, and even earlier, Bible translation became once again a mode of religious survival in a new cultural environment, as it had been in previous instances in Jewish and Christian history. It was as well the first step in biblical interpretation in the face of new challenges.[3] As in the Abbasid translation movement, so in what we might call the Judaeo-Christian Arabic translation movement the translated texts marked a new era in the intellectual lives of the Jewish, Christian, and Muslim communities living together in the Arabic-speaking World of Islam.

[1] See the magisterial study by Dimitri Gutas, *Greek Thought, Arabic Culture: the Graeco-Arabic Translation Movement in Baghdad and Early Abbasid Society (2nd–4th / 8th–10th Centuries)* (London and New York: Routledge, 1998).

[2] On the significance of this phrase in Qur'ānic usage see Daniel A. Madigan, *The Qur'ān's Self-Image: Writing and Authority in Islam's Scripture* (Princeton, NJ: Princeton University Press, 2001), esp. the appendix, "The People of the *Kitāb*," pp. 193–213.

[3] See, e.g., Tessa Rajak, Translation and Survival: The Greek Bible of the Ancient Jewish Diaspora (Oxford: Oxford University Press, 2009).

In what follows we tell the story of the first translations of portions of the Bible into Arabic and of their currency in the Jewish, Christian, and Muslim communities of the Arabic-speaking world up to Mamlūk and early Ottoman times. This story has seldom been told in a general way. Rather, accounts of its major episodes have been investigated in highly technical studies written by specialists in Judaeo-Arabic or Christian Arabic, concentrating on particular manuscript traditions or individual portions of the Bible. Nor has the story been told with a synoptic view of the role of the translations in the three main communities, living together in the same Arabic-speaking settlements, and exercising a significant measure of intellectual crosspollination. So while the present study makes no substantive contribution to the study of the Bible in Arabic per se, its purpose is to call attention to the progress that has been made by others in this undertaking, to provide an overview of the significant topics in early Islamic history in which the Bible has a major part, and not least to highlight the social and interreligious developments that resulted from the very fact of having the scriptures of the 'People of the Book' in the language of Islam.

In the beginning there is the question of the presence of the Bible among the Arabic-speaking peoples prior to the rise of Islam. The first chapter argues that in the world in which Islam was born, the Bible circulated orally in Arabic mainly in liturgical settings, and that such written biblical texts as may have been available in synagogues, churches, or monasteries in this milieu were in the liturgical languages of the several communities, Hebrew or Aramaic among the Jews, and Greek or Aramaic/Syriac among the Christians. Furthermore, given the wide range of biblical lore recollected in the Qur'ān, and the critique the Qur'ān makes of the religious beliefs and practices of the Jews and Christians, along with the actual historical evidences in hand of the communities on the Arabian periphery, the conclusion emerges that the Arabic-speaking Jews and Christians in the Qur'ān's audience were the mainstream communities of the first third of the seventh century in the Middle East in Late Antiquity and not representatives of lost or dissident groups. For the Christians, this finding means that the Arabic-speakers among them belonged to communities that in later Muslim parlance would regularly be described as Melkites, Jacobites, and Nestorians. This conclusion involves the rejection of suggestions made by many scholars that the Christians in the Qur'ān's ambience were remnants of ancient groups of Judaeo-Christians, 'Nazarenes', Elkasaites, Ebionites, or other groups whose presence in Arabia in the seventh century is otherwise unattested.

The Bible is at the same time everywhere and nowhere in the Arabic Qur'ān; there are but one or two instances of actual quotation. The second chapter of the present study advances the hypothesis that the recollections and reminiscences in the Qur'ān of the biblical and para-biblical narratives of the patriarchs and prophets are not random, but that they are selected according to Islam's distinctive 'prophetology'. It envisions a series of 'messengers' and 'prophets' sent by God to warn human communities, which 'messengers' and 'prophets' God protects from the machinations of their adversaries. The Qur'ān recalls only such biblical stories as fit the paradigm of its prophetology, and it edits the narratives where necessary to fit the pattern. Current scholarship has increasingly shown that Syriac narratives more often than not underlie the Qur'ān's recollection of Bible stories, even when they come ultimately from Hebrew or earlier Aramaic sources.

The evidence in hand suggests that the earliest written translations of portions of the Bible into Arabic were made by Jews and Christians living outside of Arabia proper after the Arab, Islamic conquest of the Fertile Crescent, from the middle of the seventh century onward. The third chapter argues that the collection and publication of the Qur'ān as a written text is the first instance of book production in Arabic and that this accomplishment in turn provided the stimulus for the production of the Bible in Arabic. Christians had written scriptures in Arabic from at least the middle of the eighth century and possibly earlier; by the ninth century Jews too were translating portions of the Bible into Judaeo-Arabic, if not somewhat earlier. Christians translated from Greek or Syriac versions; Jews translated from the original Hebrew. It is not clear where these early translations were made; the available evidence suggests that in the Christian instance the monasteries of Palestine, where most of the early manuscripts have been preserved, were also the locations of the translations.

The fourth chapter surveys what has come to light so far of translations into Arabic of biblical books and related texts under Christian auspices from the ninth century up to the Middle Ages. The effort here is not to be comprehensive or to list and describe every known Christian translation. Rather, relying on the scholarship of others, the purpose is to call attention to the many important features of the translation enterprise, and not least to call attention to the windows open to the history of the Christians living under Muslim rule that these manuscripts provide. Too often even scholars who are experts in the biblical text systematically ignore the wealth of other information the manuscripts contain, to the detriment of our knowledge of an increasingly important phase of Christian interreligious history.

The translation of the Bible, and particularly of the Torah, into Arabic beginning in the ninth century in the environs of Baghdad and in Palestine and elsewhere opened a whole new scholarly era in Jewish life and thought that extended from the eastern shores of the Mediterranean to Spain, and reached even across the Pyrenees into medieval Europe. Chapter five of the present study discusses this development, again relying on the scholarship of others. Highlighting the accomplishments of major figures such as Yaʿqūb Qirqisānī and Saʿadyah ha-Gaʾōn, the chapter calls attention not only to the importance of their scholarship for the Arabic-speaking Jews of the Islamic world, particularly in the area of the exegesis of the scriptures, but also to the important interreligious dimensions of their work. The text of the Bible in Arabic became the coin of interreligious exchange in the period under study, and it was often the case that the scriptures were the focus of arguments about religion, evoking both polemical and apologetic discourse from Jews, Christians, and Muslims alike.

The availability of the Bible in Arabic in oral or written form played an important role in the formation of early Islamic religious thought and in Muslim responses to challenges from Jews and Christians. The sixth chapter discusses the use Muslim scholars made of biblical passages and of biblical lore both to articulate Islamic convictions more convincingly and to disclose what they took to be the shortcomings of Jewish and Christian exegesis and even of their custody of the text of the scriptures. The Muslim use of the Bible suggests a more general availability of its text in Arabic than modern scholars can account for on the basis of the manuscripts that have survived. And in the study of biblical narratives, some Muslim scholars of the early Islamic period, such as the historian al-Yaʿqūbī, displayed a considerable breadth of knowledge of Jewish and Christian exegetical traditions. But in the long run, Muslim interest in the Bible in the Middle Ages focused less on the text as the Jews and Christians actually had it, than on the apologetic and polemical potential of particular biblical passages.

And yet even the apologetic and polemical use of selected passages from the Bible wove a web of enduring biblical connections between Arabic-speaking Jews, Christians, and Muslims from Late Antiquity to the Middle Ages, resulting in a situation that may be characterized as one of 'intertwined scriptures' or better, intertwined Bible history. The brief seventh chapter calls attention to this phenomenon, and to the problematic suggestions of some recent historians of religions and advocates of interreligious dialogue that the historical intertwining of scriptures in counterpoint on the part of Jewish, Christian, and Muslim religious controversialists over the centuries justifies the assumption of a common scriptural heritage.

The Bible in Arabic entered a new phase in its history with the advent of printing and the increasing involvement of Western Christians in the affairs of Arabic-speaking Christians living in the World of Islam. This is a topic that reaches beyond the chronological and topical limits of the present study. The effort here has been to call attention to a neglected area of biblical studies and to an equally neglected phase of Jewish, Christian, and Muslim interreligious history, and all along to provide sufficient bibliographic annotations to lead the interested inquirer into a deeper study of the issues raised. The hope is that the scriptures themselves may yet lead to a more appreciative interreligious understanding and to a more tolerant mutual respect.

✻ CHAPTER I ✻

The Bible in Pre-Islamic Arabia

EVEN A BRIEF PERUSAL of the Arabic Qur'ān is sufficient to convince the first-time reader that the text presumes a high degree of scriptural literacy on the part of its audience. In it there are frequent references to biblical patriarchs, prophets, and other figures of Late Antique, Jewish, and Christian religious lore. One hears of Adam, Noah, Abraham, Ishmael, Isaac, Jacob, Joseph, David, Solomon, Job, and Jonah, among others from the Hebrew Bible. Similarly, one reads of Jesus, Mary, Zecharaiah, John the Baptist, and Jesus' disciples from the New Testament, but no mention of Paul and his epistles. What is more, there are numerous echoes in the Qur'ān of non-biblical, Jewish and Christian traditions, some of them otherwise found in so-called apocryphal or pseudepigraphic biblical texts. So prominent is this scriptural material in the body of the Islamic scripture that one twentieth-century Western scholar of Islam was prompted to speak of the Qur'ān as "a truncated, Arabic edition of the Bible."[1] But in fact the Qur'ān is much more than just an evocation of earlier biblical narratives; it incorporates the recollection of those earlier scriptures into its own call to belief, to Islam and its proper observance, as it says, in good, clarifying Arabic (*lisānun 'arabiyyun mubīnun*, XVI *an-Naḥl* 103).

What attracts the attention of the historian of the Bible text in Arabic to the Qur'ān's recollection of so many biblical narratives and their *dramatis personae* is the quest for the earliest translations of the Bible or of parts of it into Arabic. In short, one wants to know if there was a pre-Islamic Arabic translation of the Bible, done by either Jews or Christians, or both, with which the Qur'ān may have been familiar? If so, was it a written translation or an oral one? If there was no such translation, how did the Qur'ān come by its high quotient of biblical knowledge?

To answer these questions one must first of all know about the Arabic-speaking Jews and Christians in the Qur'ān's milieu; who were they and

[1] Louis Massignon (1883–1962) wrote that the Qur'ān may be considered, "une édition arabe tronquée de la Bible." He went on to say, "Le Qor'an serait à la Bible ce qu'Ismael fut à Isaac." Louis Massignon, *Les trois prières d'Abraham* (Paris: Éditions du Cerf, 1997), p. 89.

what canon of scriptures did they recognize? And most importantly, do we have any evidence that they were in possession of written Arabic translations of any portion of the Jewish or Christian scriptures, made from either the original languages or from earlier versions?

JEWS AND CHRISTIANS IN PRE-ISLAMIC ARABIA

Long before the lifetime of the Arab prophet, Muḥammad ibn ʿAbd al-Allāh (c. 570–632), Arabic-speaking Jews and Christians were making their way into Arabia. Jews had lived there for centuries, and they had briefly even ruled a kingdom in South Arabia at the turn of the fifth and sixth centuries of the Christian era.[2] But the centers of Jewish religious life at the time were located outside of Arabia, in the Aramaic-speaking environs of Galilee in northern Palestine, and in the rabbinic academies of Sura and Pumbedita in southern Mesopotamia.[3] Similarly, albeit that the centers of Christianity in the East were in the Roman patriarchates of Alexandria, Antioch, and Jerusalem, and in Persia in Seleucia-Ctesiphon, and Takrīt in Iraq,[4] by the dawn of the seventh century Christians had long been pressing

[2] See Gordon D. Newby, *A History of the Jews of Arabia* (Columbia, SC: University of South Carolina Press, 1988); Christian-Julien Robin, "Himyar et Israël," *Académie des Inscriptions et Belles-Lettres*, Comptes-Rendus des Séances de l'Année 2004, avril–juin, pp. 831–908; J. Beaucamp, F. Briquel-Chatonnet, C. J. Robin (eds.), *Juifs et chrétiens en Arabie aux Ve et Vie siècles: Regards croisés sur les sources; actes du colloque de novembre 2008* (Monographies, 32; Paris: Association des Amis du Centre d'Histoire et Civilisation de Byzance, 2010); Haggai Ben-Shammai, "Observations on the Beginnings of Judeo-Arabic Civilization," in D.M. Freidenreich and Miriam Goldstein (eds.), *Beyond Religious Borders: Interaction and Intellectual Exchange in the Medieval Islamic World* (Philadelphia, PA: University of Pennsylvania Press, 2012), pp. 13–29.

[3] See Michael Avi-Yonah, *The Jews under Roman and Byzantine Rule: A Political History of Palestine from the Bar Kokhba War to the Arab Conquest* (2nd ed.; Jerusalem: Magnes Press, 1984); Robert Brody, *The Geonim of Babylonia and the Shaping of Medieval Jewish Culture* (New Haven, CT: Yale University Press, 1998); Stuart S. Miller, *Sages and Commoners in Late Antique Erez Israel: A Philological Inquiry into Local Traditions in Talmud Yerushalmi* (Tübingen: Mohr Siebeck, 2006); Catherine Hezser, *The Social Structure of the Rabbinic Movement in Roman Palestine* (Tübingen: Mohr Siebeck, 1997).

[4] For general orientation and bibliography, see Susan Ashbrook Harvey and David G. Hunter (eds.), *The Oxford Handbook of Early Christian Studies* (Oxford: Oxford University Press, 2008). For the so-called 'Oriental' Christians in particular, see Wolfgang Hage, *Das orientalische Christentum* (Die Religionen der Menschheit, Band 29, 2; Stuttgart: Verlag W. Kohlhammer, 2007). See also Jérôme Labourt, *Le Christianisme dans l'émpire perse sous la dynastie sassanide (224–632)* (Paris: V. Lecoffre,

into the Arabian heartland from all sides. Arabia was literally surrounded by Christian enclaves, in the towns and villages of South Arabia, in Ethiopia and Egypt, in Sinai, Palestine, Syria, Mesopotamia, and in Iran.[5]

While there has been some scholarly discussion about the identity of the Jews of Arabia in pre-Islamic times, scholars seem nevertheless agreed that the Arabian Jewish communities were more or less *au courant* with the modes of Jewish life and thought of their era in the broader world of Late Antiquity in the Near East. The case has been otherwise with the Arabian Christians; there has been considerable scholarly controversy about the identity of the Arabic-speaking Christians in the Qur'ān's audience. For this reason, prior to addressing the principal topic of this chapter, the Bible in pre-Islamic Arabia, a disproportionate amount of attention must be paid here to presenting the case for the author's view that contrary to prevailing scholarly consensus, the Qur'ān's Christians were in fact among the contemporary Melkites, Jacobites, and Nestorians, the dominant Christian congregations on the Arabian periphery and in Arabia proper, in the first third of the seventh century, and that the Christian Bible in Arabic would have included portions of the canonical and noncanonical scriptures, along with other ecclesiastical lore that circulated in these communities.

Arabian Jews

While some archaeological evidence suggests a Jewish presence in the Ḥijāz already in pre-Christian times,[6] much of what is known about Jewish life in the pre-Islamic Arabic-speaking world derives from much later sources in Arabic. But Arabian Jews were not confined to the Ḥijāz. Spreading throughout the peninsula for reasons of trade and sometimes for security, Jews were a familiar presence in Arabia well before the rise of Islam. They had established themselves in South Arabia, in Ḥimyar and particularly in Yemen, even prior to the common era, where they were to remain an

1904) and J. M. Fiey, "Tagrît: Esquisse d'histoire chrétienne," *L'Orient Syrien* 8 (1963), pp. 289–342.

[5]See J. Spencer Trimingham, *Christianity among the Arabs in Pre-Islamic Times* (London and New York: Longman, 1979); Theresia Hainthaler, *Christliche Araber vor dem Islam* (Eastern Christian Studies, 7; Leuven: Peeters, 2007); Yuri Arzhanov, "Zeugnisse über Kontakte zwischen Juden und Christen im vorislamischen Arabien," *Oriens Christianus* 92 (2008), pp. 79–93.

[6]See Shari Lowin, "Hijaz," in Norman A. Stillman (ed.), *Encyclopedia of Jews in the Islamic World* (5 vols.; Leiden and Boston, 2010), vol. 2, pp. 416–417.

important cultural presence until well into the twentieth century.[7] For a brief period in the sixth century, a Jewish king, Yūsuf Dhū Nuwās (517–525), reigned in Ḥimyar,[8] during which time he engaged in a military action against the city of Najrān that resulted in the tragic deaths of numerous Christians. This circumstance yielded a rich martyrological tradition in Syriac, thus bringing news of events in deepest Arabia to the notice of the wider Christian world.[9] It is significant that during his tenure in office, King Yūsuf is also said to have been in correspondence with Jewish religious authorities in Tiberias in Palestine,[10] indicating that he and his community were not isolated in Arabia from the wider world of Judaism in the sixth century, and suggesting a rabbinical consultation on the king's part.

More to the present purpose, the existence of Jewish communities in Muḥammad's immediate ambience in the Ḥijāz in the early seventh century is well attested.[11] In particular, there were Jews in the oasis communities of Khaybar as well as in Yathrib (Medina), where they were known by their tribal identities as the Banū n-Naḍīr, the Banū Qaynuqāʿ, and the Banū Qurayẓa. During his time in Yathrib/Medina, Muḥammad is credited with having composed the document that has come to be known as the 'Constitution of Medina', in which he details regulations for harmonious relationships between the several tribal groupings of Arabs in the city, the Jews prominently included.[12]

[7] See Christian Julien Robin, "Le judaïsme de Ḥimyar," *Arabia* 1 (2003), pp. 97–172; Bat-Zion Eraqi Klorman, "Yemen," in Stillman, *Encyclopedia of Jews in the Islamic World*, vol. 4, pp. 627–639.

[8] See Christian Julien Robin, "Joseph, dernier roi de Ḥimyar (de 522 à 525, ou une des années suivantes)," *Jerusalem Studies in Arabic and Islam* 34 (2008), pp. 1–124.

[9] See Irfan Shahid, *The Martyrs of Najrān: New Documents* (Subsidia Hagiographica, vol. 49; Bruxelles: Société des Bollandistes, 1971); Theresia Hainthaler, *Christliche Araber vor dem Islam*, sub voce; Robin, "Joseph, dernier roi de Ḥimyar," esp. pp. 37–72; Beaucamp et al., *Juifs et chrétiens en Arabie.*

[10] See Klorman, "Yemen," p. 629; Robin, "Joseph, dernier roi de Ḥimyar," pp. 70–71.

[11] See Michael Lecker, *Jews and Arabs in Pre-and Early Islamic Arabia* (Aldershot, UK: Ashgate, 1998); *idem, People, Tribes, and Society in Arabia around the Time of Muḥammad* (Burlington, VT: Ashgate, 2005).

[12] See Michael Lecker, *The "Constitution of Medina": Muḥammad's First Legal Document* (Princeton, NJ: Darwin Press, 2004). See also M. Gil, "The Origin of the Jews of Yathrib," *Jerusalem Studies in Arabic and Islam* 4 (1984), pp. 203–224; Michael Lecker, *Muslims, Jews and Pagans: Studies on Early Islamic Medina* (Leiden: E.J. Brill, 1995).

As mentioned earlier, there is every reason to think that the Arabian Jews, including those in the immediate environs of the early Islamic movement, were in continuous contact with Jews elsewhere, and particularly in Palestine, and that they were fully aware of current Jewish traditions, both scriptural and rabbinic. The most immediate textual evidence for this state of affairs is the Arabic Qur'ān itself. For a long time now, whatever the interpretive construction they have put upon it, Western scholars have busied themselves with calling attention to and highlighting the Qur'ān's high quotient of awareness of Jewish lore, including biblical themes and narratives, and even of the exegetical tradition.[13] Whatever else one might say about this material, including what one might think about its significance for the composition of the Qur'ān, which is another issue, it is hard to avoid the conclusion that it bespeaks a high level of Jewish biblical and traditional knowledge and awareness on the part of the Arabic-speaking Jews in the Qur'ān's audience and in the confessional milieu of Muḥammad himself. It would seem that the Jews were in regular contact and conversation with the prophet and with his companions.

As we shall see, albeit this is a more difficult case to make given the controversial character of much of the material we must discuss, the same might be said of the Arabic-speaking Christians in Muḥammad's and the Qur'an's milieu as was just said of the Arabic-speaking Jews. In both cases the question we will be seeking to answer is, does the accumulated evidence from the Qur'ān and elsewhere allow the conclusion that there was an Arabic translation of the Bible, or of parts of it, in pre-Islamic Arabia?

Arabian Christians

There is a wealth of information scattered in mainly Greek, Syriac, and Arabic texts about the Christian communities that found their way in the fifth, sixth, and seventh centuries into the Arabic-speaking milieu. In recent

[13] See in this connection, see such classical works as the following: G. Weil, *The Bible, the Koran, and the Talmud or Biblical Legends of the Musselmans* (New York: Harper, 1846); Abraham Geiger, *Was hat Mohammed aus dem Judenthume aufgenommen?* (1st ed.; Bonn: Baaden, 1833); Wilhem Rudolph, *Die Abhängigkeit des Qorans von Judentum und Christentum* (Stuttgart: Kohlhammer, 1922); Josef Horovitz, *Koranische Untersuchungen* (Berlin: De Gruyter, 1926); Anton Baumstark, "Jüdischer und christlicher Gebetstypus im Koran," *Der Islam* 16 (1927), pp. 229–248; Heinrich Speyer, *Die biblischen Erzählungen im Qoran* (Gräfenhainichen/Breslau: Schulze, 1934/1937).

years, scholars have indefatigably gathered every shred of available information they have been able to glean from all of these sources and more, thereby providing sufficient material for the composition of a more or less continuous narrative of Christian presence in Arabia and its environs from the fourth century to the time of Muḥammad.[14] And it seems clear from these sources that the major Christian communities who made headway among the Arabs in the several centuries just prior to the rise of Islam were the so-called Melkites, Jacobites, and Nestorians.[15] Their principal ecclesiastical language was Syriac, or Christian Palestinian Aramaic among the Melkites, albeit that their ecclesial identities were largely determined by the positions they adopted in the Christological controversies of the fifth and sixth centuries. These controversies in turn were largely concerned with texts translated from Greek into Syriac from the fifth century onward.[16] In

[14] In addition to the studies cited in n.4 above, and especially Hainthaler, *Christliche Araber vor dem Islam* with its rich and comprehensive bibliography, see the monumental works of Irfan Shahid, *Rome and the Arabs: A Prolegomenon to the Study of Byzantium and the Arabs* (Washington, DC: Dumbarton Oaks, 1984); *Byzantium and the Arabs in the Fourth Century* (Washington, DC: Dumbarton Oaks, 1984); *Byzantium and the Arabs in the Fifth Century* (Washington, DC: Dumbarton Oaks, 1989); *Byzantium and the Arabs in the Sixth Century* (vol. 1, parts 1–2; Washington, DC: Dumbarton Oaks, 1995); *Byzantium and the Arabs in the Sixth Century* (vol. 2, part 1; Washington, DC: Dumbarton Oaks, 2002); *Byzantium and the Arabs in the Sixth Century: Economic, Social, and Cultural History* (vol. 2, part 2; Washington, DC: Dumbarton Oaks, 2009). The series is projected to conclude with volumes on the seventh century. See too Fergus Millar, "Christian Monasticism in Roman Arabia at the Birth of Mahomet," and Robert Hoyland, "Late Roman Provincia Arabia, Monophysite Monks and Arab Tribes: A Problem of Centre and Periphery," in *Semitica et Classica* 2 (2009), pp. 97–115 and 117–139.

[15] One uses the names Melkite, Jacobite, and Nestorian with some reluctance, realizing that they are anachronistic and polemical in origin, coined by the adversaries of the communities to which they are applied, viz. the Eastern/Greek Orthodox Church, the Syrian/Oriental Orthodox Churches, and the Assyrian Church of the East, respectively. These problematic names were used for centuries by both Muslim and Christian writers and have become commonplace. See Sebastian Brock, "The Nestorian Church: A Lamentable Misnomer," *Bulletin of the John Rylands University Library of Manchester* 78 (1996), pp. 23–35.

[16] See D. S. Wallace Hadrill, *Christian Antioch: A Study of Early Christian Thought in the East* (Cambridge: Cambridge University Press, 1982); Jaroslav Pelikan, *The Spirit of Eastern Christendom (600–1700)* (The Christian Tradition, vol. 2; Chicago: University of Chicago Press, 1974); Adam H. Becker, *Fear of God and the Beginning of Wisdom: The School of Nisibis and Christian Scholastic Culture in Late Antique Mesopotamia* (Philadelphia, PA: University of Pennsylvania Press, 2006); Stephen J. Davis, *Coptic Christology in Practice: Incarnation and Divine Participation in Late Antique and Medieval*

South Arabia, there was also a significant Ethiopian presence, and while their Christological sympathies were with the Jacobites and the Copts of Egypt, their ecclesiastical language was Ge'ez.[17] The historical record preserves no memory of any other significant Christian presence among the Arabs or in their environs in the crucial period from the fifth century to the first third of the seventh century. In particular, as we shall discuss below, there is no indisputable documentary evidence for the presence of any notable Jewish Christian group thriving in Arabia in this period. Modern scholars who have postulated such a presence have done so, we shall argue, on the basis of extrapolations from their theological interpretations of certain passages in the Arabic Qur'ān.

Given the evidentiary presumption, then, that Christianity became known to the Arabic-speaking peoples by way of their contacts with Aramaic, Syriac, or Ge'ez-speaking Christians on the periphery of Arabia proper, a question arises as to the language of Christianity among the Arabs. It seems unlikely a priori that indigenous, Arabic-speaking Christians in the Arabian heartland, who would have learned their Christianity from the communities on the peninsula's periphery, would have adopted Aramaic, Syriac, or Ge'ez along with their Christian faith. Rather, the historian's presumption must be that the Arabs on the periphery translated Christianity at least orally into their own Arabic language. This would not have been a surprising development given the likely bilingualism of the Arabs living in regions bordering Arabia proper, especially in Syria and Mesopotamia. In northern Mesopotamia there was an entire region between the city of Nisibis and the Tigris River called in Syriac, Bēt 'Arbāyê, or 'the homeland of the Arabs'.[18] Here in the sixth century, the Syrian Orthodox holy man and bishop Mār Aḥūdemeh (d.575) had considerable success in evangelizing the Arab tribes, who would in due course come to have their own 'Bishop of the Arabs'.[19] Some

---

Egypt (Oxford Early Christian Studies; Oxford: Oxford University Press, 2008); Volker L. Menze, *Justinian and the Making of the Syrian Orthodox Church* (Oxford Early Christian Studies; Oxford: University Press, 2008).

[17] For a brief historical sketch and bibliography, see Wolfgang Hage, *Das orientalische Christentum* (Die Religionen der Menschheit, vol. 29, 2; Stuttgart: Verlag W. Kohlhammer, 2007), pp. 202–206.

[18] See R. Payne Smith, *Thesaurus Syriacus* (2 vols.; Oxford: Clarendon Press, 1879–1901; reprint: Hildesheim and New York: Georg Olms, 1981), vol. 2, col. 2983.

[19] See Hainthaler, *Christliche Araber vor dem Islam*, pp. 106–110. See too Jack Tannous, "Between Christology and Kalām? The Life and Letters of George, Bishop of the Arab Tribes," in George A. Kiraz (ed.), *Malphono w-Rabo d-Malphone: Studies in Honor of Sebastian P. Brock* (Piscataway, NJ: Gorgias Press, 2008), pp. 671–716.

of their number would become known in early Islamic times precisely for their bilingualism, speaking both Syriac and Arabic.[20] The situation must have been similar already in the fifth century in Palestine, where the monastic founder St. Euthymius (d.473) evangelized Arab tribesmen and established an episcopal hierarchy among them.[21] In the areas controlled by the Jacobite Ghassanids and the 'Nestorian Lakhmids' in the sixth century, Arabic may already have been the dominant language,[22] but their ties with the Syriac-speaking Jacobite and Nestorian churches were continuous. Presumably the same may be said even of the Christian communities in southern Arabia, and particularly in Najrān, where ties with the Syriac-speaking mother-churches seem to have been continuous up to the rise of Islam.[23] In the fifth and sixth centuries the south Arabian tribal group called Kinda, which included notable Christian and Jewish converts, gained ascendancy among the Arab tribes even of central and northern Arabia. And while it may well have been the case that the Christians among them played a major role in the spreading of knowledge about Christianity among the Arabic-speaking peoples, their major exploits seem to have been largely political in nature and to have transpired normally on the Arabian periphery, among the Romans in Palestine or the Persians in Mesopotamia.[24]

There is scant explicit evidence, but there is some in the Greek, Syriac, and even Arabic historical sources for a presence of Christians among the

[20] See the report of Michael the Syrian in J.–B. Chabot (ed. and trans.), *Chronique de Michel le Syrien, patriarche jacobite d'Antioche, 1166–1199* (4 vols.; Paris: Leroux, 1899–1924), vol. 2, p. 422 (Syriac) and vol. 4, p. 432.

[21] See Hainthaler, *Christliche Araber vor dem Islam*, 41–42.

[22] See the discussion of Louis Cheikho's claims for pre–Islamic, Arabic literature in Camille Hechaïmé, *Louis Cheikho et son livre: Le Christianisme et la littérature chrétienne en Arabie avant l'islam; etude critique* (Beyrouth: Dar el–Machreq, 1967. See now Irfan Shahid, *The Arabs in Late Antiquity: Their Role, Achievement, and Legacy* (The Margaret Weyerhaeuser Jewett Chair of Arabic, Occasional Papers; Beirut: The American University of Beirut, 2008); *idem, Byzantium and the Arabs in the Sixth Century*, vol. 2, part 2, pp. 297–302, 321–337. See also Elizabeth Key Fowden, *The Barbarian Plain: Saint Sergius between Rome and Iran* (Berkeley, CA: University of California Press, 1999).

[23] See René Tardy, *Najrân: Chrétiens d'Arabie avant l'Islam* (Recherches, 8; Beirut: Dar el-Machreq, 1999); C. John Block, "Philoponian Monophysitism in South Arabia at the Advent of Islam with Implications for the English Translation of '*Thalātha*' Qur'ān 4.171 and 5.73," *Journal of Islamic Studies* 23 (2012), pp. 50–75.

[24] See Irfan Shahid, "Kinda," *EI*, new rev. ed., vol. 5, pp. 118–120; Gunnar Olinder, *The Kings of Kinda of the Family of Ākil al-Murār* (Lund: H. Ohlsson, 1927). See also Irfan Shahid, "Byzantium and Kinda," *Byzantinische Zeitschrift* 53 (1960), pp. 57–73; *idem*, "Procopius and Kinda," *Byzantinische Zeitschrift* 53 (1960), pp. 74–78.

Arabic-speaking peoples of central Arabia and the Ḥijāz in the sixth and seventh centuries,[25] where presumably only Arabic was commonly spoken. And the contents of the Arabic Qur'ān that has its origins in just this Arabic-speaking milieu testifies to the fact that by the first third of the seventh century knowledge of Christianity, of its scriptures, its lore, its doctrines, and its practices must have been widespread in the Arabic-speaking heartland. For as we shall see the Qur'ān assumes that its audience has fairly detailed knowledge of these matters. So the question is, how did they acquire it? The answer seems to be that by the time of the Qur'ān, knowledge of the Christian Bible, the Christian creed, and Christian liturgy had already spread orally among the Arabs, presumably transmitted first from those Arabs living on the Arabian periphery, who were in more immediate contact with those Syriac and Ge'ez-speaking Christians whose faith and practice the Qur'ān echoes. For as we shall see, very few traces of Christian texts in Arabic prior to the rise of Islam have so far come to light.

JEWS AND CHRISTIANS IN THE QUR'ĀN

The Qur'ān and the Jews

On the face of it, the Qur'ān clearly presumes the presence of Arabic-speaking Jews in its audience.[26] It addresses them and refers to them under a number of names and titles, most straightforwardly some nine times simply as 'Jews' (*yahūdī, yahūd*), or, in its verbal form, about ten times as people who profess Judaism (*hādū*); in passages that evoke the time of Moses and the revelation of the Torah, the Qur'ān employs the biblical expression, 'Children of Israel' (*banū Isrā'īl*).[27] Otherwise, the Jews are included along with the Christians and others as 'People of the Book' or 'Scripture People' (*ahl al-kitāb*), a polyvalently inclusive phrase used some fifty-four times in the Qur'ān.[28] Unlike the case with the Christians, as we shall see, there is not

[25] See Hainthaler, *Christiliche Araber vor dem Islam*, pp. 137–142; Ghada Osman, "Pre–Islamic Arab Converts to Christianity in Mecca and Medina: An Investigation into the Arabic Sources," *The Muslim World* 95 (2005), pp. 67–80.

[26] See Uri Rubin, "Jews and Judaism," in Jane Dammen McAuliffe (ed.), *Encyclopaedia of the Qur'ān* (6 vols.; Leiden: Brill, 2001–2006), vol. 3, pp. 21 ff.

[27] See Uri Rubin, "Children of Israel," in Mc Auliffe, *Encyclopaedia of the Qur'ān*, vol. 1, pp. 303ff.

[28] See Daniel A. Madigan, *The Qur'ān's Self-Image: Writing and Authority in Islam's Scripture* (Princeton, NJ: Princeton University Press, 2001), esp. the excursus on the 'People of the Book', pp. 193–213.

much discussion in the scholarly literature about the communal or specific Jewish identity of the Qur'ānic Jews. Judging by what the Islamic scripture says about them and their religious usages by way of acceptance or criticism, and by what it evokes from their scriptures and traditions, it seems to have in mind Jews of the early seventh century, such as those well known on the Arabian periphery at the time, and especially those in Palestine and Mesopotamia. An exception to this general impression may be seen in the text's reference to a group it calls the 'People of Moses' (*qawm Mūsā*), "a group who guide by the truth, and by it act justly." (VII *al-A'rāf* 159) Some Muslim exegetes have speculated that the Qur'ān here refers to a distinct group of early Israelites, perhaps even a community of the lost tribes of Israel, but most commentators believe the phrase refers to early Jewisn converts to Islam in Muḥammad's own day and not to any otherwise unknown Jewish group living in Arabia.[29]

Given this conventional view of the identity of the Arabic-speaking Jewish communities in the Qur'ān's milieu, and given the wealth of Qur'ānic allusions to and evocations of the narratives and prophetic figures of the Hebrew Bible and Jewish tradition, one may well ask whether or not the Arabic-speaking Jews of Khaybar and Yathrib/Medina, or elsewhere in Arabia, had made translations of the scriptural and traditional texts from their original Hebrew and Aramaic into Arabic in pre-Islamic times? And if so, did these translations circulate orally or were they written? These are the questions to which this chapter seeks answers, or at least to suggest a not implausible, hypothetical suggestion as to the probable state of affairs.

The Qur'ān and the Christians

Consulting the Qur'ān as a documentary source for the history of the spread of Christianity among the Arabs, one finds evidence for the presence of Christians in the Arabic scripture's immediate purview on at least two levels. One is a purely formal, even external level of inquiry that highlights the etymologically non-Arabic vocabulary of Islamic scripture and takes account particularly of its Christian resonances. The other and more hermeneutically difficult level takes account of those passages in the Qur'ān that seem most clearly to presume a knowledge of Jewish and Christian scriptures on the part of readers, including a familiarity with biblical narratives and biblical personalities, as well as the Qur'ān's direct critiques of Christian doc-

[29] See Rubin, "Children of Israel," p. 304.

trine and practice. The aim of this inquiry is to determine which Christians and which Christian doctrines in particular the Qur'ān's text envisions, and to ask whether or not its biblical echoes and allusions reflect the presence of the Bible in Arabic in its immediate foreground?

HISTORICAL SCHOLARSHIP AND THE QUR'ĀN

Before approaching the Qur'ān as a repository of textual evidence for the spread of the knowledge of Christianity among the Arabs in the first third of the seventh century, one must take account of the current state of Qur'ān scholarship. This is a particularly important step in view of the fact that much recent research raises significant historiographical questions about the traditional view of Muḥammad, the Qur'ān, and the rise of Islam. Much of it questions the identity of the Arab prophet, including the time and place of his career, and suggests that the Qur'ān did not come into the form in which we presently have it in seventh century Arabia, as the conventional view has it, but in the early eighth century somewhere in Syria at the earliest. Along with its historicity, some have even questioned the Arabicity of the Qur'ān in its origins, postulating a so-called 'Syro-Aramaic' underpinning for the text that would later, in the eighth or even the early ninth century, be forced into the dress of a burgeoning classical Arabic.[30] Needless to say, this revisionist account of the Qur'ān would in some measure undermine its value as a source of historical information about the spread of Christianity in central Arabia and the Ḥijāz in the early seventh century.[31]

Here is not the place to engage in a review of the multiple historiographical problems surrounding the reports of the collection of the Qur'ān into its canonical form. Nevertheless the present inquiry into what the Qur'ān reveals about Christianity among the Arabs in pre-Islamic times does require a statement of the working hypothesis on the basis of which the present investigation of the Bible in Arabic proceeds. And in this connection, perhaps the most succinct statement of that basic premise is the one recently articulated by Patricia Crone, one of the most prominent historians

[30] See in particular Christoph Luxenberg, *Die syroaramäische Lesart des Koran: Ein Beitrag zur Entschlüsselung der Koransprache* (2nd rev. ed.; Berlin: Hans Schlier, 2004); English trans., *The Syro-Aramaic Reading of the Koran: A Contribution to the Decoding of the Language of the Koran* (ed. Tim Müke; Berlin: Hans Schiler, 2007).

[31] For a quick survey of these matters, see Alfred-Louis de Prémare, *Aux origines du Coran: Questions d'hier, approches d'aujourd'hui* (L'Islam en débats; Paris: Téraèdre, 2007).

of Islamic origins, who has most vigorously questioned the verisimilitude of the traditional sources. She says:

> The evidence that a prophet was active among the Arabs in the early decades of the 7th century, on the eve of the Arab conquest of the Middle East, must be said to be exceptionally good. . . . Most importantly, we can be reasonably sure that the Qur'ān is a collection of utterances that he made in the belief that they had been revealed to him by God. The book may not preserve all the messages he claimed to have received, and he is not responsible for the arrangement in which we have them. They were collected after his death—how long is controversial. But that he uttered all or most of them is difficult to doubt.[32]

On the basis of these premises one may reasonably expect that in passages that address Christians, recall biblical narratives, and reflect Christian idiom, the Qur'ān might well provide glimpses of the character of Christian thought and practice current in the Arabic-speaking milieu of the early seventh century and might offer some clues as well about the medium in which knowledge of Christianity circulated among the Arabs of that time.

THE LANGUAGES OF CHRISTIANS ON THE ARABIAN PERIPHERY

Scholars have long recognized that the Arabic vocabulary of the Qur'ān includes words and phrases that are etymologically foreign, albeit that they have been so-to-speak Arabicized and adopted into the Arabic language. Many of them are words coming ultimately from other Semitic languages such as Akkadian, Ugaritic, Hebrew, Aramaic, Syriac, or Ethiopic; but some of them may well have come originally from other, neighboring languages such as Armenian or even Greek.[33] By the time of the Qur'ān these words and phrases deemed by modern scholars to have been of foreign origin would have become simply Arabic. The interesting thing about them is that in matters pertaining to religious terminology, and especially in reference to Christian thought and practice, there is a high incidence of words with a Syriac or Ethiopic background, just what one would expect to have been the case, if, as the external historical sources suggest, Christianity first gained currency among the Arabs through their contacts with the circumambient Christian speakers of Aramaic/Syriac and Ge'ez.

[32] Patricia Crone, "What Do We Actually Know about Mohammed?" *OpenDemocracy*, June 10, 2008: http://www/opendemocracy.net.

[33] The pioneering study of this matter is by Arthur Jeffery, *The Foreign Vocabulary of the Qur'ān* (Baroda: Oriental Institute, 1938).

Ethiopian or Abyssinian Christians had come initially to Arabia in the early sixth century,[34] probably at the behest of Roman/Byzantine emissaries,[35] precisely to aid the local Christians of Najrān, who had suffered persecution at the hands of a king converted to Judaism.[36] In due course they came as well into the Ḥijāz, and approached the environs of Mecca itself when, in the later sixth century, perhaps just twenty or so years before Muḥammad's birth, Abrahah, the Christian viceroy of the Negus of Axum in Ethiopia, led an ill-fated military expedition from the Yemen toward Mecca.[37] The Qur'ān preserves a memory of the expedition's defeat by divine intervention in its *sūrat al-Fīl* (CV) 'The Elephant'. But perhaps even more suggestive of close religious contacts is the report according to which a number of Muḥammad's early followers, experiencing persecution in Mecca, fled for refuge to the court of the Negus of Abyssinia in the year AD 614/15. They were well received and returned during the prophet's Medinan years to play an important role in the life of the then burgeoning Muslim 'community of believers' among the Arabs.[38] It is therefore not surprising that Ge'ez words and turns of phrase, along with knowledge of Christianity, found their way into the diction of the Arabic Qur'ān.[39]

But Aramaic/Syriac looms largest on the list of the so-called 'foreign vocabulary' of the Qur'ān. Alphonse Mingana, writing in 1927, estimated

[34] See the convenient survey of Ethiopian Christianity, including the 'crusade' into South Arabia, with a rich bibliography, in Aloys Grillmeier, with Theresia Hainthaler, *Christ in Christian Tradition* (vol. 2, part 4, trans. O. C. Dean; London and Louisville, KY: Mowbray and Westminster John Knox Press, 1996), "Christ in a New Messianic Kingdom: Faith in Christ in Ethiopia," pp. 293–392.

[35] See Irfan Shahid, "Byzantium in South Arabia," *Dumbarton Oaks Papers* 33 (1979), pp. 23–94.

[36] See Shahid, *Martyrs of Najrān.*

[37] See M. J. Kister, "The Campaign of Ḥulubān: A New Light on the Expedition of Abraha," *Le Muséon* 78 (1965), pp. 425–436.

[38] The report appears in the biographical traditions concerning Muḥammad. See the account in William Montgomery Watt, *Muhammad at Mecca* (Oxford: Clarendon Press, 1953), pp. 109–117. See also Wim Raven, "Some Early Islamic Texts on the Negus of Abyssinia," *Journal of Semitic Studies* 33 (1988), pp. 197–218.

[39] See, e.g., Manfred Kropp, "Äthiopische Arabischen im Koran: Afroasiatische Perlen auf Band gereiht, einzein oder zu Paaren, diffuse verteilt oder an Glanzpunkten konzentriert," in Markus Groß and Karl-Heinz Ohlig (eds.), *Schlaglichter: Die beiden ersten islamischen Jahrhunderte* (Inârah, Band 3; Berlin: Hans Schiler, 2008), pp. 384–410. See also T. Fahd, "Rapports de la Mekke préislamique avec l'Abyssinie: le cas des *Aḥâbîš*," in T. Fahd (ed.), *L'Arabie préislamique et son environnement historique et culturel* (Actes du Colloque de Strasbourg, 24–27 juin 1987; Leiden: E.J. Brill, 1987), pp. 537–548.

that 70 percent of the "foreign influences on the style and terminology" of the Qur'ān could be traced to "Syriac (including Aramaic and Palestinian Syriac)."[40] Noting this high incidence of Syriac etymologies, Arthur Jeffrey wrote in 1938 that "one fact seems certain, namely that such Christianity as was known among the Arabs in pre-Islamic times was largely of the Syrian type, whether Jacobite or Nestorian."[41] He noted further that numerous early Islamic texts mention Muḥammad's contacts with both Syrian and Arabian Christians, and this observation prompted him to conclude that these texts "at least show that there was an early recognition of the fact that Muḥammad was at one time in more or less close contact with Christians associated with the Syrian Church."[42] Jeffery's conclusions, drawn from the high incidence of originally Aramaic/Syriac words and phrases that had been adopted into the Arabic of the Qur'ān, corroborate the inferences one would draw from the historical sources and from the geographical observation that sixth and seventh century Arabia was literally embraced by the territories where the largely Aramaic- and Syriac-speaking Melkite, Jacobite, and Nestorian Christians flourished, with the influence of ecclesiastical Greek traditions ever on the near horizon.[43]

The memory of Syriac as an important literary presence in Muḥammad's world is recorded even in early Islamic sources. For example, there is a tradition according to which some Syriac books had once come to Muḥammad's attention. According to the report deriving from his well-known secretary, the prophet is alleged to have asked Zayd ibn Thābit, " 'Do you know Syriac well? Some books have come to my attention'. I said, 'No'. He said, 'Learn it'. So I learned it in nineteen days."[44]

[40] A. Mingana, "Syriac Influence on the Style of the Qur'ān," *Bulletin of the John Rylands Library of Manchester* 11 (1927), pp. 77–98.

[41] Jeffery, *The Foreign Vocabulary*, pp. 20–21.

[42] Jeffery, *The Foreign Vocabulary*, p. 22. Subsequent studies of further details corroborate Jeffery's judgment. See, e.g., Guillaume Dye and Manfred Kropp, "Le nom de Jésus ('Īsā) dans le Coran, et quelques autres noms bibliques: Remarques sur l'onomastique coranique," in Guillaume Dye et Fabien Nobilio (eds.), *Figures bibliques en Islam* (Fernelmont, BE: Éditions Modulaires Européennes, 2011), pp. 171–198.

[43] Aramaic/Syriac and Ge'ez expressions of Christian thought and practice in Late Antiquity were deeply influenced by and in constant conversation with Greek Christian thought, especially in theology and Christology. For an overview of the situation among the speakers of Syriac, see Christine Shepardson, "Syria, Syriac, Syrian: Negotiating East and West," in Philip Rousseau (ed.), *A Companion to Late Antiquity* (Oxford: Wiley-Blackwell, 2009), pp. 455–466.

[44] Da'ūd ibn al-Ash'ath as-Sijistānī, *Kitāb al-Maṣāḥif* (Cairo: al-Maṭba'ah ar Raḥmāniyyah, 1355/1936), p. 6.

Among the Islamic traditions that address themselves to identifying the one whom, according to the Qur'ān, Muḥammad's adversaries said was teaching him, i.e., "the man to whom they point, whose language is foreign," (XVI *an-Naḥl* 103) a number mention that the person (or persons) in question had foreign writings at their disposal. Sometimes the traditions specify that the man was a Christian (or a Jew), and that he had read the Torah and the Gospel, or they say that he had books in his possession. They sometimes identify the 'foreign language' as 'Roman'/'Byzantine' (*rūmiyyah*), which one might take in a broad sense as a reference not just to Greek, but to one or another of the Late Antique languages of the Jews and Christians of the Roman/Byzantine Empire; and sometimes they explicitly mention Aramaic or Hebrew.[45] When all is said and done and one takes cognizance of other hints at the identities of those whom later Muslim scholars list among Muḥammad's informants—people such as Waraqah ibn Nawfal, the monk Sergius Baḥîrâ, Salmān al-Fārisī,[46] and those whom the traditions identify as Jewish or Christian slaves of well-known inhabitants

[45] See the important studies by Claude Gilliot, "Muḥammad, le Coran et les 'contraintes de l'histoire'," in Stefan Wild (ed.), *The Qur'ān as Text* (Islamic Philosophy, Theology, and Science, Texts and Studies, vol. 27; Leiden: E.J. Brill, 1996), pp. 3–26; *idem*, "Les 'Informateurs' juifs et chrétiens de Muḥammad: Reprise d'un probléme traité par Aloys Sprenger et Theodor Nöldeke," *Jerusalem Studies in Arabic and Islam* 22 (1998), pp. 84–126. See also the author's more tendentious study in Claude Gilliot, "Le Coran, fruit d'un travail collectif?" in D. De Smet et al. (eds.), *Al-Kitāb: La sacralité du texte dans le monde de l'Islam; Actes du Symposium International tenu à Leuven et Louvain-la-Neuve du 29 mai au 1 juin 2002* (Acta Orientalia Belgica, Subsidia III; Bruxelles, Louvain-la-Neuve, Leuven: Société Belge d'Études Orientales, 2004), pp. 185–231.

[46] These are three of the more prominent Christians in Muḥammad's entourage. Waraqah ibn Nawfal was the prophet's wife's cousin and one of the famed pre-Islamic, monotheist *ḥunafā'*. Pertinent to the present inquiry, Waraqah is said in some Muslim sources to have become a Christian during his travels in Syria. See C. F. Robinson, "Waraḳa b. Nawfal," *EI*, new rev. ed., vol. 11, pp. 142–143. Some recent writers have supposed that Waraqah was a priest who belonged to a 'Nazarene', 'Ebionite', Jewish Christian group in Mecca and that he exerted a considerable influence on Muḥammad. See, e.g., Joseph Azzi, *Le prêtre et le prophète: Aux sources du Coran* (trans. M. S. Garnier; Paris: Maisonneuve et Larose, 2001). The monk Sergius/Baḥīrā, a Syrian hermit, is celebrated in Islamic sources as one of the earliest religious figures to recognize Muḥammad's prophethood. See A. Abel, "Baḥīrā," in *EI*, new rev. ed., vol. 1, pp. 922–923. Salmān al–Fārisī, sometimes called Salmān Pāk, was an early Persian convert to Islam, who had previously become a Syrian Christian monk; he became a Muslim and an associate of Muḥammad in Yathrib/Medina, where he had been brought as a slave. See G. Levi della Vida, "Salmān al–Fārisī," *EI*, Supplement, pp. 701–702. Salmān has been the subject of numerous legends, particularly in Shī'ī circles. See Louis Massignon, "Salman Pak

of Mecca and Medina—at least one major modern scholar is prepared to conclude that the dominant 'foreign language' in question is none other than Aramaic in its Syriac idiom.[47]

The reports consistently mention books in connection with their accounts of those with whom Muḥammad was alleged to have been in conversation, but they never seem to have been Arabic books. Rather, they are said to be the scriptures of the Jews or the Christians in their own languages; sometimes the Torah and the Gospel are mentioned specifically. But it is the Qur'ān's special claim to have presented the earlier scriptural revelations in "clarifying Arabic" (XVI *an-Naḥl* 103; XXVI *ash-Shu'arā* 195). It is true that some reports say that Waraqah ibn Nawfal copied some Gospel passages in Arabic,[48] but nothing suggests that these, if they even existed, were more than personal notes or *aides de memoires.*[49] Some modern scholars, for reasons that we shall discuss below, have proposed that the Syriac *Diatessaron* or some other Syriac lectionary, or parts of one, was known in Medina in Muḥammad's day,[50] presumably in the hands of local, bilingual Christians. Such could well have been the case, but texts of this sort seem seldom to have been the property of individuals in Late Antiquity.[51] They would typically have been found in settings where the Divine Liturgy was celebrated, in such places as "the monasteries, churches, and oratories" (XXII *al-Ḥajj* 40), of which the Qur'ān speaks. But there are otherwise no textual reports or archaeological evidences of either churches or monasteries in central Arabia or in the Ḥijāz in Muḥammad's day, unless one is

---

et les prémices spirituelles de l'islam iranien," in Louis Massignon, *Parole donné* (Paris: Firmin-Didot, 1970), pp. 91–128.

[47] See Claude Gilliot, "Zur Herkunft der Gewährsmäner des Propheten," in Karl-Heinz Ohlig and Gerd R. Puin (eds.), *Die dunklen Anfänge: Neue Forschungen zur Entstehung und frühen Geschichte des Islam* (Berlin: Verlag Hans Schiler, 2005), pp. 148-178.

[48] See the discussion of these reports in Sidney H. Griffith, "The Gospel in Arabic: An Inquiry into its Appearance in the First Abbasid Century," *Oriens Christianus* 69 (1985), pp. 126–167, esp. pp. 144–149.

[49] See Gregor Schoeler, *Écrire et transmettre dans les débuts de l'Islam* (Paris: Presses Universitaires de France, 2002), pp. 26–29.

[50] See Gilliot, "Zur Herkunft der Gewährsmänner des Propheten," p. 166.

[51] An example of the exception that proves the rule might be seen in the sixth century story recounted in John of Ephesus' *Lives of the Eastern Saints,* according to which one famous monk was in possession of "a small Gospel book," from which he would read privately for hours in the church after the liturgy. See E. W. Brooks (ed. and trans.), *John of Ephesus, Lives of the Eastern Saints 1* (Patrologia Orientalis, vol. 17; Paris: Firmin–Didot, 1923), pp. 213–220, esp. p. 214.

disposed to accept the unlikely claim, based on a distinctive interpretation of some passages in the Qur'ān, that at one time these Gospel passages were used in the Christian liturgy celebrated in Arabic in the Ka'bah in Mecca.[52]

RECOGNIZING THE QUR'ĀN'S CHRISTIANS

The Qur'ān does in fact contain a substantial amount of evidence for the active presence of presumably Arabic-speaking Christians in Muḥammad's and the Qur'ān's own ambience. The crucial issue in this connection, however, is the hermeneutical frame of reference the interpreter brings to the construction he puts on the Qur'ānic evidence. The hypothesis suggested here is that the Qur'ān's Christians were Arabic speakers whose Christianity was representative of the confessional identities of the Syriac-speaking Christian communities living on the central Arabian periphery. It would have been transmitted among the Arabs initially by bilingual, Aramaic and Arabic-speaking tribal organizations that fostered the interests of the large neighboring Roman and Persian empires. But first we must discuss the hermeneutical issues that should be of major concern to anyone who uses the Qur'ān as a source of historical evidence.

Hermeneutics is largely about presumption. And the presumptions of the scholars of the Qur'ān have everything to do with the use they make of it. The present writer approaches the Islamic scripture not as a Qur'ān scholar but as a historian of Christianity among the Arabs and particularly of the Arabic-speaking Christian communities after the rise of Islam, which adopted Arabic as both their civil and ecclesiastical language following the Arab conquest of the Eastern Roman patriarchates: Alexandria, Antioch, and Jerusalem, and of the territories of the churches living under the jurisdiction of Persian Seleucia-Ctesiphon.[53] Inevitably the question arises about the relationship of the pre-Islamic Arabic-speaking Christians to the communities that adopted Arabic only after the rise of Islam. Actually, according to the hypothesis promoted in the present study, the Melkite, Jacobite, and Nestorian communities, which adopted Arabic after the rise of Islam and whose linguistic heritage was, as we have seen, largely Greek

[52] For this idea, see in particular Günter Lüling, *Über den Ur-Qur'ān: Ansätze zur Rekonstruction vorislamischer christlicher Strophenlieder im Qur'ān* (Erlangen: H. Lüling, 1974); *idem, Der christliche Kult an der vorislamischen Kaaba als Problem der Islamwissenschaft und christlichen Theologie* (Erlangen: H. Lüling, 1977).

[53] See Sidney H. Griffith, "From Aramaic to Arabic: The Languages of the Monasteries of Palestine in the Byzantine and Early Islamic Periods," *Dumbarton Oaks Papers* 51 (1997), pp. 11–31.

and Syriac, were the same communities from which in pre-Islamic times, and especially in the sixth and seventh centuries, Christianity had spread among the Arabic-speaking inhabitants of Arabia in the first place. But as irony would have it, and as we shall argue below, barring the possibility of a continuous, oral tradition of biblical translation, the only now traceable influence of pre-Islamic Arabic-speaking Christianity on the much larger, post-conquest Arabic-speaking communities of Islamic times came through the Arabic Qur'ān and not from any surviving, pre-Islamic, Christian Arabic texts. Hence the importance of searching out what can be known of the Qur'ān's Christians, their beliefs, their practices and, most important for the present inquiry, their scriptures.

Here is not the place for a long discussion of one's view of the Qur'ān. Suffice it to say that one approaches it as an integral text, with a history all its own. One cannot help but notice the high incidence of biblical lore in the Arabic scripture, along with numerous echoes of both Jewish, Jewish-Christian, and Christian themes and turns of phrase. But the Qur'ān seems to presume knowledge of these matters in its audience; there are hardly any extended narratives or re-tellings of biblical or other stories. We have instead only allusions to them and to their *dramatis personae*, comments on them, additional information about them, and new interpretations, as if the stories were already familiar. The Qur'ān has its own rhetoric and a distinctive stance toward those whom it calls 'People of the Book', or perhaps more accurately, 'Scripture People' (*ahl al-kitāb*), principally Jews and Christians. It is a polemical stance, critiquing the faith and practice of both communities. One is left to determine the identities of the Christians whom the Qur'ān criticizes from the distinctive traces one can discern in the language with which the Islamic scripture censures them. This is a dimension of the Qur'ān's rhetoric that many commentators on the Qur'ān's Christians and their beliefs have missed, thereby making a hermeneutical mistake. Instead of attempting to discern the Christians through the Qur'ān's rhetoric, they have looked from the other way around for Christian influences on what the Qur'ān has to say about Christians, as if the Qur'ān had no agenda of its own and were borrowing words, phrases, themes, and narratives rather than commenting on them from its own point of view. The scholars who adopted this latter approach, ignoring the Qur'ān's rhetoric, often supposed that Muḥammad and the Qur'ān had only a rudimentary or distorted view of the Bible and of Christianity.

In a search for the Qur'ān's Christians in the Qur'ān's own text, two locations immediately present themselves. The first, mostly but certainly not exclusively in Meccan *sūrahs*, is the substantial portion of the Islamic scripture that evokes biblical history, biblical *personae*, Christian lore, and echoes of Christian religious expressions. The second, mostly in Medinan *sūrahs*, are passages in which the Qur'ān directly addresses Christians, critiques their beliefs and practices, and takes issue in particular with their Christology.[54]

The Bible in the Meccan Sūrahs

The Meccan *sūrahs* that recall the Torah, the Psalms, and the Gospel, and speak familiarly of biblical personalities such as Adam, Noah, Abraham, Joseph, Moses, David, Solomon, Jonah, and Jesus the son of Mary, have long been studied by scholars looking for the origins of these themes and motifs in Jewish and Christian canonical and noncanonical sources.[55] Many problems have bedeviled their inquiries, one of the most pressing of them being the fact that in only a very few instances can one make the case for there being any actual quotations from the Jewish and Christian scriptures in the Qur'ān. Rather there are allusions to, comments on, and re-tellings of selected episodes in biblical stories. And in many passages, what the Qur'ān says is often at some variance with any extant Jewish or Christian text. This state of both harmony and disharmony in the presentations and evocations of canonical and noncanonical, Jewish and Christian prophetic history and its leading figures has in the past led many scholars, especially non-Muslims, to conclude that Muḥammad and the Qur'ān were only imperfectly or badly informed about the Bible and its contents and consequently made many mistakes in recalling biblical narratives.[56] Later Muslim scholars, following the lead of some passages in the Qur'ān itself, countered that the Jews and Christians had actually distorted their scriptures and changed them from their original form.[57] But one who is attentive to the Qur'ān's rhetoric and its homiletic style will notice that its text

[54] One notes in passing that some are questioning the chronological divisions between Meccan and Medinan *sūrahs* in the Qur'ān. See, e.g., Gabriel Said Reynolds, "Le problem de la chronologie du Coran," *Arabica* 58 (2011), pp. 477–502.

[55] See, e.g., Heinrich Speyer, *Die biblischen Erzählungen im Qoran* (reprint of 1931 ed.; Hildesheim: G. Olms, 1961).

[56] The charge of a defective and garbled knowledge of the Jewish and Christian scriptures on the part of Muḥammad and the Qur'ān was leveled against Muslims already in the early Islamic period and has been repeated by anti-Muslim polemicists down the centuries.

[57] See Jean-Marie Gaudeul, "Textes de la tradition musulmane concernant le *taḥrīf* (falsification) des écritures," *Islamochristiana* 6 (1980), pp. 61–104.

seldom, if ever, narrates Bible history. Rather, the Qur'ān assumes that its audience is thoroughly familiar with Jewish and Christian, canonical and noncanonical, scriptural and nonscriptural prophetic lore. As one recent scholar has convincingly argued, the Bible and its associated narratives can even reasonably be seen to be the Qur'ān's subtext in many passages.[58] And as we shall explore in the next chapter, a good case can also be made for the suggestion that the Qur'ān's stance in regard to the Bible is often that of a searcher for scriptural warranty, citing biblical narratives and evoking the memory of their prophetic figures for the purpose of commending a very distinctive Islamic prophetology.

The purpose now is to draw attention to the probable background of the Christian biblical lore, both canonical and apocryphal, that one can find echoed, alluded to, or evoked in the Qur'ān. Not to put too fine a point on it, most of the studies of Christian Bible history and other ecclesiastical lore reflected in the Qur'ān point to an Aramaic or Syriac provenance. Particularly noteworthy in this connection is the discernment on the part of a number of scholars of traces of familiarity with the *Diatessaron* in Qur'ānic passages that echo the New Testament.[59] Some have even pointed out that the only names of prophetic figures from the Hebrew Bible to appear are those mentioned in the *Diatessaron.*[60] Others have discerned the Syriac background even of such quintessentially Hebrew narratives as the stories of the patriarchs Abraham, Joseph, and Moses as they are evoked in the Qur'ān.[61] The same may be said for other Qur'ānic passages that comment on non-biblical, Christian stories such as the legend of the Seven Sleep-

[58] See Gabriel Said Reynolds, *The Qur'ān and Its Biblical Subtext* (Routledge Studies in the Qur'ān; London and New York: Routledge, 2010).

[59] See, e.g., Jan M. F. Van Reeth, "L'Évangile du Prophète," in De Smet, *Al-Kitāb: La sacralité du texte*, pp. 155–184.

[60] See John Bowman, "The Debt of Islam to Monophysite Christianity," in E.C.B. MacLaurin (ed.), *Essays in Honour of Griffithes Wheeler Thatcher 1863–1950* (Sydney: Sydney University Press, 1967), pp. 191–216, also published in *Nederlands Theologisch Tijdschrift* 19 (1964/1965), pp. 177–201; *idem*, "Holy Scriptures, Lectionaries and the Qur'ān," in A. H. Johns (ed.), *International Congress for the Study of the Qur'ān* (Australian National University, Canberra, May 813, 1980; Canberra: Australian National University, 1981), pp. 29–37.

[61] See, e.g., Joseph Witztum, "Joseph among the Ishmaelites: Q 12 in Light of Syriac Sources," in Gabriel Said Reynolds (ed.), *New Perspectives on the Qur'ān: The Qur'ān in Its Historical Context 2* (Routledge Studies in the Qur'ān; London and New York: Routledge, 2011), 425–448. See also the forthcoming work of Holger Zellentin on the reflections of the Syriac *Didascalia Apostolorum* in the text of the Qur'ān.

ers of Ephesus or the Alexander legends; they inevitably reveal their Syriac background.[62]

The point to be made here is not just that a large part of the biblical, apocryphal, and ecclesiastical lore in the Qur'ān has an immediate Aramaic/Syriac background, even when Greek, Coptic, or other expressions of it can also be found, but that they all had a circulation in the so-called Melkite, Jacobite, and Nestorian Christian communities of the first third of the seventh century. And all of these, on the basis of historical evidence, can arguably be found pressing into the Arabic-speaking milieu of Muḥammad and the Qur'ān in that period. In this connection one might cite the corroborating conclusion of Suleiman Mourad in his insightful study of Mary in the Qur'ān:

> Some of the Qur'ānic references to Mary and Jesus point to clear influence from canonical texts, particularly the *Gospel of Luke* or the quasi-canonical *Diatessaron*, as well as extra-canonical texts now considered apocryphal that were heavily used in the Near East before and around the time of the emergence of Islam, such as the *Protoevangelium of James*. These influences could have been exercised via popular mediums, and not necessarily through direct textual borrowing. Therefore, if one assumes that the Qur'ān does reflect the religious milieu of the prophet Muḥammad and his movement, then they were in contact with Christian groups who were using the *Gospel of Luke* or the *Diatessaron*, and the *Protevangelium of James*, among other sources. This, in my opinion, points in one direction: these Christian groups must have observed a mainstream type of Christianity, and could not have been heretical Christians.[63]

[62] See, e.g., Sidney H. Griffith, "Christian Lore and the Arabic Qur'ān: The 'Companions of the Cave' in *Sūrat al-Kahf* and in Syriac Christian Tradition," and Kevin Van Bladel, "The *Alexander Legend* in the Qur'ān 18:83–102," in Gabriel Said Reynolds (ed.), *The Qur'ān in Its Historical Context* (Routledge Studies in the Qur'ān; London and New York, 2008), pp. 109–137 and 175–203.

[63] Suleiman A. Mourad, "Mary in the Qur'ān: A Reexamination of her Presentation," in Reynolds, *The Qur'ān in Its Historical Context*, (pp. 163–174) p. 172. See also Suleiman A. Mourad, "On the Qur'ānic Stories about Mary and Jesus," *Bulletin of the Royal Institute for Inter-Faith Studies* 1 (1999), pp. 13–24; *idem*, "From Hellenism to Christianity and Islam: The Origin of the Palm-Tree Story concerning Mary and Jesus in the Gospel of Pseudo-Matthew and the Qur'ān," *Oriens Christianus* 86 (2002), pp. 206–216. See also Michael Marx, "Glimpses of a Mariology in the Qur'ān: From Hagiography to Theology via Religious-Political Debate," in A. Neuwirth,

It is the hypothesis advocated in the present study that the same may be said of the Christian doctrines and practices criticized in the Qurʾān; they were espoused by these same mainline Christian communities, whose presence among the Arabs in pre-Islamic times seems most likely. As for the so-called 'heretical Christians,' mostly Jewish Christians such as the Ebionites and Nazarenes who flourished well into the fourth century CE, while many scholars find evidence of them or of their doctrines in the Qurʾān, the present writer is skeptical of these claims. There has been a welcome crescendo in the study of Jewish Christianity ever since the work of Jean Daniélou and Hans Joachim Schoeps in the mid-twentieth century.[64] And beginning with Schoeps himself,[65] a number of scholars have since highlighted coincidences of doctrine and even of phraseology between the Qurʾān and texts of the fourth century and earlier that they believe provide evidence of the influence of Jewish Christian thought and practice. This development has prompted some to posit the existence of one or another of the Jewish Christian communities in the seventh century milieu of the Qurʾān's origins.[66] Others see a form of Jewish Christianity *redivivus* in nascent Islam.[67]

From the present writer's point of view, there are principally two methodological problems with these positions. First of all, there is little solid evidence for the persistence of Jewish Christian communities as such beyond the fourth century. Many of the texts and turns of phrase deemed reminiscent of Jewish Christianity were carried well beyond the fourth century in Late Antique Christian language traditions, and particularly in Aramaic, in communities that made every effort otherwise to accommodate themselves to various conciliar or theological, confessional formulae phrased originally in Greek. Their repertoires, like the Qurʾān's over-all reflection of Christian thought and practice, extend well beyond the resources of any given Jewish Christian community. In other words, the main Christian communities in the first third of the seventh century, especially in the realms of Aramaic and Arabic, were the most likely carriers of themes and turns of phrase

---

N. Sinai, M. Marx (eds.), *The Qurʾān in Context: Historical and Literary Investigations into the Qurʾānic Milieu* (Leiden: Brill, 2011), pp. 533–561.

64 Hans Joachim Schoeps, *Theologie und Geschichte des Judenchristentums* (Tübingen: J.C.B. Mohr (Paul Siebeck), 1949); Jean Daniélou, *Théologie du judéo-christianisme* (Paris: Desclée, 1958).

65 See Schoeps, *Theologie und Geschichte*, pp. 334–342.

66 See the studies listed in n.84 below.

67 See most recently Samuel Zinner, *The Abrahamic Archetype: Conceptual and Historical Relationships between Judaism, Christianity and Islam* (Bartlow, Camb.: Archetype, 2011).

deemed by some to be Jewish Christian. For that matter, coincidences of doctrine, especially in Christology, do not of themselves bespeak historical influences. Secondly, the drive to perceive Jewish Christianity *redivivus* in nascent Islam has the perhaps unintended effect of discounting both the integrity of the Qur'ān as a distinctive scripture and the distinctive and even critical stance it adopts toward the earlier 'People of the Book', whose diction it often reflects. This discounting effect often seems to prevent commentators from perceiving the polemical cast of the Qur'ān's language, and therefore to distort its point of view. This seems especially to be the case in regard to the Qur'ān's Christology and its view of the Christian doctrine of the Trinity, which the Qur'ān rejects. The Qur'ān critiques views contemporary with it; it is not simply a re-presentation of by-gone *theologoumena*, Jewish Christian or otherwise.

Medinan Sūrahs and the Critique of Christians

It is for the most part in the so-called Medinan *sūrahs* that the Qur'ān directly addresses the Christians polemically, criticizing their distinctive doctrines and practices.[68] While it is attractive to think that even confessed Jews and Christians might in Muḥammad's eyes have been included among the 'Believers' (*al-mu'minūn*) or the 'Community of Believers' of which the Qur'ān speaks, especially in the Meccan period of the 'Believers movement'[69] (and they were certainly within the Qur'ān's purview), the Islamic scripture never in fact directly addresses them as 'Believers'.[70] Rather, Jews and Christians were among those whom the Qur'ān calls 'People of the Book', or, perhaps more exactly, 'Scripture People' (*ahl al-kitāb*). The phrase occurs some fifty-four times in the Qur'ān, and one must determine from the context which community in particular the text is addressing in a given instance;

[68] It is very important in this context to be aware of the prominence of the Qur'ān's polemical intent. See Kate Zebiri, "Polemic and Polemical Language," in McAuliffe (ed.), *Encyclopaedia of the Qur'ān*, vol. 4, pp. 114–125. For an account of the exegesis of many of these passages in the Muslim commentary tradition, see Jane Dammen McAuliffe, *Qur'ānic Christians: An Analysis of Classical and Modern Exegesis* (Cambridge: Cambridge University Press, 1991).

[69] See Fred M. Donner, "From Believers to Muslims: Confessional Self-Identity in the Early Islamic Community," *Al-Abḥāth* 50–51 (2002–2003), pp. 9–53; *idem*, *Muḥammad and the Believers: At the Origins of Islam* (Cambridge, MA: Harvard University Press, 2010).

[70] Several verses of the Qur'ān make a clear distinction between "those who believe" and the Jews, Christians, Sabaeans, etc. Cf., e.g., V *al-Mā'idah* 51, 69, 82 and XXII *al-Ḥajj* 17.

sometimes the 'Scripture People' are all addressed together. Given the phrase's inclusive character and its resonance with the Qur'ān's formal recognition of the earlier scriptures, including the Torah, the Prophets, the Psalms, and the Gospel, one might also see in it the Qur'ān's own sense of its kinship, compatibility, and even its consonance with the earlier scriptures.[71]

In one verse the Qur'ān refers to the Christians as 'Gospel People': "Let the People of the Gospel judge in accordance with what God has revealed in it" (V *al-Mā'idah* 47).[72] But the curious thing is that the Qur'ān never calls the Christians 'Christians', even when addressing them directly. Some fourteen times, but never in direct address, the Qur'ān speaks of Christians as *an-naṣārā*, a term that seems to have both a geographical and an inner Qur'ānic resonance.[73] On the one hand, in the later Islamic exegetical literature the term is taken to be geographical and to refer to the Palestinian town of Nazareth, named in the New Testament as the hometown of Jesus and his mother Mary. On this view, and in accord with a certain usage in early Christian times in both Greek and Aramaic/Syriac, the Qur'ān is calling Christians 'Nazoreans' or 'Nazarenes'. On the other hand, pointing to a particular passage in the Qur'ān, some later Muslim commentators also postulate an etymological connection between the terms *an-naṣārā* and *al-anṣār*, 'helpers', on the basis of their shared root consonants, *n-ṣ-r*, and the Qur'ānic reference to Jesus' apostles (*al-ḥawāriyyūn*) saying in reply to Jesus' question, "Who are my helpers," "We are God's helpers (*anṣār Allah*), we believe in God. Testify that we are ones who submit (*muslimūn*)" (III *Āl 'Imrān* 52). Herewith the Muslim commentators neatly assign Jesus' true disciples, and therefore the real Christians, to the nascent Muslim community and separate them from the contemporary Melkites, Jacobites, and Nestorians, a move seconded in later times by none other than the famed literary figure, Abū 'Uthmān al-Jāḥiẓ (d.869) in his treatise 'Refutation of the Christians'. In regard to the passage in the Qur'ān that says, "You will find the closest of them in love to those who believe are those who say, 'We are *naṣārā*.'" (V *al-Mā'idah* 82), al-Jāḥiẓ remarked, "In this verse itself there is the best proof that God, exalted be He, did not mean these *an-naṣārā* [of

[71] See Madigan, *The Qur'ān's Self-Image*, esp. pp. 193–213.

[72] One commentator suggests that the phrase refers to scholars of the Gospel, in harmony with the reference to Rabbis and learned Jews in V *al-Mā'idah* 44. See Rudi Paret, *Der Koran: Kommentar und Kondordanz* (2nd ed.; Stuttgart: Verlag W. Kohlhammer, 1977), p. 122.

[73] See Jeffery, *The Foreign Vocabulary*, pp. 280–281. See also the fuller discussion in Sidney H. Griffith, "*Al-Naṣārā* in the Qur'ān: A Hermeneutical Reflection," in Reynolds, *New Perspectives on the Qur'ān*, pp. 301–322.

today] and their like, the Melkites and the Jacobites. He meant only the likes of Baḥīrā and the likes of the monks whom Salmān served."[74]

As the present writer has suggested elsewhere,[75] while from a historical point of view, it seems really to be the case that the Arabic term *an-naṣārā* in the Qur'ān is meant in the first place to reflect the sense of the Greek adjective 'Nazoraioi' via the Syriac *nāṣrāyê*, meaning Nazoreans/Nazarenes, it is not impossible that already in the time when the Qur'ān first addressed the Christians the Qur'ānic folk etymology of the later Muslim commentators was already in play orally. And if so, the Arabic-speaking Christians may well have been happy to be associated with 'God's helpers', and, with this cachet in mind, willing to say, "We are *naṣārā*" (V *al-Mā'idah* 14 and 82). In another place, the Qur'ān quotes both the local Jews and the Christians as being willing to say, "We are the children of God and His beloved" (V *al-Mā'idah* 18).

Two questions now come to the fore. Why would the Qur'ān not call Christians 'Christians', but use instead the term *an-naṣārā* for them? And who were and are the Christians so called? As the present writer has argued, it seems that the Qur'ān's choice of words in this connection is dictated by its own rhetorical, even apologetic and polemical concerns.[76] On the one hand, *an-naṣārā* receive a mild approval in the Qur'ān; they are included among the 'Scripture People', and they are the closest of the 'Scripture People' to the believers in affection. (V *al-Mā'idah* 82) On the other hand, as we shall see, a number of passages in Islamic scripture are critical of the standard Christian doctrines and of the practices typical of the contemporary Melkites, Jacobites, and Nestorians. But the appellation *an-naṣārā* does not appear in any of these critical, even polemical passages. Perhaps then, as the later Qur'ān commentators mentioned above have suggested, the Qur'ān itself makes a distinction between, on the one hand, the more acceptable, New Testament Christians, *an-naṣārā*, whom it calls by an ancient name with New Testament roots heretofore used principally by

[74] Abū 'Uthmān Amr al-Jāḥiẓ, "*Min kitābihi fī r-radd 'alā n-naṣārā*," in 'Abd as-Salām Muḥammad Hārū (ed.), *Rasā'il al-Jāḥiẓ* (4 parts in 2 vols.; Cairo: Maktabah al-Khānajī, 1399/1979), vol. 2, pp. 310–311. For Baḥīrā and Salmān, see n. 46 above.

[75] See Griffith, "*Al-Naṣārā* in the Qur'ān." For some interesting explorations in the deeper biblical and prophetic traditions in connection with the meaning of the root *n-ṣ-r*, see J.M.F. Van Reeth, "Le prophète musulman en tant que Nâsir Allâh et ses antécédents: Le 'Nazôraios' évangélique et le livre des Jubilés," *Orientalia Lovaniensia Periodica* 23 (1992), pp. 251–274.

[76] See Griffith, "*Al-Naṣārā* in the Qur'ān."

non-Christians in reference to Christians, and, on the other hand, those whose doctrines and practices it finds radically objectionable, namely the mostly Jacobite and Nestorian Christians actually within its purview, who are most often addressed more generally as 'Scripture People'.

On this reading, when the Qur'ān speaks of *an-naṣārā* it means to refer to those who, in its view, are like the followers of Jesus in his own day; perhaps those in its audience who were ready to accept the Qur'ānic message, including its critique of contemporary intra-Christian controversy, as in the passage that says:

> We also made a covenant with those who say, 'We are *an-naṣārā* and then they forgot a good portion of what was mentioned in it and so We incited enmity and anger between them to the Day of Resurrection and God will announce to them what they have been doing. (V *al-Mā'idah* 14)

In passages critical of Christian doctrines and practices, the Qur'ān is referring to the contemporary Christians, who, in its view, have gone beyond the bounds of their religion unjustly and have followed the fancies of earlier peoples who went astray. (cf. V *al-Mā'idah* 77) And the principal way they have gone astray, in the Qur'ān's judgment, is in what they say of the Messiah, Jesus, the son of Mary. The most comprehensively critical passage in the Qur'ān addressed to Christians is the following.

> O Scripture People, do not go beyond the bounds of your religion, and do not say about God anything but the truth. The Messiah, Jesus, the son of Mary, is God's messenger and His word He cast into Mary, and a spirit from Him. So believe in God and His messengers and do not say 'three'; stop it, it will be better for you. God is only one God. Glory be to Him, He has no child. His are whatever is in the heavens and whatever is on the earth. God suffices as one in whom to put one's trust. (IV *an-Nisā'* 171)

That Christians are the 'Scripture People' addressed here is evident from the nature of the critique leveled against them. That what they say about the Messiah, Jesus, Mary's son, is what leads them to speak of 'three' in reference to the one God seems equally clear. Similarly, that the Qur'ān here and consistently elsewhere speaks of Jesus as 'Mary's son', is most evidently to be taken rhetorically as a polemical corrective to the usual Melkite, Jacobite, or Nestorian habit of speaking of Jesus as 'the Son of God'. The passage furthermore, as Muslim commentators have consistently claimed, presents God's word and spirit as they are evoked here in connection with

Jesus, as referring to God's action in His messenger Jesus,[77] Word and spirit bespeak God's creative action and do not imply the 'association' (*ash-shirk*) with God that the Qur'ān thinks is meant by conventional Christian talk of God's Word and Spirit. Again, the Qur'ān's rhetoric is seen to be polemically corrective.

This point is made crystal clear in other passages. For example, in the following two verses, among several that Muḥammad is commanded to address to the 'Scripture People' (V *al-Mā'idah* 68), the Qur'ān speaks directly to current Christian usage.

> They have disbelieved who say that God is the Messiah, Mary's son. The Messiah said, 'O sons of Israel, serve God, my Lord and your Lord. God has certainly forbidden the Garden to one who gives God an associate; his abode is the fire and wrongdoers have no helpers (*anṣār*). They have surely disbelieved who say God is one of three (*thālithu thalāthatin*). There is no God save one God. If they do not stop what they are saying, a sore punishment will certainly touch those of them who have disbelieved. (V *al-Mā'idah* 72–73)

Rhetorically speaking, the two identical phrases at the beginning of the two successive verses, "They have disbelieved who say," are clearly critical of the following quotations attributed to those who say, "God is the Messiah, Mary's son," (vs. 72) and those who say, "God is one of three" (vs.73). But the quotations, while clearly meaning to censure Christian belief, do not in fact quote actual Christian usage of the era. Rather, the Christians in the Qur'ān's milieu would have said, 'the Messiah is God, the Son of God, and they would also have said, 'the Treble One, the One of Three, is God'. But for reasons of orthodoxy they would never have said that God is Jesus; rather, they would have said that Jesus is God. It seems clear, therefore, that here the Qur'ān, aware of actual Christian usage, has for its own rhetorically polemical reasons, reversed the customary Christian order of words in these formulaic phrases in order the more effectively to highlight what it considers wrong about Christian faith in Jesus, and to criticize what it regards as the objectionable Christian doctrine that God has a Son and that He is the Messiah, Jesus of Nazareth. The Qur'ān consistently and persistently teaches in varying phrases that God has no offspring; e.g., "How

[77] Elsewhere God speaks in the Qur'ān of how "Our word (*kalimatunā*) had previously come to our servants, the messengers" (XXXVII *aṣ-Ṣāffāt* 171), and of "our spirit whom We sent to her (i.e., Mary) and he seemed to her to resemble a well-shaped man" (XIX *Maryam* 17).

would He have offspring, not having a female consort" (VI *al-An'ām* 101). "It is not for God to take a child; Glory be to Him, when He determines a matter He but says to it, 'Be', and it comes to be" (XIX *Maryam* 35).[78] "God is one. . . . He has not begotten, nor is He begotten" (CXII *al-Ikhlāṣ* 1-3).

The historically troublesome term for commentators both ancient and modern in the passage quoted above from *sūrat al-Mā'idah* 73 is the phrase, *thālith thalāthatin*, 'one of three', sometimes translated as 'third of three'. Scholars have not heretofore recognized it as reflecting an epithet of Jesus the Messiah, common in mainstream Christian Syriac homiletic texts in the adjectival form *tlîthāyâ*, meaning,' one of three', 'treble', 'trine', and referring to Jesus the Son of God as 'one of three' in the Trinity, and as typologically characterized by 'three' on account of having spent three hours on the cross and three days in the tomb, just as Jonah spent three days in the belly of the whale.[79] Once the phrase is recognized as an Arabic rendering of the not uncommon Syriac epithet for Jesus the Messiah, the two verses quoted above (*sūrat al-Mā'idah* 72 and73) can be seen to be affirming the same judgment about the infidelity of those who say, in the Qur'ān's polemically inspired rendering, "God is the Messiah, Mary's son," or "God is one of three." At the same time it is clear once again that in the Qur'ān's view it is the objectionable doctrine that Christians affirm as true about Jesus, namely that he is God and the Son of God, that leads them into the further objectionable affirmation that the one God is also to be spoken of in terms of three.

The recognition of the Christian significance of the Qur'ān's phrase *thālith thalāthatin* in *sūrat al-Mā'idah* 73 effectively takes away the Qur'ānic basis for the allegation made by many commentators, ancient and modern, Muslim and non-Muslim, that since the Qur'ān speaks of the Messiah,

[78] Some half a dozen times in contexts of inter-religious controversy the Qur'ān repudiates those who say that God has taken, or adopted, a child, a son (*walad*). See II *al-Baqarah* 116; X *Yūnus* 68; XVIII *al-Kahf* 4; XIX *Maryam* 88; XXI *al-Anbiyā'* 26; XXIII *al-Mu'minūn* 91. The adversaries are either pagans or Christians, highlighting the Qur'ān likening what Christians say about Jesus to the errors of the pagans before them. See the passage addressed to the 'Scripture People' in V *al-Mā'idah* 77: "Do not follow the fancies of a people who went astray in the past and led others astray and strayed from the Right Path."

[79] For a full discussion of this matter, see Sidney H. Griffith, "Syriacisms in the Arabic Qur'ān: Who were 'those who said Allāh is third of three' according to *al-Mā'idah* 73?" in Meir M. Bar-Asher et al. (eds.), *A Word Fitly Spoken: Studies in Mediaeval Exegesis of the Hebrew Bible and the Qur'ān; Presented to Haggai Ben-Shammai* (Jerusalem: The Ben-Zvi Institute, 2007), pp. 83–110. The view espoused in this article is somewhat at variance with that of Block, "Philoponian Monophysitism."

Mary's son as 'third of three', the Qur'ān must espouse the view that the Christian Trinity consists of Allāh, the father, Mary of Nazareth, the mother, and Jesus, the Messiah, Mary's son, the 'third of three'.[80] These same commentators often cite *sūrat al-Mā'idah* 116 in support of this allegation, a verse that from the point of view of rhetorical analysis appears within a group of verses (109–120) that feature "Jesus' and his apostles' profession of monotheistic faith."[81] Here God asks, "O Jesus, son of Mary, have you said to people, 'Take me and my mother as two gods besides God?' He said, 'Glory be to You; it is not for me to say what is not for me the truth'" (V *al-Mā'idah* 116). Rhetorically speaking, the verse cannot reasonably be taken as evidence that the Qur'ān supposes that Mary, the mother of Jesus, is a member of the Christian Trinity. Rather, God's question to Jesus puts in high relief what the Qur'ān thereby highlights as being, from its point of view, the absurd corollary of the Christian belief that Jesus is the Son of God, namely that Mary his mother must therefore also somehow be divine. The passage in fact recalls the then current theological controversy dividing the largely Syriac/Aramaic-speaking, Jacobite and Nestorian Christians in the Qur'ān's own milieu over the propriety and veracity of the Marian title *theotokos*, 'Mother of God'.[82] Nestorian Christians rejected the title for much the same reason as does the Qur'ān in this verse; it would seem logically to claim too much for Jesus' human mother. The Jacobites, to the contrary, supported the propriety and orthodoxy of this title for Mary because in their view it protects the Nicene affirmation of the full divinity of Jesus of Nazareth as the consubstantial (*homoousios*) Son of God the Father. This matter was at the heart of the long drawn out, church-dividing Christological controversies that troubled the Christians of the sixth and seventh centuries. And here, as elsewhere, the Qur'ān seems very much *au courant* with precisely these matters.[83]

[80] See, e.g., Rudolph, *Die Abhängigkeit des Qorans von Judentum und Christentum*, pp. 86–88; Watt, *Muhammad at Mecca*, pp. 23–29; *idem*, "The Christianity Criticized in the Qur'ān," *The Muslim World* 57 (1967), pp. 197–201. Sometimes those who espouse this view cite the alleged presence in Arabia of a heretical sect called 'Collyridians'. See Hainthaler, *Christliche Araber vor dem Islam*, p. 55.

[81] Michel Cuypers, *The Banquet: A Reading of the Fifth Sura of the Qur'ān* (trans. Patricia Kelly; Series Rhetorica Semitica; Miami, FL: Convivium Press, 2009), pp. 395–440.

[82] This connection was suggested already by Rudolph, *Die Abhängigkeit des Qorans*, p. 87.

[83] See in particular the studies of Frank van der Velden, "Konvergenztexte syrischer und arabischer Christologie: Stufen der Textentwicklung von Sure 3, 33–64," *Oriens Christianus* 91 (2007), pp. 164–203; *idem*, "Kotexte im Konvergenztrang—die

The significance for the historian of paying close attention to the Qur'ān's polemically inspired rhetoric criticizing the major Christian doctrines in its milieu becomes apparent when one realizes that the polemic is directed at these doctrines and their customary formulae as they were actually professed by the very Melkite, Jacobite, and Nestorian Christians whose increasing infiltration into Arabia in the first third of the seventh century is historically attested. Ignoring or discounting the Qur'ān's rhetorical purposes in these passages of doctrinal critique, scholars have often taken them not as polemical characterizations and rebuttals of standard Christian teachings at the time, but somehow as reports or echoes of the views of heterodox Christians living in the Qur'ān's milieu, groups such as the ancient Nazarenes, Ebionites, and other Judeo-Christian communities,[84] for whose presence in this milieu there is virtually no historical evidence at all, save scholars' inferences from what appears to be a misreading of the relevant Qur'ānic passages and a misinterpretation of their actual polemical agenda. For, taking account of the Qur'ān's own positions in regard to the *theologoumena* espoused in the Christian teachings it criticizes, and unwarrantedly assuming that the Qur'ān must have inherited its own teachings from some Christian group in its milieu, these scholars have often looked for, and found, references to Christian groups mentioned in the ancient heresiographies. On that basis they then postulated the presence of remnants of such groups

---

Bedeutung textkritischer Varianten und christlicher Bezugstexte für die Redaktion von Sure 61 und Sure 5, 110–119," *Oriens Christianus* 92 (2008), pp. 130–173.

[84] This line of reasoning had been adumbrated in modern times already by Julius Wellhausen, *Reste arabischen Heldentumes* (Berlin: G. Reimer, 1897), p. 232. It was explicitly put forward by Hans Joachim Schoeps, *Theologie und Geschichte des Judenchristentums* (Tübingen: Mohr, 1949), pp. 334–342, where, just prior to his section on *Ebionitische Elemente im Islam,* Schoeps remarks that "ein sektirериches Christentum teilweise judenchristlichen Charaketers war es, das Muhammed am Beginn seiner Laufbahn unter dem Namen N a ṣ a r a—einer Sammelbezeichnung der Sekten Ostsyriens-Arabiens—kennenlernte." p. 334. Most recently this point of view has been most ably presented by François de Blois, "*Naṣrānī (Ναζωραιος)* and *ḥanīf (εθνικος)*: Studies on the Religious Vocabulary of Christianity and of Islam," *Bulletin of the School of Oriental and African Studies* 65 (2002), pp. 1–30; Edouard M. Gallez, *Le messie et son prophète: Aux origines de l'islam* (vol. 1: De Qumrân à Muhammad, 2nd ed.; Paris: Éditions de Paris, 2005); Joachim Gnilka, *Die Nazarener und der Koran: Eine Spurensuche* (Freiburg: Herder, 2007). See also the effort to see a recrudescence of third century CE Montanism and Manichaeism in early Islam, in J.M.F. Van Reeth, "La typologie du prophète selon le Coran: le cas de Jésus," in G. Dye and F. Nobilio, *Figures bibliques en islam* (Fernelment, BE: Éditions Modulaires Européennes, 2011), pp. 81–105.

as the Nazarenes or other Judeo-Christian communities in the Arabic-speaking milieu in the first third of the seventh century, even when there is no confirming historical evidence of their presence there at the requisite time or place, and in spite of the abundant evidence of the presence of the historically discoverable Melkites, Jacobites, and Nestorians. The mistake these scholars have made is the hermeneutical one of failing to notice the Qur'ān's polemical rhetoric against the Christian doctrines it critiques and consequently interpreting its language in these critical passages as evocations of or reflections of the teachings of Christian communities not otherwise known to have been in the Qur'ān's world. In other words, their own misreading of the pertinent Qur'ānic passages became their evidence for postulating the lingering presence of Christian groups in Arabia at a time when no other evidence supports their presence there and abundant evidence indicates that the communities whose doctrines the Qur'ān directly criticizes in its own very effective rhetorical style were present.[85] What is more, it is important to recognize the probability that themes and turns of phrase that can also be found in earlier Jewish Christian sources had long since entered the stream of mainline Christian discourse, especially in the Aramaic/Syriac-speaking communities of the early seventh century. The Qur'ān's seeming espousal of positions earlier owned by some Jewish Christians hardly constitutes evidence for the actual presence of one or another of these long-gone communities in its seventh-century Arabian milieu.

Even in the notoriously difficult case of the Qur'ān's seeming denial of Jesus' death on the cross in *sūrat an-Nisā'* 157, the text can be seen to be echoing the language of contemporary Christian controversy within the context of the Qur'ān's criticism of the Jews. The passage upbraids the Jews for, among other things, allegedly claiming to have crucified and killed "the Messiah, Jesus, son of Mary."[86] The Qur'ān says: "They did not kill him and they did not crucify him, but it was made to seem so to them (*shubbiha lahum*). Those who differ about it are certainly in doubt of it; they have no knowledge of it except the following of opinion. They certainly did not kill him. Rather, God raised him up to Himself; God is mightily wise" (IV *an-Nisā'* 157–158).

[85] See the case for this assessment made at greater length in Griffith, "*Al-Naṣārā* in the Qur'ān."

[86] Passages seeming to claim as much can be found in the Talmud and may have been known to the Arabic-speaking Jews in the Qur'ān's milieu. See Peter Schäfer, *Jesus in the Talmud* (Princeton, NJ: Princeton University Press, 2007), pp. 63–74.

While on the face of it the Qur'ānic passage would seem only to be denying that the Jews crucified and killed Jesus, in the Islamic interpretive tradition the verse is widely taken to deny that Jesus died by crucifixion at all.[87] But what has long attracted the attention of Western commentators to the passage is the 'docetic' sense of the enigmatic phrase, "it was made to seem so to them (*shubbiha lahum*)."[88] More or less ignoring the Qur'ān's reference here to the alleged Jewish claim to have been responsible for Jesus' execution, many scholars have found in this phrase an echo of the beliefs of those Christian thinkers called 'Docetists' by their adversaries because they taught that Jesus' sufferings during his passion and crucifixion were not really affecting him but were made to seem so to the onlookers.[89] And indeed it is the case that among the Jacobites of the Qur'ān's day, Syriac-speaking theologians in the tradition of Severus of Antioch (c. 465–538) were still condemning the thought of Julian of Halicarnassus (d.c. 518) and his followers, whose teachings about Christ's body, they charged, were of a 'docetic', 'phantasiast' character, claiming that the body of Christ, in accord with his single divine nature, was divine and therefore naturally incorruptible and impassible.[90] And it is certainly possible that the views of the so-called 'Julianists' were known among Arabic-speaking Christians, given their reported presence in Najrān and elsewhere on the Arabian periphery.[91] But

[87] See now Todd Lawson, *The Crucifixion and the Qur'ān: A Study in the History of Muslim Thought* (Oxford: Oneworld, 2009); Gabriel Said Reynolds, "The Muslim Jesus: Dead or Alive?" *Bulletin of the School of Oriental and African Studies* 72 (2009), pp. 237–258.

[88] One notable modern scholar, taking another tack, took the phrase to be an "unconscious memory" of Philippians 2:7, "where Jesus 'being in the form of God' was '*made in the likeness of* men'." R. C. Zaehner, *At Sundry Times: An Essay in the Comparison of Religions* (London: Faber and Faber, 1958), "Appendix: The Qur'ān and Christ," p. 211.

[89] See, e.g., Rudolph, *Die Abhängigkeit des Qorans*, p. 82; Neal Robinson, *Christ in Islam and Christianity* (Albany, NY: State University of New York Press, 1991), pp. 110–111, 127–141.

[90] See René Draguet, *Julien d'Halicarnasse et sa controverse avec Sévere d'Antioche sur l'incorruptibilité du corps du Christ: Étude d'histoire littéraire et doctrinale suivie des fragments dogmatiques de Julien; texte syriaque et traduction grecque* (Louvain: P. Smeesters, 1924); Aloys Grillmeier and Theresia Hainthaler, *Christ in Christian Tradition* (vol. 2, Part 2, trans. John Cawte and Pauline Allen; London and Louisville, KY: Mowbray and Westminster John Knox Press, 1995), pp. 79–111.

[91] See Hainthaler, *Christliche Araber vor dem Islam*, pp. 105–106, 133–134. There is no historical record of the presence in Arabia in the sixth and seventh centuries of Gnostic groups such as would have been aware of the second-century Gnostic 'Apocalypse of Peter'. This text, found at Nag Hammadi in Egypt in a Coptic version of what may have been a Greek original, records the following statement of Peter:

it seems more likely that these Christian themes would have influenced the later Muslim exegetes of the Qur'ān, who seem to have espoused a certain kind of Docetism of their own with regard to the crucifixion of Jesus, rather than to have influenced the Qur'ān itself, busy as it was in this passage with its critique of what it took as an unwarranted claim about the death of Jesus on the part of the Jews in its milieu. Nevertheless, it was indeed also the case that this matter of a docetic Christology was of interest to the Jacobite Christians, who were in all likelihood within the Qur'ān's purview. Furthermore, the death of Jesus at the instigation of the community to which he was sent as God's messenger is notably at variance with the Qur'ān's own typology of prophecy and messenger-ship, as will be explored in the next chapter of the present study.

In the end, what one wants to show is that when the Qur'ān's polemical critique of the beliefs of the Christians within its purview is taken seriously and its rhetorical character is duly taken into account, these Christians are seen to have for the most part held the views of the contemporary Melkites, Jacobites and Nestorians of the historical record and not some lost and otherwise historically unattested remnants of much earlier, so-called heretical groups not known to have been in Arabia or on its periphery in the first third of the seventh century. Accordingly, the Christian Bible known to the Qur'ān's Christians would have been the scriptures as these mainline Christians had them at the time. Their narratives, as reflected in the Qur'ān, are, as we shall see, much more extensive than the texts in the possession of the earlier Jewish Christian communities. Whereas, much that was in the hands of the Jewish Christians had long since, like most of the Jewish Christians themselves, passed into the communities and scriptural traditions of later Christian communities, especially in the Aramaic/Syriac-speaking communities.

Neither Jews nor Christians

While there is every reason to think that the Jews and Christians among the Arabic-speaking peoples in the first third of the seventh century were, as we have argued, of the mainstreams of their respective communities, there

"The Savior said to me, 'He whom you saw on the tree, glad and laughing, this is the living Jesus. But this one into whose hands and feet they drive the nails is his fleshly part, which is the substitute being put to shame, the one who came into being in his likeness. But look at him and me'." James Brashler and Roger A. Bullard, "The Apocalypse of Peter," in James M. Robinson (ed.), *The Nag Hammadi Library in English* (4th rev. ed.; Leiden: E.J. Brill, 1996), vii, 3, pp. 372–378, esp. 376.

were of course other confessional communities in the same milieu. In addition to the Jews and the Christians, the Qur'ān also mentions the Magians (*al-Majūs*) and the Sabians (*aṣ-ṣābi'ūn*) (XXII *al-Ḥajj* 17). It is widely agreed among scholars that the Magians were the Zoroastrians of the Qur'ān's day, whose presence among the Persians on the Arabian periphery and in Arabia proper is well attested.[92] The identity of the Sabians has been more difficult to establish, but there is a growing consensus that the name, which occurs three times in the Qur'ān,[93] refers to the Manichaeans.[94] They were in fact a constant presence throughout the Middle East in Late Antiquity and especially in territories on the periphery of Arabia, in Egypt, Syria, Mesopotamia, and Persia.[95] The spread of Manichaeism among Arabic-speaking communities in the early seventh century was no more unlikely than the spread of Judaism and Christianity among them. The importance of recognizing their highly probable presence for this study lies in the fact that the Manichaeans too had a canonical scripture that in many ways echoed the themes of earlier Jewish and Christian scriptures, as well as the narratives of a number of texts considered apocryphal or pseudepigraphical among the Jews and Christians.[96] It follows that the Manichaeans might also have

[92] See William R. Darrow, "Magians," in McAuliffe, *Encyclopaedia of the Qur'ān*, vol. 3, pp. 244–245.

[93] II *al-Baqarah* 62; V *al-Mā'idah* 69; XXII *al-Ḥajj* 17.

[94] See, e.g., Moshe Gil, "The Creed of Abū 'Āmir," *Israel Oriental Studies* 12 (1992), pp. 9–47; M. Tardieu, "L'arrivée des manichéens à al-Ḥīra," in Pierre Canivet and Jean-Paul Rey-Coquais (eds.), *La Syrie de Byzance à l'Islam VIIe–VIIIe siècles: Actes du colloque international, Lyon-Maison de l'Orient Méditerranien, Paris—Institut de Monde Arabe, 11–15 Septembre 1990* (Damas: Institut Français de Damas, 1992), pp. 15–24; James A. Bellamy, "More Proposed Emendations to the Text of the Koran," *Journal of the American Oriental Society* 116 (1996), pp. 196–204, esp. pp. 201–203; Róbert Simon, "Mānī and Muḥammad," *Jerusalem Studies in Arabic and Islam* 21 (1997), pp. 118–141; François de Blois, "The 'Sabians' (*ṣābi'ūn*) in Pre-Islamic Arabia," *Acta Orientalia* 56 (1995), pp. 39–61; idem, "Sabians' in McAuliffe, *Encyclopaedia of the Qur'ān*, vol. 4, pp. 511–513; idem, "*Naṣrānī* and *Ḥanīf*"; idem, "Elchasai—Manes—Muḥammad: Manichäismus und Islam in religionshistorischen Vergleich," *Der Islam* 81 (2004), pp. 31–48.

[95] See Samuel N. C. Lieu, *Manichaeism in Mesopotamia and the Roman East* (Leiden: E.J. Brill, 1994); *idem, Manichaeism in Central Asia and China* (Leiden: Brill, 1998).

[96] The echoes of and allusions to biblical and apocryphal narratives in Manichaean texts is an under-studied area of Manichaean studies. But see, e.g., L. Koenen, "Manichaean Apocalypticism at the Crossroads of Iranian, Egyptian, Jewish and Christian Thought," in Luigi Cirillo (ed.), *Codex Manichaicus Coloniensis: Atti del Simposio Internazionale (Rende–Amantea 3–7 settembre 1984)* (Cosenza: Marra Editore, 1986), pp. 285–332.

served as one of the conduits for the spread of scriptural knowledge among early-seventh-century Arabs,[97] albeit not the major conduit through which a common awareness of biblical narratives and personalities could have flowed. And in this connection one should not forget that Manichaeism persisted into early Islamic times.[98]

Was There a Pre-Islamic Arabic Bible?

Given the high level of scriptural knowledge among the Arabic-speaking peoples of the Qurʾān's era, especially as regards the biblical patriarchs and prophetical figures and their exploits, the question naturally arises of the state of the biblical text in Arabic at that time. Did Arabic-speaking Jews or Christians in pre-Islamic times produce an Arabic translation of any portion of the Bible in writing, at least for liturgical purposes? One would expect this to have been the case, especially among the Christians, given the fact that in comparable cultural situations elsewhere in Late Antiquity, Christians did produce written translations of the Bible. And they did so even where there is no appreciable evidence that the local lore had yet been put in writing, so that the Christians sometimes became the first to devise a script for the language.[99] Did the Arabic-speaking Christians do this? As Professor Irfan Shahid and others have long argued, it is certainly possible that Arabic-speaking Christians long before the early seventh century had, for the sake of the liturgy in Arabic, already translated at least the Gospel and the Psalms into Arabic.[100] The problem is that so far, aside from extrapolations scholars have made from much later material, including even from some rather inconclusive remarks found here and there in earlier Syriac or Arabic sources, no conclusive documentary or clear textual evidence of a

[97] See, e.g., the suggestions made by Cornelia B. Horn, "Lines of Transmission between Apochryphal Traditions in the Syriac-speaking World: Manichaeism and the Rise of Islam—the Case of the *Acts of John*," *Parole de l'Orient* 35 (2010), pp. 337–355.

[98] See John C. Reeves, *Prolegomena to a History of Islamicate Manichaeism* (Comparative Islamic Studies; Sheffield, UK and Oakville, CT: Equinox, 2011).

[99] In this connection, Irfan Shahid cites the example of the Armenian script devised by Mesrop Meshtots (361/2–440), who then translated the Bible into Armenian. See Shahid, *Byzantium and the Arabs in the Fifth Century*, p. 426.

[100] See in particular, Shahid, *Byzantium and the Arabs in the Fourth Century*, pp. 435–443; Shahid, *Byzantium and the Arabs in the Fifth Century*, pp. 422–429, 449–450; Shahid, *Byzantium and the Arabs in the Sixth Century*, vol. 2, part 2, p. 295.

pre-Islamic, written Bible in Arabic translation has yet come to light. Nevertheless there is overwhelming Qur'ānic evidence for a high level of awareness on the part of the Islamic scripture itself, and therefore on the part of the Qur'ān's audience, of biblical stories and even a bit of exegetical and midrashic knowledge of the Jewish and Christian scriptures and their interpretations. The latter extends to details of stories otherwise found only in apocryphal and pseudepigraphical texts, not to mention non-biblical works such as homiletic texts, saints' lives, and even liturgical and legal texts.

In this connection, one must envision the situation in which biblical passages and their interpretations would have been heard among Jews and Christians in Late Antiquity, especially those in the Aramaic and Syriac-speaking communities that were the most immediately in conversation with Arabic-speaking Christians. Texts of the scriptures or of portions of them would normally have been in the possession of synagogues, churches, shrines, and monasteries, or in the hands of rabbis, priests and monks, rather than in private hands. Aramaic, Syriac, and Arabic-speaking Jews and Christians would thus have heard scriptural passages proclaimed in the course of the celebration of the liturgies in their places of study and worship, followed by songs and homilies that unfolded the meanings of the texts for the congregants. In the Syriac-speaking communities of the early seventh century, the most common genre in which these lessons would have been put forward were the metrically composed *mêmrê,* often long meditations on the significance of some aspect of the scripture reading, interpreted within the exegetical tradition of the creedal community.[101] In this homiletic process, which was both exploratory, in a midrashic sense, and hortatory in character, biblical narratives became the starting points for exegetical stories, even dialogues, about the patriarchs and prophets, enriched by details often not found in the biblical texts themselves, but rather in oral tradition or in apocryphal or even pseudepigraphical sources that in many instances were preserved in written form in Syriac texts kept in monasteries and churches. Knowledge of the contents of these texts circulated widely in all the Christian communities of the time, and their non-biblical, or non-scriptural character was freely admitted, a circumstance that seems not to have prevented their wide circulation in the homiletic tradition. As in the case of the biblical narratives themselves, there is no surviving evidence that written translations of these homilies in Arabic were made in pre-Islamic

[101] Particularly popular in the Syriac tradition were the homilies (*mêmrê*) of Ephraem the Syrian (c. 306–373), Jacob of Serūg (c. 450–520/1) among the Jacobites, and Narsai (c. 399–c. 503) among the Nestorians.

times. But clearly they were composed to be memorable and their popular character would certainly have lent itself to the spontaneous translation of their contents in the course of a liturgy among predominantly Arabic-speaking congregants.

Given the level of writing in Arabic in pre-Islamic times, and the lack of surviving, written texts of translations of the Bible or of the Christian homiletic literature, or, for that matter, of any kind of literature, including pre-Islamic Arabic poetry,[102] one is left to conclude that knowledge of their contents normally spread orally among Arabic-speaking peoples. Originally Hebrew, Aramaic, Greek, or Syriac-speaking rabbis, monks, and Christian clergy must have transmitted the biblical and homiletic literature orally in Arabic, perhaps even functioning within traditions of oral translation. For the fact remains that, as even the most enthusiastic researchers into the history of pre-Islamic, written Arabic must admit,[103] in fact the Arabic Qur'ān remains the earliest written Arabic text of any literary length or significance that we can actually put our hands on.[104] All other compositions in Arabic, including pre-Islamic poetry, have survived in writing only in texts written well after the rise of Islam.

[102] There is a long scholarly tradition, championed most insistently in modern times by Louis Cheikho, SJ (1859–1927), and seconded by Irfan Shahid in the volumes previously cited, according to which Christian literary use of Arabic was widespread before the rise of Islam, especially in the work of the pre-Islamic Christian Arabic poets. See Camille Hechaïme, *Louis Cheikho et son livre*; Hechaïme, *Bibliographie analytique du père Louis Cheikho* (Beyrouth: Dar el-Machreq, 1978). On the importance of pre-Islamic Arabic poetry for the study of the Qur'ān, albeit preserved only in post-Islamic texts, see Thomas Bauer, "The Relevance of Early Arabic Poetry for Qur'ānic Studies, Including Observations on *kull* and on Q 22:27, 26:225, and 52:31," in Neuwirth et al., *The Qur'ān in Context*, pp. 699–732.

[103] See, e.g., Schoeler, *Écrire et transmettre*. Perhaps the best expression of the situation is: "The pre-Islamic formation and early Islamic documentation of Arabic script suggest that it was readily available at the time of the Prophet." Beatrice Gruendler, "Arabic Script," in McAuliffe, *Encyclopaedia of the Qur'ān*, vol. 1, p. 136. See also Alan Jones, "Orality and Writing in Arabia," in McAuliffe, *Encyclopaedia of the Qur'ān*, vol. 3, pp. 587 ff.; Robert Hoyland, "Mount Nebo, Jabal Ramm, and the Status of Christian Palestinian Aramaic and Old Arabic in Late Roman Palestine and Arabia," in M.C.A. Macdonald (ed.), *The Development of Arabic as a Written Language* (Proceedings of the Seminar for Arabian Studies, vol. 40; Oxford: Archaeopress, 2010), pp. 29–46; M.C.A. Macdonald, "Ancient Arabia and the Written Word," in Macdonald, *The Development of Arabic*, pp. 5–28.

[104] As Gregor Schoeler has memorably put it, "Le premier livre de l'islam et en même temps de la littérature arabe est le Coran." Schoeler, *Écrire et transmettre*, p. 26.

So where does this leave us in regard to a written Bible in Arabic in pre-Islamic times? To answer this question, one must first of all, if only briefly, take into account the proposals of those who have supported the thesis that there was a pre-Islamic, written Arabic Bible, or portions of one, which could have served as a background source for the high quotient of biblical knowledge evident in the Qur'ān and presumed in its audience. So far in modern times these proposals seem to have been made mostly in regard to the Christian Bible,[105] and particularly to the Gospel and the Psalms, texts important for the Christian liturgy. But before we consider these suggestions, we must briefly take note of reports found in early Islamic texts that mention translating portions of the scriptures into Arabic or copying down biblical passages in pre- or early Islamic times.

Perhaps the most intriguing possible reference to taking notes in Arabic from the scriptures of the 'People of the Book' in an early Islamic texts is in the Qur'ān itself, as Gregor Schoeler has recently suggested.[106] He calls attention to the following passage, in which the Qur'ān, having just ridiculed the polytheists and reaffirmed God's omnipotence (and the fact that He has neither offspring nor counterpart), goes on to say the following in reference to the adversaries' remarks about Muḥammad's message:

> Those who disbelieve say, "This is nothing but a falsehood he has concocted, with which other people have helped him, having come along deceitfully and deceptively. They say he has had the stories of the ancients written down and they are dictated to him day and night." (XXV *al-Furqān* 4-5)

Schoeler, well aware that "the stories of the ancients" in this passage are usually taken to mean ancient myths about the gods of the pagans, nevertheless points out that the text at the very least supports the view that the practice of taking notes in writing in Arabic was a commonplace in Muḥammad's time and milieu. He goes on to suggest that it is furthermore not implausible to think that those reciting "the stories of the ancients"

[105]Yosef Tobi has suggested the possibility that there was also a pre-Islamic translation of portions of the Hebrew Bible into Arabic. See Yosef Tobi, "On the Antiquity of the Judeo-Arabic Biblical Translations and a New Piece of an Ancient Judeo-Arabic Translation of the Pentateuch," in Y. Tobi and Y. Avishur (eds.), *Ben 'Ever la-'Arav: Contacts between Arabic Literature and Jewish Literature in the Middle Ages and Modern Times* (vol. 2; Tel Aviv: Afikim Publishers, 2001), pp. 17–60 [Hebrew]. I am indebted to Prof. Meira Polliack for this reference.

[106]See Schoeler, *Écrire et transmettre,* p. 28.

could just as well have been "Christian monks and missionaries who were reciting salvation history in Arabic."[107]

However plausible this suggestion might be, and one must admit its attractiveness, there are other references in early Islamic texts to individuals possessing or writing down scriptural texts in Arabic. For example, Schoeler cites traditions from the work of al-Khaṭīb al-Baghdādī (1002–1071) about the future caliph ʿUmar having copied one of the books of the 'People of the Book', presumably in Arabic, and having to abandon it on the orders of an angry Muḥammad, and of ʿUmar himself having at a later time punished a man from the Arab tribe of ʿAbd al-Qays for having a copy of the Book of Daniel in his possession, ordering him not to recite it to anyone at all.[108] But perhaps the most telling story of this sort appears in the much earlier biographical traditions about Muḥammad and refers to a Meccan Arab Christian of his time, who played a major role in his life, namely Waraqah ibn Nawfal, whom we have mentioned earlier.[109]

In the several renditions of Waraqah's story that have come down to us in early Muslim sources, the constant features are that he had become a Christian, that he was learned in the scriptures, and that when the prophet had his inaugural revelation and described the experience to Waraqah, the latter recognized immediately Muḥammad's prophetic vocation. Embedded in the several accounts about Waraqah one finds the report that "he used to write *al-kitāb al-ʿarabī* and that he would write down from the Gospel *bil-ʿarabiyyah* whatever God wanted him to write." Alternatively, one finds it said, "He used to read the Gospel *bil-ʿarabiyyah*," and even, "He used to write *al-kitāb al-ʿibrānī*, and that he would write down from the Gospel *bil-ʿibrāniyyah*."[110] What is consistent in these brief reports is that Waraqah could write and that he used this skill "to write down from the Gospel." The only significant variant concerns the language, Arabic or Hebrew. Given the fact that Waraqah was a Meccan and a native Arabic-speaker and a Christian, there was hardly any need for him to write in Hebrew. It is not unlikely that in this instance 'Hebrew' refers to an Aramaic script, perhaps Syriac,

[107] Schoeler, *Écrire et transmettre*, p. 28. It is interesting to note in passing that some have opined long ago that the Arabic root in this passage, *s-ṭ-r*, and specifically in its plural form, *asāṭīr*, "seems to be derived from the Greek ἱστορία." John Penrice, *A Dictionary and Glossary of the Kor-ân* (London: Henry S. King and Co., 1873), p. 69. See also Franz Rosenthal, "Asāṭīr al-awwalīn," in *EI*, new rev. ed., vol. 12, p. 90.

[108] See Schoeler, *Écrire et transmettre*, pp. 28–29.

[109] See n. 45 above.

[110] See these passages and their sources discussed in some detail in Griffith, "The Gospel in Arabic," pp. 144–149.

but it is even more likely that the report simply became garbled in transmission.[111] For the present purpose, the most important bit of information contained in Waraqah's story is that he was in the habit of making written notes from the Gospel. The question then becomes, is it likely that he took his notes from a written copy of the Gospel or from the oral proclamation of the scripture, perhaps in a liturgical setting? If the former was the case, given the conclusion to which we shall come below, it is more likely that he took notes in Arabic from a text written in Syriac, hence the mistaken identification of it in later Muslim reports as Hebrew. If he took notes from hearing the Gospel proclaimed, it is likely that he heard it in Arabic, as we shall argue below, and took his notes also in Arabic. The important point here is that Waraqah's story accords well with Gregor Schoeler's position that Christians may well have used written notes in Arabic as *aides de mémoire* in pre-Islamic and Qur'ānic times in the oral presentation of the scriptures, especially in liturgical settings.[112]

Islamic tradition also preserves the memory of another companion of Muḥammad, Zayd ibn Thābit, who served as the prophet's secretary and the first collector of the Qur'ān, who was literate, and who probably learned to read and write as a youngster in Yathrib/Medina "at the *midrās* of a Jewish clan called Māsika."[113] There he probably learned both Hebrew and Arabic as written languages, along with other students who studied with him in the school, "where literacy must have been taught through texts from the Old Testament in Arabic translation,"[114] presented orally. Like Waraqah ibn Nawfal, Zayd too was probably able both to read and write in Hebrew and Arabic, and to make notes for further use.

Modern scholars who have argued in behalf of the thesis that in all probability there was a pre-Islamic, written Arabic translation of the Gospels in circulation in the early seventh century have normally reasoned from two starting points. Some extrapolate backwards from the earliest dated, post-Islamic texts, positing an earlier, pre-Islamic ancestor for a given version. Others proceed diachronically, beginning with the earliest, documentable origins of widespread Christianity among the Arabs and citing bits and

[111] See Griffith, "The Gospel in Arabic," p. 145.

[112] See Schoeler, *Écrire et transmettre*, pp. 26–29.

[113] Michael Lecker, "Zayd B. Thābit, 'A Jew with Two Sidelocks', Judaism and Literacy in Pre-Islamic Medina (Yathrib)," *Journal of Near Eastern Studies* 56 (1997), pp. 259–273.

[114] Lecker, " 'A Jew with Two Sidelocks'," p. 271. See also Meir Kister, " 'Ḥaddithū 'an banī Isrā'ila wa-lā ḥaraja'," *Israel Oriental Studies* 2 (1972), pp. 215–239.

pieces of evidence for the existence of a written Bible, or portions thereof, as this evidence emerges from the historical record.

Anton Baumstark (1872–1948) was a notable proponent of the view that the Gospels, or at least lectionary pericopes drawn from them, had been prepared in Arabic well before the rise of Islam either in Sergiopolis in Syria, or more likely from his point of view, in the sixth century in the environs of the Arab city of al-Ḥīra in Mesopotamia.[115] Baumstark based his thesis on extrapolations he made from a close paleographical and textual examination of several early, post-Islamic copies of the Gospels in Arabic, of Palestinian origin. Subsequent scholarship however revealed that the manuscripts in question were members of a family of Arabic Gospel manuscripts that linguistically and liturgically originated in Palestine after the rise of Islam, perhaps as early as the late eighth century. That being the case, they could not serve credibly as evidence for the existence of a pre-Islamic, Arabic translation of the Gospels done in the sixth century in Syria or Mesopotamia, on the Arabian periphery.[116]

In his magisterial volumes on *Byzantium and the Arabs* from the fourth through the sixth centuries, Irfan Shahid has consistently argued that it was likely the case that beginning already in the fourth century, and certainly in the fifth century, Arab Christians had already produced written translations of the Bible into Arabic. Shahid proceeds diachronically and focuses his investigations on the three locations on the Arabian periphery where in pre-Islamic times cultural developments were such that one might consider it likely that translation of the Bible and other liturgically important texts might have been undertaken. The three areas are Mesopotamia, and al-Ḥīra in particular; Syria, and Palestine in particular; and South Arabia, and Najrān in particular. Basically, given the Christian practice attested elsewhere of quickly translating the scriptures into local languages as Christianity was spreading, Shahid proposes that given the state of the Arabic language

[115] See Anton Baumstark, "Die sonntägliche Evangelienlesung im vor-byzantinischen Jerusalem," *Byzantinische Zeitschrift* 30 (1929/1930), pp. 350–359; Anton Baumstark, "Das Problem eines vorislamischen christlich-kirchlichen Schrifttums in arabischer Sprache," *Islamica* 4 (1929/1931), pp. 562–575.

[116] See Georg Graf, *Geschichte der christlichen arabischen Literatur* (5 vols., Studi e Testi, 118, 133, 146, 147, 172; Città del Vaticano: Biblioteca Apostolica Vaticana, 1944–1953), vol. 1, pp. 36–146; J. Blau, "Sind uns Reste arabischer Bibelübersetzungen aus vorislamischer Zeit erhalten geblieben?" *Le Muséon* 86 (1973), pp. 67–72; Griffith, "The Gospel in Arabic," esp. pp. 153–157; Samir Arbache, *Une ancienne version arabe des Évangiles: langue, texte et lexique* (Thèse de doctorat de l'Université Michel de Montaigne; Bordeaux, 1994); Schoeler, *Écrire et transmettre*, esp. p. 28.

at the time it is unlikely, in his opinion, that in Arabia alone this practice of translation was *not* followed. Pursuing this theory, he has systematically searched everywhere for evidences of a pre-Islamic, Arabic Bible. For the fourth century he concludes, with only the evidence of a single, possibly Arabic, liturgical term reported in Jerome's *Vita S. Hilarionis*, that "A certain degree of probability attaches to the view that an Arabic liturgy and some portions of an Arabic Bible could have come into existence as early as the fourth century."[117]

For the fifth century, Shahid puts forward an important bit of evidence said to have survived in a later, Muslim Arabic work of Hishām al-Kalbī (737–819), testifying to the existence of a Bible, or at least of a Gospel, in Arabic in Najrān in the fifth century. According to the report, Hishām said that an important, fifth-century South Arabian poet, a certain Abū Naṣr ibn al-Rawḥān al-Barrāq, had associated in his childhood with a "monk (*rāhib*) from whom he learned the recitation of the Gospel (*injīl*)," and that the poet "was of the same religion as the monk."[118] The problem here, in addition to the uncertain origin of the report, is that the language of the Gospel is not specified, nor is a book mentioned. The report testifies only to the monk's knowledge of the Gospel. Shahid finds another report in a Syriac document relating to the martyrs of Najrān, according to which around the year 520, "a refugee from Arab Christian Najrān showed the Negus of Ethiopia a copy of the burnt Gospel after the persecutions which took place around that date."[119] However, there is no mention of the language of the text and Prof. Shahid argues that in all probability it was Arabic. But one could plausibly argue that the greater probability is that it was a Syriac text.

On the basis of the arguments just reviewed, Shahid assumes that in the sixth century "the Gospel and the Psalms must already have been available in Arabic," and he cites as further evidence the mention in an ode by the pre-Islamic poet al-Nābigha al-Dhubyānāī (*fl.*570–600) of a scroll (*majallat*), "which medieval commentators rightly understood to be the *injīl*, the Gospel."[120] But there is no further specification of the contents of the scroll, nor of what language was written in it. Professor Shahid promises to return to this passage in a future volume of his study of *Byzantium and the Arabs* and

[117] Shahid, *Byzantium and the Arabs in the Fourth Century*, p. 440.

[118] Shahid, *Byzantium and the Arabs in the Fifth Century*, p. 427. Prof. Shahid explains that he found this undocumented report in a work of Louis Cheikho, who failed to provide a reference for it, while Shahid has been unable independently to find it in a work of Hishām al-Kalbī. See *ibid.*, p. 427, nn. 81 and 82.

[119] Shahid, *Byzantium and the Arabs in the Fifth Century*, p. 429.

[120] Shahid, *Byzantium and the Arabs in the Sixth Century*, vol. 2, part 2, p. 295.

to examine the passage from al-Nābigha's ode in great detail. But for now it must be said that from the evidence so far adduced, there is as yet no sure basis to support the thesis that prior to the rise of Islam, Arabic-speaking Christians were in possession of a written Arabic Bible, or of portions of it, such as the Gospels or the Psalms.

More recently, and from a very different perspective, Hikmat Kachouh has made a major contribution to the study of the question of the existence, prior to the rise of Islam, of a portion of the Bible, viz. the Gospels, written in Arabic by Christian hands.[121] He carried out a careful study of some 210 Arabic manuscript copies of the Gospels, or portions of them, preserved in European and Middle Eastern libraries, apportioning them into families of translation traditions from Greek, Syriac, and even Latin. His conclusion argues forcefully for the existence of a pre-Islamic, Arabic Gospel translation done as early as the sixth century, and probably in Najrān. Kachouh's procedure is to begin with what is arguably the earliest Gospel text in Arabic now available in an extant manuscript, and on the basis of a careful scrutiny of this text, to extrapolate back to what might plausibly be its origins.

Kachouh's work is a breath of fresh air in the study of the origins of the Gospels in Arabic. His first task was to take account of previous scholarship and to discount the theories that, in the light of his own research, he found to be based on flawed reasoning or data that was incomplete or misleading. In particular, as we shall discuss in a later chapter, he deftly shows, contrary to what the present writer had proposed in an earlier study,[122] that far from beginning in the monastic communities of eighth- and ninth-century Palestine, in translations of the Gospels made from Greek, Arabic Gospel texts from this period and this milieu, should be seen not as marking the beginning of the translation process, but as part of the history of transmission of the Arabic Gospel. He puts it this way in his conclusion:

> By the end of the eighth and early ninth century, the Arabic Gospel text has been revised and corrected against different sources. All the evidence is pointing to the fact that scholars should see the second half of the eighth century not as the starting point in the history of the Arabic Gospel text, but a time during which the Arabic text has gone

[121] See Hikmat Kachouh, *The Arabic Versions of the Gospels and Their Families* (2 vols., Ph.D. Thesis; Birmingham, UK: University of Birmingham, 2008). The text is now available in a published edition: Hikmat Kashouh, *The Arabic Versions of the Gospels: The Manuscripts and their Families* (Berlin and New York: De Gruyter, 2012). In this study Kachouh's work is quoted and cited from the text of the Ph.D. thesis.

[122] See Griffith, "The Gospel in Arabic: An Inquiry into its Appearance in the First Abbasid Century."

through various revisions of more primitive exemplars. The second half of the eighth century is when we should talk of the *history of transmission* of the Arabic Gospel text and not the beginning of the Arabic translation of the Gospels.[123]

On the basis of Kachouh's careful study, the present writer heartily endorses this conclusion and more will be said about it in a later chapter. Here the question before us has to do not with the origins of the early exemplars of the eighth and ninth century, Palestinian copies of the Gospels in Arabic, but first of all with the date and probable provenance of the *earliest* Gospel text in Arabic of them all, and secondly with the question of whether or not this text, translated originally from Syriac, can reasonably be thought to pre-date the rise of Islam.

Hikmat Kachouh, on grounds that seem convincing to the present writer, singles out the Arabic translation of the Gospels contained in Vatican Arabic Manuscript 13 as "by far the earliest surviving text of the Gospels in Arabic."[124] The manuscript, which was in all probability copied at the Mar Saba monastery in the Judean desert around the year 800 CE, also contains the Pauline epistles, but these are translated from Greek and they have no relationship to the text of the Gospels, save for the fact that they have been copied into the same surviving manuscript. As for the Gospel text, Kachouh has studied it very carefully, and in some detail, and has come to the conclusion that it was translated from the Syriac Peshitta, with some Old Syriac and perhaps even *Diatessaron* readings intruding. Furthermore, given the evidences of correction and recasting in the Arabic text, the manuscript is not, in his opinion, the autograph of the original translator, but a copy of an earlier exemplar. Finally, Kachouh argues that the state of the language in this Gospel text is not the Middle Arabic of the Old South Palestinian manuscripts studied by earlier scholars, but is paleographically closer to the written state of the Arabic language as it appears in the older Ḥijāzī codices of the Qur'ān that were products of the mid to later seventh century. Therefore, in his judgment, the exemplar from which the Gospel text in Vatican Arabic Manuscript 13 was copied must have been originally written at least this early, i.e., in the mid to later seventh century and in an Arabian milieu.[125]

Actually, as he says repeatedly in the course of his discussions, Hikmat Kachouh is convinced that the original exemplar goes back at least as far as

[123] Kachouh, *The Arabic Versions of the Gospels*, vol 1, p. 333.
[124] Kachouh, *The Arabic Versions of the Gospels*, vol. 1, p. 133.
[125] See Kachouh, *The Arabic Versions of the Gospels*, vol. 1, pp. 133–167.

the sixth century and that it was originally translated from Syriac to Arabic for a Christian congregation, probably in South Arabia, perhaps in Najrān, where, as he claims, there was no knowledge of Greek, Syriac, or of the Qur'ān. Then, having cited similarities with the writing in early Arabic inscriptions, particularly that of Dayr Hind in al-Ḥīrā,[126] and accepting the conclusions of Irfan Shahid and others about the state of Arabic writing already in the fifth and sixth centuries, Kachouh concludes: "The evidence of the language itself permits us to suggest a pre-Islamic date for the origin of Vat. Ar. 13 (in Gospels only)."[127]

The problem with this conclusion from the present writer's perspective is that it is based on a series of ever more tenuous extrapolations, which have as their anchor in real time an extant text, probably copied in Palestine around the year 800 CE. The reasoning carries a good measure of plausibility as it pushes back the date for the earliest production of the original exemplar of this written Arabic translation of the Gospels to the period of the earliest texts of the Qur'ān, that is to say the mid to late seventh century, from which period we do have the earliest actual evidence of written, literary Arabic.[128] It still remains the case, as Gregor Schoeler has remarked, that in terms of actual evidence, "le premier livre de l'islam et en même temps de la littérature arabe est le Coran."[129] Wishful thinking for written literary production, as opposed to a handful of inscriptions or probable notes as *aides de mémoire*, by Arab Christians and others prior to the time of the collection of the Qur'ān, is no sound basis for postulating an earlier, written currency of either Arabic poetry or the Gospels in Arabic. All the existing, as opposed to the postulated, evidence actually suggests that prior to the literary collection of the Qur'ān in the seventh century, literary and liturgical texts alike circulated in Arabic in an oral tradition. Kachouh himself almost admits as much when he says of the instances of "phrasal transposition" he found in the Gospel text of Vatican Arabic Manuscript 13 that they "might suggest that the archetype or a portion of it was transmitted orally [rather] than in literary form."[130]

[126] See Kachouh, *The Arabic Versions of the Gospels*, pp. 368–370.

[127] Kachouh, *The Arabic Versions of the Gospels*, p. 372.

[128] As Beatrice Gruendler noted after a careful review of earlier studies of the development of the Arabic script, "The pre-Islamic formation and early Islamic documentation of Arabic script suggest that it was readily available at the time of the Prophet." Gruendler, "Arabic Script," *Encyuclopaedia of the Qur'ān*, vol. I, p. 136.

[129] Schoeler, *Écrire et transmettre*, p. 26.

[130] Kachouh, *The Arabic Versions of the Gospels*, vol. 1, pp. 164–165. The word in brackets has been supplied by the present writer; perhaps it fell out of the text in the process of revision.

The thesis defended here as expressing the more probable course of events is that Arabic-speaking Christians in Arabia, whose religious heritage was largely Aramaic/Syriac, may have first produced written translations of portions of the Bible—of the Gospels in particular—in the later seventh century, at the same time as the nascent Muslim community was bringing the hitherto largely oral Qur'ān into writing in what was to be its canonical form. This hypothesis is itself based on an extrapolation from the state of the texts of translated portions of the scriptures in copies that can plausibly be dated to the second half of the eighth century, as will be discussed in a subsequent chapter. Prior to that time, the Gospels and other Christian scriptural and ecclesiastical lore would have circulated in Arabic orally, but not haphazardly. Oral literary and liturgical traditions have been found in many cultures, and they have proved perfectly adequate to the task of transmitting complicated narratives integrally, especially in instances like the Arabic case, where one can reasonably surmise the existence of written *aides de mémoire,* not to mention the ever-present texts in the original languages, Greek, and particularly Syriac, in the Christian instance. Perhaps the best evidence in support of this hypothesis is the Arabic Qur'ān itself, in which, as we shall see in the next chapter, detailed knowledge of biblical and ecclesiastical narratives is evident, along with an almost complete lack of textual detail in the form of direct quotations or even substantial retellings of the biblical stories; the focus being instead on the patriarchal and prophetic *dramatis personae.*

As in the Christian instance, there is no compelling evidence that Arabic-speaking Jews translated any portion of the Hebrew Bible into Arabic in pre-Islamic times. As one recent scholar has put it in regard to the Arabic spoken by Jews in Arabia in Muḥammad's lifetime, "Although it is known from Muslim sources that Jews wrote letters and documents in Hebrew characters, they left behind no Judeo-Arabic literature."[131] This conclusion is in harmony with the view of Gregor Schoeler, quoted earlier, that prior to Muḥammad's time, and indeed during his lifetime, Arabic speakers made use of rough-copy, written notes and *aides de mémoire,* but did not put forward a literary text as such prior to the collection of the Qur'ān.[132] Likewise, pre-Islamic Jewish poetry in Arabic, such as that attributed to the mid-sixth-century CE al-Samaw'al ibn 'Ādiyā, did not appear in written form

[131] Norman A. Stillman, "Judeo-Arabic: History and Linguistic Description," in *Encyclopedia of Jews in the Islamic World,* Brill Online ed., September 14, 2010, *sub voce,* p.1.

[132] See Schoeler, *Écrire et transmettre,* pp. 22ff.

until well after the rise of Islam, when in the ninth and tenth centuries Arab grammarians were busy collecting their works.[133] While it is difficult to date the beginnings of Judeo-Arabic, which seems to have been flourishing already in the ninth and tenth centuries CE, there is no reason to doubt that its roots go back at least to the eighth century.[134] And in any event, the conclusion that is pertinent to the question of a pre-Islamic written translation of the Bible, or of a portion of it, is that there is no "genuine proof of the existence of Arabic versions of the Bible at this period which were initiated by Jews."[135]

Given the lack of an earlier written translation of any portion of the Bible done under Jewish or Christian auspices prior to the rise of Islam, and the consequent fact that for liturgical and other purposes, especially among Christians, translations must have been done on the spot by Arabic-speaking Christians according to an oral tradition of translation from mostly Syriac originals, the somewhat counterintuitive conclusion emerges that the Arabic Qur'ān, in the form in which it was collected and published in writing in the seventh century, is after all the first scripture written in Arabic. And as we shall suggest below, it may well have been the case that the appearance of the collected, written Qur'ān in the second half of the seventh century provided the impetus for the first written translations of the Bible into Arabic. The precipitating factor may well have been at least in part a desire to set the biblical record straight in Arabic, along with the liturgical and academic needs of the newly Arabic-speaking Christian communities.

[133] See Th. Bauer, "Al-Samaw'al b. 'Ādiyā," *EI, new rev.* ed., vol. 8, p. 1041.

[134] See Joshua Blau, *The Emergence and Linguistic Background of Judaeo-Arabic: A Study in the Origins of Middle Arabic* (Oxford: Oxford University Press, 1965).

[135] G. Vajda, "Judaeo-Arabic Literature," in *EI, new rev.* ed., vol. 4, p. 303.

✳ CHAPTER II ✳

The Bible in the Arabic Qur'ān

The Qur'ān is very conscious of the Bible and sometimes presents itself as offering once again a revelation previously sent down in the Torah and the Gospel. One verse even seems to put the Qur'ān on a par with these earlier scriptures, when it speaks of the promise of paradise for those who fight in the way of God, as already truthfully recorded in "the Torah, the Gospel, and the Qur'ān" (IX *at-Tawbah* 111). On the one hand, the Qur'ān's text insistently recalls the earlier biblical stories of the patriarchs and prophets, and even appeals to the books of the Torah, the Prophets, the Psalms, and the Gospel by name. On the other hand, Islamic scripture also pursues a reading of its own, often notably distinct from and sometimes even contrary to the biblical understandings of Jews or Christians. For the Qur'ān is in fact very selective in its approach to the Bible and to biblical lore. It ignores entirely portions of the scriptures that are very important to Jews or Christians. The New Testament Pauline epistles are a notable instance of this disinterest, as are large portions of the former and later prophets in the Hebrew Bible. What is notable is that the Qur'ān is not so much interested in the Bible per se, as it is in well-known accounts of the Bible's principal *dramatis personae*: Adam, Noah, Abraham, Ishmael, Isaac, Jacob, Joseph, Moses, Aaron, Miriam, David, Solomon, even Job and Jonah, along with Zachariah, John the Baptist, Mary and 'Jesus, son of Mary,' just to mention the major personalities. It interweaves recollections of the stories of these patriarchs and prophets into its own distinctive prophetology, culminating in Muḥammad, "the Messenger of God and the seal of the prophets" (XXXIII *al-Aḥzāb* 40), and in the presentation of God's message to the community of believers the prophet has summoned to hear it. The Qur'ān thus appears on the horizon of biblical history as a new paradigm for the reading, figuratively speaking, of a familiar scriptural narrative in an Arabic-speaking milieu, offering a new construal of a familiar salvation history, albeit not without echoes of earlier traditions.

The approach undertaken in this chapter is that of a historian of Judaism and Christianity in pursuit of understanding how the scriptural narratives and popular exegetical and communal traditions of the several Jewish and Christian communities, circulating orally in the first third of the seventh century CE in Arabic translation (from their original Hebrew, Aramaic,

Greek, Syriac, and even Ethiopic expressions), came into the frame of reference of the Arabic Qur'ān. In other words, the chapter approaches the Qur'ān as a document in evidence of the history of Jews and Christians in Arabia, along with their scriptures and traditions, rather than as a document in Islamic history. For this purpose the inquiry respects the integrity of the Qur'ān in its canonical form, as Muslims actually have it, and recognizes its distinctive kerygma. But it largely ignores later Islamic exegesis of the Qur'ān. It is an unusual approach in that almost all studies of the Qur'ān's incorporation of biblical material have heretofore come from an opposite perspective, that of a student of the Qur'ān itself and its Islamic interpretive tradition, engaged in either appreciatively or unappreciatively looking back from the Qur'ān's text on how well or ill, in the historian's opinion, the Islamic scripture has resumed earlier scriptural narratives.[1]

One of the first things that the historian of Arabian Judaism or Christianity notices on approaching the Qur'ān is that for all its obviously high degree of biblical awareness, the Qur'ān virtually never actually *quotes* the Bible. There are, of course, the exceptions that prove the rule. For example, scholars have long cited the passage from Psalm 37:29, evidently quoted in XXI *al-Anbiyā'* 105: "We have written in the Psalms after the reminder that 'My righteous servants will inherit the earth'."[2] And there is the phrase, "And God spoke directly with Moses (*wakallama Allāh Mūsā taklīman*, IV *an-Nisā'* 164), which is hauntingly close to the oft-repeated Hebrew phrase in the Torah, "And God spoke all these things to Moses, saying . . ." (*waydabber Adonay 'el Mosheh kol-haddbārîm hā'ēllê lē'mōr*, e.g., Exodus 20:1).[3] From the Gospel there is the reminiscence of Jesus' saying, "It is easier for a camel to go through the eye of a needle than for a rich man to enter the kingdom of God" (Mt. 19:24) in the Qur'ān's dictum, "Indeed, those who have denied our revelations and rejected them arrogantly – the gates of heaven shall not be opened for them and they shall not enter paradise until the camel passes through the eye of the needle." (VII *al-A'rāf* 40). Otherwise, while there are passages in the Qur'ān that are somewhat hauntingly close to passages in the Hebrew Bible or the Gospels—in the story of the patriarch Joseph (XII

[1] See in this connection the observations of Tryggve Kronholm, "Dependence and Prophetic Originality in the Koran," *Orientalia Suecana* 31–32 (1982–1983), pp. 47–70.

[2] See Anton Baumstark, "Arabische Übersetzung eines altsyrischen Evangelientextes und die Sure 21–105 zitierte Psalmenübersetzung," *Oriens Christianus* 9 (1931), pp. 164–188.

[3] I am indebted to Prof. Meir Bar Asher, who pointed out this recurring biblical phrase to me and to Prof. Adele Berlin, who helped me find the particular instance of it at the beginning of the Torah's recitation of the Ten Commandments in Exodus.

Yūsuf), for example, or the accounts of the Annunciation (III *Āl ʿImrān*; XIX *Maryam*), they are actually, as we shall see, more paraphrases, allusions, and echoes than quotations in any strict sense of the word.

For the past century and more, many Western scholars have studied the Bible in the Qurʾān, looking for its sources and the presumed influences on its text in both canonical and non-canonical, Jewish and Christian scriptures and apocryphal writings. Most often they declared the Qurʾānic readings to be garbled, confused, mistaken, or even corrupted when compared with the presumed originals. More recent scholars, however, some more sensitive than their academic ancestors to the oral character, as opposed to a 'written-text' interface between Bible and Qurʾān, have taken the point that the evident intertextuality that obtains in many places in the three sets of scriptures, Jewish, Christian, and Muslim (and in their associated literatures), reflects an oral intermingling of traditions, motifs, and histories in the days of the Qurʾān's origins. These various elements played a role in the several communities' interactions with one another within the ambience of Muḥammad's declamations of the messages he was conscious of having received for the purpose of proclaiming them in public. The Jewish and Christian texts in which scholars find them are not taken to be documentary evidences of the currency and availability of these elements in the Qurʾān's Arabic-speaking milieu. It is no longer a matter of sources and influences but of traditions, motifs, and histories retold within a different horizon of meaning. In this vein some scholars have even begun talking of the Qurʾān's role as a kind of biblical commentary in Arabic, reacting to the Bible, as one recent scholar has put it, as the Qurʾān's "biblical subtext,"[4] and developing many of its themes within its own interpretive framework.

Here the effort is not to contribute to the on-going study of individual units of the Qurʾān in which Bible-related material is to be found, but rather, from the point of view of one intent on consulting the Qurʾān as a document in evidence of Jewish and Christian history in its Arabic-speaking milieu, to study the modes of the Qurʾān's engagement, in its very formation, with the contemporary lore of the Jews and Christians, and with their biblical narratives in particular. With this purpose in mind, it is important to emphasize at the outset that one realizes that interaction with the 'People of the Book' and their scriptures is only one aspect of the Qurʾān's text in its integrity, albeit an important one. The Islamic scripture is cer-

[4] Gabriel Said Reynolds, *The Qurʾān and Its Biblical Subtext* (Routledge Studies in the Qurʾān; London and New York: Routledge, 2010).

tainly larger in scope and purpose than its interface with the Bible, albeit that its divine message is presented as continuous with the earlier scriptures.

Important recent studies of the major structures of the Qur'ān, concentrating on units of text within the framework of a given *sūrah*, well beyond the level of individual verses, where most traditional commentary, both Muslim and non-Muslim has long been focused, have called attention to the numerous prosodic features of the text. These include repeated ritual formulae, inclusions, and key indicative phrases that mark out passages of specific narrative or ritual intent.[5] Inspired by these developments, the present inquiry leaves aside a detailed examination of individual passages and their perceived indebtedness to specific Jewish or Christian *Vorlagen*, and unfolds under three more general headings. Our intent is more precisely to define from an hermeneutical point of view the historical phenomenology of the Qur'ān/Bible interface in the period of the Qur'ān's emergence into public discourse during Muḥammad's prophetic career. The three general headings are: the rubrics of scriptural recall; a distinctive Islamic prophetology; and the medium of scriptural intertextuality.

The Rubrics of Scriptural Recall

In most of the places in the Qur'ān where narratives of biblical patriarchs or prophets are evoked, or earlier scriptural passages are recalled, the text may simply name a well-known biblical figure, or employ indicative vocabulary that sets the tone and sometimes forms the structure of the text in a given unit or *sūrah*. This usage functions on both a general and a more specific level, as we shall see, and indicates the purpose and the modality of a given instance of scriptural reminiscence. But the most basic thing one notices about the Qur'ān and its interface with the Bible is the Islamic scripture's unspoken and pervasive confidence that its audience is thoroughly familiar with the stories of the biblical patriarchs and prophets, so familiar in fact that there is no need for even the most rudimentary form of introduction.

[5] One has in mind in particular the studies of Angelika Neuwirth, *Studien zur Komposition der mekkanischen Suren: die literarische Form des Koran—ein Zeugnis seiner Historizität?* (2nd ed. Studien zur Geschichte und Kultur des islamischen Orients, Band 10 (NF); Berlin: De Gruyter, 2007) and Michel Cuypers, *Le Festin: une lecture de la sourate al-Mā'ida* (Paris: Lethielleux, 2007; Eng. trans., *The Banquet: A Reading of the Fifth Sura of the Qur'ān* (trans. Patricia Kelley, Series Rhetorica Semitica; Miami, FL: Convivium, 2009).

In what follows, the immediate purpose is to call attention to both the general and the more particular horizons within which biblical recall occurs in the Qurʾān, with a view to highlighting how the Arabic Qurʾān, which is the new scripture, and hence on its own terms the primary one, calls on the authority of the older scriptures to corroborate its revelatory message, in the process making the older scriptures secondary and, in that sense, servile to the new. Here we can furnish only sufficient examples of the modalities of this intertextual phenomenon to serve the general purpose of the present study, namely to show how the Bible comes into the Qurʾān's view.

The Wider Horizon of Scriptural Recall in the Qurʾān

By the time the longer Medinan *sūrahs* had come into their final form, the general pattern of the Qurʾān's recall of the major figures and narratives in the Hebrew and Christian scriptures had been set, and the basic principles of their relationship had been enunciated. Succinctly put, the Qurʾān presents itself as confirming the truth that is in the previous scriptures and as safeguarding it. After speaking of the Torah, "in which there is guidance and light," and of Jesus, "as confirming the veracity of the Torah before him," and of the Gospel, "in which there is guidance and light," God says to Muḥammad regarding the Qurʾān: "We have sent down to you the scripture in truth, as a confirmation of the scripture before it, and as a safeguard for it" (V *al-Māʾidah* 44, 46, 48). The previous scriptures were, of course, in the Qurʾān's telling, principally the Torah and the Gospel, as is clear here and in other places, where the Qurʾān says to Muḥammad, "He has sent down to you the scripture in truth, as a confirmation of what was before it, and He sent down the Torah and the Gospel" (III *Āl ʿImrān* 3). In these and other passages one might cite, the position of the Qurʾān vis-à-vis the Jewish and Christian Bible is clear: the Qurʾān confirms the veracity of the earlier scriptures. In other words, the Qurʾān not only recognizes the Torah and the Gospel, and the Psalms too, as we shall see, as authentic scripture sent down earlier by God, but it now stands as the warrant for the truth they contain.

But the matter does not rest here. For while the Qurʾān, following both the then-current Jewish and Christian view, recognizes the Torah as the scripture God sent down to Moses—"We wrote for him in the Tablets about everything" (VII *al-Aʿrāf* 145)—the Gospel that the Qurʾān confirms is not the Gospel as Christians recognized it in the Qurʾān's own day. Rather, following the model of its own distinctive prophetology, the Qurʾān speaks of the Gospel as a scripture God gave to Jesus: "We gave him the Gospel, wherein is guidance and light, confirming what he had before him of the Torah" (V *al-Māʾidah* 46; LVII *al-Ḥadīd* 27). Here, as in other instances we have noted in the previous chapter, the Qur'ān apparently intends to criticize and correct what it regards as a mistaken Christian view of the Christians' own principal scripture. What is more, by the time of its collection, and principally in criticism of the behavior of the 'People of the Book' in regard to their scriptures, the Qur'ān is already speaking of the 'distortion' and 'alteration' of scriptural texts. This is to be found in the very passages (e.g., in II *al-Baqarah* 75–79; III *Āl 'Imrān* 78; IV *an-Nisā* 46; V *al-Mā'idah* 12–19) that in subsequent Islamic tradition will undergird the doctrine of the corruption of the earlier scriptures,[6] a development that would effectively discount the testimonies drawn by Jews or Christians from their scriptures in behalf of the verisimilitude of their teachings.

Against this background of familiarity with the major liturgical scriptures of the Jews and the Christians, the Torah and the Gospel, and the Psalms (*az-Zabūr*), "in which We wrote" (XXI *al-Anbiyā'* 105) and which "We brought to David" (IV *an-Nisā'* 163; XVII *al-Isrā'* 55), the Qur'ān even advises Muḥammad to consult "those who were reading the scripture (*al-kitāb*) before you" (X *Yūnus* 94). In context, the Qur'ān speaks of God's instructing the prophet in his discourse to his audience to "relate to them the story of Noah"(vs.71), and He goes on to speak of Moses and Aaron, the Pharaoh, the Exodus from Egypt, and the settlement of the Israelites. Within this frame of reference he also advises Muḥammad: "If you are in doubt about what We have sent down to you, ask those who were reading the scripture before you. The truth has come down to you from your Lord, so you should certainly not be in doubt" (X *Yūnus* 94). In a similar vein in another place, the Qur'ān records God's word to Muḥammad:

> We have sent out before you only men whom We have inspired, so ask the 'People of remembrance' (*ahl adh-dhikr*) if you do not know;[7] [We have inspired them] with clear evidences and texts (*az-zubur*) and We have sent down the remembrance (*adh-dhikr*) to you so that We might make clear to people what has been sent down to them; perhaps they will reflect. (XVI *an-Naḥl* 43–44)

In these passages the Qur'ān clearly commends recalling the message of the earlier scriptures, but what especially catches one's attention is the phrase 'People of remembrance' and the reference to what God sent down

[6] See Jean-Marie Gaudeul and Robert Caspar, "Textes de la tradition musulmane concernant le *taḥrīf* (falsification) es écritures," *Islamochristiana* 6 (1980), pp. 61–104; Jane Dammen McAuliffe, "The Qur'ānic Context of Muslim Biblical Scholarship," *Islam and Christian Muslim Relations* 7 (1996), pp. 141–158.

[7] This exact sentence is also found in XXI *al-Anbiyā'* 7.

to Muḥammad as 'the remembrance'. Of note is the parallel between 'the remembrance' (*adh-dhikr*) and 'the scripture' (*al-kitāb*), so in this context the 'Scripture people'/'People of the Book' (*ahl al-kitāb*) are the 'People of remembrance', and what they remember or recall is God's dealings with the patriarchs and prophets as recorded in the scriptures, the very remembrance that is also recorded in the Qur'ān. This is one reason why the Qur'ān itself is referred to in its own text as a 'remembrance', here and in the oath formula, "By the Qur'ān, possessed of remembrance (*dhī adh-dhikr*)" (XXXVIII *Ṣād* 1), and in such Qur'ānic epithets as "a blessed remembrance" (XXI *an-Anbiyā'* 50), and as being itself a "reminder" (*tadhkirah*) (XX *Ṭā Hā* 3), a 'reminder' (*dhikrā*) for the worlds "of the scripture, the judgment, and the prophethood God had previously sent down" (see VI *al-An'ām* 89–90).

On the face of it the remembrance and the recall seem to be recollections of earlier scriptures, given the repeated mention of terms such as 'book' or 'scripture' (*al-kitāb*) for the Qur'ān itself and for the earlier scriptures, as well as the use of such a term as *az-zubur*, in the sense of 'texts', as in "the texts of the ancients" (XXVI *ash-Shu'arā'* 196) or "the clear signs, the texts, and the illuminating scripture" that the messengers before Muḥammad brought (see XXXV *Fāṭir* 25). This can be seen even in the references to the 'scrolls' (*aṣ-ṣuḥuf*) of Moses, of Abraham, and of God's messengers in a general, in which there are true scriptures (see, e.g., LIII *an-Najm* 36; LXXXVII *al-A'lā* 19; XCVIII *al-Bayyinah* 2-3). The same might even be said of the 'copy' (*nuskhah*) in which God's guidance and mercy appeared on Moses' tablets (VII *al-A'rāf* 154). But a closer look reveals that it is not books, texts, scrolls, or copies that the Qur'ān actually recalls, except in such general phrases as those just quoted. Rather, the Qur'ān's actual recollections are of biblical and other narratives of patriarchs and prophets, their words and actions, in the Qur'ān's own (re)telling of the stories, for, as we have said, there are virtually no quotations in the Qur'ān from the earlier scriptures.

The Nearer Horizon of Biblical Recall in the Qur'ān

When recollections of the biblical narratives and of the words and actions of the patriarchs and prophets actually come up in the Qur'ān, the first thing that strikes the reader is, as we have seen, the high degree of familiarity with the *dramatis personae* and their stories that the text presumes in its audience. This is a feature of Qur'ānic discourse that becomes immediately evident on one's approach to any passage that brings up a biblical reminiscence. For example, the very first mention of a biblical person that one encounters on opening the Qur'ān at its canonical beginning occurs in a verse that assumes a fairly wide-ranging knowledge not only of the particular person but of Jewish and Christian lore about the scenario in which the person's name is mentioned. The text evokes the memory of God's creation of Adam and of God's teaching him the names of creatures; it approaches the topic with the affirmation that God is the Creator of all things: "It is He who created for you everything on earth, then ascended to the heavens fashioning them into seven, and He has knowledge of all things" (II *al-Baqarah* 29). Already the scenario is familiar to the 'People of the Book' whom the text is addressing, who, as we shall see, are in this instance Jews. And the next verse moves immediately into the mode of narrative recall, utilizing a key term that recurs throughout the Qur'ān in such circumstances, the simple word 'when' (*idh*), implying a preceding admonition 'to remember'; "When your Lord said to the angels, "I am going to place a deputy on earth" (II *al-Baqarah* 30). The recollection proceeds to recall the story of Adam, Eve, and Iblīs in the Garden (II *al-Baqarah* 29–38), and it does so without once quoting the scriptures, but nevertheless manages to evoke the biblical scene in details familiar not only from the Bible, but also from Jewish and Christian lore.[8] In the sequel, in the same *sūrah*, the text goes on for a hundred verses and more recalling Israelite salvation history through the remembrance of several of the major prophets, Moses in particular, three times exhorting the Israelites to *remember*, "O Sons of Israel, *remember* the grace I bestowed on you" (II *al-Baqarah* 40, 47, 122). Moreover, many subsequent verses begin with the tell-tale phrase, *wa'idh* (or *'idhā* or *lammā*), which in context many translators render as, "[Remember] when . . . ." (25x+). Often God then speaks in the imperative or recalls what He said or did on a given occasion, as in the sequence, "O Children of Israel, remember the grace I bestowed on you . . . beware of the day . . . and when Abraham was tried by his Lord . . . . And [remember] when We made the House. . . . And when Abraham said . . . And when Abraham and Ismā'īl raised the foundations of the house . . ." (II *al-Baqarah* 122, 123, 124, 125, 126, 127).

It is important to notice the prominence of the exhortation to remember or to recall, directly expressed (*idhkurū*), or implied, in Qur'ānic passages featuring the evocation of biblical figures and God's dealing with them.[9]

[8] For details and bibliography see Cornelia Schöck, "Adam and Eve," in McAuliffe, *Encyclopaedia of the Qur'ān*, vol. 1, pp. 22 ff.

[9] The evocation of biblical recollection is an aspect of the range of meaning of Qur'ānic *dhikr* that often goes unnoticed by modern scholarly commentators, most of whom put the accent simply on the recollection of God and of God's actions

Often, as in the instance just mentioned, the Qur'ān just mentions the name of a biblical person or the subject of a narrative event without any preamble, relying implicitly on its audience's ready recognition of the relevant scenario. The remembrance or recall of the tale is then most often freely phrased in its telling, or re-telling, as if from memory alone, and with no textual reference. Both narrative and dialogue on the part of both the speaker and the *dramatis personae* evoke a familiar scriptural account now woven into an almost iconic, even cinematic, narrative pattern of traditional exegetical or apocryphal details that are virtually midrashic in their generic character. What is more, even within a highly structured *sūrah,* these biblical recollections for the most part retain the feature of recalling well-known prophetic figures. In other words, it is the Qur'ān's distinctive prophetology that ultimately controls the process of scriptural recollection, determining which biblical narratives are recalled and which are ignored, a feature of the Bible in the Qur'ān that is best studied in reference to well-known instances of the phenomenon rather than merely in the abstract.

Prophetology and Scriptural Recollection

It is not to the present purpose comprehensively to review the issue of prophets and prophecy in the Qur'ān, a topic that has been widely discussed by recent scholars.[10] Rather, the interest here is to study how the Qur'ān's prophetology and its evocation of the memory of individual prophets prior to Muḥammad (particularly prophetic figures from the Bible), provides the narrative framework for the Qur'ān's recall of biblical stories in a selection of well-known passages.

But first a word must be said about the seldom-discussed difference between the Qur'ān's view of the role of prophets and prophetic history and the biblical view of their function in the Bible's unfolding history of salvation. For the difference of accent in the two overlapping narratives is a crucial one, marking the distinctive hermeneutical point of view of the Qur'ān

---

among men, an important subset of which is actually expressed in scriptural recall. See, e.g., Michael A. Sells, "Memory," in McAuliffe, *Encyclopaedia of the Qur'ān,* vol. 3, p. 372; Angelika Brodersen, "Remembrance," in McAuliffe, *Encyclopaedia of the Qur'ān,* vol. 4, pp. 419 ff.

[10] See, e.g., Brannon M. Wheeler, *Prophets in the Qur'ān: An Introduction to the Qur'ān and Muslim Exegesis* (London and New York: Continuum, 2002); Roberto Tottoli, *Biblical Prophets in the Qur'ān and Muslim Literature* (Richmond, Surrey: Curzon, 2002).

vis-à-vis the perspective of Jewish or Christian communities. Simply put, the Qur'ān evokes the memory of the biblical patriarchs and prophets within its own distinctive paradigm of prophetic significance. For the Qur'ān, the historical series of God's prophets (*al-anbiyā'*) and messengers (*ar-rusul*) from Adam to Muḥammad, "God's messenger, and the seal of the prophets" (XXXIII *al-Aḥzāb* 40),[11] is the history of God's renewed summons, in God's own words, calling people to return to their neglected, but original state of awareness of the one God, the creator of all that is, and to the God-given rule of life. The sequence of prophets envisions the end-time, the resurrection of the dead, and the consequent reward of the Garden for the just and the Fire for the sinner. For Jews and Christians, by contrast, the several divinely inspired accounts of almost the same list of prophets and messengers (though without the Islamic distinction between prophets and messengers), presents a succession of God's chosen spokesmen, whose role it was to speak God's word in particular historical situations and to summon God's chosen people to fidelity to their divine vocation and to covenant obligations in service of a distinctive eschatology, in which the coming of the Messiah would be the culmination of salvation history. Not only is there a different accent in the two conceptions of basically the same prophetic history, but the prophetic role is significantly different. In the Qur'ān's view, prophets and messengers, who are the major figures in scriptural salvation history, all transmit God's word in God's words. In the biblical view, the prophets are specially chosen individuals, who speak God's word in the human words God has inspired them to speak, usually addressing specific persons and occasions. In the biblical view, not all of the major figures of salvation history from Adam to John the Baptist and Jesus are prophets and messengers in the Qur'an's sense. In the Qur'ān's view the prophets and messengers reiterate an unchanging message, which their subsequent communities inevitably distort. In the biblical view, the prophets bear an often judgmental witness to current events in salvation history, often with a Messianic anticipation attached.[12] In the Qur'ānic view, God always vindicates

[11] In reference to a passage in XXII *al-Ḥajj* 52, which distinguishes between the messenger (*rasūl*) and the prophet (*nabī*), Uri Rubin remarks, "Muslim commentators say that in this verse *rasūl* stands for a prophet having a message, a book, which must be delivered, whereas a *nabī* has no such message or book. More specifically, al-Bayḍāwī . . . says that a *rasūl* is a prophet who establishes a new *sharī'a*, whereas a *nabī* is one who continues an old one." Uri Rubin, "Prophets and Prophethood," in McAuliffe, *Encyclopaedia of the Qur'ān*, vol. 4, p. 289.

[12] For another view of this matter see Felix Körner, "Das Prophetische am Islam," in Mariano Delgado and Michael Sievemich (eds.), *Mission und Prophetie in Zeiten*

his prophets and messengers in their struggles with their adversaries. The Qur'ān's distinct perspective exercises a determinative role in the choice of the elements of biblical history that the Qur'ān recalls.

The Typology of Qur'ānic Prophetology

The distinctive prophetology that is articulated in a number of places in the Qur'ān is well schematized in a recurring, probably liturgical, pattern of recall found in *sūrah* XXVI *ash-Shu'arā'*.[13] In the text, God apparently addresses Muḥammad's concerns about the reception of the message from God he had to deliver to his contemporaries, probably in the later Meccan phase of his public career. The *sūrah* provides a concentrated insight into the conceptual framework within which the Qur'ān recalls more particular moments of biblical and prophetic history.[14] It provides a view of the typological horizon within which particular stories are told, and it exemplifies the features of prophetic experience that in the Qur'ān's prophetology determine which specific aspects of a given biblical story are selected for recollection.

GOD'S OPENING ADDRESS TO MUḤAMMAD (XXVI:2–6)

The *sūrah* begins with God's address to Muḥammad regarding the "signs (*āyāt*) of the clarifying scripture," i.e., the Qur'ān, and the prophet's fretting over his hearers' disbelief in them (XXVI:3). God explains in regard to the hearers' reluctance to credit the 'signs' that "no new recollection (*dhikr*) [of signs] from the Merciful One would ever come to them but they would turn their backs on them." (XXVI:5) The fact that Muḥammad's hearers have 'discredited' (*faqad kadhdhabū*, XXVI:6) the signs, is presented as yet one more instance of a recurring feature in prophetic history, namely peoples' tendency to discredit God's signs. This the *sūrah* goes on to docu-

---

der Transkulturalität: Festschrift zum hundertjährigen Bestehen des Internationalen Instituts für missionswissenschaftliche Forschungen 1911–2011 (Sonderband der Zeitschrift für Missionswissenschaft und Religionwissenschaft, 95; St. Ottilien: Eos Verlag, 2011), pp. 230–244.

[13] See the schematic outline of the *sūrah* in Neuwirth, *Studien zur Komposition der mekkanischen Suren*, pp. 276–277.

[14] In this connection, see especially the very important article by Michael Zwettler, "A Mantic Manifesto: The Sūra of 'The Poets' and the Qur'ānic Foundations of Prophetic Authority," in James L. Kugel, *Poetry and Prophecy: The Beginnings of a Literary Tradition* (Ithaca, NY: Cornell University Press, 1990), pp. 75–119, 205–231.

ment in a series of recollections from prophetic history, beginning with an allusion to the prophetic potential of nature itself.

THE SEQUENCE OF THE PROPHETS

Sūrat ash-Shuʿarāʾ (XXVI) provides a sequence of eight instances of prophetic witness, which are discredited by those to whom it was addressed. Certain rhetorical features recur in the narrative that articulate the lessons the Qurʾān means to commend in its evocation of prophetic history in general, each instance in the present *sūrah* being characterized as an occasion when 'a sign' (*āyatan*) was discredited by the adversaries of a given prophet. In this connection, the 'sign' involves not only the notion of 'miracle', but it becomes as well an instance of argument and evidentiary proof of the prophet's veracity. The sign is even a prophetic revelation in its own right, in an evidently polemical moment, as when God speaks to Muḥammad of the Qurʾān's own verses recalling the story of the prophet, Jesus, "This is what we are reciting to you of the signs and the wise remembrance" (III *Āl ʿImrān* 58).[15] And the Qurʾān expresses the hope that its audience will reflect (*tafakkur*) on the 'signs' that God makes manifest, getting the point of the message, as articulated in the repeated phrase, "Perhaps you/they will engage in reflection" (e.g., in II *al-Baqarah* 219; VII *al-Aʿrāf* 176). Those who do so are often said to be people "possessed of understanding" (*uʾlī l-albāb*), as in the phrase, "Only those possessed of understanding engage in reflection" (XIII *ar-Raʿd* 19; XXXIX *az-Zumar* 9). God is said to have given the scripture to the Children of Israel, "As guidance and a reminder (*dhikrā*) for those possessed of understanding" (XL *Ghāfir* 54).

The Earth (XXVI:7–9)

The sequence begins with the rhetorical question, "Have they not considered the earth, how much We have caused every kind of noble pair to grow on it?" (XXVI:7), and the text goes on immediately to intone the refrain that will appear seven more times in the *sūrah*, after the recollection of each prophet's mission, his adversaries' discrediting of it, and God's consequent vindication of the prophet and his message: "In this there is certainly a sign and most of them did not become believers; your Lord is the mighty one, the merciful one" (XXVI:8–9). This brief passage evokes the Qurʾān's much wider suggestion of the virtually prophetic witness of nature

[15] For this wording, see Binyamin Abrahamov, "Signs," in McAuliffe, *Encyclopaedia of the Qurʾān*, vol. 5, pp. 2 ff.

at large as being almost a 'scripture' in its own right,[16] a notion the Arabic Qur'ān shares with Syriac-speaking Christian scholars of an earlier generation, who often spoke of how nature and scripture together, as the biblically warranted two witnesses (Deut. 19:15; Jn. 8:17), testify to the Creator, who is Lord of nature and Lord of Scripture.[17]

Moses (XXVI:10–68)

The Moses pericope, the longest in the *sūrah*'s recall of prophetic history, begins with the phrase, "When (*idh*) your Lord called on Moses . . . " and it proceeds to recount in some detail Moses' and Aaron's dealings with Pharoah and the subsequent exodus from Egypt. As in the other parts of the Qur'ān where Moses is recalled, so here there is a recollection of Bible history but no quotations from the Bible, albeit that scholars have been able to discover some features of the Qur'ānic story also recorded in non-biblical, Jewish and Christian texts.[18] At the end of the section, the text says, "We saved Moses and those with him altogether, and then We drowned the others" (XXVI:65–66). And the refrain follows immediately: "In this there is certainly a sign, and most of them did not become believers; your Lord is the mighty one the merciful one" (XXVI:67–68).

Abraham (XXVI:69–104)

The pericope begins with the instruction to Muḥammad: "Recite to them the account of Abraham" (XXVI:69), and it continues immediately with the phrase, "When (*idh*) he said to his father and his people, 'What are you worshipping?'" (XXVI:70). There follows the account of Abraham's rejection of the gods of his father and his ancestors, some of which is familiar from Jewish and Christian traditions and from other passages in the Qur'ān, but nowhere are there actual quotations from the Bible.[19] In the end, Abraham's people are recorded as saying, "If only we could have an-

[16] See Ian Richard Netton, "Nature as Signs," in McAuliffe, *Encyclopaedia of the Qur'ān*, vol. 3, pp. 528ff.

[17] See, e.g., Saint Ephrem, *Hymns on Paradise* (trans. Sebastian Brock; Crestwood, NY: St Vladimir's Seminary Press, 1990), p. 102. See also Sidney H. Griffith, *'Faith Adoring the Mystery': Reading the Bible with St. Ephraem the Syrian* (The Père Marquette Lecture in Theology, 1997; Milwaukee, WI: Marquette University Press, 1997).

[18] See Roberto Tottoli, *Vita di Mosè secondo le tradizioni islamiche* (Palermo: Sellerio, 1992); Brannon Wheeler, *Moses in the Quran and Islamic Exegesis* (London and New York: Routledge/Curzon, 2002).

[19] See Reuven Firestone, *Journeys in Holy Lands: The Evolution of the Abraham—Ishmael Legends in Islamic Exegesis* (Albany, NY: State University of New York Press, 1990; *idem*, "Abraham," in McAuliffe, *Encyclopaedia of the Qur'ān*, vol 1, pp. 5 ff.

other chance; then we will be among the believers" (XXVI:102), and there follows immediately the refrain: "In this there is certainly a sign and most of them did not become believers; your Lord is the mighty one, the merciful one" (XXVI:103–104).

Noah (XXVI:105–122)

The recollection of Noah's story begins abruptly with the announcement: "Noah's people discredited the messengers" (XXVI:105), and carries on with the phrase, "When (*idh*) their brother Noah said, 'Do you not fear?'" (XXVI:106). In the brief sequel, Noah bids his people to "Fear God and obey me" (XXVI:110). And he assures them, "I will not ask you for any wage; my wage is only on the Lord of the worlds" (XXVI:109). The people refuse and the text, presuming that the reader knows the story of the flood and the ark, presents God as saying of Noah, "We saved him and those with him in the fully loaded ship. Then afterwards We drowned the rest" (XXVI:119–120).[20] The refrain follows immediately: "In this there is certainly a sign and most of them did not become believers; your Lord is the mighty one, the merciful one" (XXVI:121–122).

Hūd (XXVI:123–140)

The story of the non-biblical prophet Hūd, like Noah's story, begins abruptly with the announcement that his people, "'Ād discredited the messengers" (XXVI:123), and carries on with the same phrase, "When (*idh*) their brother Hūd said, 'Do you not fear?'" (XXVI:124). And again like Noah, Hūd says, "I am a trustworthy messenger to you, so fear God and obey me" (XXVI:125–126). And he assures 'Ād, "I will not ask you for any wage; my wage is only on the Lord of the worlds" (XXVI:127). In the end his people discredit Hūd, and God says, "We destroyed them" (XXVI:129).[21] The refrain follows immediately: "In this there is certainly a sign and most of them did not become believers; your Lord is the mighty one, the merciful one" (XXVI:129–130).

Ṣāliḥ (XXVI:141–159)

Ṣāliḥ's story also begins with the abrupt announcement, "Thamūd discredited the messengers" (XXVI:141), and continues with the phrase,

[20] See Tottoli, *Biblical Prophets in the Qur'ān*, pp. 5–9, 21–23; William M. Brinner, "Noah," in McAuliffe, *Encyclopaedia of the Qur'ān*, vol. 3, p. 540.

[21] See R. B. Serjeant, "Hūd and Other Pre-Islamic Prophets of Ḥadramawt," *Le Muséon* 46 (1954), pp. 121–179; Paul M. Cobb, "Hūd," in McAuliffe, *Encyclopaedia of the Qur'ān*, vol. 2, p. 462.

"When (*idh*) their brother Ṣāliḥ said, 'Do you not fear?'" And again, like Noah and Hūd, Ṣāliḥ says, "I am a trustworthy messenger to you, so fear God and obey me" (XXVI:144). And he offers the same assurance, "I will not ask you for any wage; my wage is only on the Lord of the worlds" (XXVI:145). The text goes on to evoke the memory of the vicissitudes of the non-biblical prophet in his efforts to bring God's message to his people. In the end they disobeyed the prophet and the text says, "Punishment overtook them" (XXVI:158).[22] The refrain follows: "In this there is certainly a sign and most of them did not become believers; your Lord is the mighty one, the merciful one" (XXVI:158–159).

Lot (XXVI:160–175)

The same formula introduces the biblical prophet Lot's story as appears in the accounts of Noah, Hūd, and Ṣāliḥ: "Lot's people discredited the messengers" (XXVI:160), and again there is the phrase, "When (*idh*) their brother Lot said to them, 'Do you not fear?'" "I am a trustworthy messenger to you, so fear God and obey me" (XXVI:161–163). And he offers the assurance, "I will not ask you for any wage; my wage is only on the Lord of the worlds." (XXVI:164) Very briefly, in a succinct dialogue, the Qur'ān recalls the biblical story of Lot; there are no biblical quotations and the reader would have to know the story for its full impact to occur to him. It concludes with God's remark, "We sent a rain down upon them; wretched is the rain of those who have been warned" (XXVI:173).[23] The refrain follows straightaway: "In this there is certainly a sign and most of them did not become believers; your Lord is the mighty one, the merciful one" (XXVI:174–175).

Shuʿayb (XXVI:176–191)

Like the three previous recollections of the careers of the prophets, the same formula opens the story of the non-biblical Shuʿayb: "The companions of the thicket discredited the messengers." This introduces the recollection of "When (*idh*) Shuʿayb said to them, 'Do you not fear?'" (XXVI:177). It continues, "I am a trustworthy messenger to you, so fear God and obey me" (XXVI:178–179). Here too is the repeated assurance: "I will not ask you for any wage; my wage is only on the Lord of the worlds" (XXVI:180). Shuʿayb's

[22] See B .M. Wheeler, *Prophets in the Quran*, pp. 74–82; R. Tottoli, "Ṣāliḥ," in McAuliffe, *Encyclopaedia of the Qur'ān*, vol. 4, p. 521.

[23] See D. Künstlinger, "Christliche Herkunft der kurānischen Loṭ—Legende," *Rocznik Orientalistyczny* 7 (1929–1930), pp. 281–295; Heribert Busse, "Lot," in McAuliffe, *Encyclopaedia of the Qur'ān*, vol. 3, p. 231.

admonition to upright behavior on the part of his people earns him only their ire and they discredit him, for which punishment overtakes them.[24] There follows the refrain: "In this there is certainly a sign and most of them did not become believers; your Lord is the mighty one, the merciful one" (XXVI:190–191).

GOD'S CLOSING ADDRESS TO MUḤAMMAD (XXVI:192–227)

God's reassuring words to Muḥammad about his prophetic vocation at the end of the *sūrah* not only offer insight into the mode of Qur'ānic revelation in general, but also indicate the social and interreligious situation in which the prophet found himself. Referring to the verses that have gone before, the Qur'ān says:

> This is surely a 'sending-down' (*tanzīl*) on the part of the Lord of the Worlds; the trustworthy Spirit has brought it down upon your heart so that you might be one of the warners, with a clarifying Arabic tongue. It was already in the texts (*zubur*) of the ancients. Was it not a 'sign' (*āyatan*) for them that the learned men of the Sons of Israel would know it? Had we sent it down to a non-Arabic-speaker, and he recited it to them, they would not have become believers in it. (XXVI:192–199)

On the face of it, this passage assures Muḥammad that his experience of the disbelief of his own audience is consonant with the experience of the earlier prophets, recorded already in ancient texts, suggesting that the stories contained in such texts were known in his environs. Moreover, the fact that it was specifically the learned men of Israel who would recognize Muḥammad's experience serves both as a sign of his authenticity and presupposes the presence of these same 'People of the Book' in Muḥammad's milieu. Finally, the reference to a non-Arabic-speaker, both implies the actual presence of such persons in the Qur'ān's ambience, and at the same time bespeaks the practical necessity for their message to be translated into Arabic if it is to be accepted in the Arabic-speaking community. The purpose of highlighting the painful fate of those who in the past discredited the message of the prophets is expressed in the verse that says that the people of those days, as the people of Muḥammad's own day, "would not believe in it until they would see the dire punishment" (XXVI:201). The final verses

[24] See C. E. Bosworth, "The Qur'ānic Prophet Shu'aib and Ibn Taimiyya's Epistle concerning Him," *Le Muséon* 87 (1974), pp. 425–440; *idem*, "Madyan Shu'ayb in Pre-Islamic and Early Islamic Lore," *Journal of Semitic Studies* 29 (1984), pp. 53–64; R. Tottoli, "Shu'ayb," in McAuliffe, *Encyclopaedia of the Qur'ān*, vol. 4, p. 605.

explain how the prophetic message could never come from demons or from wandering poets, who do not practice what they preach.[25] In the end the situation in the past and the present is that the believers are "only those who do good works, remember God often, and overcome after having been wronged. The ones who have done wrong will know what sort of turmoil they will encounter" (XXVI:227).

Many other *sūrahs* offer insights into Qur'ānic prophetology and even provide fuller lists of the pre-Islamic prophets, including the biblical ones. But *sūrah* XXVI *ash-Shu'arā'*, with its highly structured format and ritualistically repeated refrains, puts the basic features of prophetic recall in the Qur'ān into high relief. And the presence of three non-biblical prophets, Hūd, Ṣāliḥ, and Shu'ayb, in this short list of seven prophets immediately calls attention to the fact that for the Qur'ān prophecy is more than a biblical phenomenon, albeit that given the high profile of biblical prophets in the scripture they can seem to dominate the others. The fact remains that in the Qur'ān, the recollection of biblical prophets does not determine the prophetology. Rather, the prophetology structures the biblical reminiscences; memories of biblical prophets are folded into a sequence that extends beyond the Bible's reach. Some figures who do appear in the Bible, but who are not normally considered prophets in the biblical tradition, are included among the prophets in the Qur'ān, e.g., Ishmael, Isaac, Jacob and the tribes, Joseph, Jesus, Job, Jonah, Aaron, Solomon, and David, among others (cf. IV *an-Nisā'* 163). From the Qur'ān's point of view, these figures are among those sent (*mursalīn*) by God to be, like Muḥammad, among the 'warners' (*mundhirīn*) of their own people; and the long, recurrent sequence stops with Muḥammad. In the sequence, as *sūrah* XXVI *ash-Shu'arā'* makes clear, the pattern is always the same. The prophet/messenger arises within his own people (he is 'their brother', *akhūhum*, XXVI:106, 124, 142, 161), delivers his message, is discredited by his audience but is vindicated by the divine punishment visited upon his adversaries, the retelling of which becomes a 'sign' for those who will believe. This pattern can be seen to determine the shape of the recall of even the most familiar of biblical figures and their stories in the Qur'ān. For this reason, the Qur'ān does not simply quote or copy earlier biblical or other narratives; it presumes its audience's familiarity with the patriarchs, prophets, and their stories. And it

[25] For more on the Qur'ān's view of the poets, see Irfan Shahid, "A Contribution to Koranic Exegesis," in G. Makdisi (ed.), *Arabic and Islamic Studies in Honor of Hamilton A.R. Gibb* (Leiden: E.J. Brill, 1965), pp. 563–580; *idem*, "Another Contribution to Koranic Exegesis: The *Sūra* of the Poets (XXVI)," *Journal of Arabic Literature* 14 (1983), pp. 1–21.

recalls them within the pattern of its own distinctive prophetology, so as to weave the recollections, echoes, and allusions to them into the patterns of discourse that the close reading of *sūrah* XXVI *ash-Shuʿarāʾ* has highlighted.

In short, the Qurʾān's distinctive prophetology, its *sunnah* as the Qurʾān itself speaks of it,[26] may be characterized as: universal (God's messengers have come to every people, not just to the people of Israel); recurrent (the pattern of prophetic experience recurs in the experience of each prophet); dialogical (the prophets interact in conversation with their people); singular in its message (there is one God, who rewards good and punishes evil on 'the Day of Judgment'); and triumphant (God vindicates His prophets in their struggles, i.e., in the so-called 'punishment stories').[27] There is also a corrective, even polemical dimension to the Qurʾān's prophetology vis-à-vis the biblical and other narratives of the Jews and Christians in its milieu. The Qurʾān means not to retell the biblical stories but to *recall* them, and to recollect them within the corrective framework of its own discourse. For this reason the Bible is not quoted; instead, the Qurʾān re-presents the stories of many of the Bible's major figures within the parameters of its own, distinctive prophetology, which is an apologetic typology in support of Muḥammad's mission. This phenomenon may best be observed by briefly reviewing several prominent instances of biblical recall in the Qurʾān, this in passages that have been widely studied by modern scholars and so may serve as brief case studies, illustrative of how we find the Bible in the Qurʾān.

Abraham in the Qurʾān

As he appears in the Qurʾān, Abraham is only a semi-biblical character. No biblical passage is quoted in the accounts of him in the Arabic scripture, and his story includes episodes that otherwise occur severally in Jewish traditions (his early history and the challenge to the polytheism of his ancestors),[28] in the Bible (his sojourn in the environs of Jerusalem), and in

[26] In reference to the messengers prior to Muḥammad, God speaks of "the *sunnah* of our messengers whom We have sent before you; you will not find that our *sunnah* has any change." XVII *al-Isrāʾ* 77. In other places the Qurʾān refers to this *sunnah* of the prophets and the '*sunnah* of the ancients' (*sunnat al-awwalīn*), as in XV *al-Ḥijr* 13; XXXV *Fāṭir* 43. See Zwettler, "A Mantic Manifesto," 106–109.

[27] See David Marshall, "Punishment Stories," in McAuliffe, *Encyclopaedia of the Qurʾān*, vol. 4, pp. 318ff. See also David Marshall, *God, Muhammad and the Unbelievers: A Qurʾānic Study* (Richmond, Surrey: Qurzon Press, 1999).

[28] See the presentation of many of these traditions in James L. Kugel, *Traditions of the Bible: A Guide to the Bible as It Was at the Start of the Common Era* (Cambridge, MA: Harvard University Press, 1998), pp. 244–274.

the Qur'ān and Islamic tradition (his sojourn with Ishmael in the environs of Mecca and the rebuilding of the Ka'bah).[29] In the Qur'ān, Abraham is presented as a subject of controversy between Jews, Christians, and Muslims at the same time as he serves as a prophetic exemplar for Muḥammad. The Qur'ān says:

> O Scripture People, why do you argue about Abraham? The Torah and the Gospel were sent down only after him; do you not know? You are those who argue with one another about that of which you have some knowledge. So why are you arguing about something of which you do not have any knowledge? God knows; you do not know. Abraham was not a Jew, nor a Christian, but he was a *ḥanīf*,[30] submissive (*muslim*), and he was not one of the polytheists (*al-mushrikīn*). The people worthiest of Abraham are surely the ones who follow him, this prophet (i.e., Muḥammad), and those who believe; God is the patron of the believers. A group of the Scripture People would love it were they to mislead you; they will mislead only themselves unawares. O Scripture People, why do you, knowing better, disbelieve God's signs? (III *Āl 'Imrān* 65–70)

The idea that Muḥammad is one of those "worthiest of Abraham" (III:68) already suggests that Abraham and his religion provided the paradigm or prototype for Muḥammad's prophetic role, a conviction that is advanced more explicitly in a long passage in another *sūrah*, II *al-Baqarah* 124–141,[31] where once again the point is argued in response to the Jews and the Christians:

> "They say, 'Become Jews or Christians; you will be rightly guided.' Say, 'No, [follow][32] the religion of Abraham (*millat Ibrāhīm*), who was

[29] See especially Firestone, *Journeys in Holy Lands.*

[30] It is very difficult properly to translate this term; on the face of it, as it is used here and elsewhere in the Qur'ān, it designates someone who is neither a Jew, a Christian, nor or a polytheist. See Uri Rubin, "Ḥanīf," in McAuliffe, *Encyclopaedia of the Qur'ān*, vol. 2, p. 402. For the interpretation of *ḥanīf* as a term equivalent to 'gentile', see François de Blois, "*Naṣrānī* (Ναζωραιος) and *ḥanīf* (εθνικος): Studies on the Religious Vocabulary of Christianity and Islam," *Bulletin of the School of Oriental and African Studies* 65 (2002), pp. 1–30.

[31] See Edmund Beck, "Die Gestalt des Abraham am Wendepunkt der Entwicklung Muhammeds. Analyse von Sure 2, 118(124)–135 (141)," *Le Muséon* 65 (1952), pp. 73–94.

[32] The verb, which is meant to be understood here, does not actually occur in the text; it is supplied on the basis of the repeated phrase, found elsewhere in the

a *ḥanīf* and not one of the polytheists. Say, 'We believe in God and what has been sent down to us and what was sent down to Abraham, Ishmael, Isaac, Jacob, and the tribes, what was brought to Moses and to Jesus, and what was brought to the prophets from their Lord. We do not single out any one of them; to Him we are submissive'." (II *al-Baqarah* 135–136)

The concept of the 'religion of Abraham' (*millat Ibrāhīm*),[33] which in the Qur'ān is explicitly presented as that religion to which the sequence of God's prophets and messengers continually call their respective peoples, is the religion to which Muḥammad and the Qur'ān were calling the Arabic-speaking people in their milieu. The Qur'ān's distinctive prophetology is ultimately determined precisely in view of commending the 'religion of Abraham', which is clearly defined negatively as being neither Judaism, Christianity, nor the indigenous Arabian polytheism. Positively it is the confession that God is one (*at-tawḥīd*). The Qur'ān says, "Who is better in religious practice (*dīnan*) than one who submits himself to God; he does well and follows the religion of Abraham (*millat Ibrāhīm*), who was a *ḥanīf*, and God took Abraham as a friend (*khalīlan*); to God belongs what is the heavens and what is on the earth; God comprehends everything" (IV *an-Nisā'* 125–126). One cannot miss the apologetic/polemic dimension of the image of Abraham as the Qur'ān's paradigmatic prophet and messenger,[34] and the role of the concept of the 'religion of Abraham' as the distinctive *theologoumenon* of the Qur'ān and of Islam is precisely to state what one might retrospectively call the Islamic difference. It is a difference defined by the corrective, even polemical stance it adopts in response to earlier claims on Abraham made by Jews and Christians.[35]

Qur'ān, "Follow the religion of Abraham, who was a *ḥanīf*," (III *Āl 'Imrān* 95; XVI *an-Naḥl* 123); see also XII *Yūsuf* 38 and XXII *al-Ḥajj* 78. Thanks to Prof. Meir Bar-Asher for this insight.

[33] The Arabic term *millah* is difficult to translate accurately into English; etymologically, given its association with the Aramaic/Syriac root *m-l-l* and the Greek λόγος, it would seem accurate to think of it as meaning 'religion' in its doctrinal aspect. See F. Buhl and C. E. Bosworth, "Milla," *EI*, 2nd ed., vol. 7, p. 61.

[34] In one passage there is even the mention of "the scrolls (*ṣuḥuf*) of Abraham and Moses." (LXXXVII *al-'Alā* 19); see also LIII *an-Najm* 36–37.

[35] On this dimension of the Qur'ān's recollection of Abraham, see Reynolds, *The Qur'ān and Its Biblical Subtext*, esp. pp. 71–87.

The Story of Joseph

As one recent scholar has said of *sūrah* XII *Yūsuf*, it is "the Qur'ān's longest sustained narrative of one character's life."[36] And in the Qur'ān it is also, like the story of Joseph in the Bible (Gen. 33–48), virtually a complete narrative unit in its own right. What is more, as M. S. Stern has pointed out, it is "the Koran's most comprehensive treatment of any specifically biblical subject."[37] Yet, as in other instances of biblical recall in the Qur'ān, so here too there are no actual quotations from the Bible, and yet the text presumes a ready familiarity with Joseph's story on the part of its audience. Moreover, in the portions of the narrative that the Qur'ān chooses to recall, the recollection more or less closely follows the outline of the story as one finds it in the book of Genesis. This selectivity in what one might call the re-telling or re-composition of the story, in turn suggests that the Qur'ān is following its own recurrent pattern of prophetic recall in this *sūrah*. It is obviously not its intention to reproduce the entire history of Joseph, or even to remain within the parameters of the story as it appears in the Bible, for it includes details and narrative embellishments that are otherwise to be found only in extra-biblical Jewish and Christian traditions, as many scholars have noted.[38]

Here is not the place to engage in a detailed discussion of the story of the biblical Joseph as it appears in *sūrah* XII *Yūsuf*. Rather, our purpose is to show that the biblical recall exhibited in the Qur'ān is a product of its distinctive prophetology, which serves as the paradigm governing the recollection. First of all, Joseph's story begins with God saying to Muḥammad: "We are going to tell you the best of stories with which We have revealed this Qur'ān to you, although prior to it you have been among the negligent" (XII:3). The narrative then takes up straightaway the telltale particle of reminiscence, "When (*idh*) Joseph said to his father . . . " (XII:4). Joseph is mentioned in only two other places in the Qur'ān, and both recall him as one in a recurrent series of prophetic figures, including non-Israelites. In one instance, in the course of recalling Moses' mission to Pharaoh, "a

[36] S. Goldman, "Joseph," in McAuliffe, *Encyclopaedia of the Qur'ān*, vol. 3, p. 55.

[37] M. S. Stern, "Muhammad and Joseph: A Study of Koranic Narrative," *Journal of Near Eastern Studies* 44 (1985), p. 193.

[38] The most sustained, recent study of the *sūrah* is that by A.-L. de Prémare, *Joseph et Muhammad: Le chapitre 12 du Coran; étude textuelle* (Aix-en-Provence: Publications de l'Université de Provence, 1989). See also Kugel, *Traditions of the Bible*, pp. 437–458; and James L. Kugel, *In Potiphar's House: The Interpretive Life of Biblical Texts* (San Francisco: HarperSanFrancisco, 1990).

believing man of the house of Pharaoh" is the speaker and he recalls a series of prophets ignored by the people to whom they were sent, including the people of Noah, ʿĀd, and Thamūd, and concluding with a mention of Joseph, who "previously brought you clear [signs], and you continued to doubt what he brought you, until, when he perished, you said, 'God will not raise up any messenger after him'" (XL *Ghāfir* 28–34). The other occurrence sees God naming Joseph in the long list of biblical prophets from Abraham onward, extending as far as John and Jesus, "whom We raise up step-by-step as We wish" (VI *al-An'ām* 83–86).

The recall proceeds dialogically, with God recounting the dialogue between Joseph and his father, and later with his brothers, with his fellow prisoners, with the women of Egypt, with the king himself, and with his father again, ending finally with his prayer to God.[39] The brothers are singled out initially as Joseph's principal adversarial interlocutors; at the outset of the account God says, "In Joseph and his brothers there are signs for those who would inquire" (XII:7); after which the story takes up again with the formula of reminiscence, "When (*idh*) they said, 'Joseph and his brother are surely the most beloved to our father . . . '" (XII:8). Along the way, at several junctures, God as narrator makes relevant comments. The final element of the narrative, Joseph's prayer of vindication, mentions the interpretation of his dream, his freedom from prison, his escape from the mischief Satan had sown among his brothers, and his family's rescue from the desert. He then prays: "Lord, you have given me dominion and taught me the interpretation of events. O creator of the heavens and the earth, you are my protector in this world and in the next. Receive me as one submissive and enlist me among the righteous" (XII:101).

The centerpiece of the Joseph story, which, on the basis of her structural analysis of the *sūrah* Angelika Neuwirth calls "the crowning keystone in the narrative arch . . . situated at the center of the central complex of scenes,"[40] is Joseph's prison speech, in which he addresses the two fellow prisoners who have asked him to interpret their dreams. A.-L. de Prémare calls it "le discours prosélyte islamique de Joseph."[41] There could hardly be

[39] See the outline of the narrative in Neuwirth, *Studien zur Komposition der mekkanischen Suren*, p. 297; *eadem*, "Zur Struktur der Yusuf-Sure," in Werner Diem and Stefan Wild (eds.), *Studien aus Arabistik und Semitistik: Anton Spitaler zum siebzigsten Geburtstag* (Wiesbaden: Harrassowitz, 1980), pp. 123–150.

[40] Neuwirth, "Zur Struktur der Yusuf-Sure," p. 14.

[41] Prémare, *Joseph et Muhammad*, p. 96.

a more explicit statement of the singular and recurrent prophetic message to be found at the heart of the Qurʾān's distinctive prophetology. Joseph says:

> I have left behind the religion of a people who do not believe in God, who disbelieve in the hereafter. I follow the religion of my fathers, Abraham, Isaac, and Jacob. It is not for us to associate anything with God. It is of God's favor for us and for [all] people, but most people are not grateful. O my fellow prisoners, are different lords better, or the one God, the omnipotent one? What you worship instead of Him are only names that you and your fathers have given them; God has not sent down any authority to them. Only God has the judgment. He has commanded that you not worship any but Him. That is the right religion, but most people are not aware. (XII *Yūsuf* 37–40)

Many commentators, including de Prémare, have put forward the view that the result of all the filtering, selecting, transforming, and recomposing of materials (biblical, rabbinical and traditional) that has gone into the Qurʾān's somewhat compact narrative of the story of Joseph is that Joseph appears now as a double for Muḥammad. As Prémare puts it in the conclusion to his book, the intention was "to reproduce in Joseph the very type of the prophet."[42] Of course, he means the prophet, Muḥammad, and it is a very apt comparison. But more to the point, it is our conclusion that in fact the story of Joseph is presented in the Qurʾān very much in view of the Qurʾān's prophetic typology and its own distinctive prophetology, and that it was perhaps even meant to correct the views of Joseph current among contemporary Jews and Christians. There is also a further point to make in connection with the Joseph story. Many earlier scholars, and Prémare cites the work of most of them, have found numerous details of the Qurʾān's account of Joseph and his adventures in earlier Jewish lore. In an insightful recent study, Joseph Witztum has convincingly shown that these same features can also by found in Syriac sources, and that they seem in fact to have been filtered into the Arabic-speaking milieu of Muḥammad and the Qurʾān through the medium of the Syriac-speaking tradition.[43]

[42] Prémare, *Joseph et Muhammad*, p. 173.

[43] See Joseph Witztum, "Joseph among the Ishmaelites: Q 12 in Light of Syriac Sources," in Gabriel Reynolds (ed.), *New Perspectives on the Qurʾān: The Qurʾān in Its Historical Context 2* (Routledge Studies in the Qurʾān; London and New York: Routledge, 2011), pp. 425–448.

Moses in the Qur'ān

Moses' name is mentioned some one hundred and thirty-six times in the Qur'ān, a number that in itself marks him as the major figure in biblical reminiscence. As Michael Zwettler has put it, "Moses is far and away the most elaborately developed character in Qur'ānic revelation." He points out that mentions of Moses appear in almost fifty separate passages and over five hundred verses.[44] Many times it is just a matter of listing Moses' name among the biblical prophets, as in the following verse: "Say, we believe in God and in what has been revealed to us and what has been revealed to Abraham, Ishmael, Isaac, Jacob and the tribes, and what was brought to Moses and Jesus and the prophets from their Lord; we do not single out any one of them; we are submissive to Him" (III *Āl 'Imrān* 84). In other places, the Qur'ān recalls a series of incidents from Moses' story in the Bible and tradition in the course of calling on the witness of prophetic history while addressing the Israelites, e.g., in II *al-Baqarah* 40–87. In several *sūrahs* the focus is on the presentation of Moses' distinctive prophetic mission in its own right (e.g., XX *Ṭā Hā* 9-99), or on his mission to Egypt and his role among the Israelites, (VII *al-A'rāf* 103–174 and XL *Ghāfir* 23–52), or Moses' story is presented to Muḥammad as a model for a prophetic career, as in XXVIII *al-Qaṣaṣ* 3–46. The focal point of the patriarch's message and his importance as a model for Muḥammad is clearly stated at the end of the Moses section in *sūrah Ṭā Hā*: Moses says to Aaron and the Israelites after the incident with the golden calf (Exodus 32), "Your God is only God, there is no other God than He, He comprehends everything in knowledge" (XX:98); and God says immediately to Muḥammad, "Like this do We narrate to you reports of what has gone before, and We have brought you a recollection (*dhikran*) from Us" (XX:99).

Just as God brought Muḥammad a recollection and a scripture, so too did He bring Moses a scripture, i.e., the Torah, to which the Qur'ān refers by name some eighteen times. A dozen times and more, however, it speaks of Torah simply as "the scripture We brought Moses" (e.g., II *al-Baqarah* 53 and 87), twice calling it *al-furqān* (II *al-Baqarah* 53 and XXI *al-Anbiyā'* 48), a term that is also used in reference to the Qur'ān itself (II *al-Baqarah* 185 and XXV *al-Furqān* 1) and is usually translated into English as 'criterion' or 'standard of judging',[45] in the sense of something by means of which one

[44] Zwettler, "A Mantic Manifesto," p. 88.

[45] See Daniel Madigan, "Criterion," in McAuliffe, *Encyclopaedia of the Qur'ān*, vol. 1, p. 486.

distinguishes true from false, right from wrong.[46] Although the Qur'ān says that "God spoke directly to Moses" (IV *an-Nisā'* 164)[47] and, seemingly in reference to the Torah, speaks of the 'scrolls' or 'pages' (*ṣuḥuf*) of Moses (and of Abraham!) (cf. LIII *an-Najm* 36–37; LXXXVII *al-A'lā* 18–19), it also evokes a recollection of God giving Moses the Torah written on tablets: "We wrote for him on the tablets," the very tablets that Moses "cast down" in anger when he discovered the apostasy of the Israelites, the tablets, "in the text of which are guidance and mercy for those who fear their Lord" (VII *al-A'rāf* 145, 150, 154). And the Qur'ān goes on in this same sequence of verses, evidently in reference to Muḥammad, to speak of "the messenger, the 'unlettered' prophet (*an-nabī al-ummī*),[48] whom they will find written down for them in the Torah and the Gospel" (VII *al-A'rāf* 157). Clearly, the Torah and the Qur'ān are mirroring one another in these passages.

As elsewhere, so in telling the story of Moses and the Torah, the Qur'ān certainly echoes the biblical narrative, but there are no actual quotations from it. This feature of the Qur'ān's recollection of the Torah extends as well to its recall of the Ten Commandments. Scholars have traditionally cited two passages in which the Decalogue is echoed: in a longer and expanded form in XVII *al-Isrā'* 22–39, and in a shorter form in VI *al-An'ām*

[46] The term *al-furqān* occurs seven times in the Qur'ān, and it seems that it both echoes the Syriac term *purqānâ*, 'salvation', 'deliverance' (and possibly *puqdānâ*, 'command'), as well as reflecting an inner Arabic sense of 'separation', 'distinction'. See Fred M. Donner, "Quranic *Furqān*," *Journal of Semitic Studies* 52 (2007), pp. 279–300; Uri Rubin, "On the Arabian Origins of the Qur'ān: The Case of *al-Furqān*," *Journal of Semitic Studies* 54 (2009), pp. 421–433. The use of the term to refer both to the Torah and the Qur'ān conveys something of the different sense of 'scripture' for the Qur'ān and the 'People of the Book', i.e., the Jews and Christians.

[47] The phrasing here, "God spoke directly to Moses (*wakallama Allāh Mūsā taklīman*)," is the one referred to in n.2 above.

[48] The expression, "the 'unlettered' prophet," appearing here and in VII:158, features a problematic translation, due to the multiple possible senses of the adjective *ummī*, a term that is almost universally taken to mean 'illiterate' in Islamic interpretations, but which many other scholars interpret in terms of a reference to the 'people' (*ummah*) from whom Muḥammad came, i.e., the Arabs, about whom various cultural assumptions are often voiced in the scholarly literature. See Sebastian Günther, "Muḥammad, the Illiterate Prophet: An Islamic Creed in the Qur'ān and Qur'anic Exegesis," *Journal of Qur'anic Studies* 4 (2002), pp. 1–26; *idem*, "Illiteracy," in McAuliffe, *Encyclopaedia of the Qur'ān*, vol. 2, pp. 492ff. and *idem*, "Ummī," in McAuliffe, *Encyclopaedia of the Qur'ān*, vol. 5, pp. 399ff.

252–253.[49] Here is the shorter form, in the translation and exposition of Sebastian Günther:

Q.6:151–153

(151) Say: 'Come, I will recite WHAT YOUR LORD HAS FORBIDDEN YOU: that you

[1] Associate not anything with Him, and to

[2] Be good to your parents, and

[3] Slay not your children because of poverty; We will provide [for] you and them; and that you

[4] Approach not any indecency outward or inward, and that you

[5] Slay not the soul God has forbidden, except by right. That they He has charged you with; haply you will understand. (152) And that you

[6] Approach not the property of the orphan, save in the fairer manner, until he is of age. And

[7] Fill up the measure and the balance with justice. We charge not any soul save to its capacity. And when you speak,

[8] Be just, even if it should be to a near kinsman. And

[9] Fulfill God's covenant. That then He has charged you with; haply you will remember. (153) And that

[10] THIS IS MY PATH, STRAIGHT;

SO DO YOU FOLLOW IT, AND FOLLOW NOT DIVERS PATHS lest they scatter you from His path. That then He has charged you with; haply you will be god-fearing.'[50]

[49] See W. M. Brinner, "An Islamic Decalogue," in W. M. Brinner and S. D. Ricks (eds.), *Studies in Islamic and Judaic Traditions: Papers Presented at the Institute for Islamic-Judaic Studies, Center for Judaic Studies, University of Denver* (Atlanta: Scholars Press, 1986), pp. 67–84; Sebastian Günther, "*O People of the Scripture! Come to a Word Common to You and Us* (Q. 3:64): The Ten Commandments and the Qur'ān," *Journal of Qur'ānic Studies* 9 (2007), pp. 28–58.

[50] Günther, "*O People of the Scripture!*," p. 35.

One readily sees in this presentation of the passage from the Qur'ān both how reminiscent it is of the biblical Decalogue, and at the same time how divergent from any previous Jewish or Christian presentation of the commandments. Indeed scholars, both ancient and modern, have had to exercise considerable ingenuity just to align the Qur'ānic text with the biblical one. It seems manifest that the Qur'ān has no written Arabic translation of either the Hebrew or the Syriac Bible behind its evocations of the Ten Commandments.

While the Moses story as it appears in the Qur'ān recognizably reflects a remodeled biblical narrative, albeit with no actual quotations, and many features found elsewhere in Jewish or even Christian tradition,[51] the Qur'ān puts them forward from its own perspective. As one modern scholar has put it, "The essential feature of the allusions to the past is a typological interpretation of the earlier narratives, by which the biography of Moses is seen in the light of the biography of Muḥammad."[52] But Angelika Neuwirth has convincingly shown that over the course of the history of the coming-to-be of the early Islamic community, the basic features of the Moses story came into the Qur'ān's narrative at different junctures, and thus reflect the prophetic concerns of the several moments in the evolution of the early community of believers, not excluding the need on the Qur'ān's part to provide corrective adjustments to the Moses story in the course of controversies with Jews and Christians in the Arabic-speaking environment.[53] In the end, of course, all the characteristics of the distinctive Qur'ānic prophetology, its *sunnah*, are evident in the Arabic scripture's recollections of Moses. In the ensemble they function in turn as the paradigm for a correct reading of the Qur'ān's own evocation of the memory of Moses, who, in its view—to judge by the number of times his story is recalled—was considered the most paradigmatic prophet of them all.

David and the Psalms in the Qur'ān

While King David does not appear as a prophet in the Hebrew Bible, in the New Testament and later rabbinical and Christian literature he assumed

[51] See Kugel, *Traditions of the Bible*, pp. 501–741.

[52] Cornelia Schöck, "Moses," McAuliffe, *Encyclopaedia of the Qur'ān*, vol. 3, p. 419.

[53] See Angelika Neuwirth, "Erzählen als kanonischer Prozess. Die Mose-Erzälung im Wandel der koranischen Geschichte," in Rainer Brunner et al. (eds.), *Islamstudien ohne Ende* (Würzburg: Ergon, 2000), pp. 322–344.

this role,[54] an identity that carries over into the Qur'ān. The longest of the the sixteen passages that mention him occurs in *sūrah* XXXVIII *Ṣād* 17–30, which resumes a number of the themes associated with David in other parts of Arabic scripture, particularly David and Solomon's wise perspicuity as judges (cf. XXI *al-Anbiyā'* 78–79; XXVII *an-Naml* 15–16), David's ability to understand the speech of the birds (XXVII:16), and how the mountains and the birds sang God's praises with him (XXXIV *Sabā* 10). In other places one hears of David's killing of Goliath (II *al-Baqarah* 251) and of how "those who disbelieved of the children of Israel were cursed on the tongue of David and Jesus, son of Mary" (V *al-Mā'idah* 78). In one passage God says to David, "We made you a vicegerent (*khalīfatan*) on earth" (XXXVIII *Ṣād* 26), While one can recognize in these themes echoes, allusions to, and re-workings of features from the extended cycle of David and Solomon stories that circulated in Jewish and Christian tradition,[55] the most notable feature from the perspective of David's role as a prophet is his receipt of a scripture from God intended for people's reflection: "A blessed scripture We have sent down to you, so that they might ponder on its signs/verses (*ayātihi*) and those possessed of understanding might engage in recollection (*yatadhakkara*)" XXXVIII *Ṣād* 29. The reference is of course to the Psalms; in another place in the Qur'ān God makes it clear to Muḥammad that He brought the Psalms to David as one in the sequence of His prophets and messengers: "We have revealed to you as We revealed to Noah and the prophets after him, and We revealed to Abraham, Ishmael, Isaac, Jacob and the tribes, Jesus, Job, Jonah, Aaron, and Solomon, and We brought David Psalms (*zabūran*)"[56] (IV *an-Nisā'* 163; see also XVII *al-Isrā'* 55).

Modern scholars have looked very intensively for the Psalms in the Qur'ān. So far, the only quotation to which we can point with confidence is one that the Qur'ān itself identifies: God says, "We wrote in the Psalms (*az-zabūr*) after the recollection (*adh-dhikr*) that 'My righteous servants will inherit the earth'" (XXI *al-Anbiyā'* 105), a phrase that on the face of it partially quotes Psalm XXXVII:29, "The righteous shall possess the land, and dwell

[54] See James L. Kugel, "David the Prophet," in James L. Kugel (ed.), *Poetry and Prophecy: The Beginnings of a Literary Tradition* (Ithaca, NY: Cornell University Press, 1990), pp. 45–55.

[55] See Jacob Lassner, *Demonizing the Queen of Sheba: Boundaries of Gender and Culture in Postbiblical Judaism and Medieval Islam* (Chicago: University of Chicago Press, 1993); Jean-Louis Déclais, *David raconté par les musulmans* (Paris: Éditions du Cerf, 1999).

[56] For etymological reasons, the term *az-zabūr* in these passages is sometimes translated as 'a book' or 'a text', albeit that the reference here is in fact to the book of Psalms. See J. Horovitz and R. Firestone, "Zabūr," *EI*, rev. ed., vol. 11, p. 372.

upon it for ever" (RSV). But for many researchers the matter does not rest there. On the basis of this partial quotation, one scholar did not hesitate to speak of Muḥammad's "spezielle Kenntnis des Psalters überhaupt, den er ja allein von allen biblischen Büchern 21, 105 ausdrücklich zitiert."[57] Anton Baumstark went on in his very influential article to say that in all likelihood Muḥammad had encountered the Psalter orally, in Jewish and Christian liturgical settings. And it is in the burgeoning liturgical rites of the developing Muslim community in the middle to late Meccan periods that scholars have sought the influences of the Psalter in compositions that, according to their hypotheses, then made their way into the collected Qur'ān. A classic case in point is found in *sūrah* LV *ar-Raḥmān*, where as early as the late nineteenth century Western scholars have perceived an imitation of Psalm 136.[58] The strongest case for this hypothesis in current scholarship has been made by Angelika Neuwirth,[59] who readily speaks of the formative role that the reception of the Psalms played in the formation of Qur'ānic language and of the degree to which one might assume Psalm inter-texts, even echoes of the Psalms, in early portions of the Qur'ān.[60] Neuwirth makes it clear that she has in mind a wider presence of Psalm language in the Qur'ān than just quotations or echoes of particular Psalms or Psalm verses. Rather, she speaks of a "common liturgical language that was communicated through oral tradition, and which in only a few instances is so narrow as to be tied to particular Psalm texts."[61] Interestingly, Neuwirth finds this postulated infusion of Psalm language and expression into the early *sūrahs* to be the medium through which the Qur'ān came by its mentions of agricultural phenomena such as fruit-bearing trees and the vegetative cycle that are foreign

[57] Anton Baumstark, "Jüdischer und christlicher Gebetstypus im Koran," *Der Islam* 16 (1927), pp. 229–248.

[58] M.A.S. Abdel Haleem cites in this connection the work of E. M. Wherry, *A Comprehensive Commentary on the Qur'ān* (4 vols.; London: K. Paul, Trench, Trübner and Co., 1896), vol 4, p. 104. See M.A.S. Abdel Haleem, "Context and Internal Relationships: Keys to Quranic Exegesis; a Study of *Sūrat al-Raḥmān*" (Qur'ān chapter 55), in G. R. Hawting and Abdul-Kader A. Shareef (eds.), *Approaches to the Qur'ān* (London and New York: Routledge,), p. 98, n.36.

[59] See in particular her important study, Angelika Neuwirth, "Psalmen—im Koran neu gelesen (Ps 104 und 136)," in Dirk Hartwig et al. (eds.), *"Im vollen Licht der Geschichte": Die Wissenschaft des Judentums und die Anfänge der kritischen Koranforschung* (Ex Oriente Lux, vol. 8; Würzburg: Ergon Verlag, 2008), pp. 157–189.

[60] See Neuwirth, "Psalmen—im Koran," pp. 158–159.

[61] Neuwirth, "Psalmen—im Koran," p. 160.

to the Arabian Ḥijāz, but common features in the Psalms and characteristic of the geography of the land of the Psalms' origins.[62]

Beyond these more general observations, Neuwirth goes on in her article to study in considerable detail what she takes to be two instances of intertextual relationship between passages in the Qur'ān and particular Psalms. She reads *sūrah* LXXVIII *an-Nabā'* 1–16 as a reprise of Psalm 104:5ff., "one of the few instances in which a non-narrative, biblical subtext lies clearly evident;"[63] and *sūrah* LV *ar-Raḥmān* as a corrective re-reading of Psalm 136, an echo of the Psalm that is its subtext, effectively a 'new reading' (*Neulektüre*) of the Psalm as Neuwirth presents it. Here is not the place to go into the details of the analyses; suffice it to say that the evidence for the postulated relationship between the *sūrahs* and the Psalms does not go so far as direct quotations of the biblical text in the Qur'ān. Rather, the two Psalms are taken to be the subtexts to the challenges of which the *sūrahs* are taken to be intended responses. What is clear is that if we do in fact have here reminiscences of the Bible in the Qur'ān, it is still the Qur'ān's distinctive prophetology that determines the nature of the recollection. For in both *an-Nabā'* and in *ar-Raḥmān*, in the verses that are alleged to recall the Psalms, the beauties of creation, here and hereafter, both terrestrial and celestial, are evoked. Their function is as signs in witness of the one God's power and presence, of man's discrediting of the signs ("So which of your Lord's bounties do you discredit" LV *passim*), and of man's disinclination to believe, just as in the paradigm of Qur'ānic prophecy announced in *sūrah* XXVI *ash-Shu'arā'*, and especially in connection with the earth's own prophetic witness, set at the head of the list of prophetic witnesses in the *sūrah* (XXVI:7–9).

Jesus and Mary in the Qur'ān

Of the twenty-five times Jesus (*'Īsā*) is named in the Qur'ān,[64] twenty-one relate that he is said to be "the son of Mary" (*ibn Maryam*); twice this epithet

[62] Neuwirth, "Psalmen—im Koran," p. 160. This observation puts one in mind of the conundrum posed by the Qur'ān's evocations of agricultural and geographical scenarios alien to its Arabian environment as studied by Patricia Crone, "How Did the Quranic Pagans Make a Living?" *Bulletin of the School of Oriental and African Studies* 68 (2005), pp. 387–399.

[63] Neuwirth, "Psalmen—im Koran," p. 164.

[64] Of the many explanations for the form of Jesus' name as it appears in the Qur'ān, the most reasonable one from this writer's point of view is that it reflects an Arabic speakers's spelling of what he hears in an Arabic articulation of the common East

is used alone to refer to him, and eleven times he is accorded the title 'Messiah' (*al-masīḥ*),[65] which is used alone to refer to him three times. But it is abundantly clear that in the Qur'ān, Jesus, the son of Mary and the Messiah, is presented as one of God's prophets and messengers, a status that is highlighted by the Qur'ān's regularly naming him as one among a long list of prophets and messengers familiar from the Old and New Testaments (see, e.g., VI *al-An'ām* 83–86).[66] Jesus' exact place in the Qur'ān's sequence, as confirming the Israelite prophets who came before him and anticipating the coming of Muḥammad after him, can be seen in the following passage in which the memory of both Moses and Jesus is evoked:

> When (*wa'idh*) Moses said to his people, "O my people, why do you offend me; you know that I am God's messenger (*rasūl*) to you." When they turned aside, God turned their hearts aside; God will not guide aright wicked people. And when (*wa'idh*) Jesus, son of Mary, said 'O sons of Israel, I am God's messenger (*rasūl*) to you, confirming what was before me of the Torah, and announcing a messenger who will come after me, whose name is Aḥmad, when he comes to them with clear [signs], they say, "This is manifest sorcery." (LXI *aṣ-Ṣaff* 5–6)

In another passage, when the Qur'ān speaks of Muḥammad's place among his own people as a prophet, once again the memory of Jesus among other prophets is evoked as God addresses Muḥammad: "When we made

---

Syrian form of the name: *Îshô'*. See Arthur Jeffery, *The Foreign Vocabulary of the Koran* (Baroda: Oriental Institute, 1938), pp. 218–220. See the other opinions presented in Neal Robinson, "Jesus," in McAuliffe, *Encyclopaedia of the Qur'ān*, vol. 3, pp. 7ff. See too the ingenious, if ultimately unconvincing suggestion of James A. Bellamy, according to which "'Īsā is a corruption of the Arabic al-Masīḥ, from which the definite article was dropped when the prophet rejected the regular name for Jesus, Yasū'," to avoid an inappropriate urological connotation. See James A. Bellamy, "A Further Note on *'Īsā*," *Journal of the American Oriental Society* 122 (2002). pp. 587–588. Most convincingly, see G. Dye and M. Kropp, "Le nom de Jésus ('Īsā) dans le Coran, et quelques autres noms bibliques: remarques sur l'onomastique coranique," in Guillaume Dye et Fabien Nobilio (eds.), *Figures bibliques en islam* (Religion et Alterité; Fernelmont, BE: Éditions Modulaires Européennes, 2011), pp. 171–198.

[65] There is no reason to assume that the title means anything other than 'Messiah', in the Christian sense of the word, in the Qur'ān. In the later Islamic exegetical tradition, other interpretations have been put forward. See A. J. Wensinck and C. E. Bosworth, "Al-Masīḥ," in *EI*, rev. ed., vol. 6, p. 726.

[66] For a very different view of the role of Jesus in the Qur'ān from the one espoused here, see J.M.F. Van Reeth, "La typologie du prophète selon le Coran; le cas de Jésus," in Dye and Nobilio, *Figures bibliques en islam*, pp. 81–106.

a covenant with the prophets, and with you, with Noah, Abraham, Moses, and Jesus, son of Mary, We made a strong covenant with them" (XXXIII *al-Aḥzāb* 7). And as in the case of the other major prophets and messengers, so too is the Qurʾān concerned with Jesus' origins and with his mission to his own people.

In two places the Qurʾān recalls the Gospel accounts of the birth annunciations and early lives of John the Baptist and Jesus (XIX *Maryam* 1–34; III *Āl ʿImrān* 35–59. In both instances the account stays close to the main outline of the stories in Christian lore, without actually quoting from the Gospel or any other Christian text, and in both instances the narratives present the story in the context of the Qurʾān's wider prophetic vision, in that the narratives go on to recall other prophets and their stories. In XIX *Maryam*, the story stays close to the Annunciation scene in Luke (1:5–2:40), with features otherwise found in the so-called 'Gospel of Pseudo-Matthew', but without once actually quoting the texts. In III *Āl ʿImrān*, the recollection of the story seems more to reflect traditions otherwise found in the apocryphal Protoevangelium of James. These accounts have been studied many times, with reference to Christian sources in which similar narrative features are also to be found,[67] and it is beyond the purpose of the present undertaking to rehearse the matter once again. Rather, the point to be made here is that the Qurʾān's purpose is selectively to recall the stories of Jesus and Mary within the parameters of its own distinctive prophetology. This purpose is most evident in the many passages that critique and correct non-Qurʾānic views of Jesus, thereby bespeaking what must have been a considerable countervailing Christian discourse in the Qurʾān's own milieu.

A remarkably clear statement of the Qurʾān's view of Jesus' prophetic role is recorded in *sūrah* XLIII *az-Zukhruf*. It is bracketed between two sections of polemical verses expressing outrage at the treatment accorded to the prophets before Muḥammad and verses describing unbelievers'

[67] For bibliography and an excellent survey of the material, see Neal Robinson, "Jesus," in McAuliffe, *Encyclopaedia of the Qurʾān*, vol. 3, pp. 7ff. See too the studies by Suleiman A. Mourad, "On the Qurʾānic Stories about Mary and Jesus," *Bulletin of the Royal Institute for Inter-Faith Studies* 1 (1999), pp. 13–24; *idem*, "From Hellenism to Christianity and Islam: The Origin of the Palm Tree Story concerning Mary and Jesus in the Gospel of Pseudo-Matthew and the Qurʾān," *Oriens Christianus* 86 (2002), pp. 206–216; Angelika Neuwirth, "Mary and Jesus: Counterbalancing the Biblical Patriarchs; a Re-Reading of Sūrat Maryam in Sūrat Āl ʿImrān (Q 3:1–62)," *Parole de l'Orient* 30 (2005), pp. 332–359. See also Reynolds, *The Qurʾān and Its Biblical Subtext*, pp. 130–147.

misconceptions about the hereafter. In the middle section, the Qurʾān evokes the memory of Abraham, Moses, and Jesus.[68] Of the latter the text says:

> When Jesus brought clear [signs], he said, "I have come to you with wisdom, and to clarify for you some of what you are differing about. So fear God and obey me.[69] God is my Lord and your Lord, so worship Him; this is a straight path." But the parties differed with one another. Woe betide those who do wrong, due to the punishment of a painful day. (XLIII *az-Zukhruf* 63–65)

The source of the "differing" regarding Jesus, the Messiah, the son of Mary, is the doctrine promoted by the Arabic-speaking Christians in its milieu that Jesus is the 'Son of God', a doctrine the Qurʾān rejects time and again.[70] The Qurʾān proposes that this allegation is an instance of exceeding the bounds in one's religion and of following "the fancies of a people who went astray in the past and led many astray and they strayed from the even path" (V *al-Māʾidah* 77). The most comprehensive passage in the Qurʾān that rejects the principal Christian teaching about Jesus, and which records the Qurʾān's recognition that what the Christians say about Jesus is at the root of what they say about God (wrongly in the Qurʾān's view), also clearly insists that Jesus is God's messenger. The text says:

> O Scripture People, do not go beyond the bounds in your religion and do not say about God anything but the truth. The Messiah, Jesus, the son of Mary, is only God's messenger (*rasūl*), His word (*kalimatuhu*) that God put into Mary, and a spirit from Him.[71] So believe in God

[68] See the outline of the *sūrah* in Neuwirth, *Studien zur Komposition der mekkanischen Suren*, p. 283.

[69] Note this phrase that recurred some five times in the prophetic typology presented in *sūrah* XXVI *ash-Shuʿarāʾ* 108, 126, 144, 163, 179.

[70] See the numerous passages cited in Wheeler, *Prophets in the Quran*, pp. 311–314.

[71] The Qurʾān's corrective, that Jesus is God's (created) word (*kalimah*) and spirit (*rūḥ*), as expressed here, is to be taken together with the passage in the recollection of the Annunciation which speaks of the angel telling Mary that "God is announcing to you the good news of a word (*kalimatin*) from Him, whose name is the Messiah, Jesus, the son of Mary" (III *Āl ʿImrān* 45). In another passage in the Qurʾān, God speaks of how "Our word (*kalimatuna*) has come to our servants, the messengers." (XXXVII *aṣ-Ṣāffāt* 171), implying that it came to all of them. Regarding Jesus as God's spirit, God says of Mary, daughter of ʿImrān, that "She guarded her womb and so we breathed into it of Our spirit." (LXVI *at-Taḥrīm* 12) See Sidney H. Griffith, "Holy Spirit," in McAuliffe, *Encyclopaedia of the Qurʾān*, vol. 2, pp. 442–443.

and His messengers, and do not say 'three'; stop it; it is better for you. God is only one God. Praise be to Him, far be it that He should have a son (*walad*); what is in the heavens and on the earth belongs to Him; God suffices as a guardian. The Messiah would not disdain to be a worshipper of God, nor would the near-by angels. He will gather up all together those who disdain His worship and who vaunt themselves. (IV *an-Nisā'* 171–172)

On the face of it, this passage both rejects what the Arabic-speaking Christians in Muḥammad's and the Qur'ān's milieu were accustomed to say about Jesus and implicitly rejects as well their saying that God is Father, Son (Word), and Holy Spirit. It affirms that Jesus is God's messenger. Here is not the place to go further into the Qur'ān's critique of Christian beliefs and practices; the present purpose is to affirm that what the Qur'ān recalls from the Christian scriptures and traditions is in service to its claims about Jesus as God's messenger and that its critique and anti-Christian polemic is designed to dispel any current Christian ideas to the contrary. Elsewhere the present writer has argued, contrary to many current scholarly opinions, that the Christian doctrines and practices the Qur'ān rejects are in fact those affirmed by the contemporary, Arabic-speaking Christian Melkites, Jacobites, and Nestorians, whose theological heritage and scriptures were in Aramaic/Syriac, translated from the original Greek.[72] But there remains one more feature of the Jesus story in the Qur'ān that must be mentioned as an integral part of the Qur'ān's presentation of Jesus according to the paradigm of its distinctive prophetology.

The prophetic typology displayed in *sūrah* XXVI *ash-Shu'arā'* consistently mentions the vindication of God's prophets and messengers in the face of the discrediting of their signs and messages by adversaries among the people to whom they were sent. Accordingly, it is not surprising to find this feature also in the Qur'ān's recall of the story of Jesus, whom God had sent as a messenger (*rasūl*) to the Israelites (cf. III *Āl 'Imrān* 49). In two places, the Qur'ān speaks of God's raising Jesus up to Himself. In one place God says to Jesus, "I will bring about your demise (*innī mutawaffika*), raise you up

[72] See Sidney H. Griffith, "Christians and Christianity," in McAuliffe, *Encyclopaedia of the Qur'ān*, vol. 1, pp. 307–316; *idem*, "Syriacisms in the Arabic Qur'ān: Who were 'those who said "Allāh is third of three"' according to *al-Mā'idah* 73?" in Meir M. Bar-Asher et al. (eds.), *A Word Fitly Spoken: Studies in Mediaeval Exegesis of the Hebrew Bible and the Qur'ān; presented to Haggai Ben-Shammai* (Jerusalem: The Ben-Zvi Institute, 2007), pp. 83–110; *idem*, "*al-Naṣārā* in the Qur'ān: A Hermeneutical Reflection," in Reynolds, *New Perspectives on the Qur'ān*, pp. 301–322.

to Me, purifiy you of those who have disbelieved, and I will put those who follow you above those who have disbelieved, to the day of resurrection" (III *Āl 'Imrān* 55). In the other place, after specifying that God took Jesus up to Himself, the text goes on to say of Jesus in regard to the disbelievers that "the Scripture People will most certainly believe in him before his death, and on the day of resurrection he will be a witness against them" (IV *an-Nisā'* 159). Just previous to this verse the text had been speaking of a number of ways in which the people to whom Jesus was sent had misbehaved in God's eyes (IV:153–157), the last example being their claim, "We killed the Messiah, Jesus, the son of Mary, the messenger of God." The Qur'ān says immediately, "They did not kill him, nor did they crucify him, but it was made to seem so to them (*walākin shubbiha lahum*)" (IV *an-Nisā'* 157). The last phrase has long been a *crux interpretum* for both Muslim and non-Muslim commentators on the Qur'ān,[73] but it need not distract the reader from noticing that however the phrase is to be understood, the verse clearly states *inter alia* that in fact Jesus' Israelite/Jewish adversaries "did not kill him, nor did they crucify him." It is a declaration clearly in accord with the requirements of the Qur'ān's distinctive prophetology.

Regarding the meaning of the much discussed phrase, "but it was made to seem so to them" (IV:157), suffice it to say here that much of the controversy surrounding it hinges on one's view of the historical reality of the crucifixion of Jesus, which then determines the significance of the phrase. On the face of it, the Qur'ān's insistence that Jesus' Israelite/Jewish adversaries were not in fact responsible for his crucifixion and death, as the Qur'ān says they claimed, is not obviously incompatible with the Christian confession of his death on the cross. And that confession was common to all of the Arabic-speaking Christian communities in the Qur'ān's milieu, however differently some of them may have expressed themselves theologically about Jesus' experience of the event.[74] That this verse outright denies the historicity of Jesus' death by crucifixion is an exegetical conclusion drawn by post-Qur'ānic Muslim commentators, some of whom may well have been inspired by the final vindication of God's prophets and messengers that Qur'ānic prophetology envisions. Alternatively, some commentators may

[73] See Neal Robinson, "Crucifixion," in McAuliffe, *Encyclopaedia of the Qur'ān*, vol. 1, p. 487; Todd Lawson, *The Crucifixion and the Qur'ān: A Study in the History of Muslim Thought* (Oxford: One World, 2009); Gabriel Said Reynolds, "The Muslim Jesus: Dead or Alive?" *Bulletin of the School of Oriental and African Studies* 72 (2009), pp. 237–258.

[74] See Reynolds, "The Muslim Jesus," esp. pp. 251–258.

well also have been familiar with the so-called 'phantasiast' or 'docetic' views of Jesus' suffering and death on the cross, a view current in some strains of Christian theology at the time. Such notions could have put them in mind of the 'likening' or 'seeming' involved in the Qurʾān's expression *walākin shubbiha lahum*, but that understanding, which may well have come to the attention of the commentators, would not necessarily have been on the Qurʾān's horizon.[75]

The Medium of Scriptural Intertextuality

The quick review of Qurʾānic presentations of biblical patriarchs and prophets just rehearsed, selective and schematic as it is, nevertheless makes three things fairly clear: biblical personalities and their stories are recalled according to the paradigm of Qurʾānic prophetology and not according to Jewish or Christian narrative patterns. The narratives *are* sometimes hauntingly close to the biblical versions, but they frequently incorporate non-biblical, Jewish or Christian apocryphal and traditional lore; and there are almost never any actual quotations from a known biblical text or, for that matter, from any other text. These observations give rise to three preliminary conclusions: the sources of the Qurʾān's biblical and traditional reminiscences were oral; the Qurʾān's recollections of the biblical patriarchs and prophets according to the paradigm of its own prophetology bespeaks the Arabic scripture's corrective, even polemical stance toward Jewish and Christian scriptures and traditional lore; and, given the lack of actual quotations from the Bible, the presence of the Bible in the Qurʾān is not textual; in its own words, it is present but by way of allusion and re-presentation. In short, the Qurʾān mirrors in writing the unwritten modes of transmission of the biblical and traditional lore circulating among the Arabic-speaking Jews and Christians in Arabia prior to the rise of Islam. In turn, as we shall argue in the next chapter, the collection and production of the Qurʾān as a written Arabic text from the mid to late seventh century, the very first written literary or rhetorical text in Arabic, was one of the factors that provided the impetus for the translation of the Jewish and Christian scriptures into Arabic in early Islamic times.

[75] See the discussion of this matter in the previous chapter and the bibliographical references in nn.84–86 of chapter 1.

The Written and the Oral

As far as the available evidence allows us clearly to see, Jews and Christians in the Arabic-speaking milieu of Muḥammad and the Qur'ān were in possession of the scriptures of their respective communities in their original languages, Hebrew and Aramaic for Jews, and Greek and Aramaic/Syriac for Christians. These texts would be found in synagogues, churches, and monasteries, and in the hands of rabbis, monks, and priests. Most people, including Arabic-speaking Jews and Christians, would have encountered their scriptures in liturgic oral presentations and interpretations. In this setting, as we saw in the previous chapter, it is not inconsistent with the available evidence for the currency of written Arabic in Muḥammad's day to think that some people, including rabbis, churchmen, and companions of the Arab prophet might have made use of notes, *aides de mémoire,* and even more extensive records in written Arabic.[76] Nevertheless, as we have seen, there is as yet no convincing evidence for the existence of any extended part of the Bible in written Arabic prior to the rise of Islam. And as we shall argue in the next chapter, the earliest time at which it would have been feasible for Arabic-speaking Jews and Christians to undertake a translation of the Bible (or parts of it) into written Arabic was the mid to late seventh century. The project would at that point have been possible either in tandem with, or in response to the Muslim project after Muḥammad's death to collect and to publish the Arabic Qur'ān as a fully written scripture. But it is more likely that the first written Bible translations were made in the eighth century, and outside of Arabia. And yet, as among the Jews and Christians of Arabia, so too among the early followers of Muḥammad, and even in the as yet uncollected Qur'ān, the concept of 'scripture' (*al-kitāb*) as the repository of divine revelation was already invested with enormous religious significance.[77]

[76] See in particular the studies of Gregor Schoeler, Beatrice Gruendler, Robert Hoyland, and others, cited in chapter 1, p. 44, n.96.

[77] See in this connection the studies by William A. Graham, *Divine Word and Prophetic Word in Early Islam: A Reconsideration of the Sources; with Special Reference to the Divine Saying or Ḥadīth Qudsī* (The Hague: Mouton, 1977); *idem, Beyond the Written Word: Oral Aspects of Scripture in the History of Religion* (Cambridge: Cambridge University Press, 1987); Daniel A. Madigan, *The Qur'ān's Self-Image: Writing and Authority in Islam's Scripture* (Princeton, NJ: Princeton University Press, 2001); Gregor Schoeler, *The Oral and the Written in Early Islam* (trans. Uwe Vagelpohl, ed. James E. Montgomery; London and New York: Routledge, 2006).

The prominence of the concept of scripture as text in the Qurʾān, and the numerous references to earlier scriptures such as the Torah, the Psalms, and the Gospel, contrasts with the virtual non-existence of the text of the Bible in any of the Qurʾān's biblical reminiscences. And yet, as we showed earlier in this chapter, in our consideration of the 'wider horizon' of biblical recall in the Qurʾān, the prominence of terms such as 'scripture' (*al-kitāb*), 'scrolls' (*aṣuḥuf*), 'texts' (*az-zubur*), and 'copy' (*an-nuskah*) to refer to records of divine revelation bespeaks both the Qurʾān's recognition of the special significance of 'holy scripture' and its own conception of itself as becoming a 'scripture'. Revealing in this regard are its references to itself as a 'sending down of scripture from God' (*tanzīl al-kitāb min Allāh*; XXXIX *az-Zumar* 1, XL *Ghāfir* 2). But when it comes to the concrete reminiscence of biblical stories, (and the Qurʾān conceives of itself as an instrument of reminiscence as it engages in biblical recall; cf. IIIVIII *Ṣād* 1), as we saw in our consideration of the 'nearer horizon' of biblical recall, it is a matter of the memory, recollection, and reflective pondering of the stories of both biblical and non-biblical patriarchs and prophets, their words and deeds, not textually but narratively. The source material for this enterprise was drawn not only from earlier scriptures, but also from traditions found elsewhere only in non-biblical, apocryphal, or pseudepigraphical texts. And the recall is not governed by the paradigms of the earlier scriptures and traditions themselves but, as we have shown, by the requirements of the Qurʾān's own prophetology, its prophetic typology. What is more, it is clear that the whole process of biblical recall in the Qurʾān is reflective of an originally oral phenomenon. Albeit now preserved in writing in the Arabic scripture, it has its roots in a biblically oriented colloquy between the Qurʾān and the Arabic-speaking 'Scripture People' in its milieu. The recognition of this presumed *Sitz im Leben* calls for a consideration of the medium of the transmission of biblical knowledge in this situation.

The Interpreted Bible

To judge by the reminiscences of its narratives as we find them in the Islamic scripture, the Bible that came within the purview of the Qurʾān was not simply the canonical scripture of either the Jews or the Christians, nor was it a written text. Rather, in a number of its *sūrahs* the Qurʾān is in dialogue with narratives about a number of biblical figures, which narratives had circulated both orally and in writing in Late Antique Jewish and Christian communities. According to the hypothesis being proposed here, they came into Arabic orally. They can be described as 'inter-textual' in that while the full stories they tell cannot be found in any one particular text, they exist inter-textually in the texts and memories of the communities in which they circulated. As narratives they are not the Bible as such, but one may think of them as composing in the ensemble a kind of oral 'interpreted Bible', to borrow an apt phrase from scholars who study the history of interpretation in regard to another body of 'biblical' material that is not altogether dissimilar to what is recollected in the Qur'ān, albeit that it is preserved in texts.[78]

In both the Jewish and the Christian communities of the Qur'ān's day and beyond, numerous texts and traditions were in circulation in Greek, Aramaic, Syriac, Coptic, and Ethiopic that were not part of the canonical scriptures of either community but which often provided retellings of biblical narratives with embellishments and narrative realignments suitable to the circumstances in which they were composed and adopted and adapted.[79] One often finds their traces in midrashic, targumic, and homiletic texts in the major languages of the Jewish and Christian communities and, locally, their themes and motifs can readily be detected in what we might call the preaching traditions.

Preaching is a function of the liturgical life of Jews and Christians, and while it is essentially an oral function, homilies, sermons and instructions also circulated in writing and, like the scriptures which they sought to interpret and apply to daily life, they could also be recited in liturgical settings. And so it is that in the Syriac-speaking Christian communities, with whom the Arabic-speaking Christians of Muḥammad's and the Qur'ān's milieu were largely in communion, a fairly large body of written homiletic mate-

[78] One thinks in this connection of the concept 'interpreted Bible' as it is used in a more carefully defined way in the work done by James L. Kugel, in books like *Traditions of the Bible: A Guide to the Bible as it Was at the Start of the Common Era* (Cambridge, MA: Harvard University Press, 1998); *The Bible As It Was* (Cambridge, MA: Harvard University Press, 1999); *How to Read the Bible: A Guide to Scripture Then and Now* (New York: Simon and Schuster, 2008).

[79] From the Syriac tradition one thinks in this connection of the 'Bible history' presented in the Syriac *Cave of Treasures*, a work of the sixth century in its final form, which has survived in numerous manuscripts in both eastern (i.e., Nestorian) and western (i.e., Jacobite) recensions. The modern edition of the Syriac text, along with a French translation, is by Su-Min Ri, *La caverne des trésors: les deux recensions syriaques* (CSCO vols. 487 and 488; Louvain: Peeters, 1987). See also Su-Min Ri, *Commentaire de La Caverne des Trésors: étude sur l'histoire du texte et de ses sources* (CSCO vol. 581; Louvain: Peeters, 2000). There has long been an English translation in E. A. Wallis Budge, *The Book of the Cave of Treasures* (London: Religious Tract Society, 1927).

rial has been preserved, attributed to the major literary figures of the tradition. The latter include Ephraem the Syrian (306–373), who was esteemed among all the communities, Jacob of Serug (c. 450–520/1), cherished by the Jacobites, and the long-lived Narsai (399–c. 503), beloved of the Nestorians.[80] While these texts, like the Bibles themselves, would have been found only in churches and monasteries, and then only in Syriac, they seem in addition to the Bible, and perhaps the ever popular *Cave of Treasures*, to have been the main reading of bishops, priests, and monks, and so to have been the channels through which the 'interpreted Bible' came to the attention of the monks and missionaries who likely conducted liturgies among pre-Islamic-period Arabic-speaking Christians. Tutored by their familiarity with these texts and traditions in Syriac, it is likely that in liturgical celebrations in Arabia the local priests and monks, or their interpreters, would then have presented the scripture readings and homilies *viva voce* in Arabic translation.[81] It is not out of the question that they may even have employed written notes or other textual helps, as discussed above, but documentary evidence for this practice is lacking.

The interesting thing to observe at this juncture is that the stories of the biblical patriarchs and prophets as they circulated in Syriac homiletic traditions, especially in the *mêmrê* composed most notably by Ephraem, Jacob of Serug, and Narsai,[82] are suffused with biblical recall, and that often they

[80] See these and other important Syriac exegetical writers and their works discussed, with ample bibliography, in Lucas Van Rompay, "The Christian Syriac Tradition of Interpretation," in Magne Sæbø (ed.), *Hebrew Bible/Old Testament: The History of Its Interpretation* (vol. 1; Göttingen: Vandenhoeck and Ruprecht, 1996), Part 1, chap. 17, pp. 612–641.

[81] One thinks in this connection of the fourth-century practice in Jerusalem, in the church of the Anastasis, as described by the pilgrim Egeria between 381 and 384. She wrote: "In this province there are some people who know both Greek and Aramaic; but others know only one or the other language. The bishop may know Aramaic, but he never uses it. He always speaks in Greek and has a presbyter beside him who translates the Greek into Aramaic so that everyone can understand what he means." John Wilkinson (trans.) *Egeria's Travels to the Holy Land: Newly Translated, with Supporting Documents and Notes* (Jerusalem: Ariel Publishing House and Warminster, UK: Aris and Phillips, 1981), p. 146.

[82] These *mêmrê* were composed in verse and declaimed in a liturgical setting, with the speaker often addressing the congregants in a direct homiletic style. See, for example, the studies of the *mêmrê* of Jacob of Serug by Thomas Kollamparampil, *Jacob of Serug: Selected Festal Homilies* (Bangalore: Dharmaram and Rome: Center for Indian and Inter-Religious Studies, 1997); *idem, Salvation in Christ according to Jacob of Serug* (Bangalore: Dharmaram Publications, 2001) or the *mêmrê* of Narsai studied by R. H. Connolly, *The Liturgical Homilies of Narsai* (Cambridge: Cambridge

are designed to explore the significance of particular biblical passages read out in the liturgy.[83] Collections of them are normally arranged according to the liturgical cycles. Scholars who study the Syriac *mêmrê* regularly point out their interpretive strategies, such as typologies, echoes of alternate biblical texts such as the *Diatessaron*, allusions to non-biblical narrative features, non-scriptural legends involving biblical characters, and even tropes and turns of phrase otherwise found only in Jewish traditions. In other words, the 'interpreted Bible' as we find it in these homiletic compositions bears an uncanny resemblance in many of its details to the reminiscences of Bible history as we find them in the Qur'ān. Scholars have only begun to explore the riches of the Syriac *mêmrê* as sources of insight into the religio-cultural and intellectual history of the Arabic-speaking audience addressed by Muḥammad and the Qur'ān. But their initial forays have clearly shown the considerable potential of this large body of homiletic and paranaetic material to offer a broader horizon for interpretation and a deeper contextual understanding of a number of passages of the Qur'ān than were previously available.[84]

For a century and more in the West a regular scholarly industry has been dedicated to the search for analogues in various bodies of early Jewish and Christian literature for narrative features involving biblical personalities in the Qur'ān; very often the suggestion of literary dependence has been made, citing the analogous passages as sources or influences on

University Press, 1909); Philippe Gignoux (ed. and trans.), *Homélies de Narsai sur la création: édition critique du texte syriaque, introduction et traduction française* (Patrologia Orientalis, vol. 34, facls. 3–4; Turnhout: Brepols, 1968); Frederick G. McLeod, *Narsai's Metrical Homilies on the Nativity, Epiphany, Passion, Resurrection and Ascension* (Patrologia Orientalis, vol. 40, fasc. 1, n. 182; Turnhout: Brepols, 1979).

[83] For example, Jacob of Serug's *mêmrâ* 109, "On Abraham and his Types," an extended homiletic meditation on Genesis 22, is keyed to the Gospel passage in which Jesus says to the Jews: "Your father Abraham rejoiced that he was to see my day; he saw it and was glad." (John 8:56. See Paulus Bedjan, *Homiliae Selectae Mar-Jacobi Sarugensis* (vol. 4; Paris and Leipzig: Via Dicta and Otto Harrassowitz, 1908), pp. 61–103.

[84] See, e.g., Sidney H. Griffith, "Christian Lore and the Arabic Qur'ān: The 'Companions of the Cave' in *Sūrat al-Kahf* and in Syriac Christian Tradition," and Kevin van Bladel, "The Alexander Legend in the Qur'ān 18:83–102," in G. S. Reynolds (ed.), *The Qur'ān in Its Historical Context* (London: Routledge, 2007), pp. 109–137 and 175–203. See also Kevin van Bladel, "Heavenly Cords and Prophetic Authority in the Quran and its Late Antique Context," *Bulletin of the School of Oriental and African Studies* 70 (2007), pp. 223–246; Reynolds, *The Qur'ān and Its Biblical Subtext*, pp. 230–253.

Qur'ānic narratives. Only relatively recently have the Syriac *mêmrê* in particular been considered as providing possible 'subtexts' for a deeper understanding of certain passages in the Qur'ān, an inquiry that seems to be particularly promising. But it seems even more likely that study of the *mêmrê* may help the historian gain an understanding of how familiar features of the 'interpreted Bible' found their way into the Arabic-speaking milieu of Muḥammad and the Qur'ān, where they became integral parts of the religious public domain addressed by the Qur'ān, especially in its enterprise to correct the views of the local 'Scripture People'.

Ironically, when the historian of Judaism or Christianity looks at the matter from this perspective, given the absence of preserved textual evidence from the Arabic-speaking Jewish or Christian communities themselves of the sixth and early seventh centuries, the Arabic Qur'ān becomes a unique piece of surviving documentary evidence. Its significance extends beyond the question of the currency of an Aramaic- or a Syriac-inspired, 'interpreted Bible' in the preaching of the Arabian Jews and Christians prior to the rise of Islam, for it is also, and perhaps more, important for assessing the very presence and active participation of these Arabic-speaking Jews and Christians in the Qur'ān's conversations with the 'Scripture People' about the real meaning and proper interpretations of the signs and messages delivered by their own patriarchs and prophets, and recorded in their Bibles.

The Bible Encountered in the Qur'ān

The Bible is both in the Qur'ān and not in the Qur'ān. That is to say, it has virtually no textual presence, but the selective presence of an 'interpreted Bible' in Islamic scripture is undeniable. And the selection process involved in the inclusion of biblical reminiscences in the Qur'ān, according to the hypothesis advanced here, is one determined by the Qur'ān's own distinctive prophetology. That is to say, recollections of biblical patriarchs and prophets, and references to the earlier scriptures that tell their stories, appear as integral components of the Qur'ān's advancement of its own prophetic message. And what is more, the Qur'ān is corrective of, even polemical toward the earlier readings of the 'Scripture People', to the point that it can even accuse Jews of distorting the scripture God sent to them (cf. IV *an-Nisā'* 46; V *al-Mā'idah* 13, 41). This dimension of the Qur'ān's reprise of the Bible bespeaks the opening of a new book altogether in the growing library of books on the 'interpreted Bible'. Or perhaps it bespeaks not so much a new book, as a corrected, alternate scripture, one that recalls the

Tanakh and the Bible but ultimately rejects them in the forms in which the Jews and Christians actually have them. It is no wonder then that for later Muslim scholars there has for the most part been little interest over the centuries in the Bible as the Jews or the Christians actually have it;[85] the Qur'ān has made it irrelevant. And one might argue that this circumstance itself became one of the factors that prompted the 'Scripture People' in a world newly become Arabophone and Islamic in its public culture to translate their scriptures into Arabic—to counter the challenge posed by the Arabic Qur'ān.

[85] The exception that proves the rule here is the fifteenth-century writer al-Biqā'ī's eccentric insistence on consulting the Bible as the Jews and Christians have it, an undertaking that earned him obloquy in the Muslim community. See Walid A. Saleh, *In Defense of the Bible: A Critical Edition and an Introduction to al-Biqā'ī's Bible Treatise* (Islamic History and Civilization, vol. 73; Leiden: Brill, 2008).

✻ CHAPTER III ✻

The Earliest Translations of the Bible into Arabic

IT WAS NOT LONG after the death of the Arab prophet Muḥammad in 632 CE that the burgeoning Muslim Community of Believers began the task of collecting the Qur'ān into the form in which it would become the written scripture of the Muslims. As most scholars agree, it was destined also to be the first book properly so called to appear in the Arabic language.[1] The processes surrounding the collection of the Qur'ān were such that they summoned the energies of Muslims to draw such skills as the Arabic-speaking populace had already developed to make the quantum leap from note-taking to book production. And not too long after the production and wide circulation of the written Qur'ān, no more than a century later the scholarly project to systematize and codify the Arabic language in its literary phase was undertaken outside of Arabia, in the newly occupied territory of Iraq. The work, which flourished in the eighth century was done largely by newly Islamized Persians, not least for the purpose of aiding the reading and interpretation of the Qur'ān. Meanwhile, during the century and more between the years 640 and 750 CE, the gradual Arabicization and cultural Islamicization of the hitherto non-Arabic speaking, conquered populations of the Near East had long been under way. At some point along this temporal spectrum of a hundred years or so, the first Islamic century and a half, Jews and Christians began to translate their scriptures and other religious literature into Arabic, and to write original works in the new *lingua franca* of the new Islamic commonwealth.

A discussion of the appearance of the earliest translations of the Bible into Arabic requires first a brief consideration of the cultural developments just mentioned as the framework within which the translations were first undertaken, as well as a consideration of how the biblical translation movement later became a catalyst for the major Graeco-Arabic translation movement of the eighth to tenth centuries CE.

[1] See Gregor Schoeler, *Écrire et transmettre dans les débuts de l'Islam* (Paris: Presses Universitaires de France, 2002), p. 26.

After Muḥammad: Islam's First Two Centuries

Arguably, from the cultural point of view, the three most important developments of the first two centuries of Islam were those just mentioned above: the collection of the Qur'ān; the Arabicization of religious and intellectual life beyond the confines of Arabia following the Arab conquests; and the birth of theoretical Arabic grammar and lexicography, standardizing a linguistic ideal. The three are inter-related, with the Qur'ān assuming a central place in both the processes of Arabicization and Islamicization, as well as serving as the beacon of *'Arabiyyah* and the interpretive horizon for religious thought expressed in Arabic. For Jews and Christians, the Arabic Bible hurried to meet the Qur'ān's challenge.

The Collection of the Arabic Qur'ān

In the first chapter of the present inquiry, the conclusion was reached, counterintuitive as it might seem from the perspective of especially Late Antique Christian religious history, that there is so far no reliable evidence for the existence of a written Arabic version of any portion of the Bible done under Jewish or Christian auspices prior to the rise of Islam. The argument was advanced that the hypotheses to the contrary so far put forward are based on extrapolations from evidence that first of all is too fragmentary or too far removed in time to logically bear the weight of the conclusions drawn from it, and secondly that the hypotheses run counter to current scholary views of the development of literary Arabic and the Arabic script prior to the seventh century. But the absence of a written Arabic version of any portion of the Bible does not mean that there was no Bible in pre-Islamic Arabia. To the contrary, it is highly probable that the Jewish communities had the Hebrew Bible and the Aramaic Targums in their possession, just as the Christians most likely had their scriptures in Greek and Aramaic/Syriac, for the most part in the keeping of synagogues, churches, and monasteries. Moreover, in both communities there was a lively oral tradition in circulation, undoubtedly in Arabic, that included Bible history and large amounts of Jewish and Christian lore, composing in the ensemble a sizeable narrative installment of what, borrowing a phrase, we have called the 'interpreted Bible'. The Qur'ān itself is the single best piece of historical evidence for this state of affairs. And the very existence of the oral Arabic 'scripture' in a largely oral culture may well be one of the reasons why there was no felt need for a written Arabic Bible prior to the appearance and circulation in writing of the collected Arabic Qur'ān, with its open challenge to the 'Scripture People' and their scriptures.

Here is not the place for an extended discussion of the collection of the Qur'ān, but given its importance as a precipitating moment for the production of written, literary texts in Arabic, not to mention its fundamental role more generally in the formation of religious culture, a brief discussion of its highlights is important to the story of the Bible in Arabic. For the need to bring out the *muṣḥaf*, "the written corpus of the Qur'ān,"[2] historically provided an impetus and a definite focus to the development of Arabic writing skills and textual production, which would have been pre-requisites for the making and circulation of Arabic biblical translations in writing. Not surprisingly, the undertaking was tied to the earlier exercises in literacy in Yathrib/Medina, mentioned earlier in connection with the names of Waraqah ibn Nawfal and Zayd ibn Thābit. And as fate would have it, Zayd was destined to become a major player in the collection and publication of the Qur'ān.

As with almost everything else in early Islamic history, considerable controversy has attended the traditional accounts of the collection of the Qur'ān, with different scholars assigning widely divergent dates to the undertaking, ranging all the way from the first third of the seventh century in Arabia to early in the ninth century CE in Mesopotamia.[3] Suffice it for now to say that more recent scholarship, based on more recently available evidence and interpretive methodologies, dates the traditional reports on the collection of the Qur'ān to "the last decades of the first century AH,"[4] i.e., around 700 CE. These reports attribute the first collection to the initiative of the caliph Abū Bakr (632–634), and the production of an official edition to the orders of the caliph 'Uthmān (644–656), who sent exemplars of the finished product to the important Islamic centers of the day. Zayd ibn Thābit is said to have been involved in both undertakings, and some other companions are said to have been in possession of at least portions of the text in writing, taken down earlier from the prophet's recitations. On the basis of these reports, the conclusion is then drawn that "an official written corpus must have already existed in the second half of the seventh century."[5] Corroborating these conclusions, and taking the matter a giant step further, are two recently available, early copies of portions of

[2] Harald Motzki, "Muṣḥaf," in McAuliffe, *Encyclopaedia of the Qur'ān*, vol. 3, p. 463.

[3] See the survey of the divergent views in Harald Motzki, "The Collection of the Qur'ān: A Reconsideration of Western Views in Light of Recent Methodological Developments," *Der Islam* 78 (2001), pp. 1–34.

[4] Motzki, "The Collection of the Qur'ān," p. 31.

[5] Motzki, "Muṣḥaf," in McAuliffe, *Encyclopaedia of the Qur'ān*, vol. 3, p. 464.

the Qur'ān's text that have been shown to date from the mid-first century AH. Both demonstrate the early currency of some form of the Qur'ānic text and show how even earlier 'companion codices' indicate that memory and orality must have figured in their composition.[6] All of this suggests a priori that a point in the middle of the seventh century CE might well serve as the likeliest *terminus post quem* for the appearance of a written, Arabic translation of some portion of the Bible. This now raises the question of which Arabic-speaking Jews and Christians were the more likely to have first translated portions of the Bible into Arabic in the period after the mid-seventh century? Was it those already living among the Arabs in pre-Islamic times in Arabia, or those living outside of Arabia who adopted the Arabic language only after the conquest?

Arabicization and Islamicization outside of Arabia

The evidence so far adduced is inadequate to substantiate the claim that Arabic-speaking Jews or Christians had translated the Bible into written Arabic in Arabia before the mid-seventh century, a subject to which we shall return below. This, coupled with the fact that there are for this period in Arabia no surviving texts at all written in Arabic by Jews or Christians, and moreover no references by later Arabic-speaking Jews or Christians to any such texts, the search for the first Bible written in Arabic necessarily turns to the newly Arabic-speaking Jews and Christians who lived outside of Arabia after the conquest. For the Jews, the earliest evidence comes from ninth-century Karaite and Rabbanite sources originating in Palestine and Mesopotamia. Similarly for the Christians, there are two areas from which the available evidence comes, Syria/Palestine and Mesopotamia, the centers in which Christianity in its Graeco-Aramaic and Graeco-Syriac expressions flourished prior to the Arab conquest. Chronologically, the first written translations of biblical books into Arabic were done by Christians, as we shall see. In addition to the evidence coming from the Jewish and Christian

[6] See especially the important study by Behnam Sadeghi and Uwe Bergman, "The Codex of a Companion of the Prophet and the Qur'ān of the Prophet," *Arabica* 57 (2010), pp. 343–436. See also the conclusions of François Déroche, *La transmission écrite du coran dans les débuts de l'islam* (Leiden: Brill, 2009), who, on the basis of his study of the Codex Parisino-Petropolitanus, concludes that the Qur'ān was substantially complete as a text within forty to sixty years after the death of the prophet. For another view see Karl-Friedrich Pohlmann, *Die Entstehung des Korans: Neue Erkenntnisse aus Sicht der historisch-kritischen Bibelwissenschaft* (Darmstadt: Wissenschaftliche Buchgesellschaft, 2012).

communities themselves about their translations and their use of Arabic more generally, there is evidence from Islamic history about the times and places in which the twin processes of Arabicization and Islamicization had progressed sufficiently that circumstances were ripe for serious translation efforts in the conquered and occupied territories.

As many studies have shown, it was during the Umayyad period, and particularly during the reigns of the caliph ʿAbd al-Malik (685–705) and his sons and successors that Arabicization and Islamicization began in earnest in the territories that the Muslim Arabs had conquered and occupied by the mid-seventh century.[7] As recent scholars have said of Syria/Palestine at the time, where many Christian communities flourished, it was "a land in which a combination of a well established Aramaean, Hellenistic, Byzantine, Christian legacy interacted with the new Arab Islamic rule and cultural values." And as a result, "Syria underwent a 180-degree reorientation in strategic and geopolitical terms."[8] Most notable was the determined campaign that Muslim authorities undertook around the turn of the eighth century to claim the occupied territories for Islam and to register the new Islamic hegemony in the public sphere.[9] The most dramatic and monumental projects were sited in Jerusalem and Damascus, where the Dome of the Rock and the Umayyad Mosque, respectively, were constructed.[10] Of a whole host

[7] For the broad picture, see Chase F. Robinson, *ʿAbd al-Malik* (Makers of the Muslim World; Oxford: One World, 2005); Garth Fowden, *Empire to Commonwealth: Consequences of Monotheism in Late Antiquity* (Princeton, NJ: Princeton University Press, 1993).

[8] Ahmad Shboul and Alan Walmsley, "Identity and Self-Image in Syria-Palestine in the Transition from Byzantine to Early Islamic Rule: Arab Christians and Muslims," *Mediterranean Archaeology* 11 (1998), pp. 255–256.

[9] See Sidney H. Griffith, "Images, Islam and Christian Icons: A Moment in the Christian/Muslim Encounter in Early Islamic Times," in Pierre Canivet and Jean-Paul Rey-Coquais (eds.), *La Syrie de Byzance à l'islam VIIe-VIIIe siècles: Actes du colloque international, Lyon—Maison de l'Orient Méditerranien, Paris—Institut de Monde Arabe, 11–15 Septembre 1990* (Damas: Institut Français de Damas, 1992), pp. 121–138; *idem*, "Images, Icons and the Public Space in Early Islamic Times: Arab Christians and the Program to Claim the Land for Islam," in Kenneth Holum and Hayim Lapin (eds.), *Shaping the Middle East: Jews, Christians, and Muslims in an Age of Transition, 400–800* CE (Studies and Texts in Jewish History and Culture, 20; Bethesda, MD: University Press of Maryland, 2011), pp. 197–210; Robert Schick, *The Christian Communities of Palestine from Byzantine to Islamic Rule: A Historical and Archaeological Study* (Princeton, NJ: The Darwin Press, 1996).

[10] See K.A.C. Cresswell, *Early Muslim Architecture: Umayyads A.D. 622–750* (2nd ed. in two parts, vol. 1, pt. .2; Oxford: Oxford University Press, 1969), esp. pp. 246–290; Julian Raby and Jeremy Johns (eds.), *Bayt al-Maqdis: ʿAbd al-Malik's Jerusalem* (Part 1;

of other developments, the most significant for the present inquiry was the decree by the caliph al-Walīd (705–715) that henceforth all official records were to be kept in the Arabic language.[11] It was against this background that Christians first responded to the challenge of Islam in writing, first in Greek and Syriac, but very soon in Arabic.[12] It would seem that the first Arabic texts were prepared in the environs of Jerusalem and the cosmopolitan monastic establishments of the Judean desert, but very soon work was also underway in the hitherto Aramaic and Syriac-speaking milieu of Mesopotamia. And it was not long, as we shall see, before Christians were translating important texts into Arabic, including the Bible.

There was analogous movement among the Jews, particularly in Mesopotamia and Palestine where Jewish culture and learning flourished somewhat later. Texts written in Arabic and the development of 'Judeo-Arabic' date perhaps a half-century after similar developments among the Christians in the same areas.[13] But the socio-cultural circumstances backgrounding these development would have been comparable in both communities, although the need for religious texts in Arabic may have initially been more pressing among Christians than among newly Arabic-speaking Jews, due to the fact that Christians in the areas under discussion, and particularly in Syria/Palestine, had been much more integrated into Byzantine civil and ecclesiastical life, and therefore into Hellenism, than was the case among Jews in the same areas. And, as the present writer has argued elsewhere, it is not unlikely that the virtual disappearance of Greek as a scholarly and an everyday language in the area after the eighth century was a contributing factor to the early adoption of Arabic among the Christians for religious purposes,[14] a need that would not have been so pressing among Jews in the

---

Oxford: Oxford University Press, 1992); Oleg Grabar, *The Shape of the Holy: Early Islamic Jerusalem* (Princeton, NJ: Princeton University Press, 1996).

[11] See the report in J. B. Chabot, *Anonymi Auctoris Chronicon ad Annum Christi 1234 Pertinens* (CSCO, vol. 81; Paris: J. Gabalda, 1920), pp. 298–299.

[12] See Sidney H. Griffith, "The Monks of Palestine and the Growth of Christian Literature in Arabic," *The Muslim World* 78 (1988), pp. 1–28; *idem*, "From Aramaic to Arabic: The Languages of the Monasteries of Palestine in the Byzantine and Early Islamic Periods," *Dumbarton Oaks Papers* 51 (1997), pp. 11–31; *idem, The Church in the Shadow of the Mosque: Christians and Muslims in the World of Islam* (Princeton: Princeton University Press, 2008).

[13] See Joshua Blau, *The Emergence and Linguistic Background of Judaeo-Arabic: A Study of the Origins of Neo-Arabic and Middle Arabic* (3rd rev. ed.; Jerusalem: Ben-Zvi Institute for the Study of Jewish Communities in the East, 1999).

[14] See Sidney H. Griffith, "Byzantium and the Christians in the World of Islam: Constantinople and the Church in the Holy Land in the Ninth Century," *Medieval*

same early period. But as a number of scholars have noted, it may well be the case that the lack of documentation for Judeo-Arabic earlier than the mid-ninth century prevents our seeing an earlier phase in its development, and especially in the area of Bible translations.[15]

The States of the Arabic Language in Early Islamic Times

It was in the second half of the eighth century, well outside the boundaries of Arabia in the conquered and occupied territories, and largely in the famously intellectual, Iraqī city of Baṣrah,[16] that Muslim scholars composed the first systematic grammars and dictionaries of the Arabic language. They took the Qur'ān as their standard and sought informants among the native speakers of Arabic, principally among Bedouin reciters of pre-Islamic poetry.[17] Khalīl ibn Aḥmad (d.791) is usually credited with having produced the first dictionary (*Kitāb al-ʿAyn*), albeit that he left it unfinished, as well as with systematizing the prosody of Arabic poetry,[18] while his student Sibawayhī (d.793) composed the first theoretical grammar of the Arabic language (*al-Kitāb*), completed by his student, al-Akhfash al-Awsaṭ (d.835).[19] Their accomplishments and those of their students and successors established

---

Encounters 3 (1997), pp. 231–265; *idem*, "What Has Constantinople to Do with Jerusalem? Palestine in the Ninth Century: Byzantine Orthodoxy in the World of Islam," in Leslie Brubaker (ed.), *Byzantium in the Ninth Century: Dead or Alive? Papers from the Thirtieth Spring Symposium of Byzantine Studies, Birmingham, March 1996* (Aldershot, UK and Brookfield, VT: Variorum, 1998), pp. 181–194. *Pace* Maria Mavroudi, *Bilingualism in Greek and Arabic in the Middle Ages: Evidence from the Manuscripts*, a forthcoming study.

[15] See Meira Polliack, "Arabic Bible Translations in the Cairo Genizah Collections," in Ulf Haxen et al. (eds.), *Jewish Studies in a New Europe: Proceedings of the Fifth Congress of Jewish Studies in Copenhagen 1994* (Copenhagen: C.A. Reitzel, Det Kongtelge Bibliotek, 1998), pp. 395–620.

[16] See the now classic study by Charles Pellat, *Le milieu basrien et la formation de Gāḥiẓ* (Paris: Librairie d'Amérique et d'Orient Adrien-Maisonneuve, 1953).

[17] See Wolfdietrich Fischer, "Classical Arabic," in Kees Versteegh et al. (eds.), *Encyclopedia of Arabic Language and Linguistics* (Leiden: Brill, 2005–2009), vol. 1, pp. 397ff.

[18] See Stefan Wild, *Das Kitāb al-ʿAyn und die arabische Lexikographie* (Wiesbaden: Harrassowitz, 1965); Raphael Talmon, *Arabic Grammar in Its Formative Age: Kitāb al-ʿAyn and Its Attribution to Ḳalīl ibn Aḥmad* (Leiden: Brill, 1997); Karin C. Ryding (ed.), *Early Medieval Arabic: Studies on al-Khalīl ibn Aḥmad* (Washington, DC: Georgetown University Press, 1998).

[19] See Michael G. Carter, *Sībawayhi* (New Delhi and New York: Oxford University Press, 2004).

the rules, systematized the grammar, and defined the terms that made up Classical Arabic, the literary language in which Islamic thought and belles lettres were often written and published by the normalizing scribal industries in the formative period of classical Islamic culture.[20] But in the beginning, the language of the Bible translations made by Jews and Christians was not Classical Arabic, for they by and large did not have access to the standard scribal services of the Islamic establishment. Rather, Jewish and Christian Arabic texts often exhibited the features of Middle Arabic, a state of the language hovering between the Classical Arabic of high culture and the colloquial Arabic of the spoken language, with its regional variations.[21]

Middle Arabic was not rule free, nor did it lack normalizing tendencies of its own, but these tended to be dictated by the autonomous literary traditions of the communities that produced texts in Middle Arabic. In the Jewish and Christian communities, the state of the language employed not infrequently reflected syntactic and lexical uses characteristic of the earlier languages still current in those communities, such as Hebrew, Aramaic, Syriac, Coptic, or even Greek. Under the general rubric of Middle Arabic, modern scholars have distinguished among others, Judaeo-Arabic and a so-called 'Christian Arabic', each with its own distinguishing characteristics. Most of the early translations of portions of the Bible into Arabic display features of either Judaeo-Arabic or 'Christian Arabic', and the editors of modern editions of these texts almost always discuss these distinctive features, as we shall see below.

A distinguishing feature of Judaeo-Arabic is that most of the texts written in this vein of Arabic use the Hebrew script, at first somewhat phonetically but eventually in a regularized fashion that, where possible, accords with the cognate letters in Arabic script.[22] There is a large archive of material in Judaeo-Arabic, including a number of important original compositions in addition to translations of biblical texts.[23] Due to the conditions of their

[20] Of course the codification of the classical language did not mean that all Arabic was thereafter written according to these rules. See Simon Hopkins, *Studies in the Grammar of Early Arabic: Based upon Papyri Datable to before 300* AH/*912* AD (Oxford: Oxford University Press, 1984).

[21] See Jérôme Lentin, "Middle Arabic," in Versteegh, *Encyclopedia of Arabic Language and Linguistics*, vol. 3, pp. 215ff.

[22] See Joshua Blau and Simon Hopkins, "On Early Judaeo-Arabic Orthography," *Zeitschrift für Arabische Linguistik* 12 (1984), pp. 9–27.

[23] See Blau, *The Emergence and Linguistic Background of Judaeo-Arabic*; Meira Polliack, "Genres in Judaeo-Arabic Literature," (The Irene Halmos Chair of Arabic Literature Annual Lecture; Tel Aviv: Tel Aviv University, 1998). See also the following general

preservation, many of the earliest biblical translations survive only in fragments, and most of them come from the treasure trove of the Cairo Geniza, which still yields remarkable finds long years after its first discovery.[24] One special feature of Judaeo-Arabic seems to have been its ability to provide a consistent idiom of scholarly expression for Jewish communities living in the World of Islam from Baghdad in the east to al-Andalus in the west, and from its first flourishing early in the ninth century to its virtual disappearance as a scholarly language among Jews by the thirteenth century.

'Christian Arabic' designates a much less consistent state of the language than does Judaeo-Arabic, and a number of scholars have even questioned the adequacy of the expression,[25] given the variety of features that are evident in the earliest Arabic texts written by Christians. These texts originated in a wide variety of earlier language communities and therefore display variations on Classical Arabic commonly found in texts written by many peoples, not just Christians, but including even Muslims who had access to the established modes of book production.[26] Nevertheless, the designation serves the useful purpose of calling attention to the fact that Arabic texts written by Christians, devoted to Christian topics, and circulating in the several Christian communities of early Islamic times were often written in an Arabic that betrayed the fact that for their writers, and presumably for their readers as well, Arabic was often a second language. For the 'Christian

essays, with accompanying bibliography: Geoffrey Khan, "Judaeo-Arabic," in Versteegh, *Encyclopedia of Arabic Language and Linguistics*, vol. 2, pp. 526ff.; Abraham Solomon Halkin and Hava Lazarus-Yafeh, "Judeo-Arabic Literature," and "Judeo-Arabic Culture," in M. Berenbaum and F. Skolnik (eds.), *Encyclopaedia Judaica* (2nd ed.; 22 vols.; Detroit, MI: Macmillan, 2007), vol. 11, pp. 530–545; Norman A. Stillman, "Judeo-Arabic: History and Linguistic Description," in Norman A. Stillman (ed.), *Encyclopedia of Jews in the Islamic World* (5 vols.; Leiden: Brill, 2010), Brill Online ed., September 14, 2010, *sub voce.*

[24] See Polliack, "Arabic Bible Translations in the Cairo Genizah Collections."

[25] The expression 'Christian Arabic' seems to have come into common parlance with the publication of Joshua Blau's *A Grammar of Christian Arabic Based Mainly on South-Palestinian Texts from the First Millennium* (CSCO, vols. 267, 276, 279; Louvain: Secrétariat du CorpusSCO, 1966–1967), a ground-breaking study of the grammatical features characteristic of the Middle Arabic found in an archive of 'old, south Palestinian texts' found principally in the manuscript collections of the Monastery of St. Catherine at Mount Sinai.

[26] See in particular the remarks of Kh. Samir in Kh. Samir (ed.), *Actes du premier congrès international d'études arabes chrétiennes, Goslar, Septembre 1980* (Orientalia Christiana Analecta, 218; Rome: Pontifical Institute for Oriental Studies, 1982), pp. 52–59.

Arabic' so deployed is usually described in terms of its deviations from the standard or classical Arabic usages current in the dominant society, thereby achieving a modicum of notoriety among some by reason of its 'mistakes'.[27]

The Earliest Bible Translations into Arabic

The most important evidence for the earliest translations of the Bible into Arabic is to be found in the surviving manuscripts that have preserved these translations down to modern times. But there are also references in the historical literature, which is for the most part of Muslim origin, that speak of the early translations, and it seems best to mention them in the first place and then to discuss the evidence of preserved manuscripts.

Reports of Bible Translations

According to the Muslim historian, Abū l-Ḥasan ʿAlī al-Masʿūdī (d.956 CE), one of the best-known Christian translators of the Baghdad translation movement, Ḥunayn ibn Isḥāq (808–873), translated a portion of the Bible into Arabic from the Greek of the Septuagint. As al-Masʿūdī put it in regard to the Septuagint, "This text has been translated a number of times into Arabic by earlier and more recent scholars, among them Ḥunayn ibn Isḥāq. For most people it [i.e., the Septuagint] is the soundest of the texts of the Torah."[28] While no trace of Ḥunayn's translation seems to have survived, al-Masʿūdī's remark that by his time the Bible had been translated a number of times into Arabic certainly rings true. The famous bio-bibliographer, Abū l-Faraj Muḥammad ibn Isḥāq ibn an-Nadīm (d.995/8), speaks in his *Kitāb al-Fihrist* of the translations made by one Aḥmad ibn ʿAbd Allāh ibn Salām, a scholar of the time of Harūn ar-Rashīd (786–809). According to Ibn an-Nadīm, Salām said, "I have translated . . . the Torah, the Gospels, and the books of the prophets and disciples from Hebrew, Greek, and Sabian,

[27] See the discussion and brief description of the major traits in Jacques Grand'Henry, "Christian Middle Arabic," in Versteegh, *Encyclopedia of Arabic Language and Linguistics*, vol. 1, pp. 383ff. See also the discussion in Griffith, "The Monks of Palastine and the Growth of Christian Literature in Arabic," esp. pp. 7–11.

[28] Abū l-Ḥasan ʿAlī al-Masʿūdī, *Kitāb at-Tanbīh wa l-Ishrāf* (ed. M.M. de Goeje, Bibliotheca Geographorum Arabicorum, 8 vols.; Leiden: E.J. Brill, 1967), vol 8, p. 112.

which are the languages of the people of each book, into Arabic, letter for letter."[29]

Early Muslim authors who quoted passages from the Bible in their works provide indirect evidence for the availability of translations in their time. One of the earliest of these was a certain Abū r-Rabī' Muḥammad ibn al-Layth, who wrote a letter in the name of the caliph Harūn ar-Rashid addressed to the Byzantine emperor, Constantine VI (780–797), arguing on behalf of the truth claims of Islam, in which he quoted loosely from the Old and New Testaments in a way that suggests a translation was available to him.[30] Other early writers whose works contain such quotations include those of the traditionist Wahb ibn Munabbih (d. betw. 725 and 737),[31] the Zaydī *imām*, Abū Muḥammad al-Qāsim ibn Ibrāhīm al-Ḥasanī (785–860),[32] the historian Aḥmad ibn Abī Ya'qūb ibn Ja'far ibn Wahb ibn Wadīḥ al-Ya'qūbī (d.897),[33] the philologist, Abū Muḥammad 'Abd Allāh ibn Muslim ibn Qutaybah (828–889),[34] and the Muslim apologist, a convert from

[29] Bayard Dodge (trans.), *The Fihrist of al-Nadīm* (2 vols.; New York: Columbia University Press, 1970), vol. 1, p. 42.

[30] See D. M. Dunlop, "A Letter of Harūn arRashīd to the Emperor Constantine VI," in Matthew Black and Georg Fohrer (eds.), *In Memoriam Paul Kahle* (Beiheft zur ZAW, vol. 103; Berlin: A. Töpelmann, 1968), pp. 106–115.

[31] See R. G. Khoury, "Quelques réflexions sur les citations de la Bible dans les prémieres générations islamiques du premier et du deuxième siècles de l' Hégire," in *Mélanges H. Laoust* in *Bulletin d'Études Orientales* 29 (1977), pp. 269–278; *idem*, "Quelques réflexions sur la première ou les premières Bibles arabes," in T. Fahd (ed.), *L'Arabie préislamique et son environnement historique et culturel: Actes du colloque de Strasbourg, 24–27 juin 1987* (Travaux du Centre de Recherche sur le Proche-Orient et la Grèce Antiques, 10; Leiden: E.J. Brill, 1989), pp. 549–561. See also the interesting study by Wolfhart Heinrichs, "The Meaning of *Mutanabbī*," in James L. Kugel (ed.), *Poetry and Prophecy: The Beginnings of a Literary Tradition* (Ithaca, NY and London: Cornell University Press, 1990), pp. 120–139, nn. pp. 231–239.

[32] See David Thomas, "The Bible in Early Muslim Anti-Christian Polemic," *Islam and Christian-Muslim Relations* 7 (1996), pp. 29–38.

[33] See Sidney H. Griffith, "The Gospel, the Qur'ān, and the Presentation of Jesus in al-Ya'qūbī's *Ta'rīkh*," in John C. Reeves (ed.), *Bible and Qur'ān: Essays in Scriptural Intertextuality* (Symposium Series, 24; Atlanta: Society of Biblical Literature, 2003), pp. 133–160.

[34] See G. Vajda, "Judaeo-Arabica: Observations sur quelques citations bibliques chez Ibn Qotayba," *Revue des Études Juives* 99 (1935), pp. 68–80; G. Lecomte, "Les citations de l'Ancien et du Nouveau Testament dans l'oeuvre d'Ibn Qutayba," *Arabica* 5 (1958), pp. 34–46; Raimund Köbert, "Die älteste arabische Genesis-Übersetzung," in Franz Altheim and Ruth Stiehl (eds.), *Die Araber in der alten Welt* (5 vols.; Berlin: Walter de Gruyter, 1965), vol. 2, pp. 333–343.

Christianity to Islam, ʿAlī ibn Rabbān al-Ṭabarī (*fl.*mid-ninth c.),[35] just to name the most prominent of those who quoted more or less accurately from the Bible and thus likely had access to translations of the Jewish and Christian scriptures.

The question naturally arises, where would Muslim writers such as those just mentioned have found translations of the Bible in Arabic? One suspects that they may have sought out Jewish or Christian informants, or alternatively, that they visited synagogues, churches, or monasteries in search of texts they could consult. There is in fact some evidence of the latter practice in a report cited by R. G. Khoury from Abū Nuʿaym al-Isbahānī's (948–1038) *Ḥilyat al-awliyāʾ wa-Ṭabaqāt al-aṣfiyāʾ*, according to which the traditionist Mālik ibn Dīnār (d.748), who lived in Baṣrah and was reportedly a bibliophile and an associate of Ḥasan al-Baṣrī (642–728), paid regular visits to Christian monasteries in search of books and at least once went away with one of their books. Khoury observes, "If one believes such texts, and basically what could be more natural than to imagine comparable encounters through the centuries, he [i.e., Mālik ibn Dīnār] could have come upon an Arabic version of the Old and New Testament, or at least a part of one. The pages that Abū Nuʿaym devotes to him mention not only the Torah, but also *al-Ḥikma* and the Psalms of David."[36] As we shall see, it was precisely in Christian monasteries that the first translations of the Bible into Arabic seem to have been undertaken, and arguably in the late seventh and early eighth centuries, the very period of time within which Mālik ibn Dīnār went looking for them.

The Earliest Christian Translations of the Bible into Arabic

The need on the part of the Christians to translate their scriptures into the languages of peoples newly evangelized has in a number of historic instances provided the impetus for the development of a script and a writing culture suitable for the undertaking. The case of the Armenians in the fifth century,[37] and the devising of Old Church Slavonic at the hands of Sts. Cyril and Methodius in the ninth century are two well-known instances

[35] See Thomas, "The Bible in Early Muslim Anti-Christian Polemic," pp. 29–38.

[36] Khoury, "Quelques réflexions sur les citations de la Bible," pp. 275–276. The Qurʾān mentions *al-Ḥikmah*, along with the Torah and the Gospel, as one of God's scriptures. See III *Āl ʿImrān* 48 and V *al-Māʾidah* 110.

[37] Irfan Shahid cites the Armenian instance in Irfan Shahid, *Byzantium and the Arabs in the Fifth Century* (Washington, DC: Dumbarton Oaks, 1989), p. 426.

of the phenomenon. As for the Arabs, as we have mentioned in chapter 1, scholars are agreed that by the time of Muḥammad the Arabic script was "readily available."[38] And, as Robert Hoyland has noted on the basis of his detailed studies of early Arabic inscriptions, "We must infer that there had been much writing of the Arabic language in the Nabataean script on parchments and papyri that very sadly have not survived."[39] He goes further to say that it might even have been the case already among the Ghassanids "that certain Christian texts were translated into Arabic for the purpose of instructing new Arabophone converts."[40] These too, unfortunately have not survived (if indeed they ever existed), nor have any other pre-Islamic texts written in Arabic by Christians, including any of the notes or *aides de mémoire* written in Arabic that we may reasonably suppose were used by Jews and Christians in the milieu of Muḥammad and the Qur'ān.[41] One can only conclude that it was not Arabic writing by Christians that provided the impetus for the cultural transition from the oral tradition to the written among the Arabs. Rather, as the hypothesis espoused here proposes, it was the Muslim Arabs' need, after the death of Muḥammad, to collect the Qur'ān into a written scripture on the order of the Torah, the Psalms, and the Wisdom of the Jews, and the Gospel of the Christians (cf. III *Āl 'Imrān* 48 and V *al-Mā'dah* 110), that encouraged the rise of a widespread culture of writing among the Arabs.[42] And it was this very development that yielded the written and edited Qur'ān and the attendant early Islamic religious literature, one further surmises, that during the processes of Arabization and

[38] Beatrice Gruendler, "Arabic Script," in McAuliffe, *Encyclopaedia of the Qur'ān*, vol. 1, p. 137.

[39] Robert Hoyland, "Mount Nebo, Jabal Ramm, and the Status of Christian Palestinian Aramaic and Old Arabic in Late Roman Palestine and Arabia," in M.C.A. Macdonald, *The Development of Arabic as a Written Language: Papers from the Special Session of the Seminar for Arabian Studies Held on July 24, 2009* (Supplement to the Proceedings of the Seminar for Arabian Studies, vol. 40; Oxford: Archaeopress, 2010), p. 35.

[40] Hoyland, "Mount Nebo, Jabal Ramm," p. 35. See also Robert Hoyland, "Epigraphy and the Linguistic Background to the Qur'ān," in Gabriel Said Reynolds (ed.), *The Qur'ān in Its Historical Context* (London and New York: Routledge, 2008), pp. 51–69.

[41] See the discussion in chapter 1 and the references cited in nn. 96–105.

[42] In this connection, one notes the following observation by Robert Hoyland: "The change from oral to written tends only to happen to a language when its speakers (or one particular group of them, which thereby make its dialect into the high form of the language) acquire sufficient common identity and sufficient political power to promote their own tongue." Hoyland, "Mount Nebo, Jabal Ramm," p. 35.

Islamicization in the conquered and occupied territories outside of Arabia eventually provided the cultural and religious imperative for the adoption of Arabic among Jews and Christians as a written medium for their own religious expression.[43]

To judge by information that can be gleaned from the few colophons attached to surviving manuscripts, the city of Damascus in Syria and the monasteries of Jerusalem, the Judean desert, and the Sinai were the places outside of Arabia where Christians wrote and copied most of the earliest, surviving manuscripts containing Christian texts in Arabic. From the colophons of some of the manuscripts we are able to learn something of the monastic scribes who copied the manuscripts, and something of the monasteries in which they lived, particularly Mar Saba, Mar Chariton, and the monastery at Mt. Sinai.[44] These monasteries were still flourishing, cosmopolitan institutions in the early years of the Islamic conquest, peopled by monks from all over the Christian world.[45] While Greek was the standard language of liturgy and theology in the pre-Islamic Patriarchate of Jerusalem, many other languages flourished in the monastic communities, and were used in the liturgies to interpret the scriptural readings that were proclaimed in Greek. Among the languages for which textual evidence survives in the manuscript collections of several of the monasteries are Syriac, Armenian, Georgian, and the local Christian Palestinian Aramaic (CPA); the latter seems to have been devised by monks in the Jerusalem monastic establishment specifically to accommodate the needs of the local

[43] See David J. Wasserstein, "Why Did Arabic Succeed Where Greek Failed? Language Change in the Near East after Muḥammad," *Scripta Classica Israelica* 22 (2003), pp. 257–272; Robert Hoyland, "Language and Identity: The Twin Histories of Arabic and Aramaic (and: Why Did Aramaic Succeed Where Greek Failed?)," *Scripta Classica Israelica* 23 (2004), pp. 183–199.

[44] See Sidney H. Griffith, "Stephen of Ramlah and the Christian Kerygma in Arabic in Ninth-Century Palestine," *Journal of Ecclesiastical History* 36 (1985), pp. 23–45; *idem*, "The Monks of Palestine;" and *idem*, "Anthony David of Baghdad, Scribe and Monk of Mar Sabas: Arabic in the Monasteries of Palestine," *Church History* 58 (1989), pp. 7–19.

[45] See the studies by Yizhar Hirschfeld, *The Judean Desert Monasteries in the Byzantine Period* (New Haven, CT: Yale University Press, 1992); *idem* (ed.), *The Founding of the New Laura* (New York: Oxford University Press, 1995); Joseph Patrich, *Sabas—Leader of Palestinian Monasticism* (Dumbarton Oaks Studies, 32; Washington, DC: Dumbarton Oaks, 1995; *idem, The Sabaite Heritage: The Sabaite Factor in the Orthodox Church—Monastic Life, Theology, Liturgy, Literature, Art and Archaeology (Fifth Century to the Present)* (Orientalia Lovaniensia Analecta; P. Peeters: Leuven, 2001). See also Schick, *The Christian Communities of Palestine from Byzantine to Islamic Rule.*

Christians. But with the exception of a number of remaining inscriptions, all of the surviving documents in this language contain texts translated from Greek.[46]

When in the second half of the eighth century CE, as we shall see, Arabic began to take its place among the languages of the Church of Jerusalem,[47] it gradually grew in importance to the point that its use in theological discourse became one of the distinguishing features of a distinct Christian confessional community that emerged in the territories of the Caliphate, the Melkites. By the ninth century in the Melkite community, it would seem that Arabic had already effectively replaced Greek for a century and more as the preferred ecclesiastical language from Alexandria in Egypt, to Jerusalem in Palestine, and even reaching to Antioch in Syria.[48] Indeed, Jerusalem became the effective ecclesiastical center for the Arabic-speaking, Melkite church throughout the Oriental Patriarchates.[49] And by the end of the first half of the ninth century, the use of Arabic had also become commonplace in the Syriac-speaking communities of the Jacobite and Nestorian Christians as well.[50] In Coptic-speaking Egypt, it was not until the late tenth or early eleventh century that Arabic became an ecclesiastical language, and

[46] See Griffith, "From Aramaic to Arabic." From 1997, Michael Sokoloff and Christa Moeller-Kessler have been publishing a *Corpus of Christian Palestinian Aramaic* (Leiden: Brill, 1997–), currently at 5 vols., with the intention of including all the extant texts.

[47] It is interesting to note that on the basis of a careful study of inscriptions in the Syro-Palestinian area, Leah Di Segni could conclude that "by the end of the eighth century, Greek as an epigraphic medium had ceased to be relevant." Leah Di Segni, "Greek Inscriptions in Transition from the Byzantine to the Early Islamic Period," in Hannah M. Cotton et al. (eds.), *From Hellenism to Islam: Cultural and Linguistic Change in the Roman Near East* (Cambridge: Cambridge University Press, 2009), p. 352.

[48] See Sidney H. Griffith, "Melkites, Jacobites and the Christological Controversies in Arabic in Third/Ninth-Century Syria," in David Thomas (ed.), *Syrian Christians under Islam: The First Thousand Years* (Leiden: Brill, 2001), pp. 9–35; *idem*, "Theology and the Arab Christian: The Case of the Melkite Creed," in David Thomas (ed.), *A Faithful Presence: Essays for Kenneth Cragg* (London: Melisende, 2003), pp. 184–200; *idem*, "The Church of Jerusalem and the Melkites: The Making of an 'Arab Orthodox' Christian Identity in the World of Islam, 750–1050," in Ora Limor and G. G. Stroumsa (eds.), *Christians and Christianity in the Holy Land: From the Origins to the Latin Kingdom* (Turnhout: Brepols, 2006), pp. 173–202.

[49] See Sidney H. Griffith, "The *Life of Theodore of Edessa*: History, Hagiography, and Religious Apologetics in Mar Saba Monastery in Early Abbasid Times," in Patrich, *The Sabaite Heritage*, pp. 147–169.

[50] See Griffith, *The Church in the Shadow of the Mosque*, esp. pp. 60–68.

when it did enter the Christian mainstream there it eventually eclipsed Coptic altogether as the public language of the church.[51]

The earliest text written in Arabic by a Christian that attests to the date of its composition is a work preserved in an old parchment manuscript from Sinai (Sinai Arabic MS 154), called by its original editor and translator, Margaret Dunlop Gibson, 'On the Triune Nature of God'.[52] At one point in the text the now unknown author provided an indication of the date of his writing. Speaking of the endurance of Christianity against all odds, even up to his own day, he wrote, "If this religion were not truly from God, it would not have stood so unshakably for seven hundred and forty-six years."[53] If we reckon the beginning of the Christian era from the beginning of the year of the Incarnation, according to the computation of the Alexandrian world era, which Palestinian scribes were likely to use prior to the tenth century, we arrive at a date not too far removed from 755 CE for the composition of the treatise. This text remains the earliest written by a Christian in Arabic that contains an internal indication of the date of its composition. Another early documentary source that refers to a Christian text in Arabic and gives a date for its composition is contained in a note appended to the end of an Arabic version of the story of the "Fathers who were killed at Mount Sinai." It says that the text of the martyrdom was originally translated from Greek into Arabic in the Hijrah year 155, which corresponds to 772 CE.[54] While some other texts, as we shall see, contain scribal notes in their colophons that mention the dates of their copying, for the most part the dates of Christian Arabic manuscripts are established by modern scholars on the basis of paleographical considerations. The earliest actually recorded dates are for the most part from the second half of the eighth century and the ninth century.

The translation of the scriptures was high on the agenda of the early Arabic-speaking Christians outside of Arabia, but unfortunately the very earliest surviving manuscripts seldom carry the dates of their copying. A case in point is the text of Psalm 78 (77 in the LXX), found in the treasury

[51] See Tonio Sebastian Richter, "Greek, Coptic and the 'Language of the Hijra': The Rise and Decline of the Coptic Language in Late Antique and Medieval Egypt," in Cotton, *From Hellenism to Islam,* pp. 401–446.

[52] See the discussion and bibliography in Griffith, *The Church in the Shadow of the Mosque,* pp. 53–57.

[53] Sinai Arabic MS 154, f. 100v. Unaccountably, Margaret Gibson omitted this leaf from her edition of the text.

[54] See the text discussed in Griffith, "The Monks of Palestine," p. 17 and Sidney H. Griffith, "The Arabic Account of ʿAbd al-Masīḥ an-Na[rānī al-Ghassānī," *Le Muséon* 98 (1985), esp. pp. 337–342.

of the Umayyad Mosque in Damascus.[55] It is a dual-language text, in which the Psalm is written in Greek along with an Arabic version written alongside it in Greek script. It seems that the intended reader or interpreter, presumably in a liturgical setting, was expected to be fluent in Arabic but more familiar with the Greek script. On paleographical grounds, most scholars have dated the text to the late eighth century at the earliest, though some have more recently opted for a later date in the ninth century.[56]

Not surprisingly, the Gospels seem to have been among the earliest biblical texts translated by Arabic-speaking Christians, and there are several translations that may well have been among the very earliest. Before we discuss them in any detail, however, we must first consider the general state of the manuscript evidence. The so far earliest known dated manuscript containing an Arabic translation of a Christian biblical text is a copy of the four Gospels in Arabic now in the library of the Monastery of St. Catherine at Mt. Sinai, which, according to a scribal note, was completed on the feast of St. George in the year AD 859.[57] Sinai Arabic MS 151 contains an Arabic version of the Epistles of St. Paul that according to its colophon was copied in Damascus in the year 867.[58] For the rest, the earliest dated manuscripts

[55] See Bruno Violet, "Ein zweisprachiges Psalmfragment aus Damaskus," *Berichtigter Sonderabzug aus der Orientalistischen Literatur-Zeitung* (Berlin: Akademie-Verlag, 1902). The text is re-presented in Joshua Blau, *A Handbook of Early Middle Arabic* (Jerusalem: The Max Schloessinger Memorial Foundation, The Hebrew University, 2002), pp. 68–71.

[56] See the discussions by Anton Baumstark, "Der älteste erhaltene Griechisch-Arabische Text von Psalm 110 (109)," *Oriens Christianus* 9 (1934), pp. 55–66; Rachid Haddad, "La phonétique de l'arabe chrétien vers 700," in Pierre Canivet and Jean-Paul Rey-Coquais (eds.), *La Syrie de Byzance a l'Islam: VIIe–VIIIe siècles; Actes du Colloque International Lyon-Maison de l'Orient Méditerranéen, Paris—Institut du Monde Arabe, 11–15 Septembre 1990* (Damas: Institut Français de Damas, 1992), pp. 159–164; Maria Mavroudi, "Arabic Words in Greek Letters: The Violet Fragment and More," in Jérôme Lentin and Jacques Grand'henry (eds.), *Moyen arabe et variétés mixtes de l'arabe à travers l'histoire: Actes du premier colloque international (Louvain-la-Neuve, 10–14 mai 2004)* (Université Catholique de Louvain, Institut Orientaliste; Leuven: Peeters, 2008), pp. 321–354.

[57] See Ιωαννου Εμμ. Μειμαρη, Καταλογος των Νεων Αραβικων Χειρογραφων της Ιερας Μονης Αγιας Αικατερινης του Ορους Σινα (Αθηναι: Εθνικον Ιδυμα Ερευνων, 1985), parchment no. 16; see also photos 19–21. See the beautiful photograph of the two pages from this MS, including an illustration of St. Luke, in Michelle P. Brown, *In the Beginning: Bibles before the Year 1000* (Washington, DC: Smithsonian Institution, 2006), pp. 166–167, 274–275.

[58] See H. Staal, *Mt. Sinai Arabic Codex 151: I Pauline Epistles* (CSCO, vols. 452 and 453; Louvain: Peeters, 1983).

cluster in the second half of the ninth century.[59] But it is clear from numerous studies that these dated manuscripts are not in fact the earliest manuscripts, nor are the translations of the Bible they contain necessarily the earliest translations.

Judging on the basis of paleographical considerations, scholars have identified several manuscripts containing copies of Arabic translations of the Gospels that in their opinion can reasonably be dated to the eighth century, and in one or two instances they even make a case for the seventh century. However, it is important to understand from the outset the distinction that must be made between the original Arabic translation of a given scriptural text and the surviving copy of that translation that one finds in the manuscripts. In each of the instances that we shall discuss here, scholars have shown that the surviving manuscripts they have studied contain a copy of the original Arabic translation of a biblical text; in no case is it thought that one is dealing with the autograph of the translation as it left the hand of the original translator. The earliest translations of the Gospels were made from Syriac and Greek *Vorlagen* into Arabic,[60] and, as we shall argue, in the first instance they were most likely all produced in the multilingual monastic communities of Syria/Palestine, and particularly in the environs of Jerusalem and the Judean desert, where the first large-scale Arabic translation movement under Christian auspices was undertaken as early as the second half of the eighth century, if not a bit earlier.

GOSPELS TRANSLATED FROM SYRIAC

Hikmat Kachouh has recently made the case that the Arabic translation from a Syriac *Vorlage* of the Gospels of Matthew, Mark, and a portion of Luke, now preserved in Vatican Arabic MS 13, is arguably the earliest surviving Arabic version of the Gospels.[61] The extant manuscript also includes the Epistles of St. Paul translated from Greek, but in its present state, in addition to lacking all of the Gospel of Luke, the manuscript also lacks the Acts of the Apostles and the Catholic Epistles, which it presumably once contained. Based on paleographical considerations, scholars have agreed that the manuscript itself was copied around the year 800 AD, in all prob-

[59] See Griffith, "The Monks of Palestine," esp. pp. 13–20.

[60] See H. Kachouh, "The Arabic Versions of the Gospels: A Case Study of John 1:1 and 1:18," in David Thomas (ed.), *The Bible in Arab Christianity* (The History of Christian-Muslim Relations, vol. 6; Leiden: Brill, 2007), pp. 9–36.

[61] See Kachouh, *The Arabic Versions of the Gospels*, vol. 1, esp. pp. 133–167.

ability at the monastery of Mar Saba in the Judean desert.[62] But as Kachouh has very convincingly argued, evidently the text of the Gospels had been edited and copied from an earlier exemplar before being copied into the existing Vatican Arabic MS 13. On the evidence of the copy's paleographical features, it is clear to Kachouh that the text of the Gospels was translated from the Syriac Peshitta, with, as he says, perhaps some indirect connection with the *Diatessaron* and pre-Peshitta readings. He also speaks of what he calls 'phrasal transposition' in the text, suggesting the influence of orally transmitted wording, and he notes that the translation has not been corrected against Greek readings, and that the spellings of the proper names reflect Syriac and not Greek formulations. As for the characteristics of the Arabic language itself in the translation, there are many archaic usages in the form of unfamiliar vocabulary, unusual orthography, and a want of diacritical points.[63] None of these are in themselves unusual linguistic traits in very early Arabic texts.

Given the premise that the translated Arabic text of the Gospels in Vatican Arabic MS 13 was copied from an earlier exemplar, one reasonably concludes that the translation itself was made earlier, perhaps at some earlier point in the eighth century; and the question then arises, how much earlier? Could it have been done as early as sometime in the seventh century? Then, as one is caught up in the current of extrapolation, one's thoughts run to the sixth century and to pre-Islamic times; could the translation have been made among the Arabic-speaking Christians of Arabia, who had for the most part inherited their Christianity from Syriac-speaking Christians, such as the Christians of al-Ḥīrā, of the Ghassanid confederation, or even the Christians of Najrān in south Arabia? Kachouh's reasoning follows this path, going back and forth from the sixth century to the early eighth century. In the end, he settles for a pre-Islamic date and surmises that the original translation may even have been done in Najrān.[64]

Hikmat Kachouh finds corroborating evidence for the hypothesis that the translation of the Gospels in Vatican Arabic MS 13 is pre-Islamic in origin in a comparison of the 'Arabicity' of the translated text with that found

[62] See the descriptions of the MS in A. Mai, *Scriptorum Veterum Nova Collectio e Vaticanis Codicibus Edita* (vol. 4; Romae: Rypis Vaticanis, 1831), pp. 11–13, who had mistakenly maintained that the Gospel translation had been made from Greek, and I. Guidi, *Le Traduzioni degli Evangelii in Arabo e in Etiopico* (Reale Accademia dei Lincei, Anno 285; Roma: Tipografia della R. Accademia dei Lincei, 1888), pp. 8–10.

[63] See Kachouh, *The Arabic Versions of the Gospels*, vol. 1, esp. pp. 162–165.

[64] See Kachouh, *The Arabic Versions of the Gospels*, vol. 1, pp. 140–146, 364–370.

in an early Qur'ān manuscript, and even in a reference to a pre-Islamic Christian inscription in Arabic, now vanished but reported to have been at Dayr Hind in al-Ḥīrā,[65] as well as in the form of the letter 'alif', which he takes to be characteristic of the shape of the letter as it is found in South Arabia. For Kachouh, historical corroboration for his hypothesis comes in the form of the supposition that Syriac itself would not have been current in a place like Najrān (hence the need for the translation) and in the perception that there is no evidently Qur'ānic phrasing in the translated Gospel text. Kachouh's conclusion is: "The evidence of the language itself permits us to suggest a pre-Islamic date for the origin of Vat. Ar. 13 (in the Gospels only)."[66]

There are a number of problems with this conclusion and the line of reasoning used to support it. The primary obstacle, as we have seen above, is that there is no independent, pre-Qur'ānic evidence for the existence of any extended writing in Arabic prior to the rise of Islam. The Qur'ān is itself in all likelihood the earliest Arabic book. Moreover, as we have also seen, oral transmission of the scriptures in Arabic in pre-Islamic Arabia seems to have been the preferred medium, even for the Qur'ān prior to its collection following the death of Muḥammad. The 'evidence of the language', which Kachouh cites in favor of the hypothesis is also unconvincing. First of all, the only Arabic text cited in comparison is an Ḥijāzī Qur'ān manuscript of the later seventh century, indubitably a text produced in Islamic times.[67] The facts that the vocabulary in the original exemplar of the translated Gospels seems to have been strange to the later copyist, that the script lacked vowel marks, that there is no evidence of Qur'ānic language in the translation, and that the Arabic writing does not feature many of the characteristics that Joshua Blau described as typical of 'old south Palestinian' Christian Arabic,[68] do not add up to evidence that the translation was done originally in Najrān, or anywhere else in the Arabic-speaking milieu prior to the rise of Islam in the fifth or sixth century. Alternatively, remembering that the text we actually have in hand dates from around the year 800 and that it was copied at Mar Saba monastery in the Judean desert provides the strong suggestion that the origin of the archaic translation of the Gospels in Vatican

[65] On this now vanished inscription in al-Ḥīrā, the text of which is preserved in later Muslim texts, see Shahid, *Byzantium and the Arabs in the Fourth Century*, pp. 355–357, 460.

[66] Kachouh, *The Arabic Versions of the Gospels*, vol. 1, p. 372.

[67] See Kachouh, *The Arabic Versions of the Gospels*, p. 138.

[68] The reference is to Blau, *A Grammar of Christian Arabic*.

Arabic MS 13 was most likely also in Syria/Palestine, where, as we shall see, the other earliest Gospel translations into Arabic were made. Furthermore, the likeliest period for the first translation could indeed have been some time in the late seventh or early eighth century, which, as we shall also see, is the period within which a number of other early Bible translations can plausibly be thought to have been done. This period falls well within the time frame proposed above, namely a most likely *terminus post quem* for the appearance of a written, Arabic translation of some portion of the Bible at a point in the middle of the seventh century CE. To extrapolate further back in time, and to postulate a location outside of Syria/Palestine for the translation, is both to stretch the available evidence beyond its reach, and to run up against the counter evidence, such as the time frame for the development and deployment of written, literary Arabic. It is also to ignore the force of the challenge posed to the Arabic-speaking 'Scripture People' by the collection and publication of the Arabic Qur'ān in the mid to late seventh century. It is reasonable to suppose that the Qur'ān's idiosyncratic recollection of biblical narratives and themes (discussed in the previous chapter) served to some degree, along with liturgical necessity, as an inducement to the 'Scripture People' to undertake their own Bible translations into Arabic. Furthermore, it is a mistake to neglect or discount Syria/Palestine's strong claim as the likeliest place for the first translation of the Gospels in Vatican Arabic MS 13. To the case for that argument we now turn.[69]

On the basis of the evidence actually in hand, the work of producing the original Arabic translation of the Gospels that was later copied into Vatican Arabic MS 13 was most likely done in Palestine and Syria, in the monastic communities of the seventh and eighth centuries, and at Mar Sabas monastery in particular, where Vatican Arabic MS 13 was copied. In the first place, the requisite languages, Greek and Syriac, were actually cultivated in these communities, and the monasteries were, already in the seventh and eighth centuries, at the center of an early translation movement devoted precisely to the translation of biblical and other ecclesiastical texts from Greek into Christian Palestinian Aramaic and from Greek and Syriac into Arabic. Not to mention that the monasteries were also the source of original

[69] Kachouh avers, not very convincingly and without any persuasive discussion, that it is unlikely that the original exemplar of the Arabic translation of the Gospels copied in Vat. Ar. MS 13 was done in Mar Saba. See Kachouh, *The Arabic Versions of the Gospels*, vol. 1, p. 140, n. 50.

compositions in Arabic from the eighth century onward.[70] Furthermore, the surviving, early Arabic translations of non-biblical ecclesiastical texts, such as versions of saints' lives and patristic homilies, show the same archaic linguistic features that one finds in the Bible translations. It is no more than supposition, based on modern theological ideas of scriptural sufficiency (*sola scriptura*), to think that the Bible translations were made first and the other texts followed in time. In short, one would require more convincing reasons than have so far been advanced to conclude that the original exemplar of the Arabic version of the Gospels translated from Syriac and copied into Vatican Arabic MS 13 around the turn of the ninth century was made anywhere else than in the monasteries of Palestine, let alone anywhere in pre-Islamic Arabia.

It is interesting to note that the Arabic version of the Gospels preserved in Vatican Arabic MS 13 in all probability had an afterlife. Hikmat Kachouh has found evidence for its persistence even into modern times, in manuscripts in which over the centuries later hands have corrected or otherwise modified the text to improve it or to make it more serviceable to later users.[71] This observation calls attention to a feature of the Bible translation enterprise that we shall meet again; the tendency to build on or to improve older, familiar translations rather than to produce altogether new ones. In all probability this practice attests to the liturgical contexts in which the translations were used, where continuity and familiarity would be desirable.

GOSPELS TRANSLATED FROM GREEK

Hikmat Kachouh has also recently shown that among the very earliest of the translations of the Gospels from Greek into Arabic there is one that has only recently come to the attention of scholars. This is a single text contained in a manuscript now divided into two portions, each with its own shelf number, Sinai ar. N.F. parch. 8 and 28, a manuscript that Kachouh proposes to call 'Codex Sinaiticus Arabicus (CSA)'.[72] Like a number of the

[70] See Griffith, "From Aramaic to Arabic." A detailed study of the wide-ranging ecclesiastical translation movement into Arabic in early Islamic times is long overdue.

[71] See Hikmat Kachouh, "The Arabic Gospel Text of Codex Beirut, Bibliothèque Orientale, 430: Is It Recent or Archaic?" *Parole de l'Orient* 32 (2007), pp. 105–121.

[72] See Hikmat Kachouh, "Sinai Ar. N.F. Parchment 8 and 28: Its Contribution to Textual Criticism of the Gospel of Luke," *Novum Testamentum* 50 (2008), pp. 28–57. It is a bit unfortunate that Kachouh has chosen to call this important manuscript 'Codex Sinaiticus Arabicus', because it facilitates confusion with another Sinai Arabic manuscript, also a palimpsest, which Aziz Atiya called 'Codex Arabicus', viz.

early Sinai manuscripts, this one is a palimpsest and it contains, among other interesting items in the topmost text, an Arabic translation of the four Gospels that Kachouh argues is "undoubtedly one of the earliest surviving Arabic Gospel manuscripts . . . possibly copied in the second half of the eighth century or early ninth century."[73] In addition to the translation of the Gospels, the manuscript also contains what Kachouh calls simply, "an apology" as the first work in the text, then the Gospels, followed by a sermon of St. John Chrysostom, an Arabic translation of the Apostolic Canons, and an exhortation for monks.[74] Its omnibus character calls attention to an important feature of the Sinai manuscripts in general; texts of different works, by different copyists, and even of different provenance, are often bound together by later hands, with custodial markings made by still later curators or librarians. On the one hand, this phenomenon reminds the scholar that each text must be studied individually, with reference to its own origins, but on the other, it also calls attention to the fact that it behooves the researcher to remember that in the Christian translation movement of early Islamic times, there was a simultaneous need for Arabic translations of works in various genres. Consequently, one should not presume the priority of any one sort of text over another without corroborating evidence. It is not, for example, self evident that the translation of biblical texts into Arabic would have had the highest priority, to the degree that one could suppose that they would antedate translations of other sorts of texts, or even original compositions in Arabic.

Among the earliest translations of the Gospels from Greek into Arabic are those associated with a particular family of Gospel manuscripts, the later exemplars of which all seem to go back to an earlier, undated text now preserved in Sinai Arabic MS 74. Scholars have assigned that manuscript to the eighth century on paleographical grounds. The translation was in all likelihood done in the Palestinian monastic milieu and, interestingly, while it was surely translated from Greek, the text reveals features otherwise

---

Sinai Arabic MS 514. See A. S. Atiya, "The Monastery of St. Catherine and the Mount Sinai Expedition," *Proceedings of the American Philosophical Society* 96 (1952), pp. 578–586; *idem*, "The Arabic Palimpsests of Mount Sinai," in J. Kritzeck and R. B. Winder (eds.), *The World of Islam: Studies in Honor of Philip K. Hitti* (London and New York: Macmillan and St. Martin's Press, 1959), pp. 109–120; *idem*, "Codex Arabicus (Sinai Arabic MS No. 514)," in H. Lehmann-Haupt (ed.), *Homage to a Bookman: Essays on Manuscripts, Books, and Printing written for Hans P. Kraus on his 60th Birthday, October 12, 1967* (Berlin: Mann, 1967), pp. 75–82.

[73] Kachouh, "Sinai Ar. N.F. Parchment 8 and 28," p. 30.

[74] See Kachouh, "Sinai Ar. N.F. Parchment 8 and 28," p. 31.

found only in the so-called Syro-Palestinian Lectionary, a version itself done from Greek for use among the Christians in the same Syro-Palestinian milieu as the Arabic translation. What is more, in these manuscripts, liturgical notices are interspersed in the Gospel text, indicating the times and seasons in the liturgical year when the particular pericopes are to be read. Clearly the texts were meant for practical use. A notable feature in their transmission history is that the later manuscripts in the family provide numerous instances of textual revisions, corrections, and improved readings vis-à-vis the earlier ones, testifying to the not unusual practice of carrying on with a particular translation rather than commissioning a new one.[75]

OTHER BIBLICAL BOOKS

The Gospels were of course not the only portions of the Bible translated by Christians into Arabic in the early period of the ecclesiastical translation movement though, as we mentioned above, the oldest surviving and dated translation is in fact a Gospel text. In the same era translations of the Epistles of St. Paul were made, as well as translations under Christian auspices of the Torah, the Psalms and other portions of the Bible. These will be the subject of a later chapter. The purpose here is simply to give some indication of the range covered by the earliest translations made by Christians. Our conclusion, based on the available evidence, is that in all probability the earliest Christian translations of the Bible into Arabic appeared in the eighth century in Syria/Palestine. It is not unreasonable to suppose that in one or two instances one might extrapolate from the evidence in hand back to a date in the late seventh century for the production of the original exemplar of a particular text, such as that of the Gospels in Vatican Arabic MS 13, but this remains an undocumented supposition. Many historians of Christianity among the Arabic-speaking peoples have wanted to find evidence for a pre-Islamic Arabic translation of the Bible. The trouble is that not only is there so far no completely convincing evidence for such a translation, but the existing evidence argues against its probability. A later chapter will explore the likelihood that the publication of the Arabic Qur'ān

[75] See Sidney H. Griffith, "The Gospel in Arabic: An Inquiry into its Appearance in the First Abbasid Century," *Oriens Christianus* 69 (1985), pp. 126–167; Samir Arbache, *Une ancienne version arabe des Évangiles; langue, texte et lexique* (Thèse de doctorat de l'Université Michel de Montaigne; Bordeaux, 1994); Jean Valentin, "Les Évangéliaires arabes de la bibliothèque du monastère ste. Catherine (Mont Sinaï): Essai de classification d'après l'étude d'un chapitre (*Matth.* 28); traducteurs, réviseurs, types textuels," *Le Muséon* 116 (2003), pp. 415–477.

itself served as one of the catalysts for both Jews and Christians to undertake Arabic translations of their scriptures.

BIBLICAL QUOTATIONS IN CHRISTIAN ARABIC TEXTS

As noted above, the earliest, surviving text written in Arabic by a Christian that includes some textual indication of the date of its composition is the treatise now called 'On the Triune Nature of God'.[76] Its author speaks of the seven hundred and forty-six years that had elapsed from the foundation of Christianity to his own day, a reckoning that suggests he composed his treatise somewhere around the year 755 CE. A striking feature of the treatise is the large number of quotations from both the Old Testament and the New Testament that it contains. A recent study documents some eighty-one biblical quotations and allusions to Genesis, Deuteronomy, Job, the Psalms, Isaiah, Jeremiah, Daniel, Ezekiel, Micah, Habakkuk, Zechariah, Malachi, and Baruch, along with the Gospels of Matthew, Luke, and John.[77] Famously, the author also names and quotes from the Qur'ān, citing its verses along with testimonies from the Bible in attestation of the credibility of Christian doctrines. He speaks of "the Law and the Prophets and the Psalms and the Gospel" in ways reminiscent of the Qur'ān's own evocation of these scriptures, even listing the prophets in Qur'ānic order.[78] And the leitmotiv of the whole composition is the repeated echoing of a verse from the Qur'ān that speaks of Jesus, the Messiah, and of God's Word and Spirit (IV *an-Nisā'* 171). But in the end, for all of the obvious recollections of the Qur'ān and Qur'ānic idiom in the text, the work is in its essence composed of a carefully chosen series of biblical testimonies quoted in Arabic translation. In the context of the present inquiry, the question arises, what is the source of these

[76] M. D. Gibson, *An Arabic Version of the Acts of the Apostles and the Seven Catholic Epistles, from an Eighth or Ninth Century MS in the Convent of St Catherine on Mount Sinai, with a Treatise on the Triune Nature of God, with a Translation, from the Same Codex* (Studia Sinaitica, 7; Cambridge: Cambridge University Press, 1899; reprinted Piscataway, NJ: Gorgias Press, 2003); Samir Khalil Samir, "The Earliest Arab Apology for Christianity (c. 750)," in Samir Kh. Samir and Jørgen S. Nielson (eds.), *Christian Arabic Apologetics during the Abbasid Period (750–1258)* (Leiden: E.J. Brill, 1994), pp. 57–114; Mark N. Swanson, "Beyond Prooftexting: Approaches to the Qur'ān in Some Arabic Christian Apologies," *The Muslim World* 88 (1998), pp. 297–319.

[77] See Thomas W. Ricks, "Developing the Doctrine of the Trinity in an Islamic Milieu: Early Arabic Christian Contributions to Trinitarian Theology," (Ph.D. Dissertation; Washington, DC: The Catholic University of America, 2012).

[78] See Gibson, *An Arabic Version*, pp. 3 (English) and 75 (Arabic); 14 (English) and 86 (Arabic), cf. III *Āl 'Imrān* 33.

eighty-some biblical quotations in Arabic? Did this mid-eighth century, probably Palestinian monastic author make his own translations as he went along, as Theodore Abū Qurrah seems to have done a generation later?[79] Or did he make use of previously existing, translated texts, ready to hand? No systematic study of the quotations has yet been done, and a quick survey shows no obvious dependence on known translations, all of which are available only in manuscript copies made a century and more after the composition of 'On the Triune Nature of God'.

As Hikmat Kachouh has shown, even the earliest surviving portions of the Bible in Arabic are copies of earlier texts. We have already seen that this conclusion warrants the assumption that the translations themselves were first made perhaps quite early in the eighth century. On the presumption that the author of the mid-century 'On the Triune Nature of God' most likely made use of ready-made Arabic translations of the Bible passages he quoted, his work becomes evidence that the readily available translations were already current well before he composed his treatise. It is not unreasonable therefore to think that the Bible translations into Arabic were being made in the Holy Land monastic communities as early as the turn of the eighth century, if not already in the waning years of the seventh century. It is also from this period that we have evidence of the earliest Christian awareness of the text of the Qur'ān outside of Arabia, just in time for it to have exerted the influence it did have on the author of 'On the Triune Nature of God'. It is no wonder then that he was anxious to set the prophetic record straight by including numerous Arabic translations of Bible passages in his apologetic treatise on the articles of Christian faith critiqued in the Qur'ān, and by doing so to put aright the Qur'ān's understanding of prophets foretold in earlier scriptures.

THE EARLIEST JEWISH TRANSLATIONS OF THE BIBLE INTO ARABIC

Without a doubt, the most notable early translation of the Hebrew Bible into Arabic is that done by Saadia Gaon (882–942), a work that will receive considerable attention in a later chapter. But Saadia's was certainly not the earliest biblical translation done under Jewish auspices in the early Islamic period, albeit that in all probability Arabic-speaking Jews outside of Arabia proper did not perceive a need to have a Bible in Arabic as early as newly Arabic-speaking Christians. Among Christians, translating the scriptures into the languages of their several communities, largely for liturgical pur-

[79] See Khalil Samir, "Notes sur les citations bibliques chez Abū Qurrah," *Orientalia Christiana Periodica* 49 (1983), pp. 184–191.

poses, had been an imperative long before the rise of Islam, whereas among Jews the Hebrew, along with the Aramaic (the language of the *Targumīm*), had long sufficed as the liturgical languages in the synagogues of Syria/Palestine and Mesopotamia. But circumstances seem to have changed in the course of the ninth century as more and more Jews in the Levant adopted Arabic and began to develop the linguistically distinctive 'Middle Arabic' state of the language that scholars have come to call Judaeo-Arabic, not only because it was employed by Jews, but also because it was written in Hebrew characters and was in many other ways influenced by Hebrew grammar, syntax, and lexicography.[80] The earliest texts in Judaeo-Arabic have been preserved in the Cairo Genizah, an archive that has provided abundant documentation for the study of Jewish communities and their interactions with others in the Mediterranean milieu in the early Islamic period and well beyond.[81]

As was the case among the Arabic-speaking Christians, so too among the Jews, the earliest texts in Arabic include both translations and original compositions. The earliest are dated to the ninth century, and a number of the original compositions are in the apologetic and polemical genres characteristic of the interreligious controversies of the early Islamic period.[82] The earliest Bible translation so far confidently identified seems to be a passage from the book of Proverbs, identified by Joshua Blau in a Cairo Genizah fragment.[83] Blau points out that the manner of transcription of the Arabic letters into Hebrew ones in the text, the usage characteristic of Judaeo-Arabic reflects the practice of phonetic spelling common in pre-tenth century manuscripts, rather than the standard system of transliteration in use

[80] Blau, *The Emergence and Linguistic Background of Judaeo-Arabic: A Study of the Origins of Neo-Arabic and Middle Arabic*; *idem*, *A Dictionary of Mediaeval Judaeo-Arabic Texts* [Hebrew and English] (Jerusalem: The Israel Academy of Sciences and Humanities, 2006).

[81] See the classic study by S. D. Goitein, *A Mediterranean Society: The Jewish Communities of the Arab World as Portrayed in the Documents of the Cairo Geniza* (6 vols.; Berkeley, CA: University of California Press, 1967–1993).

[82] See, e.g., Daniel J. Lasker, "*Qiṣṣat Mujādalat al-Usquf* and *Neṣṭor Ha-Komer* The Earliest Arabic and Hebrew Jewish anti-Christian Polemics," in J. Blau and S. C. Reif (eds.), *Genizah Research after Ninety Years: The Case of Judaeo-Arabic; Papers Read at the Third Congress of the Society for Judaeo-Arabic Studies* (Cambridge: Cambridge University Press, 1992), pp. 112–118; Simone Rosenkranz, *Die jüdisch-christliche Auseinandersetzung unter islamischer Herrschaft: 7.–10. Jahrhundert* (Judaica et Christiana, vol. 21; Bern and Berlin: Peter Lang, 2004).

[83] See Joshua Blau, "On a Fragment of the Oldest Judaeo-Arabic Bible Translation Extant," in Blau and Reif, *Genizah Research after Ninety Years*, pp. 31–39.

from Saadia's time onward. This observation pushes the date of the text back into the ninth century. What is more—and again not unlike the case with the earliest surviving Christian Arabic texts—on the basis of his study of the text of Proverbs preserved in the fragment, Blau was able to conclude that "its heterogeneous character makes it quite likely that it based itself on other translations preceding it."[84] This probability allows one reasonably to assume that the first translations of portions of the Hebrew Bible were carried out quite early in the ninth century. In the meantime, other scholars have identified more fragments of early Bible translations into Judaeo-Arabic in the Cairo Genizah archive, and again, as in the instance of the earliest Gospel translations, some scholars of the Judaeo-Arabic translations have yielded to the temptation to extrapolate from the state of the texts surviving from the ninth century and to postulate the not impossible existence of earlier translations, possibly even pre-Islamic ones.[85]

The problem with extrapolating from the probable ninth century dating of the earliest surviving Judaeo-Arabic translations of portions of the Bible to a date earlier than the second half of the seventh century as the *terminus post quem* for written Bible translations in Arabic is that the historian encounters a number of countervailing factors. These push the probable date forward from that point, and well into the ninth century for the earliest Judaeo-Arabic translations. There is first of all the fact that the late seventh century is the earliest period to which the available evidence would warrant dating any substantial body of written Arabic, as explored above. But perhaps even more telling in the instance of the Hebrew Bible is the accumulating evidence that even in Arabic-speaking Jewish communities, the Torah would not have been read individually but proclaimed orally in synagogues and in Hebrew, or in Aramaic targums. Moreover, it appears that the early Bible translations into Judaeo-Arabic were in fact contemporaneous with, and perhaps integral parts of the cultural shift in Jewish reading and writing practices that began in the late eighth century and continued throughout the ninth century, a development that one recent

[84] Blau, "On a Fragment of the Oldest Judaeo-Arabic Bible Translation Extant," p. 32.

[85] See, e.g., Yosef Tobi, "On the Antiquity of Ancient Judeo-Arabic Biblical Translations and a New Piece of an Ancient Judeo-Arabic Translation of the Pentateuch," [Hebrew] in Y. Tobi and Y. Avishur (eds.), *Ben 'Ever la-'Arav: Contacts between Arabic Literature and Jewish Literature in the Middle Ages and Modern Times* (vol. 2; Tel Aviv: Afikim Publishers, 2001), pp. 17–60.

scholar calls the 'codexification' of Judaism.[86] This cultural phenomenon provides a context for the Judaeo-Arabic translation movement of the same period within the framework of Jewish adjustment to early Islam. Among the challenges Judaism now faced were the many factors that gave rise to burgeoning controversies within the Jewish communities between Rabbanites and Karaites.[87]

The Impetus to Translate

The processes of Arabicization and Islamicization that occurred in the territories conquered and brought under Islamic hegemony during the first two centuries after the death of Muḥammad doubtless provided the major social and cultural impetus for the adoption of Arabic among Jews and Christians living in the new World of Islam. But there were other motivations as well, especially in regard to the Bible translations. While the processes of enculturation mentioned above would have been sufficient inducements for the translation of the non-Muslim communities' intellectual heritage and for their adoption of Arabic as a suitable language for original compositions in the new common language of the Muslim polity, there were some special concerns attached to the Bible translations that become evident already in the earliest Arabic versions of the scriptures.

It seems reasonable to suppose that the Arabic Qur'ān, published in the late seventh century, had already come to the notice of the newly Arabic-speaking Jews and Christians living in the Levant by the early eighth century. For by the second half of the century, a now unknown Christian writer explicitly quoted from it several times, in the earliest dated Christian Arabic text so far known, i.e., the apologetic work written not long after 755 CE and called by its first modern editor 'On the Triune Nature of God'.[88] It would not have escaped the first Jewish and Christian hearers or readers

[86] See David Stern, "The First Jewish Books and the Early History of Jewish Reading," *The Jewish Quarterly Review* 98 (2008), pp. 163–202, esp. p. 198.

[87] Here is not the place to discuss this very important topic. See Daniel Lasker, "Rabbinism and Karaism: The Contest for Supremacy," in R. Jospe and S.M. Wagner (eds.), *Great Schisms in Jewish History* (New York: Ktav Publishing House, 1981), pp. 47–72; Meira Polliack, "Rethinking Karaism: Between Judaism and Islam," *AJS Review* 30 (2006), pp. 67–93.

[88] For the details and further bibliography, see Griffith, *The Church in the Shadow of the Mosque*, pp. 53–57.

of the Qur'ān that the Islamic scripture has a biblical subtext and that its presentation of biblical lore and its 'take' on the stories of the patriarchs and prophets offer a reading of the biblical narratives notably at variance with that which was common within either of their communities. One might imagine that it did not take the Arabic-speaking Jews and Christians long to take exception to the Qur'ān's prophetology and to its interpretation of many aspects of the Bible stories, especially in those passages that implied a correction or objection to Jewish or Christian beliefs and teachings. These matters undoubtedly came up in interreligious conversations and controversies. Why else would one find among the stipulations already included in the early recensions of the so-called 'Covenant of 'Umar' such a provision as 'We shall not teach the Qur'ān to our children'?[89] It follows that one inducement for Jews and Christians to translate the Bible into Arabic already in early Islamic times may well have been the concern to, as it were, set the biblical record straight in Arabic. On this view, the Qur'ān itself provided Jews and Christians with an impetus to translate the Bible into Arabic.

It seems evident already from a perusal of the early translations that the Arabic Bible played a different role in the Jewish and Christian communities respectively. The earliest Christian translations obviously had a liturgical function as well as a role in theology and controversy; the earliest Jewish translations seem to have been made more for study, for discussion and controversy rather than for liturgical proclamation. In the following chapters, we shall discuss in more detail some of the important aspects of the translations of the Bible into Arabic among Jews, Christians, and Muslims alike.

[89] See A. S. Tritton, *The Caliphs and their Non-Muslim Subjects: A Critical Study of the Covenant of 'Umar* (London: Frank Cass, 1930/1970), p. 8. See also Mark R. Cohen, "What Was the Pact of 'Umar? A Literary-Historical Study," *Jerusalem Studies in Arabic and Islam* 23 (1999), pp. 100–157.

✻ CHAPTER IV ✻

Christian Translations of the Bible into Arabic

As we have seen, all the evidence points to the late seventh century and, with a greater degree of certainty, to the eighth century for the origin of Bible translations into Arabic done under Christian auspices. It was, however, the ninth century that counts as the heyday of the Christian translation movement more generally. Translations were now produced not only of biblical texts, but of all sorts of ecclesiastical literature, not excluding philosophical and logical works. Moreover, the ecclesiastical translation movement was not confined to the monasteries of the Judean desert where it seems to have begun already in the eighth century.[1] By the beginning of the ninth century, the schools and monasteries of the largely Syriac-speaking communities of northern Syria and Mesopotamia and their associated scholars had already taken up their role in the now famous Graeco-Arabic translation movement on-going in Baghdad in early Abbasid times.[2] Modern historians of the movement have usually concentrated only on the translation into Arabic of Greek philosophical, medical, scientific, and mathematical texts, to the exclusion of biblical or other ecclesiastical works, but translations of the Bible into Arabic were nevertheless done within the same time frame and sometimes even by the same translators. Biblical translations into Arabic were produced under the auspices of all the main Christian churches in the Islamic world, the Melkites, the Jacobites, the Copts, and the Nestorians. And to a greater or lesser extent in each community, translations were made principally from originally Greek, Aramaic/Syriac, and, later, Coptic originals; in Syria/Palestine, including the Judean desert, and in Mesopotamia, Aramaic/Syriac was a common idiom in all three communities. What

[1] See Sidney H. Griffith, "The Monks of Palestine and the Growth of Christian Literature in Arabic," *The Muslim World* 78 (1988), pp. 1–28.

[2] See the now standard study by Dimitri Gutas, *Greek Thought, Arabic Culture: The Graeco-Arabic Translation Movement in Baghdad and Early 'Abbasid Society (2nd–4th/8th–10th Centuries)* (London: Routledge, 1998). See also Adam H. Becker, *Fear of God and the Beginning of Wisdom: The School of Nisibis and Christian Scholastic Culture in Late Antique Mesopotamia* (Philadelphia: University of Pennsylvania Press, 2006).

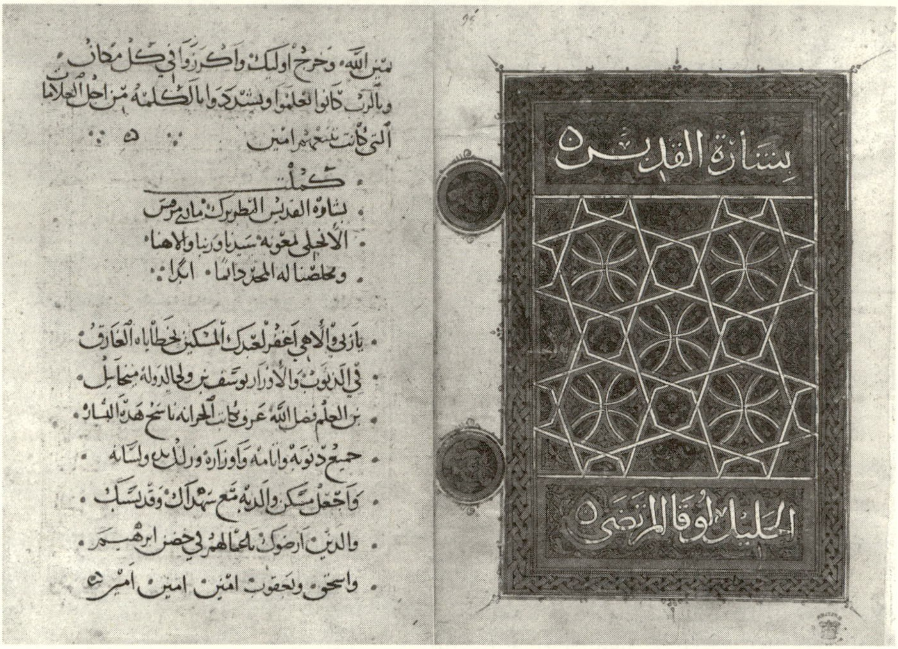

Fig. 1. Four Gospels in Arabic, Palestine, 1337, Gospel of Luke.
Left: © The British Library Board. All rights reserved. Add. 11856, f.94v 202.
Right: © The British Library Board. All rights reserved. Add. 11856, f.95 205.

is more, as we shall see, Arabic translations done by members of one community often found their way into the life of another of the churches, in spite of their confessional estrangements in the area of Christology.

In the present chapter, we shall review some of the features of the numerous Bible translations into Arabic done by Christians in the period from the ninth century to the beginning of the sixteenth century. We make no effort to list and describe all or even most of the Christian translations. Rather, our concern is two-fold. First, we will call attention to a number of notable features of the translations, highlighting the circumstances in which they were accomplished, the distinctive characteristics one finds in them, and the uses to which they were put. In addition, we will consider the usefulness of these translations to modern scholars who wish to gain better insight into the fortunes of a number of para-biblical, apocryphal, and even pseudepigraphical texts that often circulated alongside the canonical scriptures in Eastern Christian communities.

Translations of the whole Bible into Arabic in one perhaps multivolume work seem not to have been undertaken under Christian auspices until the sixteenth century. Perhaps this state of affairs is best explained by the fact that in the life of the churches in the Arabic-speaking world, as elsewhere in the early centuries, people most often encountered the Bible in their everyday languages as it was proclaimed in the liturgy, following the reading of the day's scriptural pericopes in the traditional liturgical language, be it Greek, Syriac, or Coptic.[3] For this purpose, as well as for study, Arabic translations of the scriptures done by Christians before the 1500's consisted almost entirely of translations of individual books or of compilations of related books, such as the books of the Torah, the Psalms, the Gospels, the Epistles of St. Paul, or the Acts of the Apostles, along with the so-called 'Catholic Epistles'.[4] To judge by the number of surviving manuscripts containing these translations, the Pentateuch,[5] the Psalms, and the Gospels were the most popular, but translations were also made of less popular books, as we shall see. Some of the translations, as noted in the previous chapter, were continually copied and corrected over a very long period of time. Some, especially among the Gospels, have transmission histories reaching from the ninth or tenth centuries all the way into modern times.[6] Similarly, a number of surviving early manuscripts containing an Arabic translation of the Pentateuch from the Syriac Peshitta can be traced back to a common source; the several recensions offering corrections and improvements to the common text in the course of their transmission. Richard

[3] This practice is reported as early as the fourth century. See, e.g., the remarks of Egeria, the fourth-century Spanish pilgrim to the Holy Places, on the liturgy in the Holy Sepulchre in John Wilkinson (trans.), *Egeria's Travels to the Holy Land: Newly Translated, with Supporting Documents and Notes* (rev. ed.; Warminster, UK: Aris and Phillips,1981), p. 146.

[4] See the extensive catalog of texts, including apocrypha and pseudepigrapha, in Georg Graf, *Geschichte der christlichen arabischen Literatur* (5 vols.; Studi e Testi, 118, 133, 146, 147, 172; Città del Vaticano: Biblioteca Apostolica Vaticana, 1944–1953, vol. 1, pp. 85–297. See also Michel van Esbroeck, "Les versions orientales de la Bible: Une orientation bibliographique," in Margaret Davis et al. (eds.), *Interpretation of the Bible* (Ljubljana: Slovenska Academija Znanosti in Umetnosti; Sheffield, UK: Sheffield Academic Press, 1998), pp. 399–415.

[5] One scholar has made a list of about 150 Arabic translations of the Torah alone, done under Christian auspices prior to the thirteenth century. See Ronny Vollandt in a message posted on the list–serve of the North American Society for Christian Arabic Studies, March 8, 2010: nascas@googlegroups.com.

[6] See, e.g., Hikmat Kachouh, "The Arabic Gospel Text of Codex Beirut, Bibliothèque Orientale, 430: Is It Recent or Archaic?" *Parole de l'Orient* 32 (2007), pp. 105–121.

Steiner has recently even proposed that the common source for one family of these Pentateuch translations, surviving now in Sinai Arabic MSS 2 and 4, and copied in the tenth century, was itself originally translated by none other than the famed Baghdadī translator of Greek and Syriac logical and medical texts into Arabic, Ḥunayn ibn Isḥāq. As we noted earlier, the Muslim historian al-Mas'ūdī had credited Ḥunayn with translating the whole Bible from the Greek Septuagint, mistakenly according to Steiner, who has shown that the translation was in fact made from the Syriac Peshitta version of the Pentateuch, originally done under Jewish auspices in Edessa in the mid-second century CE.[7] This is the version that would have been the most familiar to Ḥunayn as it was the standard translation in use in his Nestorian community.

While earlier scholars have surveyed Arabic translations of the Pentateuch,[8] it has not been until very recently, in Ronny Vollandt's Cambridge dissertation, that a systematic study of Christian-Arabic translations of the Pentateuch has been undertaken, this within the context of a wide-ranging and bibliographically rich survey of previous scholarly work on the whole phenomenon of Arabic Bible translations.[9] One might mention at the outset that Vollandt has shown that while the Melkite and Nestorian Christian communities possessed what he calls "preferred, quasi-canonical versions of the Pentateuch,"[10] done under community auspices from the Septuagint and Peshitta versions respectively, the Jacobite and Coptic communities were more inclined to adopt and adapt translations made by translators from other communities, including, as we shall see in the next chapter, the widely appreciated Arabic translation of the Torah made in the tenth century by the Jewish scholar, Sa'adyah Ga'ōn (882–942). Vollandt reasonably suggests that this more eclectic approach was due to the relatively

[7] See Richard C. Steiner, *A Biblical Translation in the Making: The Evolution and Impact of Saadia Gaon's* Tafsīr (Cambridge, MA: Harvard University Center for Jewish Studies/Harvard University Press, 2010), pp. 52–68. See also Michael Weitzmann, *The Syriac Version of the Old Testament: An Introduction* (University of Cambridge Oriental Publications, vol. 56; Cambridge: Cambridge University Press, 1990).

[8] See Joseph Francis Rhode, *The Arabic Versions of the Pentateuch in the Church of Egypt* (Washington, DC: The Catholic University of America, 1921); Graf, *Geschichte der christlichen arabischen Literatur*, vol. 1, pp. 101–108).

[9] See Ronny Vollandt, "Christian-Arabic Translations of the Pentateuch from the 9th to the 13th Centuries: A Comparative Study of Manuscripts and Translation Techniques," (PhD Thesis; Cambridge: St. John's College, University of Cambridge, 2011).

[10] Vollandt, "Christian-Arabic Translations of the Pentateuch," p. 102.

slower pace of the adoption of Arabic as an ecclesiastical language among the Jacobites and 'Copts'.[11] Similarly, Juan Pedro Monferrer-Sala has found evidence for the use of a Nestorian Arabic Pentateuch among the Arabic-speaking Christians of al-Andalus,[12] noting that with the exception of the Arabic translation of the Psalms by one Ḥafṣ ibn Albar al-Qūṭī,[13] little is known of the translation of the scriptures into Arabic in the Islamic West.

Apparently, the earliest datable Christian-Arabic translation of the Pentateuch is one done under Nestorian auspices in the latter decades of the ninth century. It is preserved in a family of three surviving manuscripts copied variously at later times, the earliest one of which carries the date 939/40 CE, making it, in Ronny Vollandt's words, "the first dated manuscript copy of an Arabic Pentateuch of any provenance."[14] Vollandt convincingly argues that the translation was first made in the second half of the ninth century at the latest, based on the fact that quotations from the Pentateuch found quoted in the works of a Muslim scholar who died in the year 889 (i.e., Abū Muḥammad ibn Qutaybah [828-889]), can be traced to this Arabic version. Furthermore, on the basis of his close and extensive study of this version of the Pentateuch, Vollandt draws attention to its high literary quality and classical Arabic style. With reference to the original translator, he says that his work "suggests that he was a trained professional."[15] This conclusion puts one in mind of Richard Steiner's suggestion, cited above, proposing Ḥunayn ibn Isḥāq (808–873) as the translator, precisely in reference to the earliest manuscript in the family.

Ronny Vollandt's study includes an inventory of all the manuscripts he could find containing Christian-Arabic translations of the Pentateuch; he includes in it as complete a description of the texts as accessibility to the manuscripts or published accounts would allow, including bibliographical references to earlier studies. An interesting observation emerged from this exercise, namely the fact that in a given manuscript, the Arabic translation of every book of the Pentateuch did not always derive from the same

[11] See Vollandt, "Christian-Arabic Translations of the Pentateuch," pp. 101–103.

[12] See Juan Pedro Monferrer-Sala, "A Nestorian Arabic Pentateuch Used in Western Islamic Lands," in Thomas, *The Bible in Arab Christianity*, pp. 351–368.

[13] See Marie-Thérèse Urvoy, *Le Psautier mozarabe de Hafs le Goth* (Toulouse: Presses Universitaires du Mirail, 1994).

[14] Vollandt, "Christian-Arabic Translations of the Pentateuch," p. 104.

[15] Vollandt, "Christian-Arabic Translations of the Pentateuch," pp. 179–180. See also R. Köbert, "Die älteste arabische Genesis-Übersetzung," in Franz Altheim and Ruth Stiehl (eds.), *Die Araber in der alten Welt* (5 vols. in 6; Berlin: Walter De Gruyter, 1965), vol. 2, pp. 333–343.

source. Vollandt put it this way: "Not a few codices merge texts from varying provenances."[16] This textual eclecticism suggests that scribes were more concerned with practical matters, such as the suitability of a given text for liturgical proclamation, or its faithfulness in rendering the original for study purposes, than they were interested in textual consistency.

The Circumstances of Translation and Transmission

The liturgy's need for translations of the scriptures into Arabic seems to have been among the most important of the factors prompting the initial production and then the continuous copying of the earliest versions of the Gospels in Arabic. Unfortunately for scholarship, most recent studies of Arabic Gospel manuscripts ignore this circumstance and in their descriptions of the texts systematically leave out any attention to liturgical markings or exegetical remarks contained in rubrics or marginal glosses. They are interested only in the scriptural text and are willing to jettison all of the other information that many biblical manuscripts do contain, this to the detriment of our understanding of the translating, copying, and transmission of the scriptures in Arabic.

This neglect continues even with the study of the family of manuscripts that contains the arguably earliest Arabic translation of the Gospels from Greek, a work mentioned in the previous chapter. While Sinai Arabic MSS 72 and 74, along with Vatican Borgia MS 95, and Berlin Orient. Oct. MS 1108, present the four Gospels in a continuous text and not in a lectionary format, the text is nevertheless marked off with liturgical rubrics assigning pericopes to the appropriate days in the temporal cycle of the old Jerusalem liturgy.[17] This information is important both for the insight it affords the historian into the use to which the translations were put and for the study of the history of the liturgy. As Georg Graf pointed out, some readings included in the translation reflect expressions unique to the so-called 'Palestinian Syriac' version of the Gospels, which also rests on a Greek *Vorlage*.[18] Consider, for example, the addition to Mt. 6:34 found only in this family of Arabic Gospel manuscripts and the 'Palestinian Syriac' version: "Let the

[16] Vollandt, "Christian-Arabic Translations of the Pentateuch," p. 181.

[17] This was precisely the circumstance that prompted Anton Baumstark to date this Arabic translation of the Gospels to pre-Islamic times. See Anton Baumstark, "Das Problem eines vorislamischen christlich-kirchlichen Schrifttums in arabischer Sprache," *Islamica* 4 (1929–1931), pp. 562–575; *idem*, "Die sonntägliche Evangelienlesung im vor-byzantinischen Jerusalem," *Byzantinische Zeitschrift* 30 (1929–1930), pp. 350–359.

[18] See Graf, *Geschichte der christlichen arabischen Literatur*, vol. 1, p. 146.

day's own trouble be sufficient for the day, and the hour's difficulties for the hour." The last phrase is an *agraphon* not found in any surviving Greek Gospel manuscript.[19] This coincidence of readings points to a concern on the Arabic translators' part for textual continuity in readings destined for the liturgy, consistent with the earlier translation of the same text from a Greek *Vorlage* into what is now called Christian Palestinian Aramaic, the local language in the Jerusalem patriarchate that Arabic gradually replaced.

Another historically interesting feature in the Jerusalem family of Gospel manuscripts in Arabic, which scholars narrowly focused only on the scripture text ignore, is the bit of traditional lore about each evangelist and his text that the translator included in notes at the end of each Gospel. For example, at the end of the Gospel according to Mark one finds the following note: "The holy gospel is finished. Mark, the disciple of Peter, spoke 'Roman' (*ar-rūmiyyah*) in the city of Rome. The holy church reads from Mark from the feast of the Cross to the Birth."[20] While there is no such note at the end of Matthew in Sinai Arabic MS 72, at the end of Luke, the copyist noted that Luke spoke Greek in Alexandria,[21] and at the end of John he remarked that the evangelist wrote the Gospel in Ephesus of the Romans (*ar-Rūm*) and that he preached it in Greek (*al-yūnāniyyah*).[22] Such details, while they are of no use to the scholar interested only in the textual criticism of the Gospel, do shed considerable light on the interests of the translators and their times. Other manuscripts contain similar information.

Sinai Arabic MS 151 contains the oldest portion of the Bible in Arabic so far published in a modern edition; namely, the fourteen Epistles attributed to St. Paul (with some marginal commentaries); as well as the Acts of the Apostles, and the Catholic Epistles.[23] A colophon at the end of the text of

[19] The addition appears in Sinai Arabic MSS 72 and 74, Vatican Borgia Arabic MS 95, and Berlin Orient. Oct. 1108, all family members featuring the same basic translation. See Agnes Smith Lewis and Margaret Dunlop Gibson, *The Palestinian Syriac Lectionary of the Gospels, Re-Edited from Two Sinai MSS. and from P. de Lagarde's Edition of the 'Evangeliarium Hierosolymitanum'* (London: K. Paul, Trench, Trübner and Co., 1899), p. 71. See also Bruce M. Metzger, "A Comparison of the Palestinian Syriac Lectionary and the Greek Gospel Lectionary," in E. Earle Ellis and Max Wilcox (eds.), *Neotestamentica et Semitica: Studies in Honour of Matthew Black* (Edinburgh: T and T Clark, 1969), pp. 209–220.

[20] Sinai Arabic MS 72, f. 57v.

[21] See Sinai Arabic MS 72, f.91v.

[22] See Sinai Arabic MS 72, f.116v.

[23] See Harvey Staal, *Mt. Sinai Arabic Codex 151: I Pauline Epistles* (CSCO, vols. 452 and 453; Lovanii: In Aedibus E. Peeters, 1983). Photographs of two pages and a description of this Sinai MS are also available in Michelle P. Brown, *In the Beginning: Bibles before the Year 1000* (Washington, DC: Smithsonian Institution, 2006), pp. 158–161 and 272. See

the Pauline Epistles gives the year 867 CE for the completion of the copying. A closer consideration of this colophon is useful for the information it gives about the social circumstances of early Bible translations into Arabic in general. It reads:

> The poor sinner, Bishr ibn as-Sirrī, translated these fourteen Epistles from Syriac into Arabic, and provided an explanation of their interpretation, as much as his inadequate abridgement would allow, for his spiritual brother Sulaymān. He finished it in the city of Damascus in the month of Ramaḍān in the year two hundred and fifty-three. Praise be to God the Father, and the Son, and the Holy Spirit, forever and ever, Amen. May God have mercy on anyone who prays for mercy and forgiveness for the author, translator, and possessor [of this book].[24]

First of all, it is notable that a Christian copyist working in Damascus in the middle of the ninth Christian century is already dating his text, a text obviously intended for Christian readers, according to the Islamic calendar, with no corresponding Christian dating. This usage bespeaks an already high degree of enculturation into the prevailing, public conventions of the World of Islam on the part of Arabic-speaking Christians in this milieu. Secondly, the translation was made from Syriac, indicating that the Melkite translator and scribe, Bishr ibn as-Sirrī, was himself a Syriac-speaker, who belonged to an ecclesial community with an originally Syriac patristic and liturgical heritage, albeit that he was a congregant in an Arabic-speaking church, which professed the orthodoxy of the Greek-speaking Byzantine church of the Roman Empire.[25] Thirdly, the colophon refers to abbreviated exegetical material, which Bishr ibn as-Sirrī himself included with the translation of the Pauline Epistles in the form of interlinear and marginal notes; one can still read them in the manuscript, even though they are not

---

also Paul Féghali, "Les Épîtres de Saint Paul dans une des premières Traductions en Arabe," *Parole de l'Orient* 30 (2005), pp. 103–130.

[24] Staal, *Mt. Sinai Arabic Codex 151*, vol. 452, p. 248, n. 23 (Arabic text); vol. 453, p. 260, n. 23 (English translation). The English version quoted in the present text is by the author.

[25] On Bishr ibn Sirrī, see the remarks of Joseph Nasrallah, "Deux versions Melchites partielles de la Bible du IXe et du Xe siècles," *Oriens Christianus* 64 (1980), pp. 202–215, esp. 203–206. See also Khalil Samir, "Michel, évêque melkite de Damas au 9e siècle: a propos de Bišr ibn al-Sirrī," *Orientalia Christiana Periodica* 53 (1987), pp. 439–441.

included in the modern, published edition of the text.[26] It is interesting to note in this connection that a number of these annotations concern differences between the texts of the Epistles as they were transmitted in Greek and Syriac, along with points of confessional significance to the on-going controversies between Melkites, Jacobites, and Nestorians.

Beyond the testimony of the colophon following the Pauline Epistles, Sinai Arabic MS 151 provides even further information about the transmission of Arabic translations of biblical texts made by Christians in early Islamic times. At various junctures and by different hands, further exegetical and commentary material was added in the margins of the text and between the lines. One such annotator, who even left his own colophon, dated to the year 1030 CE and signed Jirjis ibn Yuḥanna ibn Sahl, also inserted Melkite liturgical annotations.[27] Taken in the ensemble, these added remarks indicate that the manuscript had an active life in the church; it was intended to serve both homiletic, even catechetical, as well as liturgical purposes. Since these features are readily observable even in the several published photographs of pages from Sinai Arabic MS 151, the manuscript may serve as a more or less accessible exemplar for the numerous other, unpublished manuscripts of Christian translations of portions of the Bible into Arabic in early Islamic times, many of which have similar features. Taken together, these numerous texts enable us to surmise that translations of portions of the Bible were first made in the several Arabic-speaking Christian communities in the territories occupied by the conquering Muslims after the mid-eighth century, and that their primary purpose was to serve the liturgical needs of the churches. This may help explain the large variety of the Arabic versions of portions of the Bible. For example, Ronny Vollandt has made a list of about one hundred and fifty Arabic translations of the Pentateuch/Torah alone, done under Christian auspices prior to the thirteenth century.[28]

Seldom do the published descriptions of the manuscripts or of their colophons furnish us with the names of the translators of the biblical books or

[26] See Sebastian Brock, "A Neglected Witness to the East Syriac New Testament Commentary Tradition: Sinai Arabic MS 151," in Rifaat Ebied and Herman Teule (eds.), *Studies on the Christian Arabic Heritage* (Eastern Christian Studies, 5; Leuven: Peeters, 2004), pp. 205–215.

[27] On this name and the proper identity of the annotator, see J. Nasrallah, "Abū l-Farağ al-Yabrūdī: médecin chrétien de Damas (Xe–XIe s.)," *Arabica* 23 (1976), pp. 13–22.

[28] Ronny Vollandt in a message posted on the list-serve of the North American Society for Christian Arabic Studies, March 8, 2010, nascas@googlegroups.com.

the dates of their work; Sinai Arabic MS 151 is one of the rare exceptions. But occasionally other bits of information can be extracted from the often meager reports, allowing the scholar to identify some of the professional translators. For example, we learn from the manuscripts that sometime in the tenth century, the presumably Jacobite scholar from Ḥarrān, al-Ḥarith ibn Sinān ibn Sinbāṭ,[29] is said to have translated the Torah into Arabic from the Syro-Hexapla, Paul of Tella's (d.617) Syriac version of the Septuagint text in Origen's Hexapla, and that in the introduction to the translation, al-Ḥarith discussed the several Greek translations, along with their variants, and the peculiarities of the Hebrew textual tradition.[30] In another source this same scholar is named as the translator of the books of Solomon, and there he is explicitly called, *al-Ḥarrānī,* a tidbit of information that allows the modern scholar to know al-Ḥarith's hometown.[31]

At least one popular Muslim writer of the ninth century took notice of the new Arabic translations of the Bible. In his essay in refutation of the Christians, Abū ʿUthmān al-Jāḥiẓ (d.868/9) complained of the lack of knowledge of the Arabic language on the part of the translators, be they Jews or Christians, and of their bad translations. He remarked, "If, along with their fluency in Hebrew, they had the knowledge of the Muslims and their understanding of what is possible in the language of the Arabs, and of what it is possible [to say] about God, they would have found for that language a good interpretation, an easy expression, and an accessible presentation."[32]

A Muslim Cast to the Language

Speaking of the language of the Arabs, a very noticeable feature of early Christian translations of the Bible into Arabic is what one scholar has called the 'Muslim cast' to the language. By this he meant the recurrence of Qurʾānic diction and obvious Islamic phraseology in the translations. Richard M. Frank first called attention to this phenomenon in his study

[29] Interestingly, the Syrian Orthodox Patriarch, Ignatius Aphram I Barsoum, on the authority of the Muslim al-Masʿūdī, identifies al-Ḥarith as a Melkite. See Ignatius Aphram Barsoum, *History of Syriac Literature and Sciences* (ed. and trans., Matti Moosa; Pueblo, CO: Passeggiata Press, 2000), pp. 19 and 121. See also Vollandt, *Christian-Arabic Translations of the Pentateuch,* p. 32.

[30] See Graf, *Geschichte,* vol. 1, p. 107.

[31] See Shams ar-Riʾāsah Abū l-Barakāt, Ibn Kabar, *Misbāḥ aẓ-Ẓulmah fī Īḍāḥ al-Khidmah* (2 vols.; Cairo: Maktabat al-Karūz, 1971), vol. 1, p. 236.

[32] Joshua Finkel (ed. and trans.), *Three Essays of Abu ʿOthman ʿAmr ibn Baḥr al-Jaḥiẓ* (Cairo: The Salafyah Press, 1926), p. 28.

of the translations of portions of the Bible from Syriac into Arabic by the Nestorian Pethion ibn Ayyūb as-Sahhār, who flourished in Baghdad in the mid-ninth century.[33] The famed Muslim bio-bibliographer of the tenth century, Muḥammad ibn Isḥāq ibn an-Nadīm (d.905), said in his *Fihrist* that of all the Christian scholars of his day, Pethion "was the most accurate of the translators from the point of view of translation, also the best of them for style and diction."[34] However true this might have been, Pethion is on record as having translated the biblical books of Job, the Wisdom of Ben Sirach, and the Prophets, all from Syriac into Arabic.[35] Richard Frank edited and translated a portion of Pethion's version of Jeremiah and his version of a Palestinian recension of Ben Sirach into English,[36] and it was in the course of these undertakings that he remarked on the 'Muslim cast' of the language. He observed this phenomenon not only in Pethion's translations, but also in those by other early translators, and he called attention to what must have been the translators' dilemma in the matter of language:

> To render the Peshitta literally into Arabic or simply to Arabize the Syriac . . . would be to produce a rather barbarous Arabic in which the religious tone of the text would be altogether lacking, since the words would have no associations and overtones within themselves but only as seen through another language (Hebrew or Syriac). The book would thus be colorless and devoid of the solemnity which belongs to it.[37]

The translators solved this dilemma by consistently using Arabic terms with a noticeable 'Muslim cast'. That is to say, they consistently used terms which, though not perhaps exclusively Islamic or Qur'ānic, are nevertheless thoroughly Muslim in their resonance, being in fact often stock phrases or oft-repeated invocations from the Qur'ān that soon became common wherever Arabic was spoken. This process inevitably imparted a certain Islamic or Qur'ānic ring to biblical diction in the Arabic translations.

[33] On Pethion see Graf, *Geschichte*, vol. 2, pp. 120–121.

[34] Bayard Dodge (ed. and trans.), *The Fihrist of al-Nadīm: A Tenth Century Survey of Muslim Culture* (2 vols.; New York: Columbia University Press, 1970), vol. 1, p. 46.

[35] Graf, *Geschichte* vol. 2, pp. 120–121.

[36] Richard M. Frank, "The Jeremias of Pethion ibn Ayyūb al-Sahhār," *The Catholic Biblical Quarterly* 21 (1959), pp. 136–170; *idem*, (ed. and trans.), *The Wisdom of Jesus Ben Sirach (Sinai ar. 155, IXth/Xth cent.)* (CSCO, vols. 357 and 358; Louvain: Secrétariat du Corpus SCO, 1974).

[37] Frank, "The Jeremias of Pethion," pp. 139–140.

Middle Arabic

In common with the broader range of texts written in Arabic by Jews and Christians in the early Islamic period, the biblical translations, whether they were made from Hebrew, Greek, Syriac, or Coptic *Vorlagen*, display a range of grammatical and syntactical features and usages that in the ensemble, and in virtue of their consistency and constancy, can be seen to be important elements in the development of Middle Arabic. Broadly speaking, it is a state of the Arabic language that linguists see emerging into view in the Judaeo-Arabic and the so-called 'Christian Arabic' texts of the ninth and tenth centuries. Some of these distinctive elements of Middle Arabic seem to have owed their origins to linguistic features of the Hebrew, Greek, or, especially, the Aramaic and Syriac dialects originally spoken by the newly Arabic-speaking Muslim and non-Muslim populations of the Levant in early Islamic times.[38] The recognition of these Middle Arabic elements in the Jewish and Christian translations of books of the Bible in the early Islamic period has enhanced the scholarly importance of these translations as sources for the study of Middle Arabic and as documentation for the study of the textual transmission of books of the Bible more generally in Arabic translation. For this reason, as we shall see in the works cited below, most recent publications of the Arabic versions of biblical books have included studies of the state of the Arabic language they display.

Arabic Versions and the Biblical Text

While the early Arabic translations of books of the Bible, often themselves translations of translations, are not always of immediate significance for the study of the text of the scriptures in their original languages, they are nevertheless valuable for the evidence they can provide about the state of the biblical text in the earlier translations from which the Arabic versions were made. So, for example, the Arabic versions of biblical books made from Syriac *Vorlagen* can inform the study of the textual history of the Peshitta. What is more, these same Arabic versions are also valuable sources for the study of the history of biblical interpretation, especially in the context of

[38] See especially Joshua Blau, *The Emergence and Linguistic Background of Judaeo-Arabic: A Study of the Origins of Middle Arabic* (London: Oxford University Press, 1965); Joshua Blau, *A Grammar of Christian Arabic, Based Mainly on South-Palestinian Texts from the First Millennium* (CSCO vols. 267, 276, 279; Louvain: Secrétariat du Corpus SCO, 1966–1967).

the religious challenge of Islam. They often include numerous glosses, marginal comments, longer commentaries, and even prologues to the biblical books, which are a rich source of evidence for how the texts were read and understood by Christians living in the Islamic milieu.

In the instance of some apocryphal or pseudepigraphical biblical books, hitherto known only from a single Syriac source or from scattered fragments in Greek and/or Syriac, early Arabic versions have sometimes provided scholars with a further access to their contents. A case in point is provided by Sinai Arabic MS 389, preserved today in the library of the monastery of St. Catherine at Mount Sinai, a text that may well date from as early as the ninth century.[39] It contains three Arabic translations, made from Syriac *Vorlagen*, of three pseudepigraphic scriptural texts: the Apocalypse of Baruch, the accompanying Epistle of Baruch, and IV Ezra.[40] The story of the scholarly editions and studies of these texts provides a telling glimpse into the history of the vicissitudes surrounding the translation and transmission of biblical texts in the early Islamic Arabic-speaking milieu, as well as insight into the travails of modern textual historians.

The *Apocalypse of Baruch* was the first text from Sinai Arabic MS 589 to be published and compared with the previously known Syriac version of the work.[41] There are a number of places in the text where the Arabic translator treated the Syriac *Vorlage* somewhat loosely. Sometimes he even failed to understand it correctly, and more than once he seemingly misunderstood or altogether missed allusions to other biblical passages in the work from the Old and New Testaments. The editors of the text note that at the same time the Arabic translator's knowledge of the Qur'ān and of Islamic Arabic usage is more than adequate; quotations from Islamic scripture and typically Islamic turns of phrase appear here and there in the translation. This state of affairs prompted Fred Leemhuis to advance the hypothesis that the Arabic translator of the *Apocalypse of Baruch* was in fact a Muslim, whose version of this pseudepigraphic scripture was subsequently bound together in Sinai Arabic MS 589 with another translation, by another translator, of

[39] See Adrianna Drint, *The Mount Sinai Arabic Version of IV Ezra* (CSCO, vols. 563 and 564; Lovanii: Peeters, 1997), vol. 563, pp. vi–vii.

[40] See the contents described in Drint, *The Mount Sinai Arabic Version*, vol. 563, p. vii.

[41] See F. Leemhuis, A. F. Klijn, and G.J.H. van Gelder (eds. and trans.), *The Arabic Text of the Apocalypse of Baruch: Edited and Translated with a Parallel Translation of the Syriac Text* (Leiden: E.J. Brill, 1986). See also Fred Leemhuis, "The Mount Sinai Arabic Version of the Apocalypse of Baruch," in Khalil Samir (ed.), *Actes du deuxième congrès d'études arabes chrétiennes (Oosterhesselen, Septembre 1984)* (Orientalia Christiana Analecta, 226; Roma: Pont. Institutum Studiorum Orientalium, 1986), pp. 73–79.

another such book, viz., *IV Ezra.* Leemhuis even offers suggestions regarding which Muslim community in the ninth or tenth century might have had an interest in such a scripture.[42]

While some Muslims are indeed reported to have translated biblical texts into Arabic, and other early Muslim scholars show remarkable familiarity with Christian sources in Syriac, Leemhuis' hypothesis is not the only plausible construction one might put on the evidence he found in the Arabic translation of *Apocalypse of Baruch.* First, it is a not uncommon feature of biblical texts in Arabic translation that they manifest a certain 'Muslim cast' of language in their Arabic diction, as mentioned above. Then, there is also the often-noted historical complaint on the part of some Christian writers in Islamic times that as Christians became more fluent in Arabic, they lost their earlier command of the traditional languages of their communities, and with it the ready recall of biblical phrases and even traditional theological formulae. One may therefore also plausibly surmise that the Arabic translator of the *Apocalypse of Baruch* was not a Muslim, but a successfully acculturated and assimilated Arab Christian, whose skills in the traditional language and lore of his church had gone rusty.

Adriana Drint has now published the Arabic text of the translation of *IV Ezra* from Syriac, as it is found in Sinai Arabic MS 589, along with an annotated English translation.[43] Her studies show that the translator was not the same person who translated the *Apocalypse of Baruch.* Rather, the translator of *IV Ezra* remained fairly faithful to the Syriac *Vorlage,* which he gives every indication of having understood reasonably well. What is more, the text of *IV Ezra* is presented in its Arabic translation in Sinai Arabic MS 589, with a descriptive introduction and with interpolated subtitles indicating the subject matter of the successive portions of the text. In the process, these editorial additions show how the text was read in the Arab Christian community in which it was used, shedding light on the Christological interpretation it received.[44] These features are common in other Arabic translations of apocryphal or pseudepigraphical works, and they illustrate the importance of the Arabic versions for the preservation of such texts. Another case in point is the so-called *Apocalypse of Peter,* edited long ago by Alphonse Mingana.[45] A

[42] See Fred Leemhuis, "The Arabic Version of the Apocalypse of Baruch: A Christian Text?" *Journal for the Study of the Pseudepigraphica* 4 (1989), pp. 19–26.

[43] See Drint, *The Mount Sinai Arabic Version of IV Ezra.*

[44] See Drint, *The Mount Sinai Arabic Version of IV Ezra,* vol. 564, pp. xvii–xxxii.

[45] A. Mingana, *Woodbrooke Studies: Christian Documents in Syriac, Arabic and Garshuni* (vol. 2; Cambridge: W. Heffer and Sons, 1931, pp. 70ff.

recent study underlines the importance of such a work for Arabic-speaking Christians living in the Islamic milieu.[46]

The Diatessaron

A special case in which the surviving Arabic translation of a biblical work is crucial for the recovery of the original text is the Arabic Gospel Harmony that purports to be an Arabic version of the *Diatessaron* attributed to the Mesopotamian Tatian (*fl*150–175 CE), a work that many modern scholars think was originally composed in Syriac.[47] It circulated widely in Syriac-speaking Christian communities, and it may well have been the best known form of the Gospel among the Arabic-speaking Christians in the Qur'ān's milieu, whose patristic and liturgical heritage was largely Syriac. It was these Christians who were in all likelihood the immediate source of biblical lore for Muḥammad and the Qur'ān.[48] It is clear that the Arabic Gospel Harmony, which has survived in a number of manuscripts from a fairly early period, was translated from a Syriac *Vorlage*,[49] albeit that many of its readings had already been brought into agreement with the Peshitta prior to its translation into Arabic.[50] The current scholarly consensus is that the original Arabic translation was done by the famous Baghdadī Christian polymath, Abū l-Faraj ʿAbd Allāh ibn aṭ-Ṭayyib (d.1043) on the basis of a

[46] See Emmanouela Grypeou, "The Re-Written Bible in Arabic: The Paradise Story and its Exegesis in the Arabic *Apocalypse of Peter*," in David Thomas (ed.), *The Bible in Arab Christianity* (The History of Christian-Muslim Relations, vol. 6; Leiden: Brill, 2007), pp. 113–129.

[47] See William L. Peterson, *Tatian's Diatessaron: Its Creation, Dissemination, Significance and History in Scholarship* (Supplements to *Vigiliae Christianae*, vol. 25; Leiden: E.J. Brill, 1994), esp. p. 397.

[48] See John Bowman, "The Debt of Islam to Monophysite Syrian Christianity," in E.C.B. MacLaurin (ed.), *Essays in Honour of Griffithes Wheeler Thatcher 1863–1950* (Sydney: Sydney University Press, 1967), pp. 191–216; Jan M. F. Van Reeth, "L'Évangile du Prophète," in D. De Smet et al. (eds.), *Al-Kitāb: La Sacralité du texte dans le monde de l'Islam* (Acta Orientalia Belgica, Subsidia III; Bruxelles, Louvain-la-Neuve, Leuven: Société Belge d'Études Orientales, 2004), pp. 155–174.

[49] There are so far only two editions of the whole text: A. Ciasca, *Tatiani Evangeliorum Harmoniae Arabice nunc primum ex duplici codice edidit et translatione Latina donavit p. Augustinus Ciasca* (Romae: Typographia Polyglotta S.C. de Propaganda Fide, 1888, repr. 1914 and 1934); and A.-S. Marmardji, *Diatessaron de Tatien: Texte arabe établi, traduit en français, collation avec les anciennes versions syriaques, suivi d'un évangéliaire syriaque* (Beyrouth: Imprimerie Catholique, 1935).

[50] See the summary and comprehensive bibliography of the many studies on the Arabic Gospel Harmony in Petersen, *Tatian's Diatessaron*, pp. 133–138, 448–451.

Syriac manuscript copied by the late-ninth-century Syriac/Arabic lexicographer, ʿĪsā ibn ʿAlī,[51] who was in turn a student of the master translator of the ninth century, Ḥunayn ibn Isḥāq, whom we mentioned above as the reputed translator of a portion of the Bible into Arabic.[52]

In passing, one should note that in addition to his role as a translator of the *Diatessaron* into Arabic, Ibn aṭ-Ṭayyib was one of the foremost Christian biblical scholars writing in Arabic in early Islamic times.[53] Not only did he produce an important commentary on the Psalms and the Gospels, the latter complete with an introduction in which he discusses the necessity for critical biblical scholarship,[54] but he was also the author of a monumental Christian theological commentary on the whole Bible, his *Firdaws an-Naṣrāniyyah*, a work still largely unstudied.[55]

Continuing close study of Ibn aṭ-Ṭayyib's Arabic Gospel harmony shows that it has value for the on-going search for original Diatessaronic readings,[56] and that the probably originally Syriac *Diatessaron* continued to be of interest and of use to the Arabic-speaking Syrian and Egyptian churches well up to and beyond the thirteenth and fourteenth centuries.[57] What is more, the *Diatessaron* seems to have been important to some medieval Christian controversialists in their encounters with Muslims, for "it did not exhibit the discrepancies of the separate Gospels,"[58] and thus play into the hands of the Muslim disputants who argued against the Gospels' textual dependability. As if to corroborate this observation, continuing research suggests that in

[51] See Graf, *Geschichte der christlichen arabischen Literatur*, vol. 2, pp. 131 and 157.

[52] See Tjitze Baarda, "The Author of the Arabic Diatessaron," in T. Baarda et al. (eds.), *Miscellanea Neotestamentica* (vol. 1, Supplements to Novum Testamentum, vol. 47; Leiden: E.J. Brill, 1978), pp. 61–103.

[53] See Graf, *Geschichte*, vol. 2, pp. 160–184, esp. pp. 162–169.

[54] See Samir Khalil-Kussaim, "Nécessité de la science: Texte de ʿAbdallā ibn aṭ-Ṭayyib (m. 1043)," *Parole de l'Orient* 3 (1972), pp. 241–259; Samir, K., "Nécessité de l'exégèse scientifique: Texte de ʿAbdallāh ibn aṭ-Ṭayyib," *Parole de l'Orient* 5 (1974), pp. 243–279.

[55] See Samir Khalil Samir, "La place d'Ibn aṭ-Ṭayyib dans la pensée arabe," *Journal of Eastern Christian Studies* 58 (2006), pp. 177–193; Julian Faultless, "Ibn al-Ṭayyib," in David Thomas and Alex Mallett (eds.), *Christian-Muslim Relations: A Bibliographical History* (vol. 2 (900–1050); Leiden: Brill, 2010), pp. 667–697.

[56] See Nanne Pieter George Joosse, "The Sermon on the Mount in the Arabic Diatessaron," (PhD Dissertation, Free University of Amsterdam; Amsterdam: Centrale Houisdrukkerij, 1997).

[57] See the descriptions of the MSS in Joosse, "The Sermon on the Mount," pp. 10–16.

[58] Joosse, "The Sermon on the Mount," p. 16.

the sixteenth century the Muslim author of the spurious *Gospel of Barnabas* made significant use of Diatessaronic readings in his production of a Gospel that he clearly hoped would fulfill Islamic requirements for the Gospel that, in Islamic thought, Jesus is supposed to have brought to mankind, as Moses brought the Torah and Muḥammad the Qurʾān.[59] More will be said about the *Gospel of Barnabas* in a later chapter on the Muslims and the Bible.

Testimony Collections

Citations of biblical passages translated into Arabic from both the Old and New Testaments are found in many apologetic works written in Arabic by Christians in early Islamic times. 'Arguing from scripture' and 'arguing from reason' were the twin approaches that Jews, Christians, and Muslims all used in the treatises they composed to commend the truth of the confessions of faith they championed. As for 'arguing from scripture', the Christian theologian Theodore Abū Qurrah (c. 755–c. 730) spelled out the principle he espoused in his treatise, 'On the Authority of the Mosaic Law, and the Gospel, and on the Orthodox Faith'. He wrote as follows:

> Christianity is simply faith in the Gospel and its appendices,[60] the Law of Moses, and the books of the prophets in between. Every intelligent person must believe in what these books we have mentioned say, and acknowledge its truth and act on it, whether his own understanding attains it or not.[61]

It is noticeable that Abū Qurrah here refers to the whole Bible in mentioning only the Law and the Gospel, in accordance with Qurʾānic usage (III:48; V:110) He and other Christian apologists often quote long passages from the scriptures in the course of their works. Unfortunately, only a few studies of these quotations have been undertaken to determine if they derive from one or another of the known Arabic translations of the

[59] See Jan Joosten, "The Gospel of Barnabas and the Diatessaron," *Harvard Theological Review* 95 (2002), pp. 73–96.

[60] By the Gospel's 'appendices (*tawābiʿihi*)' Abū Qurrah means the New Testament books, Acts to Revelation, which follow the Gospels according to the four evangelists in the canonical scriptures. Similarly, in speaking of the prophets who come 'in between' the Law and the Gospel, as he says in the next phrase, he means all the books from Joshua to Malachi, which follow the Law in the Septuagint editions of the Bible.

[61] Constantin Bacha, *Les oeuvres arabes de Théodore Aboucara, évêque d'Haran* (Beyrouth: Imp. Alfawïd du Journal Alawal, 1904), p. 27.

scriptures, or if the apologists simply made *ad hoc* translations of the passages they employed, or, even more simply, just quoted and translated them from memory.[62] Often they bundled together a sequence of passages from the Law, the Gospel, and other scriptures, scarcely identifying the conflated quotations.[63]

There is good evidence in a number of Christian Arabic apologetic texts for the circulation of testimony lists or collections of scriptural passages in Arabic for use in Christian/Muslim controversies.[64] Such a list is in fact included in the anonymous and still un-published, ninth-century Christian Arabic treatise entitled, 'The Summary of the Ways of Faith in the Trinity of the Unity of God and in the Incarnation of God the Word from the Pure Virgin Mary'.[65] Chapter XIII of the 'Summary of the Ways of Faith' consists entirely of a collection of scriptural testimonies from the Old Testament and the New Testament,[66] while chapter XVII is made up of a collection of *scholia* on passages from the Gospels, delivered in the form of thirty-three questions and answers focused on as many Gospel passages.[67] Many of the Gospel passages discussed in Chapter XVII are in fact the very ones that are to be found quoted in Islamic refutations of the Christians.[68] For the most

[62] See, e.g., Samir Khalil Samir, "Note sur les citations bibliques chez Abū Qurrah," *Orientalia Christiana Periodica* 49 (1983), pp. 184–191.

[63] See Sidney H. Griffith, "Arguing from Scripture: The Bible in the Christian/Muslim Encounter in the Middle Ages," in T. J. Heffernan and T. E. Burman (eds.), *Scripture and Pluralism: Reading the Bible in the Religiously Plural Worlds of the Middle Ages and Renaissance* (Studies in the History of Christian Traditions, vol. 123; Leiden: Brill, 2005), pp. 29–58.

[64] See David Bertaina, "The Development of Testimony Collections in Early Christian Apologetics with Islam," in Thomas, *The Bible in Arab Christianity*, pp. 151–173. See also Mark Swanson, "Beyond Prooftexting (2): The Use of the Bible in Some Early Arabic Christian Apologies," in Thomas, *The Bible in Arab Christianity*, pp. 91–112.

[65] This unpublished text is available in its entirety in British Library, MS Or. 4950, a text copied in the year 877 by Stephen of Ramleh. See Khalil Samir, "La 'Somme des aspects de la foi'," and Sidney H. Griffith, "A Ninth Century Summa Theologiae Arabica," in Khalil Samir, (ed.), *Actes du deuxième congrès international d'études arabes chrétiennes* (Orientalia Christiana Analecta, 226; Rome: Pontifical Institute of Oriental Studies, 1986), pp. 93–121; 123–141.

[66] BL MS Or. 4950, fols. 54v–76v.

[67] BL MS Or. 4950, fols. 96r–114v.

[68] See the lists published in Martin Accad, "The Gospels in the Muslim Discourse of the Ninth to the Fourteenth Centuries: An Exegetical Inventorial Table," *Islam and Christian-Muslim Relations* 14 (2003), pp. 67–91, 205–220, 337–352, 459–479. See also Camilla Adang, "A Rare Case of Biblical 'Testimonies' to the Prophet

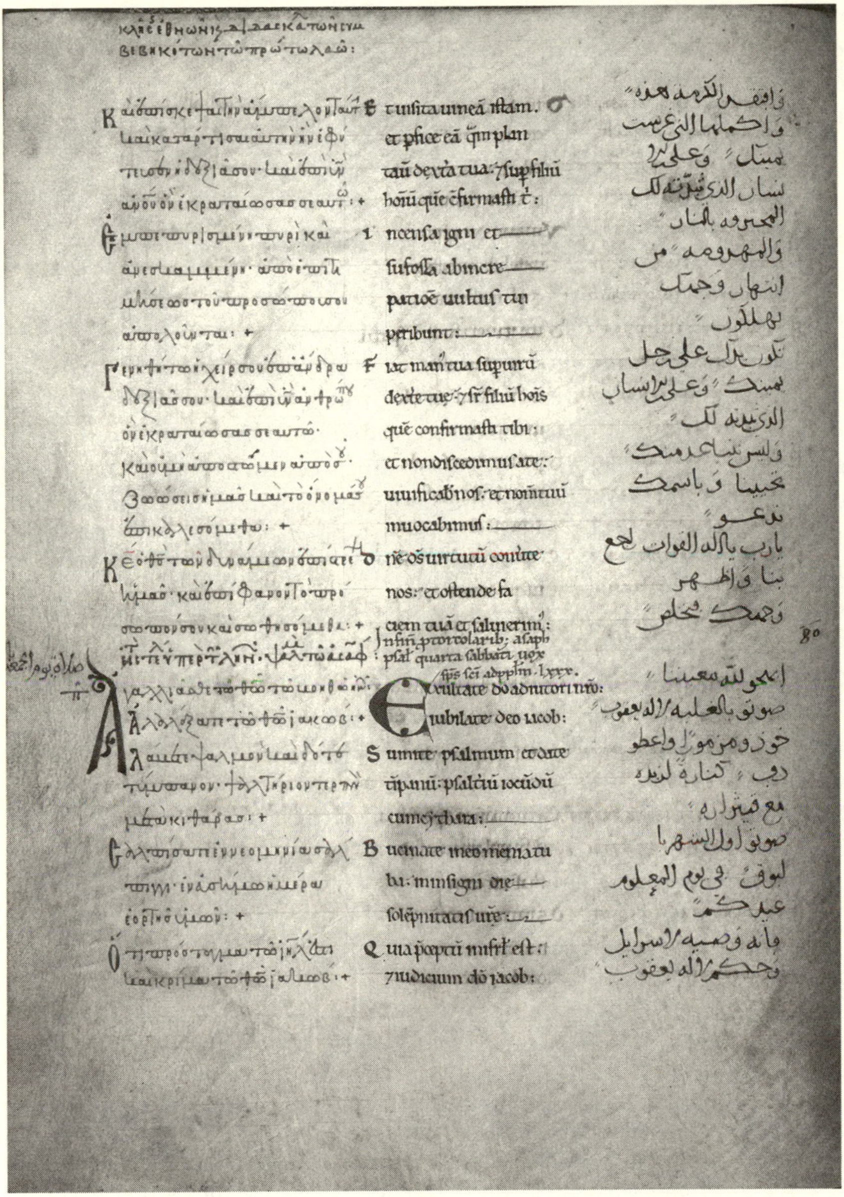

Fig. 2. Trilingual Psalter, Greek/Latin/Arabic, Palermo, 1130–1154, Ps. 81. Or. 2540, f18v–19v.

part, but not exclusively, they are sayings of Jesus recorded in the Gospel, mostly in the Gospel according to John, that on the face of it bespeak Jesus' complete humanity. The author explains in each instance how he thinks they should properly be interpreted, consistent with the church's teachings about the divinity and humanity of Christ.

Bilingual Bible Texts

As mentioned earlier, many Arabic translations of the scriptures were made for service in the liturgy as well as for study. So it is not surprising to find bilingual biblical texts, including both the original language and an Arabic translation. These texts seem to have been peculiarly, but not exclusively popular in the Coptic Church, where Arabic did not succeed in becoming an ecclesiastical language until the tenth century,[69] long after Christian communities in Syria/Palestine and Mesopotamia had adopted the common language of the Islamic world. Already in the eighth and ninth centuries, for example, bilingual Greek/Arabic Psalm books meant for the liturgy were in use in the Palestinian desert monasteries, as three surviving bilingual Psalters from Sinai testify.[70] It was not until later centuries in Egypt, however, that the use of bilingual biblical texts came to full flower.

When the Copts turned their attention to the production of Arabic translations of the Bible, both from their native Coptic and from other versions, they showed a remarkable eclecticism, as was mentioned earlier, in adopting and adapting Arabic translations already circulating in other, even rival confessional communities. As a result, both Copto-Arabic and Arabic ver-

---

Muḥammad in Muʿtazilī Literature: Quotations from Ibn Rabban al-Ṭabarī's *Kitāb al-dīn wa-l-dawla* in Abū l-Ḥusayn al-Baṣrī's *Ghurar al-adilla*, as Preserved in a Work by al-Ḥimmaṣī al-Rāzī," in C. Adang et al. (eds.), *A Common Rationality: Mutazilism in Islam and Judaism* (Istanbuler Texte und Studien, 15; Würzburg: Ergon Verlag, 2007), pp. 297–330.

[69] See Samuel Rubenson, "Translating the Tradition: Some Remarks on the Arabization of the Patristic Heritage in Egypt," *Medieval Encounters* 2 (1996), pp. 4–14; *idem*, "The Transition from Coptic to Arabic," *Égypte/Monde Arabe* 27–28 (1996), pp. 77–92. See also Tonio Sebastian Richter, "Language Choice in the Qurra Dossier," in Arietta Papaconstantinou (ed.), *The Multilingual Experience in Egypt, from the Ptolemies to the Abbasids* (Farnham, Surrey, UK: Ashgate, 2010), pp. 189–220.

[70] See the photograph of a page from one of these manuscripts and the accompanying description in Brown (ed.), *In the Beginning: Bibles before the Year 1000*, no. 46, pp. 192–193 and 285.

sions of the scriptures circulated in the churches of Egypt.[71] The study of these texts in the surviving manuscripts is in its infancy, but the sheer variety of their sources is already evident.[72]

There are numerous surviving bilingual, Coptic/Arabic texts among the Christian Arabic biblical manuscripts from Egypt, dating from the twelfth century onward and including portions of both the Old and New Testaments. It appears that Arabic came gradually into Coptic liturgical and biblical works, beginning as marginal notes and section headings, and ending in parallel-column texts.[73] Unfortunately, the Arabic versions of the biblical texts in these bilingual manuscripts have not yet been much studied by modern textual scholars, but this state of affairs is changing. For example, recent studies of the Coptic/Arabic text of the Pentateuch in Paris MS Copt. 1, copied in the year 1356 CE,[74] have yielded some interesting observations touching on the Arabic translation and the translator's technique. In this manuscript the Coptic and Arabic versions are written in parallel columns. It seems that the Coptic text was the first to be written because, as Ofer Livne-Kafri has explained, "in most cases where the text exceeds the lines it is the Arabic text."[75] Furthermore, while the Arabic translator stays close to the Coptic text he is translating, so much so that Livne-Kafri wants

[71] See Rubenson, "The Transition from Coptic to Arabic," p.4; Rhode, *The Arabic Versions of the Pentateuch in the Church of Egypt*, p. 117.

[72] See Khalil Samir, "Old Testament, Arabic Versions of the," in Aziz Z. Atiya (ed.), *The Coptic Encyclopedia* (8 vols.; New York: Macmillan, 1991), vol. 6, pp. 1827–1836; Bruce M. Metzger, *The Early Versions of the New Testament, their Origin, Transmission and Limitations* (Oxford: Oxford University Press, 1977), pp. 257–268. See also the detailed description of NT MSS, including many Copto/Arabic texts in George W. Horner, *The Coptic Version of the New Testament in the Northern Dialect, Otherwise Called Memphitic and Bohairic; with Introduction, Critical Apparatus, and Literal English Translation* (4 vols.; Oxford: Clarendon Press, 1898–1905), vol 1, pp. xxxvii–cxxvi.

[73] See Hanny N. Takla, "Copto (Bohairic)-Arabic Manuscripts: Their Role in the Tradition of the Coptic Church," in M. Immerzeel and J. van der Vliet (eds.), *Coptic Studies on the Threshold of a New Millennium: Proceedings of the Seventh International Congress of Coptic Studies* (Leuven: Uitgeverij Peeters en Departement Osterse Studies, 2004), pp. 639–646.

[74] See the description of the MS in Rhode, *The Arabic Versions of the Pentateuch in the Church of Egypt*, pp. 46–52.

[75] Ofer Livne-Kafri, "Some Notes Concerning the Arabic Version," in A. Shisha-Halevy, *Topics in Coptic Syntax: Structural Studies in the Bohairic Dialect* (Orientalia Lovaniensia Analecta, 160; Leuven: Uitgeverij Peeters en Departement Oosterse Studies, 2007), Appendix 2, p. 685.

to speak of it as 'Coptic Christian Arabic',[76] it is nevertheless clear that he strove for good, classical Arabic expression albeit that his usage also admits some of the features of the Middle Arabic we have seen in other Arabic Bible translations.[77] Not surprisingly given the eclecticism of Copto-Arabic, Livne-Kafri in his close examination of Paris MS Copt.1 also finds reflections of the Coptic version's Septuagint *Vorlage*, along with reflections of earlier Arabic translations from the Hebrew, and possibly even traces of influences from the Judaeo-Arabic of Egypt.[78]

There arises in connection with the bilingual Copto-Arabic biblical translations, the question as to their purpose and the uses to which they were put. We have already mentioned in connection with Paris MS Copt. 1 the perception that the Coptic text was written first and the Arabic version then set down in a second column, sometimes exceeding the usual number of lines on the page. In other manuscripts one can see the Arabic text squeezed into the margins of the Coptic text, sometimes even curling up the side of a page. Is the Arabic text included just for reasons of clarification, or secondary, liturgical proclamation, while the Coptic text is the principal one? Or is it the case that the Coptic text is presented largely for iconic, traditional reasons, or just for reference, and the Arabic text is the practical one, intended for Bible study and liturgical proclamation? The opinions of scholars are divided on this issue; some, like Hany Takla, favor the first option,[79] while others have wondered if in these manuscripts the Arabic does not stand in relation to the Coptic in the same way as Coptic stands in relation to the Greek in some Greek/Coptic bilingual biblical texts, in which the Greek seems to have more of an honorific than a practical presence, exhibiting what one scholar characterizes as "a somewhat 'fossilized' usage."[80]

[76] Ofer Livne-Kafri, "Some Notes on the Vocabulary in a Coptic-Arabic Translation of the Pentateuch," *Al-Karmil: Studies in Arabic Language and Literature; University of Haifa* 30 (2009), p.27 (17–27).

[77] See Livne-Kafri, "Some Notes Concerning the Arabic Version," pp. 686–687; Ofer Livne-Kafri, "A Note on the Enegeticus in a Coptic-Arabic Translation of the Pentateuch," *Acta Orientalia Academiae Scientiarum Hung.* 62 (2009), pp. 405–411.

[78] See Livne-Kafri, "Some Notes Concerning the Arabic Version," pp. 687–689; O. Livne-Kafri, "A Note on Coptic and Judeo-Arabic on the Basis of Bilingual Manuscript to the Pentateuch," *Massorot* 12 (2002), pp. 97–101 [Hebrew].

[79] See Takla, "Copto (Bohairic)-Arabic Manuscripts," p. 645.

[80] See Anne Boud'hors, "Toujours honneur au grec? À propos d'un papyrus gréco-copte de la region thébaine," in Papaconstantinou, *The Multilingual Experience in Egypt*, p. 187 (179–188).

In addition to the bilingual biblical texts, Greek and Arabic, Coptic and Arabic, there is also a surviving trilingual Psalter (Greek, Latin, and Arabic) that was produced in the Kingdom of Sicily in the reign of the Norman king, Roger II (1130–1154).[81] The Psalms are presented in parallel columns in Greek from the Septuagint, in Latin from the Latin Vulgate, and in an Arabic translation from Greek made by a deacon of the Melkite church of Antioch. That the Psalter was intended for liturgical use is indicated by the presence of rubrics and marginal notes in Arabic alongside the Greek text. One can only speculate on the make-up of the congregation for which the Psalter was intended, its sumptuous presentation suggests it was used by a fairly sophisticated community. It is possible that by the mid-twelfth century in Sicily the use of Arabic had become sufficiently widespread that scripture readings in the local Greek Orthodox liturgy had to be repeated in Arabic.[82]

Christian Arabic Commentaries on the Bible

Biblical commentary was no less a concern for Arabic-speaking Christian scholars in the early Islamic period than it had been for their Syriac-speaking predecessors, especially in the East Syrian or Nestorian communities in which the commentary tradition had flourished in Syriac in earlier times. It was arguably the primary vehicle for the transmission of the church's distinctive doctrines, couched in the exegetical tradition of Theodore of Mopsuestia (c. 350–428).[83] In fact, in the Islamic milieu, the earliest comprehensive theological response to the new religious challenge to be composed in Syriac was a summary of Christian teaching by the East Syrian scholar Theodore bar Kônî (*fl.*c. 792). He published his work in the form of a commentary on the Old and New Testaments called simply *Scholion*. It is in fact a compendium of commentaries on selected scriptural passages, definitions of philosophical terms, and explanations of theological formulae,

[81] See the description of the MS, and the reproduction of the page featuring the text of Psalm 81 at http://www.qantara-med.org/qantara4/public/show_document.php?do_id=1132&lan=en.

[82] In this connection, see J. Johns, "The Greek Church and the Conversion of Muslims in Norman Sicily," *Byzantinische Forschungen* 21 (1995), pp. 133–157.

[83] See Lucas van Rompay, "The Christian Syriac Tradition of Interpretation," in Magne Sæbø (ed.), *Hebrew Bible/Old Testament: The History of Its Interpretation* (vol. 1, part 1; Göttingen: Vandenhoeck and Ruprecht, 1996), pp. 612–641; *idem*, "The Development of Biblical Interpretation in the Syrian Churches of the Middle Ages," in Sæbø, *Hebrew Bible/Old Testament*, vol. 1, part 2, pp. 559–577.

along with appendices devoted to controversy with Muslims, and Christian heresiology.[84] Similarly, in the west Syrian tradition in Islamic times scholars such as Dionysius bar Ṣalībī (d.1171), with his commentary on the Old Testament, and Bar Hebraeus (d.1286), with his 'Storehouse of Mysteries', continued the Jacobite tradition of scripture commentary.[85]

In Islamic times biblical commentary in Syriac thus continued in the several Arabophone Christian communities living in the Islamic world, sometimes reflecting Muslim concerns in its shifts of emphasis.[86] In Arabic the commentary traditions appeared most prominently in the 'proofs from scripture' sections of theological or apologetic works,[87] in Arabic translations of some of the earlier Syriac commentaries,[88] and eventually in independent works of exegesis composed in Arabic.

The only complete commentary in Christian Arabic on the whole Bible that has survived to modern times is the *Firdaws an-Naṣrāniyyah*, or 'Paradise of Christianity', a work still unedited and unpublished in its entirety, composed by the well-known Nestorian scholar, Abū l-Faraj ʿAbdullāh ibn aṭ-Ṭayyib (d.c. 1043).[89] So far only the commentary on Genesis from this work has been published and studied in full. It is interesting to note that, according to the modern scholar who has studied it the most closely, this commentary, while it mentions no earlier writers other than the fathers of the Nestorian tradition, nevertheless displays a reliance on the ninth-century Syriac Genesis commentary by Ishôʿdad of Merv.[90] This feature tes-

[84] See Sidney H. Griffith, "Theodore bar Kônî's *Scholion*: A Nestorian *Summa contra Gentiles* from the First Abbasid Century," in N. Garsoïan et al. (eds.), *East of Byzantium: Syria and Armenia in the Formative Period* (Washington, DC: Dumbarton Oaks, 1982); *idem*, "Chapter Ten of the Scholion: Theodore bar Kônî's Apology for Christianity," *Orientalia Christiana Periodica* 47 (1981), pp. 158–188; Van Rompay, "Development of Biblical Interpretation," p. 566.

[85] See Van Rompay, "Development of Biblical Interpretation," pp. 573–576.

[86] See, e.g., Martin Accad, "Did the Later Syriac Fathers Take into Consideration their Islamic Context When Reinterpreting the New Testament?" *Parole de l'Orient* 23 (1998), pp. 13–32.

[87] See, e.g., the several studies in Thomas, *The Bible in Arab Christianity*.

[88] For example, portions of the sixth-century, Jacobite Daniel of Ṣalaḥ's (*fl.* 541/42) commentary on the Psalms were included in Arabic translation in later exegetical compilations. See Graf, *Geschichte der christlichen arabischen Literatur*, vol. 1, p. 453.

[89] On Ibn aṭ-Ṭayyib, see Faultless, "Ibn al-Ṭayyib"; on the *Firdaws*, see pp. 681–683.

[90] See Faultless, "Ibn al-Ṭayyib," p. 681, citing J.C.J. Sanders (ed. and trans.), *Ibn aṭ-Taiyib, Commentaire sur la Genèse* (CSCO vols. 274 and 275; Louvain: Secrétariat du Corpus SCO, 1967); *idem, Inleiding op het Genesis kommentaar van de Nestoriaan Ibn*

tifies to Ibn aṭ-Ṭayyib's concern to transmit the traditional biblical commentary of his Nestorian ecclesial community, that of Theodore of Mopsuestia and the Antiochene school generally. The same fidelity is evident as well in what survives of his other known commentaries, on the Psalms[91] and the Gospels, which were apparently later folded into the *Firdaws* in abbreviated form.[92]

He was one of the more notable Christian intellectuals of Baghdad in the first half of the eleventh century, prominent as both a physician and philosopher. It is interesting to note that Ibn aṭ-Ṭayyib included in the introduction to his commentary on the Four Gospels a spirited defense of a scholarly approach to biblical exegesis against the more simplistic views of some of his anti-intellectual, Christian contemporaries. It is a rare moment in Arabic biblical commentary when one finds such a text, in which the author discusses and defends 'scientific' methodology in exegesis. Indeed he spells out exactly what he means in reference to specific biblical passages and pays particular attention to how difficult it is even to discern the literal meaning of a passage without careful lexicographical study.[93]

Some Arab Christian authors also wrote commentaries on individual books of the Bible. Unfortunately, not many of these have been carefully studied or even published and translated into a Western scholarly language. Particularly interesting are two commentaries on the Book of Revelation, written by two thirteenth-century Arabophone Copts, Būlus al-Būshī (*fl.* c. 1250) and Ibn Kātib Qayṣar,[94] about whom little is known other than

---

at-Taiyib (Proefschrift-Amsterdam; Leiden: E.J. Brill, 1963). See also Paul Féghali, "Ibn at-Tayib et son commentaire sur la Genèse," *Parole de l'Orient* 16 (1990–1991), pp. 149–162.

91 A. Chahwan, "Le commentaire de Psaumes 33–60 d'Ibn at Tayib reflet de l'exégèse syriaque orientale," (Th.D. Dissertation; Rome: Pontifical Gregorian University, 1997). See also R. Köbert, "Ibn at-Taiyib's Erklärung von Psalm 44," *Biblica* 43 (1962), pp. 338–348.

92 See Faultless, "Ibn al-Ṭayyib," pp. 669–670.

93 An account of Ibn aṭ-Ṭayyib's scientific work appears among the biographies of the famous physicians of the era, and as a philosopher he was known to his presumably older contemporary, the famed Persian physician and philosopher Abū 'Alī Ḥusayn ibn 'Abd Allāh ibn Sīnā (980–1037). For his concern with lexicography, see four particularly significant sections of the introduction edited, discussed, and translated into French in Samir Khali-Kussaim, "Nécessité de la science"; idem, "Nécessité de l'exégèse scientifique.

94 See Stephen J. Davis, "Introducing an Arabic Commentary on the Apocalypse: Ibn Kātib Qayṣar on Revelation," *Harvard Theological Review* 101 (2008), pp. 77–96. See also Shawqi N. Talia, "Būlus al-Būshī's Arabic Commentary on the Apocalypse

what is revealed of their scholarly interests in their surviving, but unpublished Arabic writings. Their Apocalypse commentaries are notable because of the general scarcity of interest in this biblical book in the Christian East. It is perhaps not an accident that this interest surfaced in a Christian community under Muslim rule in early Mamlūk times.

Illustrations in Arabic Biblical Texts

Illustrations are not common in Christian Arabic biblical manuscripts, but there are nevertheless some notable ones. Among the most fascinating are the depictions of the four evangelists, each on a separate page preceding the text of their Gospel, in what may well be one of the earliest dated manuscripts of the Gospels in Arabic (859 CE). They are full-page, simple drawings in color, with the evangelists in their traditional presentations. Only the image of St. Luke has been published. It shows the evangelist standing in an archway, with the traditional ascription to 'St. Luke' in Greek characters above the figure, and just his name (Luke) inscribed in Arabic characters below.[95]

Most illustrated Arabic Bible texts come from Egypt, and they most often appear in bilingual, Coptic-Arabic manuscripts of the thirteenth and fourteenth centuries.[96] Not all the illustrations are figural; many of them feature geometric or calligraphic patterns, or elaborate designs framing the scriptural text, not unlike those familiar from contemporary Islamic book art.[97] A particularly interesting use of illustration is provided by two manuscripts from early Mamlūk times that feature the Gospels in Arabic

---

of St. John: An English Translation and Commentary," (Ph.D. Dissertation; Washington, DC: The Catholic University of America, 1987).

[95] See Brown (ed.), *In the Beginning: Bibles before the Year 1000*, no. 35, pp. 166–167, 274–275.

[96] See Jules Leroy, *Les manuscrits coptes et coptes-arabes* (Institut Français d'Archéologie de Beyrouth, Bibliothèque Archéologique et Historique, vol. 96; Paris: P. Geuthner, 1974).

[97] See Leslie S.B. Maccoull, "Illustrated Manuscripts in the Coptic Museum: Language and History," *Parole de l'Orient* 19 (1994), pp. 391–399; Lucy-Anne Hunt, "Introducing the Catalogue, in Progress, of the Illustrated Manuscripts in the Coptic Museum," *Parole de l'Orient* 19 (1994), pp. 401–413. See also Lucy-Anne Hunt, *Byzantium, Eastern Christendom and Islam: Art at the Crossroads of the Medieval Mediterranean* (London: Pindar Press, 1998); *eadem*, "Cultural Transmission: Illustrated Biblical Manuscripts from the Medieval Eastern Christian and Arab Worlds," in J. L. Sharpe and K. Van Kampen (eds.), *The Bible as Book: The Manuscript Tradition* (London: British Library, 1998), pp. 123–136.

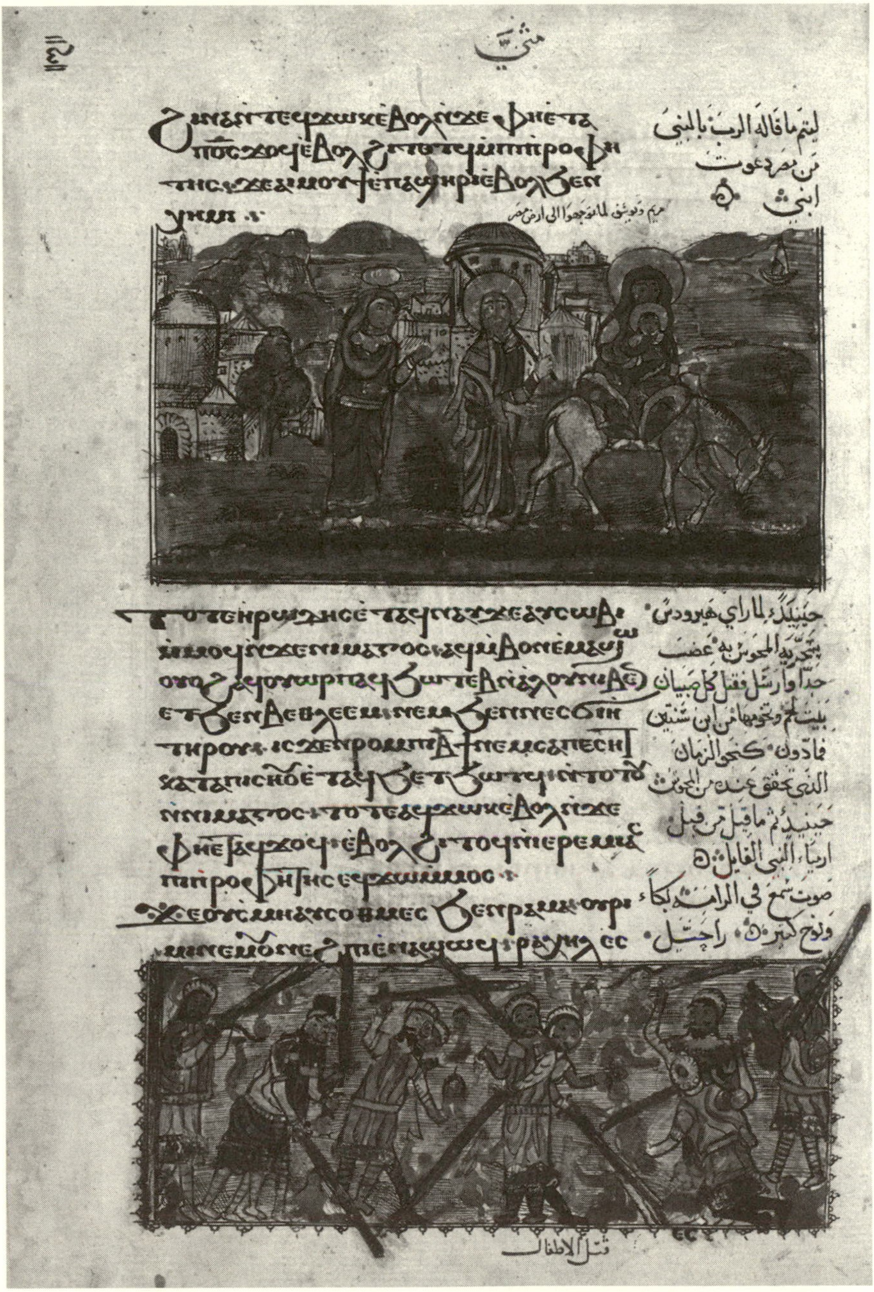

Fig. 3. Bilingual Gospel MS, Coptic & Arabic, 1663, with illustrations of the Flight into Egypt and the Massacre of the Innocents. © The British Library Board. All rights reserved. Or. 1316, f.5v 204.

along with Byzantine illustrations of the four evangelists.[98] Lucy-Anne Hunt has suggested that they come from a period in Mamlūk Egypt "when there were different versions available," and that the function of "such Greek, or Greek-style, illustrations was . . . to offer a seal of respectability to the text."[99] It is notable that these manuscripts were in the possession of Coptic Orthodox persons and not Egyptian Melkites, as one might expect from the use of Byzantine models.

There are also of course other illustrated Arabic biblical manuscripts that one might mention,[100] but for the most part biblical texts in Arabic in the medieval period seem to have had a very practical, even subsidiary liturgical or academic purpose. They were produced for use in communities that were largely Arabic-speaking, but where the traditional languages of liturgy and scholarship—Greek, Syriac, Coptic, or Armenian—enjoyed an almost iconic status. Texts in these languages were more likely to receive a sumptuous presentation.

[98] See Lucy-Anne Hunt, "Illustrating the Gospels in Arabic: Byzantine and Arab Christian Miniatures in Two Manuscripts of the Early Mamlūk Period in Cambridge," in Thomas, *The Bible in Arab Christianity*, pp. 315–349.

[99] Hunt, "Illustrating the Gospels in Arabic," p. 315.

[100] See, e.g., pages from an illustrated lectionary of the Epistles from the eighteenth century in Agnès-Mariam de la Croix and François Zabbal, *Icônes arabes: Art chrétien du Levant* (Méolans-Revel: Éditions Grégoriennes, 2003), no. XIV, B 42.

✻ CHAPTER V ✻

Jewish Translations of the Bible into Arabic

It was in early Islamic times, perhaps as early as the first decades of the eighth century, that Jewish scribes began producing books in the codex form. The earliest surviving dated Hebrew Bibles written in this format appeared between the early tenth and mid-eleventh centuries.[1] It was a development that in the judgment of David Stern provided "our first evidence for 'professional' Jewish readers of the Bible."[2] It was also around the eighth century, as Stern goes on to say, that building on earlier exercises "there developed distinct schools of masoretes, in both Babylonia and Palestine,"[3] who produced biblical codices in which the text was displayed on the page in a manner that both evidenced and encouraged study of the text precisely as a *written* text, as opposed to a 'heard' text. He speaks of the development as "an early medieval cultural epiphenomenon which we might call the 'codexification' of Judaism."[4] Stern, along with some other scholars writing before him,[5] also draws attention to the fact that this development occurred at a time and in a place in which the textual study of the Qur'ān was gaining ground among the Muslims.[6] And one might add that it was also the time and the place in which Jews, Christians, and Muslims, now fully integrated into a new Arabophone intellectual culture, were beginning to engage in debates with one another in the Arabic language, often involving disagreements over the wording and the interpretation of scriptural testimonies alleged to support one or another of the creedal or confessional formulae that were favored by the different communities.[7] It was in the wake of these

[1] See David Stern, "The First Jewish Books and the Early History of Jewish Reading," *The Jewish Quarterly Review* 98 (2008), pp. 163–164 (163–202).

[2] Stern, "The First Jewish Books," p. 165.

[3] Stern, "The First Jewish Books," p. 172.

[4] Stern, "The First Jewish Books," p. 198.

[5] Notably Rina Drory, *Models and Contacts: Arabic Literature and its Impact on Medieval Jewish Culture* (Leiden: E.J. Brill, 2000).

[6] Stern, "The First Jewish Books," esp. pp. 197–199. It is notable in this connection that Muqātil ibn Sulaymān (d. 767), the earliest scholar to write a full *tafsīr* of the Qur'ān, flourished in Baṣrah in the middle third of the eighth century.

[7] See Daniel J. Lasker, "*Qiṣṣat Mujādalat alUsquf* and *Neṣṭor Ha-Komer*: The Earliest Arabic and Hebrew Jewish anti-Christian Polemics," in J. Blau and S.C. Reif (eds.),

developments, and perhaps in no small part due to them, that the first written Jewish translations of the scriptures into Arabic appeared in the course of the ninth century CE.

While the earliest translations of the scriptures into Judaeo-Arabic in all likelihood appeared early in the ninth century CE, as we saw in an earlier chapter, it was in the latter part of the century, and particularly in the first half of the tenth century in the environs of Baghdad that the translation of the scriptures into Arabic became a major project in the Jewish communities. By the first third of the tenth century, Baghdad had become an intellectual center for Jews, Christians, and Muslims alike: it had been the seat of the patriarch of the Nestorian Church of the East since the early ninth century at the latest;[8] by the end of the first third of the tenth century, the Geonim of the Jewish academies of Sura and Pumbedita had relocated to Baghdad;[9] and among the Muslims by the early years of the tenth century the city had long been the center of the flourishing *majlis* culture that not infrequently featured encounters between the scholars and intellectuals of all three of the major religious traditions.[10] Jews and Christians were very attentive to these currents of thought and readily brought them into the life of their own communities.[11]

Jewish initiatives to translate the Bible into Arabic seem to have had their origins in this cosmopolitan, Arabic-speaking milieu of Baghdad with its rich intellectual and cultural networks. They coincided in time with another important development in Jewish history, the emerging and on-going controversies between the Rabbanites and the Karaites.[12] Here is not the

---

Genizah Research after Ninety Years: The Case of Judaeo-Arabic (Cambridge: Cambridge University Press, 1992), pp. 112–118.

[8] See Sidney H. Griffith, "Patriarch Timothy I and an Aristotelian at the Caliph's Court," in Erica C. D. Hunter (ed.), *The Christian Heritage of Iraq: Collected Papers from the Christianity of Iraq I–V Seminar Days* (Gorgias Eastern Christian Studies, 13; Piscataway, NJ: Gorgias Press, 2009), pp. 38–53.

[9] See Robert Brody, *The Geonim of Babylonia and the Shaping of Medieval Jewish Culture* (New Haven, CT: Yale University Press, 1998), p. 36.

[10] See most notably Joel L. Kraemer, *Humanism in the Renaissance of Islam: The Cultural Revival during the Buyid Age* (Leiden: Brill, 1986).

[11] See Steven M. Wasserstrom, *Between Muslim and Jew: The Problem of Symbiosis under Early Islam* (Princeton, NJ: Princeton University Press, 1995); Sidney H. Griffith, *The Church in the Shadow of the Mosque: Christians and Muslims in the World of Islam* (Princeton, NJ: Princeton University Press, 2008).

[12] See Daniel Lasker, "Rabbinism and Karaism: The Contest for Supremacy," in R. Jospe and S. M. Wagner (eds.), *Great Schisms in Jewish History* (New York: Ktav Publishing House, 1981), pp. 47–72; Michael Cook, "Anan and Islam: The Origins

place to discuss these controversies in themselves, albeit that the translation and interpretation of the scriptures were major topics in the disputes between the two groups. But it is important to take cognizance of the fact that even the earliest Judaeo-Arabic translations, done perhaps in the early ninth century (as discussed in chapter 3), were produced against the background of the Rabbanite/Karaite debates.

Perhaps the earliest name that emerges in connection with the translation into Arabic of biblical passages, or biblical words and phrases, is that of the Karaite Daniel al-Qūmisī (*fl.*c. 870–910), who is known as a commentator on various books of the Hebrew Bible, and who normally wrote in Hebrew. But Arabic glosses appear in his work, along with what Meira Polliack calls "general lapses into Arabic terminology." She describes these 'lapses' as "paraphrases or lexical definitions which are embedded within the continuous Hebrew text of the commentary," and she writes: "They represent a transitory stage between a method of commentary which is devoid of translation to one which requires Arabic rendering as an integral part of the interpretive process."[13]

An important point emerges here and it is that unlike the scripture translations of Arabic-speaking Christians, those done by Jews were not for the purpose of official, liturgical proclamation in the vernacular language, nor were they in any way intended to replace the original scriptural language for public purposes. They functioned, rather, as means to interpretation and commentary. In the beginning this interpretation seems to have been oral, following the liturgical proclamation of the appointed Torah portions in synagogues in Hebrew, on the model of the traditional use of the Aramaic targums. Surviving evidence shows that although there was initial

---

of Karaite Scripturalism," *Jerusalem Studies in Arabic and Islam* 9 (1987), pp. 161–172; Haggai Ben Shammai, "The Karaite Controversy: Scripture and Tradition in Early Karaism," in B. Lewis and F. Niewöhner (eds.), *Religionsgespräche im Mittelalter* (Wiesbaden: Harrassowitz, 1992), pp. 11–26; *idem*, "Return to Scriptures in Ancient and Medieval Jewish Sectarianism and in Early Islam," in E. Patlagean and A. Le Boulluec (eds.), *Les retours aux écritures: Fondamentalismes presents et passes* (Leuven: Peeters, 1993), pp. 313–339; Meira Polliack, "Rethinking Karaism: Between Judaism and Islam," *AJS Review* 30 (2006), pp. 67–93; Sagit Butbul, "Translations in Contact: Early Judeo-Arabic and Syriac Biblical Translations," in D. M. Freidenreich and M. Goldstein, *Beyond Religious Borders: Interaction and Intellectual Exchange in the Medieval Islamic World* (Philadelphia, PA: University of Pennsylvania Press, 2012), pp. 57–64.

[13] Meira Polliack, *The Karaite Tradition of Arabic Bible Translation: A Linguistic and Exegetical Study of Karaite Translations of the Pentateuch from the Tenth and Eleventh Centuries* C.E. (Études sur le Judaïsme Médiéval, vol. 17; Leiden: E.J. Brill, 1997), p. 31.

Fig. 4. Karaite Book of Exodus, Palestine/Egypt, tenth century.

resistance on the part of the rabbinical authorities to the oral interpretation of scriptural passages in Arabic, due to congregational demand the practice, along with the use of the traditional targums, was eventually allowed in ninth-century Arabophone synagogues.[14] Nevertheless, Arabic-speaking Jews, and in the first instance particularly Karaites, required Arabic translations principally for the purpose of Bible study, along with personal and congregational biblical interpretation. The translations did not do away with or substitute for the original Hebrew texts. To the contrary, to judge by some surviving fragments from the Cairo Geniza, there was a Karaite "practice of transliterating the Hebrew Bible in Arabic characters and 'outfitting' them with the traditional Hebrew signs for the vowels above and below the characters."[15] In other words, Jewish translators of the Bible into Arabic thought of themselves primarily as exegetes, and transliteration and translation were the first steps in the process of exegesis.[16]

Around the year 880 CE, Daniel al-Qūmisī moved to Palestine, and it was there in the tenth century that eventually a circle of Karaite Bible translators emerged who produced Arabic translations, in particular very literally rendered versions of the Torah or portions of it. Much of their work was done in the tenth century, and the community seems to have flourished in Jerusalem until the coming of the Crusaders at the end of the eleventh century. They included well-known scholars: Yefet ha-Levi ben ʿElī, Yeshuʿah ben Yehudah, David ben Boʿaz, and David ben Abraham al-Fāsī, to name only a few.[17] Their work has been studied in some detail by numerous scholars, many of them writing in Modern Hebrew, but it would go beyond

[14] See Haggai Ben-Shammai, "The Tension between Literal Interpretation and Exegetical Freedom: Comparative Observations on Saadia's Method," in J. D. McAuliffe et al. (eds.), *With Reverence for the Word: Medieval Scriptural Exegesis in Judaism, Christianity, and Islam* (Oxford: Oxford University Press, 2003), p. 34 (33–50).

[15] Adina Hoffman and Peter Cole, *Sacred Trash: The Lost and Found World of the Cairo Geniza* (Jewish Encounters; New York: Nextbook/Schocken, 2011), p. 159.

[16] Lenn E. Goodman made this point in connection with his study of Saʿadyah's translation of the Book of Job, as we shall see below. He spoke of Saʿadyah's purpose as being "not to make the work accessible to nonreaders of Hebrew. . . . He expects his reader to be familiar with the text and its expressions. . . . An interpretive translation leaves nothing unresolved." Lenn E. Goodman, "Saadiah Gaon's Interpretive Technique in Translating the Book of Job," in *Translation of Scripture: Proceedings of a Conference at the Annenberg Research Institute, May 15–16, 1989* (A Jewish Quarterly Review Supplement; Philadelphia: Annenberg Research Institute, 1990), p. 49 (47–75)

[17] See the discussion of these 'Karaite' scholars and their work discussed in Polliack, *The Karaite Tradition of Arabic Bible Translation*, 37–64.

the scope of the present essay to describe their studies in detail. Suffice it to say that these Karaite Arabic translations were done in a very self-conscious way, which a number of the translators themselves have actually described in some detail.[18] Their versions were meant to serve the exegetical interests of their Karaite communities and were not without polemics against their Rabbanite adversaries.[19] Some of the translators achieved a considerable measure of scholarly authority in the Karaite movement at large. A case in point is Yefet ben Elī (*fl.* 950–1000 CE), much lauded in the later tradition, who seems to have produced commentaries on all of the books in the Hebrew Bible, consisting of "alternating (section-by-section) Arabic translations and commentaries."[20] It is interesting to note further that modern scholars have found in his works "a theological-philosophical perspective that was in many respects consistent with, and to a certain extent influenced by, the views of the Islamic Muʿtazila."[21]

Meira Polliack, whose scholarly study of the Karaite translations provides extensive bibliographical references as well as studies of the syntactic and lexical features of these works, offers the following assessment. She says that for these Karaite translators, "an acceptable Bible translation [was] one . . . based on the correct understanding of the Hebrew language. . . . Arabic Bible translation [was] first and foremost a medium for expressing the accurate structure—whether grammatical or lexical—of biblical Hebrew, in order to arrive at a clear comprehension of the meaning, or meanings, of the biblical text."[22] In other words, these translations, largely products of the 'Jerusalem school', were meant to be first steps in the exegetical process.

Meanwhile, back in the cosmopolitan environs of Baghdad, Abū Yūsuf Yaʿqūb al-Qirqisānī (*fl.*c. 940) was advancing the Karaite view of Arabic biblical translation within a much wider intellectual frame of reference.[23] In his Arabic works he took into account not only the multiple strains of Jew-

[18] See the several statements on translation by a number of 'Karaite' scholars published in Polliack, *The Karaite Tradition of Arabic Bible Translation*, Appendix One, pp. 293–296.

[19] See Fred Astren, *Karaite Judaism and Historical Understanding* (Columbia, SC: University of South Carolina Press, 2004), pp. 66–76.

[20] Michael G. Wechsler, "Japheth (Abū ʿAlī Ḥasan) ben Eli," in Norman A. Stillman (ed.), *Encyclopedia of Jews in the Islamic World* (5 vols.; Leiden: Brill, 2010), vol. 3, p. 12 (11–13).

[21] Wechsler, "Japheth (Abū ʿAlī Ḥasan) ben Eli," in Stillman, *Encyclopedia of Jews in the Islamic World*, vol. 3, p 12.

[22] Polliack, *The Karaite Tradition of Arabic Bible Translation*, p. 64.

[23] See Astren, *Karaite Judaism and Historical Understanding*, pp. 98–123.

ish thought of the time, but also engaged with issues that were the concern of Christian and Muslim scholars in the same milieu, issues high on the topical agendas of the contemporary *mutakallimūn*, especially among the Muʿtazilah, with their emphasis on the role of reason in religious thinking. He is even remembered to have written a treatise with the decidedly Muʿtazilī title, *Kitāb at-tawḥīd*. His main works were two: *Kitāb al-anwār wa-l-marāqib*, a systematic presentation and defense of his Karaite legal views, defended in *kalām* style in response to his intellectual adversaries, both Jewish and non-Jewish;[24] and a commentary on the non-legal portions of the Torah, *Kitāb ar-riyāḍ wa-l-ḥadā'iq'iq*. Prominent in these works are Qirqisānī's ideas about the role of Arabic translation in the interpretation of the scriptures. His particular concern was that in contrast to the traditional Jewish interpretive translations in other languages, works such as the Aramaic targums of Onkelos and Jonathan, the Arabic translations should as accurately—and even as literally—as possible reflect the underlying Hebrew text. Qirqisānī moreover espoused the view that the Arabic translations should express the consensus of the Arabic-speaking Jewish people instead of representing just the views of individual scholars.[25]

The important point that one wants to emphasize here is that Qirqisānī articulated his views on Arabic Bible translation within the Jewish community, which was itself well within the horizon of the cosmopolitan, multi-confessional, intellectual life of Baghdad in his day. One must take that wide horizon into account; it highlights the fact that the Arabic translations of the Bible done by Jews had an intellectual relevance that reached beyond internal Jewish concerns, albeit they were written in Judaeo-Arabic in Hebrew script. These translations had a role to play in the Jewish scholars' encounters with their Arabic-speaking Christian and Muslim interlocutors, who were also busy with the biblical text in Arabic in the midst of the

[24] See Haggai ben Shammai, "Qirqisani on the Oneness of God," *Jewish Quarterly Review* 73 (1982), pp. 105–111; Bruno Chiesa and Wilfrid Lockwood (eds. and trans.), *Yaʿqūb al-Qirqisānī on Jewish Sects and Christianity* (Frankfurt: Peter Lang, 1984); H. Ben-Shammai, "Major Trends in Karaite Philosophy and Polemics in the Tenth and Eleventh Centuries," in M. Polliack (ed.), *Karaite Judaism: A Guide to Its History and Literary Sources* (Leiden: Brill, 2003), 339–362. See also the presentation of the topics of the *Kitāb al-anwār* in Fred Astren, "Qirqisānī, Jacob al-," in Stillman, *Encyclopedia of Jews in the Islamic World*, vol. 4, pp. 136–140.

[25] See Polliack, *The Karaite Tradition of Arabic Bible Translation*, pp. 65–77; Geoffrey Khan, "Al-Qirqisānī's Opinions Concerning the Text of the Bible and Parallel Muslim Attitudes towards the Text of the Qur'ān," *The Jewish Quarterly Review* 81 (1990), pp. 59–73.

current interreligious controversies. Scriptural quotations, proof-texts, and their interpretations formed an integral part of the intercommunal controversial agendas of the day. These debates, as well as the principal intra-Jewish concerns of the day, must also have influenced the ways in which the translators chose to phrase their versions, precisely to foil non-Jewish interpretations of passages used by adversaries in an attempt to discredit Jewish claims to true religion, the principal topic on the interreligious agenda of Jewish, Christian, and Muslim apologists alike.[26]

The major Jewish voice in this religiously contentious intellectual scene in Baghdad in the first half of the tenth century was undoubtedly that of Qirqisānī's older contemporary, the famous Rabbanite scholar, Sa'adyah ben Yosef al-Fayyūmī ha-Ga'ōn (882–942).[27] As his name indicates, Sa'adyah came originally from Egypt to Babylonia, with an intervening sojourn in Palestine. He was well known as a scholar even before his arrival in Iraq, and in due course, in 928 CE, he was appointed *ga'ōn* of the academy of Sura, now removed to Baghdad. Sa'adyah held this position, not without struggle and controversy, until the end of his life. He made major contributions to Jewish religious and intellectual life, which it is not to the present purpose to rehearse, since his accomplishments have been and continue to be much studied by specialists in the Jewish history and culture of the early Islamic period. But in several areas in particular Sa'adya's work achieved a significance that reached well beyond the confines of his time and place, and, as we shall see, even beyond the confines of the Jewish communities. The most pertinent of his works for the present study include his translation of the Torah and other books of the Bible into Judaeo-Arabic, his biblical commentaries, and his philosophical/theological masterpiece, *The Book of Beliefs and Opinions.*

Beyond a doubt, Sa'adyah's *Tafsīr*, as he called his Arabic translations of the Hebrew Bible, stands as an enduring monument of his scholarship; in addition to the Torah, he translated the books of Isaiah, Psalms, Proverbs, Job, Lamentations, Esther, and Daniel.[28] The Arabic title for the transla-

[26] See Miriam Goldstein, "Arabic Composition 101 and the Early Development of Judeo-Arabic Bible Exegesis," *Journal of Semitic Studies* 55 (2010), pp. 451–478.

[27] See still Henry Malter, *Saadia Gaon: His Life and Works* (The Morris Loeb Series; Philadelphia: Jewish Publication Society of America, 1921). See also Brody, *The Geonim of Babylonia*, pp. 235–248; Haggai Ben-Shammai, "Sa'adya Gaon," in Stillman, *Encyclopedia of Jews in the Islamic World*, vol. 4, pp. 197–204.

[28] Sa'adyah's *Tafsīr* and his other works are published in Joseph Derenbourg (ed.), *Oeuvres complètes de R. Saadia Ben Josef al-Fayyoûmī* (5 vols.; Paris: Ernest Leroux, 19893–1899). For further bibliography on more recent editions of Sa'adyah's

tions, a term that means 'interpretation', 'explanation', or 'commentary', bespeaks Sa'adyah's understanding of his project as an effort to promote a better understanding of the Hebrew Bible among Jews living in the new Arabic-speaking milieu. Unlike the Karaites, however, Sa'adyah was concerned not only with using good, clear Arabic, but was also intent on transmitting traditional Jewish understandings of the biblical text. As Haggai Ben-Shammai has noted, "his translation of the Pentateuch often follows the Aramaic translation of Onkelos, but not consistently. In matters of lexicography he occasionally follows earlier Judeo-Arabic translations."[29] But it is noteworthy that by means of his biblical translations, which soon became popular throughout the Arabic-speaking Jewish communities, Sa'adyah succeeded not only in overcoming the excessive literalism in the earlier versions and their perceived stylistic clumsiness and infelicity,[30] but also in standardizing Judaeo-Arabic spelling, moving it away from the earlier phonetic Hebraized orthography to a standard system of transliteration.[31] Moreover, it was Sa'adyah who first introduced Arabic "into the discourse of the rabbinic elite. . . . He also followed the structure of Arabic works, especially in providing systematic theoretical introductions to all his writings."[32]

The perceived infelicity of earlier Judaeo-Arabic biblical translations, along with a number of concerns with translation technique, some of them dictated by important religious considerations, seem to have been among the motives that prompted Sa'adyah to undertake work on his *Tafsīr*. He says himself of his project:

> For a long time, in my hometown, I dwelled constantly on my desire, which was to have a translation of the Torah composed by me in use among the people of the true religion, a proper translation that would not be refuted by speculative knowledge or rebutted by tradition; but

---

translations see Richard C. Steiner, *A Biblical Translation in the Making: The Evolution and Impact of Saadia Gaon's Tafsīr* (Harvard University Center for Jewish Studies; Cambridge, MA: Harvard University Press, 2010), esp. pp. 169–170.

[29] Ben-Shammai, "Sa'adyah Gaon," p. 199.

[30] Joshua Blau speaks of what he calls "the carelessness" of Judaeo-Arabic style as one of its "chief characteristics." See J. Blau, *The Emergence and Linguistic Background of Judaeo-Arabic: A Study in the Origins of Neo-Arabic and Middle Arabic* (3rd rev. ed.; Jerusalem: Ben-Zvi Institute, 1999), pp. 97–98. On these and related issues connected with the earlier Jewish Bible translations, see Steiner, *A Biblical Translation in the Making*, esp. pp. 5–31.

[31] See Joshua Blau, "On a Fragment of the Oldest Judaeo-Arabic Bible Translation Extant," in Blau and Reif, *Genizah Research after Ninety Years*, pp. 31–32.

[32] Ben-Shammai, "Sa'adyah Gaon," p. 198.

I refrained from taking that on . . . because I thought that in the lands far from my hometown there were translations that were clear and formulated precisely.[33]

Saʿadyah's hometown was in Egypt, and it seems to have been the case that no sooner had he arrived in Palestine than he discovered that the clear and precisely formulated Arabic translations of which he speaks did not in fact yet exist. In all likelihood it was already then, during his sojourn in Tiberias, that he began his own long-dreamed of project. Richard Steiner makes the case for this position, and he argues that "Saadia's *Tafsīr* was originally nothing more than an annotated translation, perhaps only on the beginning of Genesis." He goes on to explain that on this hypothesis, as Saʿadyah continued work on his project during his years in Baghdad, the annotations in due course became a substantial commentary, leaving the translation engulfed within. Subsequently, he believes, Saʿadyah was persuaded by a request from others,[34] and "rectified the situation by reissuing the translation (in a revised version) without any notes at all."[35] And so was born the Arabic version of the Torah and other biblical books that quickly found their way throughout the Arabic-speaking Jewish communities in the Islamic world and beyond.

To take one's cue from Saʿadyah's statement quoted above, a proper translation would be one "that would not be refuted by speculative knowledge or rebutted by tradition." Left out of account for the moment is an explicit concern for felicity of expression in the target language, i.e., Arabic in this instance. But that concern might well be understood to lie behind what Saʿadyah meant by his further mention of translations that are "clear and formulated precisely." As for the requisite respect for 'speculative knowledge', in the intellectual milieu in which Saʿadyah lived and worked, one may consider it to be summed up in the phrase, "knowledge triumphant" that Franz Rosenthal famously used to characterize the intellectual life of medieval Islam.[36] One thing that Saʿadyah no doubt had much in mind in

[33] Quoted from the preface of Saʿadyah's edition of the *Tafsīr* published without commentary, in Richard Steiner's English translation; Steiner, *A Biblical Translation in the Making*, p. 1.

[34] See Saʿadyah's own remarks on this request and his response to it in the English translation of the relevant passage from the Foreword to the unencumbered *Tafsīr*, in Brody, *The Geonim of Babylonia*, pp. 302–303.

[35] Steiner, *A Biblical Translation in the Making*, p. 93; see also the discussion on pp. 76–93.

[36] See Franz Rosenthal, *Knowledge Triumphant: The Concept of Knowledge in Medieval Islam* (Leiden: E.J. Brill, 1970).

this connection was the contemporary Muʿtazilī concern about the unreasonableness of using anthropomorphic language and thought in reference to God. As Richard Steiner has pointed out, "Saadia is particularly concerned with anthropomorphisms and anthropopathisms, which, he says, contradict both reason and explicit, unambiguous scriptural statements."[37] Steiner also calls attention to Saʿadyah's concern to translate Genesis 1:1 in a way that would avoid any possibility of its seeming to support the Aristotelian view of the eternity of the world, one of the major intellectual issues facing Christian and Muslim thinkers of the day. Indeed, Steiner makes the case that in this matter Saʿadyah may even have been influenced by a contemporary Christian Arabic translation of Genesis.[38]

A translation that is not "rebutted by tradition" would, in Saʿadyah's view, be one done in accord with traditional rabbinic understandings of the scriptures. And it is here that his concern for felicitous Arabic brought him into difficulties that he mastered with aplomb, albeit not without arousing some controversy. To begin with, there was the question of literalism versus freedom in the rendering, specifically freedom from the necessity to reflect in the target language (Arabic) every particle, tense, and part of speech of the original Hebrew. This was an important matter because from the religious point of view, every jot and tittle of the sacred text was significant. Compelled therefore to deal with issues of abbreviation and repetition, not to mention seemingly anthropomorphic language in his *Tafsīr*, Saʿadyah rose to the challenge with considerable creativity. To avoid the obloquy that earlier Arabic translations had garnered in the new cultural milieu, he made use of periphrasis, varied the language in biblical repetitions, supplied subordinate clauses, used pronouns in place of proper nouns, and even omitted superfluous words. This he did for the sake of fluency and accuracy in the Arabic rendering, not just for style's sake but also, and perhaps principally, so that the traditional meanings and interpretations would emerge in the new language.[39]

Earlier Judaeo-Arabic translations of the scripture had in fact been ridiculed by no less a personage than the great Muslim Muʿtazilī, Abū ʿUthmān Amr al-Jāḥiẓ (777–868 CE), who in his 'Refutation of Christians' excoriated

[37] Steiner, *A Biblical Translation in the Making*, p. 72.

[38] Steiner, *A Biblical Translation in the Making*, pp. 69–70. One will recall Steiner's view, cited in the previous chapter, that the earliest extant Christian Arabic translation of the Pentateuch was in all likelihood done by Ḥunayn ibn Isḥāq (see pp. 52–68), who, like Saʿadyah, and the Muslim Ibn Qutaybah, had translated the opening phrase of Genesis 1:1 "The first of what God created . . . ."

[39] See the insightful study of these matters in Steiner, *A Biblical Translation in the Making*, esp. pp. 13–51.

Jewish interpretations of the scriptures not only for their want of good Arabic, but also for what he considered to be their misunderstanding of figures of speech.[40] Some modern scholars have plausibly called attention to al-Jāḥiẓ's unwonted criticisms as evidence of an attitude of condemnation in the wider culture that, along with other, internal Jewish reasons, could well have been among the motives that prompted Saʿadyah to produce his *Tafsīr*.[41]

Buttressing this line of reasoning is the fact that not only in the *Tafsīr* and the 'Book of Beliefs and Opinions' but in the biblical commentaries as well, Saʿadyah is seen to be very much au courant with the contemporary concerns in Baghdad's scholarly and intellectual circles, and not least with the philosophical issues that interested Jews, Christians, and Muslims alike. Henry Malter put it well years ago when he wrote, "The appreciation of Saadia as a master of philosophy should not be based merely on those of this writings that are specially devoted to the subject, but on the general trend of his works in all other branches of Jewish literature as well."[42] A case in point is his approach to the translation of Genesis 1:1 in the *Tafsīr*, mentioned above. Saʿadyah was dissatisfied with the usual interpretation, "In the beginning God created . . ." because in light of the ideas current in his world, it implied that God created the world in time, time being the measure of motion, as the Aristotelians understood it, and motion implying the existence of matter. In other words, it implied the existence of matter prior to the creation, a position unacceptable to Jewish, Christian, and Muslim thinkers. So Saadia, like Ibn Qutaybah before him, and Ḥunayn ibn Isḥāq before either of them on Richard Steiner's view, translated the phrase, "The first of what God created . . ."[43]

In most of Saʿadyah's surviving biblical commentaries or portions of commentaries, one finds introductions in which he sets forth the ideas and concerns, often in essence philosophical ones, that he will address in the course

[40] See Abū ʿUthmān Amr al-Jāḥiẓ, *Rasāʾil al-Jāḥiẓ* (4 parts in 2 vols.; Cairo: Maktabah al-Khānajī, 1399/1979), vol. 3, pp. 303–351, esp. pp. 334–338.

[41] See, e.g., the discussion in Steiner, *A Biblical Translation in the Making*, pp. 100–108. See also Miriam Goldstein, "Saadya's *Tafsīr* in Light of Muslim Polemic against Ninth-Century Arabic Bible Translations," *Jerusalem Studies in Arabic and Islam* 37 (2010), forthcoming.

[42] Malter, *Saadia Gaon, his Life and Works*, p. 176.

[43] See n.35 above; see also Richard C. Steiner, "Philology as the Handmaiden of Philosophy in R. Saadia Gaon's Interpretation of Gen 1:1," *Israel Oriental Studies* 19 (1999), pp. 379–389.

of the composition.[44] A good example, and one that has been studied in detail from this perspective and even translated into English, is the commentary on the Book of Job.[45] Lenn Evan Goodman, the English scholar and translator of Saʿadyah's commentary on this biblical book, highlighted the philosophical aspect of the work by the very title he chose for his translation, *The Book of Theodicy*.[46] But of course Saʿadyah's most forthright book on matters of contemporary philosophy is his *Kitāb al-amanāt wa-l-itiqādāt*, usually translated the 'Book of Beliefs and Opinions'.[47] It is clear that he wrote this work to address the religious and philosophical issues being debated among Jews, Christians, and Muslims in the Baghdad of his day.[48] Quotations from and allusions to the Bible and rabbinic works are a notable part of the book, demonstrating that the proper interpretation and application of these texts to the issues under discussion were important to Saʿadyah's systematic defense of Jewish life and thought. The philosophical controversies that stirred Baghdad were almost always also interreligious in nature, and so interreligious as well as intra-Jewish polemics found their way into his exegeses.[49]

[44] See Erwin I. J. Rosenthal, "Saadya Gaon: An Appreciation of his Biblical Exegesis," in E. I. J. Rosenthal, *Studia Semitica* (2 vols., vol. 1, Jewish Themes; Cambridge: Cambridge University Press, 1971), vol. 1, pp. 86–96.

[45] See the over-all description of the work in Erwin I. J. Rosenthal, "Saadya's Exegesis of the Book of Job," in Rosenthal, *Studia Semitica*, vol. 1, pp. 97–125. Here the author shows Saʿadyah's concern in the commentary with earlier Jewish tradition and understandings, as well as with contemporary philosophical problems.

[46] L. E. Goodman, *The Book of Theodicy: Translation and Commentary on the Book of Job by Saadiah ben Joseph alFayyūmī* (Yale Judaica Series, vol. 25; New Haven, CT: Yale University Press, 1988).

[47] The text is also known by its Hebrew title: *Emunot ve-Deʿot.* The Arabic edition is published by S. Landauer, *Kitāb al-Amânât wa'l-Iʿtiqâdât von Saʿadja b. Jûsuf al-Fajjûmî* (Leiden: E.J. Brill, 1880); the Arabic with a Hebrew translation by Yosef Kafaḥ, *Sefer ha-Nivhar ba-Emunot ufa-deʿot le-Rabenu Seʿadyah ben Yosef Fiumi: Makor vetargum tirgem le-ʿIvrit* (Jerusalem: Sura; New York: Yeshivah University, 1969/1970); an English translation by Samuel Rosenblatt, *Saadia Gaon: The Book of Beliefs and Opinions* (Yale Judaica Series, vol. 1; New Haven, CT: Yale University Press, 1948).

[48] See Steiner, *A Biblical Translation in the Making*, pp. 109–117.

[49] See A. S. Halkin, "Saadia's Exegesis and Polemics," in Louis Finkelstein (ed.), *Rab Saadia Gaon: Studies in His Honor* (New York: Jewish Theological Seminary of America, 1944), pp. 117–141; Andrew Rippin, "Saʿadya Gaon and Genesis 22: Aspects of Jewish-Muslim Interaction and Polemic," in W. M. Brinner and S. D. Ricks (eds.), *Studies in Islamic and Judaic Traditions: Papers Presented at the Institute for Islamic-Judaic Studies; Center for Judaic Studies, University of Denver* (Atlanta, GA: Scholars Press, 1986), pp. 33–46.

It would be impossible to overstate the importance of Saʿadyah's contribution to the phenomenon that is the Bible in Arabic. Not only did his *Tafsīr* circulate widely in Arabic-speaking Jewish communities, but his translation of the Torah was also adopted and adapted in Christian churches in the Islamic world, particularly among the Copts. Much later it even found its way into the great European polyglot Bibles of the sixteenth and seventeenth centuries.[50] Similarly, Muslim scholars such as Abū l-Ḥasan al-Masʿūdī (d.956), who knew Saʿadyah personally, and ʿAlī ibn Aḥmad ibn Ḥazm (994–1064), among others, seem to have known Saʿadyah's *Tafsīr* and to have consulted it.[51] This wide distribution outside of the Jewish world invites a look at the script in which Saʿadyah wrote.

The early Jewish translations of the Bible into Arabic, and particularly Saʿadyah's *Tafsīr* were certainly intended for use in Jewish communities, and consequently were composed in Judaeo-Arabic, which normally involved writing the Arabic texts in Hebrew characters adapted to the purposes of transliteration. We mentioned earlier that Saʿadyah himself played a role in the regularization of the system of transliteration. Yet there is a report in Abraham ibn Ezra's (1089–1164) commentary on Genesis 2:11 that Saʿadyah had "translated the Torah into the language and script of the Ishmaelites."[52] This remark has aroused a considerable difference of opinions about the script in which Saʿadyah wrote the *Tafsīr*.[53] It remains a vexed question, albeit that some fragments preserved in the Cairo Geniza have passages from the text in Arabic writing. Perhaps the so far most reasonable solution is the one proposed by Richard Steiner, according to which either Saʿadyah himself arranged for the *Tafsīr* to be produced in both the Hebrew and Arabic scripts, which was seemingly Ibn Ezra's position, or that others, be they Christians, Muslims, or Maghribī Jews, very soon transcribed the

[50] See Georg Graf, *Geschichte der christlichen arabischen Literatur* (5 vols. Studi e Testi, 118, 133, 146, 147, 172; Città del Vaticano: Biblioteca Apostolica Vaticana, 1944–1953) vol. 1, pp. 101–103. Note Graf's curious remark, "Seine Uebersetzung zeigt im allgemeinen den Charakter einer Paraphrase" (p. 101).

[51] See Camilla Adang, *Muslim Writers on Judaism and the Hebrew Bible: From Ibn Rabban to Ibn Ḥazm* (Islamic Philosophy, Theology, and Science, vol. 22; Leiden: E.J. Brill, 1996), pp. 122–126, 133–138.

[52] Quoted from Steiner, *A Biblical Translation in the Making*, p. 94.

[53] The issue has been discussed in Blau, *The Emergence and Linguistic Background of Judaeo-Arabic*, pp. 39–44; Leon Nemoy, "The Factor of Script in the Textual Criticism of Judeo-Arabic Manuscripts," *Jewish Quarterly Review* 66 (1975–1976), pp. 148–159; Rippin, "Saʿadya Gaon and Genesis 22," pp. 33–34.

text from the customary Judaeo-Arabic script into conventional Arabic writing for use in their own circles.[54]

Once the Jewish translations of the Bible into Arabic, and Sa'adyah's *Tafsīr* in particular, gained a purchase in the Arabic-speaking Rabbanite communities, an era of Jewish biblical scholarship in Arabic emerged that was to have a major impact. It extended from the Near East, Egypt, and North Africa all the way to Spain, and its echoes would be heard well to the north of the Pyrenees in the scholarly worlds of Rashi (1040–1105), Rambam (c. 1080–1160), and the great Ashkenazi scholars of medieval Europe. To make the point one need only mention the names of the most prominent of the Arabophone scholars after Sa'adyah, who flourished in the wake of the Jewish adoption of Arabic in the ninth century CE: Samuel ben Ḥofnī Gaon (d.1013), Jonah ibn Janaḥ (*fl.*early eleventh cent.), Moses ibn Ezra (c. 1055–1138), Abraham ibn Ezra (1089–1164), Moses Maimonides (1135–1204), and David Kimḥī (c. 1160–1235). They all contributed substantially to the grammatical, linguistic, and exegetical study of the Bible in ways that are still discussed with verve in contemporary Jewish scholarship.[55] Similarly, in the Karaite communities after the time of Qirqisānī, biblical translation continued to be a major step in exegesis, and was supplemented by the production of word lists and other philological tools intended to enhance the understanding of the Hebrew text. The Karaites flourished in Jerusalem at least up to the coming of the crusaders from the West at the end of the eleventh century and they continued thereafter in Byzantium and later in Turkey and elsewhere.[56]

Meanwhile, from the ninth century onward into the fourteenth and fifteenth centuries, the translation of biblical texts into Judaeo-Arabic continued apace among the many Jews in the Arabic speaking world. They continued to be considered helps to the understanding of the Hebrew text, and for this reason were often called 'expositions' or 'explanations', *ash-shurūḥ* in Arabic. Many of them were very literal in character, eschewing the literary grace that distinguished the Arabic of Sa'adyah's *Tafsīr* and made it,

[54] See Steiner, *A Biblical Translation in the Making*, pp. 94–99.

[55] See the survey in Mordechai Cohen, "Bible Exegesis, 1. Rabbanite," in Stillman, *Encyclopedia of Jews in the Islamic World*, vol. 1, pp. 442–457. See also Mordechai Z. Cohen, *Three Approaches to Biblical Metaphor: From Abraham ibn Ezra and Maimonides to David Kimhi* (Études sur le Judaïsme Médiéval, vol. 26; Leiden: Brill, 2008).

[56] See the survey in Daniel Frank, "Bible Exegesis, 2. Karaite," in Stillman, *Encyclopedia of Jews in the Islamic World*, vol. 1, pp. 457–461. See also Meira Polliack (ed.), *Karaite Judaism: A Guide to its History and Literary Sources* (Handbuch der Orientalistik, vol. 73; Leiden: Brill, 2003).

as we have seen, popular even beyond the boundaries of the Jewish communities. Most modern scholars seem to put an emphasis on the role of *ash-shurūḥ* in the Bible-study of those who had no command of Hebrew or Aramaic, the traditional languages of Jewish scholarship and intellectual life.[57] One wonders if in addition to this role, and perhaps subsidiary to it, these explanatory versions of biblical texts, with their literalness and even word-for-word equivalencies, were not also intended to aid the Jewish response to the interreligious polemics of the day.[58]

In the interreligious milieu of the Arabic-speaking world, novel anti-Jewish polemical issues arose, chief among them the charge that in the new scriptural dispensation of the Qur'ān, the Jewish law was abrogated. It was a charge that had its origins in Islamic anti-Jewish polemic, but somewhat surprisingly was soon adopted by Arabophone Christian anti-Jewish polemicists as well. It is not unlikely that in addition to the Jewish communities' time-honored study of the details of the Torah's Hebrew text, there would have been added attention paid in early Islamic times to the proper translation and interpretation of those passages from the Torah and the books of the prophets that Christian and Muslim anti-Jewish polemicists regularly cited, either in support of their distinctive Messianic or prophetic claims, or as evidence alleged to support the abrogation (*an-naskh*) of the precepts of the Torah.

The so far earliest known text written by a Muslim in which the claim of such abrogation is voiced seems to have been written by the early Muʿtazilī *mutakallim* an-Naẓẓām (d.846), arguing against an otherwise unknown Jewish opponent named Manassā ibn Ṣāliḥ.[59] Eventually the allegation that the Qur'ān abrogates Mosaic Law became such a commonplace in both Muʿtazilī and Ashʿarī anti-Jewish polemics,[60] that both Saʿadyah and

[57] See the brief discussion of these texts, with an attendant bibliography, in Benjamin Hary, "Judeo-Arabic Shurūḥ (Since the Fourteenth Century)," in Stillman, *Encyclopedia of Jews in the Islamic World*, vol. 1, pp. 469–472, and p. 475 (bibliography).

[58] In this connection, see Sarah Stroumsa, "The Impact of Syriac Tradition on Early Judaeo-Arabic Bible Exegesis," *ARAM* 3 (1991), pp. 83–96.

[59] See Camilla Adang and Sabine Schmidtke, "Polemics (Muslim-Jewish)," in Stillman, *Encyclopedia of Jews in the Islamic World*, vol. 4, pp. 82–90.

[60] See Binyamin Abrahamov, "Some Notes on the Notion of *Naskh* in the *Kalām*," in Anna Akasoy and Wim Raven (eds.), *Islamic Thought in the Middle Ages: Studies in Text, Transmission, and Translation, in Honour of Hans Daiber* (Islamic Philosophy, Theology and Science, Texts and Studies, vol. 75; Leiden: Brill, 2008), pp. 3–19.

Qirqisānī devoted considerable attention to refuting the charge in the apologetic sections of their philosophical works.[61]

The earliest Christian Arabic writer to argue philosophically in behalf of what he called "the necessity of the abrogation (*naskh*) of the Mosaic *sharī'ah*,"[62] was Abū 'Alī 'Īsā ibn Zur'ah (943–1008), who made his argument in a letter addressed in the year 997 CE to a now unknown Jewish correspondent, one Bishr ibn Finḥās ibn Shu'ayb al-Ḥāsib, in which the author discussed a number of topics at issue between Jews and Christians.[63] In the long section of the letter in which he advanced what he called rational proofs for the abrogation of the Mosaic *sharī'ah*, Ibn Zur'ah also included a brief presentation of what he considered to be scriptural proof of the allegation. He claimed that the abrogation was, as he put it to Bishr ibn Finḥās, "already mentioned for you in your own scriptures," and he cited the prophet David, who said, "God does not have a predilection for the sacrifice that passes away; God's sacrifice is only the humble, submissive soul" (Ps. 51:16–17). In response, Ibn Zur'ah immediately poses the following rhetorical question:

> Do you not consider this quotation from David in conjunction with Moses' text about God's pleasure, exalted be He, in the sacrifice of lambs and bulls,[64] to be an abrogation on [David's] part of what Moses said? I think there is no one who does not know it. For there is nothing more to abrogation than that it removes the one and imposes the other, Just as David said, on whom be peace. For he spoke about something which Moses said, namely, about the sacrifice pleasing to God, that the one sacrifice does not please God, and that God's sacrifice is a humble, submissive heart.[65]

What is notable in this remark is what Ibn Zur'ah says about abrogation; that it is a matter of one thing in scripture abrogating another, an idea that is at the heart of the Islamic doctrine of *an-naskh*.[66] He cites one more

[61] Sa'adyah in his *Kitāb al-amānāt wal-i'tiqādāt* and Qirqisānī in his *Kitāb al-anwār wa l-marāqib.*

[62] Paul Sbath (ed.), *Vingt traités philosophiques et apologétiques d'auteurs arabes chrétiens du IXe au XIVe siècle* (Cairo: Friedrich and Co., 1929), p. 22.

[63] See the text published in Sbath, *Vingt traités,* pp. 19–52.

[64] Presumably a reference to such passages in the Torah as Gen. 8:20 and Lev. 1:9 that speak of the odor of animal sacrifices being pleasing to the Lord.

[65] Sbath, *Vingt traités,* pp. 29–30.

[66] See the discussion in John Burton, "Naskh wa 'l-Mansūkh, in *EI,* 2nd ed., vol. 7, pp. 1009 ff.; *idem,* "Abrogation," in Jane Damen McAuliffe, *Encyclopaedia of the Qur'ān* 6 vols.; Leiden: Brill, 2001–2006), vol. I, pp. 11–19.

scriptural passage to the same point, from the prophet Jeremiah: "God says that the days are coming and I will make a new covenant for you, not like the covenant I made for your fathers when I brought them out from the Land of Egypt" (Jer. 31:31-32). Ibn Zur'ah asks, "Is there not in this quotation an evident statement of the abrogation of the *sharī'ah* of Moses?"[67] Clearly by the tenth century, Ibn Zur'ah was taking his cue from developments in Islamic thought about a later passage of scripture abrogating an earlier one and putting it to use in his arguments against the Jews and their claim to be professing the true religion.[68]

While 'Īsā ibn Zur'ah embedded his arguments in largely philosophical and political terms, later Arab Christian writers would concentrate on searching the scriptures in an effort to multiply what they claimed to be instances of just such scriptural abrogation as Ibn Zur'ah alleged in the two passages quoted above. They compiled lists of precepts from the Torah and paired them with seemingly contradictory precepts or contrary behavior from the Prophets, thereby alleging abrogation. In many instances these are inconsistencies or seeming contradictions in the biblical texts that the Rabbis had that had already engaged the Rabbis' attention, and sometimes Christian writers took notice of rabbinical opinions on these texts and argued against them. One compilation of this sort is the probably eleventh- or twelfth-century text wrongly attributed to the Melkite bishop of Sidon, Paul of Antioch, 'On the Abrogation of the *Sharī'ah* of the Jews from the Torah and the Prophets.'[69] Here, for example, the author cites and takes issue with the opinion of an unnamed Exilarch regarding the impossibility of abrogation when the scripture text speaks of a precept as binding forever (*'alaykum ilā l-abad*), as in the instance of the keeping of the Sabbath, a perpetually controversial subject dividing Jews and Christians.[70]

[67] Sbath, *Vingt traités*, p. 30.

[68] See the discussion in Shlomo Pines, "La loi naturelle et la société: La doctrine politico-théologique d'Ibn Zur'a, philosophe chrétien de Bagdad," in Uriel Heyd (ed.), *Studies in Islamic History and Civilization* (Scripta Hierosolymitana, vol. 9; Jerusalem: The Magnes Press, The Hebrew University, 1961), pp. 154–190, including a French translation of the section of the letter dealing with the abrogation of the Mosaic law, pp. 173–178.

[69] The text is published in Louis Cheikho (ed.), *Vingt traités théologiques d'auteurs arabes chrétiens (IXe–XIII siècles)* (Beyrouth: Imprimerie Catholique, 1920), pp. 63–70. See the brief discussion of this still unstudied text in Graf, *Geschichte der christlichen arabischen Literatur*, vol. 2, p. 77; Paul Khoury, *Paul d'Antioche, évêque melkite de Sidon (XIIe siècle.)* (Beyrouth: Imprimerie Catholique, 1964), p. 43.

[70] See Cheikho, *Vingt traités*, p. 66.

Given these attacks by Bible-quoting Christian opponents, along with the similar polemical habits of apostate Jews, such as those found in the *Ifḥām al-yahūd* of Samaw'al ibn Yaḥyā al-Maghribī (d.1174),[71] and, as we shall see in the next chapter, the scriptural interpretations advanced by contemporary Muslim controversialists, it is no wonder that in mid-March of the year 1280/81 CE, the preeminent Jewish philosopher of Baghdad, 'Izz ad-Dawlah Sa'd ibn Manṣūr ibn Kammūnah (d.1284),[72] published his famous book, *Tanqīḥ al-abḥāth lilmilal al-thalāth.*[73] In it he argued the case for the Jews precisely in reference to the issue of prophecy and the right reading of the Bible, comparing the understandings of the matter on the part of scholars in the three communities, Jews, Christians, and Muslims. No small part of his discussion concerned the proper construction to be put on key biblical passages customarily cited by the opponents of the Jews. Then some years later a Jacobite Christian, Ḥasan ibn Ibrāhīm ibn Yaqūb ibn Nakhtūmā al-Khabbāz ibn al-Maḥrūmah (d. before 1354), wrote a series of *Ḥawāshī*, or marginal notes, some quite long, on the sections of Ibn Kammūnah's *Tanqīḥ* that concerned the views of the Jews and Christians.[74] Speaking favorably of the views of Samaw'al al-Maghribī, Ibn al-Maḥrūmah's comments focused for the most part on refuting the interpretation of biblical passages offered by Ibn Kammūnah in the section of the *Tanqīḥ* on Jewish beliefs. Al-Maḥrūmah concentrated in particular on arguments meant to demonstrate to his satisfaction the wisdom of abrogating *sharī'ah.* But he also argued, like

[71] See Moshe Perlmann (ed. and trans.), *Samau'al al-Maghribī, Ifḥām al-Yahūd; Silencing the Jews* (Proceedings of the American Academy for Jewish Research, vol. 32; New York: American Academy for Jewish Research, 1964); Ibrahim Marazka, Reza Pourjavady, and Sabine Schmidtke (eds.), *Samaw'al al-Maghribī's (d.570–1175) Ifḥām al-Yahūd* (Wiesbaden: Harrassowitz, 2006).

[72] See Reza Pourjavady and Sabine Schmidtke, *A Jewish Philosopher of Baghdad: 'Izz al-Dawla ibn Kammūna (d.683/1284) and his Writings* (Islamic Philosophy, Theology and Science, vol. 65; Leiden: Brill, 2006).

[73] See Moshe Perlmann (ed.), *Sa'd b. Manṣūr ibn Kammūna's Examination of the Inquiries into the Three Faiths: A Thirteenth-Century Essay in Comparative Religion* (University of California Publications, Near Eastern Studies, 6; Berkeley and Los Angeles, CA: University of California Press, 1967); *idem* (trans.), *Ibn Kammūna's Examination of the Three Faiths: A Thirteenth-Century Essay in the Comparative Study of Religion, Translated from the Arabic, with an Introduction and Notes* (Berkeley and Los Angeles, CA: University of California Press, 1971).

[74] See Ḥabīb Bacha, *Ḥawāshī (Notes) d'Ibn al-Maḥrūma sur le Tanqīḥ d'ibn Kammūna* (Patrimoine Arabe Chrétien, 6; Jounieh, Liban and Roma: Librairie Saint-Paul and Pontificio Istituto Orientale, 1984).

some polemicists before him, that "The Torah incites to bad morals."[75] And of the Jews he claims that their Law was "taken from the Jewish *'ulamā'*, not from Moses. They follow neither Moses nor the Torah, but the Rabbis."[76] As for the Torah itself, he says that the Christians, in contradistinction to the Muslims, "do not believe in the corruption (*taḥrīf*) of the Torah. Rather, they believe only in its abrogation (*naskh*)."[77]

The apologetic/polemical horizons defined by the interreligious controversies between Jews, Christians, and Muslims, as well as between rival circles of thought within the Jewish communities themselves must have been an important factor in Jewish projects to translate the Bible into Arabic from the ninth to the thirteenth centuries. The translations then provided the first steps in the larger enterprise of biblical exegesis that flowered in Arabic in these centuries and became in that language one of the all-time monuments of Jewish scholarship. The inter-communal dimension to this achievement, while it may not have been of the essence, was nevertheless not one to be ignored by historians in search of a fuller appreciation of the accomplishment.

[75] Bacha, *Ḥawāshī*, p. 96.
[76] Bacha, *Ḥawāshī*, p. 101.
[77] Bacha, *Ḥawāshī*, p. 123.

✻ CHAPTER VI ✻

Muslims and the Bible in Arabic

IN THEIR QUEST to articulate and commend a distinctive Islamic religious view of the world and of the Muslim's place in it, Muslim scholars in the early Islamic period were quick to take their cue from the Qur'ān's multiple recollections and reminiscences from the Torah, the Prophets, the Psalms, and the Gospel. In addition to articulating principles of polity and government for the new political reality,[1] they constructed a view of sacred history that subtly and perhaps somewhat subconsciously wove traditional scriptural language, with its characteristically Jewish and Christian idiom, into an Arabic expression of a distinctively Islamic narrative. As John Wansbrough pointed out so clearly, early Muslim Qur'ān interpretation, the earliest Muslim historical works, the early biographies of Muḥammad and his companions, and the genealogies linking the early Muslim heroes to the preexisting biblical and folkloric record, all utilized the biblical idiom and exegetical strategies familiar from the lore of the Jews and Christians. But they did so with a new hermeneutical purpose, namely, to define the religious identity and underwrite the legitimacy of nascent Islam in terms that would resonate with the scripture-based theologies of those whom the Qur'ān, some fifty-four times, pointedly calls 'People of Scripture' (*ahl'al-kitāb*).[2] Within this horizon we find the earliest Muslim interest in the text of the Jewish and Christian Bible.

MUSLIMS AND THE AUTHENTICITY OF THE BIBLE

Already in the Qur'ān, disparities between the interpretations given the scriptural narratives by the several communities of Jews, Christians, and Muslims gave rise to the charge that the text of the Bible was corrupt. The

[1] See Patricia Crone, *God's Rule: Government and Islam* (New York: Columbia University Press, 2004).

[2] See J. Wansbrough, *Quranic Studies: Sources and Methods of Scriptural Interpretation* (London Oriental Series, vol. 31; Oxford: Oxford University Press, 1977); *idem, The Sectarian Milieu: Content and Composition of Islamic Salvation History* (London Oriental Series, vol. 34; Oxford: Oxford University Press, 1978).

alteration of words, for example, and the concealment of meanings was cited (cf., e.g., III *Āl 'Imrān* 78). From the early Islamic period onward, the charge and countercharge of corrupting (*at-taḥrīf*) the scriptures became a staple in arguments about religion between Jews, Christians and Muslims.[3] On the one hand, Muslim writers were concerned to claim the authority of the Bible to warrant the scriptural authenticity of Muḥammad, the Qur'ān, and Islamic teaching more generally; one may call this process the 'Biblicizing' of the Islamic prophetic claims. On the other hand, given the concomitant Islamic contention that the earlier scriptures were corrupt and therefore of questionable authenticity, along with the divergent cast of many Islamic presentations of Biblical narratives, one might also speak of a simultaneous process of 'Islamicizing' the biblical material.[4]

The biblical interests of Muslim religious writers underwent a certain evolution over the centuries. In the earlier period, when the primary concern was to 'Biblicize' Islamic prophetology, some writers, as we shall see, showed a keen interest in the Biblical text familiar to Jews and Christians. By the tenth century however, the interests of many Muslim scholars seem to have shifted away from quotations as such from the earlier scriptures, however attentively they once 'corrected' the wording of these texts, and to have turned their focus more toward the 'Islamicization' of whole biblical narratives. These stories they retold, paying concomitantly less interest to the wording of the texts, which were of course familiar to Jews and Chris-

[3] See Jean-Marie Gaudeul and Robert Caspar, "Textes de la tradition musulmane concernant le *taḥrīf* (falsification des Écritures," *Islamochristiana* 6 (1980), pp. 61–104; Camilla Adang, *Muslim Writers on Judaism and the Hebrew Bible: From Ibn Rabban to Ibn Ḥazm* (Islamic Philosophy, Theology and Science, vol. 22; Leiden: E.J. Brill, 1996), esp. pp. 223–248; Gordon Nickel, *Narratives of Tampering in the Earliest Commentaries on the Qur'ān* (History of Christian-Muslim Relations, vol. 13; Brill: Leiden, 2011); Martin Whittingham, "The Value of *taḥrīf ma'nawī* (Corrupt Interpretation) as a Category for Analysing Muslim Views of the Bible: Evidence from *Al-radd al-jamīl* and Ibn Khaldūn," *Islam and Christian-Muslim Relations* 22 (2011), pp. 209–222. See also the interesting study on the background of the early Muslim concern with the corruption of scripture by Gabriel Said Reynolds, "On the Qur'ānic Accusation of Scriptural Falsification (*taḥrīf*) and Christian Anti-Jewish Polemic," *Journal of the American Oriental Society* 130 (2010), pp. 189–202.

[4] Brian Hauglid called attention to these processes in B. Hauglid, "Al-Tha'labī's *Qiṣaṣ alAnbiyā'*: Analysis of the Text, Jewish and Christian Elements, Islamization, and Prefiguration of the Prophethood of Muḥammad," (Ph.D. Dissertation; Salt Lake City, UT: The University of Utah, 1998). See also Jane Dammen McAuliffe, "The Qur'ānic Context of Muslim Biblical Scholarship," *Islam and Christian–Muslim Relations* 7 (1996), 141–158.

tians—as for example the large body of popular tales of the prophets (*qiṣaṣ al-anbiyā'*) and the so-called, *Isrā'īliyyāt* that circulated widely in the World of Islam.[5]

Muslim scholars in the earliest period were anxious to show that Muḥammad's coming had been foretold in the Bible, and they assembled lists of quotations in support of this contention. An early case in point is the work of Wahb ibn Munabbih (d.732), who in his accounts of the prophets before Muḥammad alluded to the Torah, the Psalms, and once or twice to the Gospel, including a reference to a long paraphrase of Jesus' Sermon on the Mount, following along the lines of Matthew chapters 6 through 7.[6] Wahb was careful to present his recollections of the narratives of the earlier scriptures in accordance with what the Qur'ān teaches about their message. Nevertheless, it is clear that he and others must have consulted Jewish and/or Christian sources for his information.[7] Given a report from Mālik ibn Dīnār (d.748) that Wahb took a book that interested him from a Christian monastery, R. G. Khoury has pointed out that ". . . if one can believe such texts, and basically what could be more natural than to think of such encounters all across the centuries, [Wahb] could have come upon an Arabic version of the Old and of the New Testaments, or at least of a part."[8] In an earlier chapter we have seen that in all likelihood, Christians were in fact producing the earliest Arabic translations of the Bible in the

[5] See Roberto Tottoli, "Origin and Use of the Term *Isrā'īliyyāt* in Muslim Literature," *Arabica* 46 (1999), pp. 193–210; *idem, I Profeti Biblici nella Tradizione Islamica* (Brescia: Paideia Editricee, 1999). Brannon Wheeler, *Prophets of the Qur'ān: An Introduction to the Qur'ān and Muslim Exegesis* (London and New York: Continuum, 2002). One of the most popular texts is available in English translation: W. M. Thackston (trans.), *The Tales of the Prophets of al-Kisa'ī* (Boston: Twayne Publishers, 1978). See also Tarif Khalidi, *The Muslim Jesus: Sayings and Stories in Islamic Literature* (Cambridge, MA: Harvard University Press, 2001).

[6] See R. G. Khoury, "Quelques réflexions sur les citations de la Bible dans les premières générations islamiques du premier et du deuxième siècles de l'hégire," *Bulletin d'Études Orientales* 29 (1977), pp. 269–278; *idem,* "Quelques réflexions sur la première ou les premières Bibles arabes," in T. Fahd (ed.), *L'Arabie préislamique et son environnement historique et culturel: Actes du Colloque de Strasbourg 24–27 juin 1987)* (Leiden: E.J. Brill, 1989), pp. 549–561; M. E. Pregill, "*Isrā'īliyyāt,* Myth, and Pseudepigraphy: Wahb b. Munabbih and the Early Islamic Versions of the Fall of Adam and Eve," *Jerusalem Studies in Arabic and Islam* 34 (2008), pp. 215–284.

[7] See in this connection the important studies of Jean-Louis Déclais, *David raconté par les musulmans* (Paris: Éditions du Cerf, 1999); *idem, Un récit musulman sur Isaïe* (Paris: Les Éditions du Cerf, 2001).

[8] Khoury, "Quelques réflexions sur les citations," pp. 275–276.

eighth century. What is more, there are persistent reports in other Islamic sources of Arabic versions of portions of the Bible available to early Muslim scholars, beginning with the traditions about translations made by the pre-Islamic *ḥanīf*, Waraqah ibn Nawfal.[9] The earliest suggestion in Islamic times of Arabic translations of the Bible made by a Muslim comes in the *Fihrist* of Muḥammad ibn Isḥāq ibn an-Nadīm (d.995/8), who cited the work of one Aḥmad ibn ʿAbd Allāh ibn Salām, a scholar of the time of the caliph Harūn ar-Rashīd (786–809). According to Ibn an-Nadīm, Salām said, "I have translated the Torah, the Gospels, and the books of the prophets and disciples from Hebrew, Greek, and Sabian, which are the languages of the people of each scripture, into Arabic letter for letter."[10] While one may be tempted simply to discount such a report, one should not be so hasty. There is no inherent reason why a Muslim scholar of the period could not at the very least have composed a chrestomathy of passages from the earlier scriptures, perhaps based on Arabic translations made by Jews or Christians already to hand, a practice already well in evidence, as we shall see.

Subsequently, in consequence of the aforementioned doctrine of the Jewish and Christian falsification and corruption of the scripture text, it quickly became the practice in debates between Jews, Christians, and Muslims from the tenth century onwards for Muslim scholars to impugn the authenticity of the Bible text as Jews and Christians actually have it and interpret it. Against Jews they argued from scripture that with the coming of the Qurʾān, the Mosaic *sharīʿah* had been abrogated, as we saw in the previous chapter. Against Christians, Muslim scholars argued from scripture that Jesus, son of Mary, was just like Adam, someone whom God had created from the dust (III *Āhl ʿImrān* 59), and that therefore he was neither God nor the son of God. Appeals to passages in the Gospel according to St. John were often put forward in support of both of these latter points,[11] but in due course scholars assembled an impressive arsenal of passages from all four Gospels.[12]

[9] Regarding these traditions, see the discussion in Griffith, "The Gospel in Arabic," pp. 144–149.

[10] Quoted in the translation of Bayard Dodge (trans.), *The Fihrist of al-Nadim: A Tenth-Century Survey of Muslim Culture* (2 vols.; New York, Columbia University Press, 1970), vol. 1. p. 42.

[11] See Mark Beaumont, "Muslim Readings of John's Gospel in the ʿAbbasid Period," *Islam and Christian Muslim Relations* 19 (2008), pp. 179–197.

[12] See Martin Accad, "The Gospels in the Muslim Discourse of the Ninth to the Fourteenth Centuries: An Exegetical Inventorial Table," *Islam and Christian-Muslim Relations* 14 (2003), pp. 67–91, 205–220, 337–352, 459–479.

Biblical Quotations in Muslim Texts

Perhaps the earliest explicit quotation and translation of a biblical passage to be found in early Islamic scholarship is the passage from the Gospel according to John 15:23–16:1, which records Jesus' words about the 'paraclete' (ὁ παράκλητος whom he would send from the Father; the Spirit of Truth, who would bear witness to him. Heeding the Qur'ān's recollection of Jesus' announcement of "a messenger who will come after me, whose name is Aḥmad," (LXI *aṣ-Ṣaff* 6), Abū 'Abd Allāh Muḥammad ibn Isḥāq (d.c. 767) quoted the entire Gospel passage in Arabic translation in his biography of Muḥammad, which has come down to us in the recension of Abū Muḥammad 'Abd al-Malik ibn Hishām (d.834).[13] Ibn Isḥāq quoted the passage from an Arabic version that was made from the same Greek original that lay behind the so-called 'Syro-Palestinian Lectionary', as was the case with the family of manuscripts that contain the earliest known Arabic Gospel text translated from Greek discussed in an earlier chapter. But what is notable about this quotation is that while it is an obvious, line by line quotation and not just an allusion or a reminiscence of the original text, the translator (or his later editor?) has changed words in the passage that might offend Muslim sensibilities, e.g., using 'the Lord' in place of the original 'Father'. This, along with other adjustments, are revealing of early suspicions that the biblical text was corrupt, and of a tendency on the part of Muslim scholars already to 'Islamicize' their cited versions of earlier scriptural narratives.[14] A similar tendency may be observed in the use made by early Muslim writers of the passage in Isaiah 21: 6–7, which speaks of the watchman who sees "riders, horsemen in pairs, riders on asses, riders on camels," a text taken to be a biblical prophecy of the coming of Muḥammad and the Muslims.[15]

[13] See Abū Muḥammad 'Abd al-Malik ibn Hishām, *Sīrat an-nabī* (ed. Muḥammad Muḥyī ad-Dīn 'abd al-Ḥamīd, 4 vols.; Cairo: Maṭba'ah Ḥijāzī bil-Qāhirah, 1356), vol. 1, p. 251.

[14] See the full discussion of Ibn Isḥāq's quotation in Sidney H. Griffith, "The Gospel in Arabic: An Inquiry into its Appearance in the First Abbasid Century," *Oriens Christianus* 69 (1985), pp. 126–167, esp. 137–143; *idem*, "Arguing from Scripture: The Bible in the Christian/Muslim Encounter in the Middle Ages," in Thomas J. Heffernan and Thomas E. Burman (eds.), *Scripture and Pluralism: Reading the Bible in the Religiously Plural Worlds of the Middle Ages and Renaissance* (Studies in the History of Christian Traditions, vol. 123; Leiden: Brill, 2005), pp. 29–58, esp. 36–45.

[15] See John C. Reeves, "The Muslim Appropriation of a Biblical Text: The Messianic Dimensions of Isaiah 21:6–7," in Kenneth G. Holum and Hayim Lapin

Many early Muslim scholars writing in defense of Muḥammad's status as a prophet who was foretold in the scriptures of the Jews and Christians quoted from the Bible extensively in support of this position, thereby providing evidence of the general accessibility of the Bible in Arabic already in the ninth century, and even earlier. In addition to Ibn Hishām's (d.834) edition of Ibn Isḥāq's *Sīrah*, there are several other texts by Muslim authors of the ninth century that include quotations of Bible passages in Arabic from the texts more or less as the Jews and Christians actually had them. A particularly notable case is the work of the Christian convert to Islam, ʿAlī ibn Rabbān aṭ-Ṭabarī (c. 780–c. 860), who, in addition to other works, composed two apologies in Arabic in defense of the prophethood of Muḥammad, *Kitāb ad-dīn wa dawlah*,[16] and in refutation of the Christians, *Al-Radd ʿalā n-naṣārā*.[17] In these works, ʿAlī ṭ-Ṭabarī quoted liberally and literally from the Bible—from the Torah, the Psalms, Isaiah and other prophets, as well as from the Gospels. It is unclear if he made his own translations from the underlying Syriac or from a ready-to-hand translation already in circulation, perhaps in the form of a standard list of biblical testimonies commonly said by earlier Muslim apologists to refer to Muḥammad.[18] Whatever may have been the case, it has become clear from recent studies that Rabbān aṭ-Ṭabarī's selection of biblical testimonies itself had an influence on subsequent Muslim authors with an interest in finding proof-texts in the scriptures of the Jews and Christians indicative of Muḥammad's prophetic mission.[19] Their interest in the biblical text came just as it was becoming generally available in Arabic translation in the ninth century. For example, al-Qāsim ibn Ibrāhīm ar-Rassī (c. 785–860), a Zaydī *imām*, included numer-

(eds.), *Shaping the Middle East: Jews, Christians, and Muslims in an Age of Transition 400–800 CE* (Bethesda, MD: University Press of Maryland, 2011), pp. 211–222.

[16] On the authenticity of this work, which some earlier scholars had questioned, see David Thomas, "Tabari's Book of Religion and Empire," *Bulletin of the John Rylands University Library of Manchester* 69 (1986), pp. 1–7.

[17] For further information and bibliography, see David Thomas, "Alī l-Ṭabarī," in David Thomas and Barbara Roggema (eds.), *Christian-Muslim Relations: A Bibliographical History* (History of Christian-Muslim Relations, vol. 11; Leiden: Brill, 2009), vol. 1, pp. 669–674. See also Adang, *Muslim Writers on Judaism and the Hebrew Bible*, pp. 23–30.

[18] See Adang, *Muslim Writers on Judaism and the Hebrew Bible*, pp. 110–111.

[19] See, e.g., Ronny Vollandt, "Christian-Arabic Translations of the Pentateuch from the 19th to the 13th Centuries: A Comparative Study of Manuscripts and Translation Techniques," (Ph.D. dissertation; Cambridge: St. John's College, University of Cambridge, 2011), pp. 63–68.

ous quotations from the Old and New Testaments in his *Kitāb ar-radd ʿalā n-naṣārā*, a general refutation of the Christians and their doctrines.[20]

One of those who seems to have come under the influence of Rabbān aṭ-Ṭabarī, and whose work would surpass that of his predecessor in significance in the Muslim community, was Abū Muḥammad ʿAbd Allāh ibn Qutaybah (828–889),[21] an important Muslim scholar interested in the study of the 'signs of prophecy' (*dalāʾil an-nubuwwah*) among other topics. In his *Aʿlām an-nubuwwah*, Ibn Qutaybah quoted often from the Bible, particularly from the Old Testament,[22] and recent scholars have made the case that his quotations from the Pentateuch were derived at least in part from one of the earliest known of the Christian translations of the Torah from Syriac,[23] the very version that Richard Steiner has sought to attribute to none other than Ḥunayn ibn Isḥāq and which, as we saw in the last chapter, Steiner thinks might even have had an influence on Saʿadyah Gaʾōn's *tafsīr* of the beginning of Genesis.[24] Clearly, by the second half of the ninth century the Bible in Arabic had become available to the Arabic-speaking, scholarly public, be they Jews, Christians, or Muslims, and the translations played an important role in intellectual life across denominational and interreligious lines. The Bible, its integrity, and its interpretation were topics of common interest to the scholars of all three communities. And while they approached them

[20] See Wilferd Madelung, "Al-Qāsim ibn Ibrāhīm," in Thomas and Roggema, *Christian-Muslim Relations: A Bibliographical History*, vol. 1, pp. 540–543. Lesser known apologetic pamphlets by Muslim writers of the period also contained biblical quotations; see, e.g., B. Roggema, "Ibn al-Layth," and "Pseudo-ʿUmarʾ II's Letter to Leo III," in Thomas and Roggema, *Christian Muslim Relations: A Bibliographical History*, vol. 1, pp. 347–353 and 381–385.

[21] See G. Vajda, "Judaeo-Arabica: Observations sur quelques citations bibliques chez ibn Qotayba," *Revue des Études Juives* 99 (1935), pp. 68–80; G. Lecomte, "Les citations de l'Ancien et du Nouveau Testament dans l'oeuvre d'Ibn Qutayba," *Arabica* 5 (1958), pp. 34–46; Adang, *Muslim Writers on Judaism*, pp. 112–117; D. Thomas, "Ibn Qutayba," in Thomas and Roggema, *Christian-Muslim Relations: A Bibliographical History*, vol. 1, pp. 816–818.

[22] See the analyses of Said Karoui, "Die Rezeption der Bibel in der frühislamischen Literatur am Beispiel der Hauptwerke von Ibn Qutayba (gest. 276/889)," (Ph.D. Dissertation; Heidelberg: Ruprecht-Karls Universität Heidelberg, 1996). See now the edition of Ibn Qutaybah's *Aʿlām an-nubuwwah* in Sabine Schmidtke, "The Muslim Reception of Biblical Materials: Ibn Qutayba and his *"Aʿlām al-nubuwwa,"* *Islam and Christian-Muslim Relations* 22 (2011), pp. 249–274.

[23] See Vollandt, "Christian-Arabic Translations of the Pentateuch," pp. 68–73.

[24] See Richard C. Steiner, *A Biblical Translation in the Making: The Evolution and Impact of Saadia Gaon's Tafsīr* (Harvard University Center for Jewish Studies; Cambridge, MA: Harvard University Press, 2010), esp. pp. 52–75.

from the perspective of their own particular concerns, the scholarship and biblical lore of one community nevertheless often found an echo in that of the other two communities.

Muslim Scholars and Bible History: A Case Study

Muslim scholars were not slow to take advantage of the wealth of biblical scholarship, including translation and commentary, that Jews and Christians made accessible to them in Arabic from the ninth century CE onward. While not many Muslim texts have been carefully studied from the point of view of their indebtedness to the biblical traditions of the 'Scripture People', there are nevertheless some notable instances in which researchers have shown just how successfully some early Muslim writers made the biblical material, newly available in Arabic, their own. An example, and one that shows this accomplishment at its most highly integrated level is the work of the Muslim historian Aḥmad ibn Abī Ya'qūb ibn Wāḍiḥ al-Ya'qūbī (d.betw. 897–905). We may take his presentation of biblical *personae* in his world history as a case study in the integration of biblical traditions into Islamic intellectual history.

Al-Ya'qūbī's *Ta'rīkh*, or 'History', was written sometime in the third quarter of the ninth century.[25] The work is organized in two major sections. The first, devoted to pre-Islamic history, includes cameo presentations of the major figures of Bible history from Adam to Jesus, along with accounts of the other peoples of the then-known world, their rulers, institutions, and major cultural accomplishments. The second part of the *History* presents the story of Muḥammad and his companions, followed by an account of the successive caliphs and their accomplishments, down to the year 872.[26] The

[25] Al-Ya'qûbî's *Ta'rīkh* is published in Arabic in two editions: M. Th. Houtsma (ed), *Ibn-Wādhih qui dicitur al-Ja'qubî, Historiae* (2 vols.; Leiden: E.J. Brill, 1883); Aḥmad al-Ya'qûbî, *Ta'rīkh al-Ya'qûbî* (2 vols.; Beirut: Dar Sadir and Dar Bayrut, 1379/1960). An English translation of the *Ta'rīkh* is in preparation, by a team of scholars under the general editorship of Lawrence Conrad, Matthew Gordon, and Chase Robinson.

[26] No major study of the *Ta'rīkh* has yet appeared, but general discussions of the work's major characteristics may be found in studies of Islamic historiography. See, e.g., Franz Rosenthal, *A History of Muslim Historiography* (Leiden: E.J. Brill, 1952), pp. 114–116; D. M. Dunlop, *Arab Civilization to AD 1500* (Arab Background Series; London: Longman; Beirut: Librairie du Liban, 1971), pp. 87–88; Yves Marquet, "Le Shi'isme au IXe siècle à travers l'histoire de Ya'qûbî," *Arabica* 19 (1972), pp. 1–45, 101–138; A. A. Duri, *The Rise of Historical Writing among the Arabs* (ed. and trans. L. I. Conrad; Princeton, NJ: Princeton University Press, 1983), pp. 64–67; M.J.L.

Ta'rīkh is characterized by al-Ya'qûbî's close attention to the sources available to him, including the canonical scriptures of the Jews and the Christians. While his reading of the Bible is guided by the Qur'ān, as we shall see, he nevertheless is almost unique among his co-religionists of the time in allowing the canonical biblical text to speak for itself when he has need of it. In the section of the *Ta'rīkh* devoted to Bible history, he quotes from it, paraphrasing liberally in some places. Bible history constitutes a major part of al-Ya'qûbî's *Ta'rīkh*; as it remains to us, the narrative begins with the story of Adam and Eve and, in the Bible history section of the work, it extends to the story of 'the Messiah, Jesus, son of Mary'.[27] Originally, according to al-Ya'qûbî's own testimony, the text began with a now-lost creation story, which he describes as an "abbreviated account" of the "beginning of the coming to be of this world and reports of the most important ancient peoples, of the various kingdoms and of their manifold affairs."[28] In the work as we now have it, the biblical material is presented under the names of the principal figures in Bible history.[29] They appear in order as follows: Adam, the descendants of Adam, Noah, the descendants of Noah, Abraham, Isaac, Jacob, the descendants of Jacob, Moses, the prophets after Moses, David, Solomon, the kings after Solomon up to the destruction of Jerusalem,[30] and

Young et al. (eds.), *Religion, Learning and Science in the 'Abbasid Period* (Cambridge: Cambridge University Press, 1990), pp. 184–201; Bernd Radtke, *Weltgeschichte und Weltbeschreibung im mittelalterlichen Islam* (Beiruter Texte und Studien, 51; Beirut and Stuttgart: Franz Steiner Verlag, 1992), pp. 11–15; Tarif Khalidi, *Arabic Historical Thought in the Classical Period* (Cambridge Studies in Islamic Civilization; Cambridge: Cambridge University Press, 1994), pp. 115–132; Fred M. Donner, *Narratives of Islamic Origins; the Beginnings of Islamic Historical Writing* (Princeton: The Darwin Press, 1998), p.134.

[27] A Dutch translation of the Bible history section of the *Ta'rīkh* is available in G. Smit, *'Bijbel en Legende'; bij den arabischen Schrijver Ja'qubi; 9th Eeuw na Christus* (Leiden: E. J. Brill, 1907). A French translation of the entire Bible history section of the *Ta'rīkh*, with the Arabic text on the facing page, is available in André Ferré, *L'histoire des Prophètes d'après al-Ya'qûbî; d'Adam à Jésus* (Rome: Pontificio Istituto di Studi Arabi e d'Islamistica, 2000).

[28] Al-Ya'qûbî, *Ta'rīkh*, vol. 2, p. 5; Houtsma, *Historiae*, vol. 2, p. 2.

[29] In the manuscript transmission of the *Ta'rīkh* the names of biblical characters have become hopelessly garbled, save in those cases where Islamic tradition preserves a common Arabic form for some of the names, usually those that appear in the Qur'ān. In order to avoid confusion and undue puzzlement, in the present essay the names of biblical characters are always given in the form in which they appear in the Revised Standard Version of the Bible in English.

[30] An English translation of the section dealing with the kings after Moses, up to the excursus on the laws and practices of the Jews is available in R. Y. Ebied and L. R.

finally Jesus.[31] Just after the account of the destruction of Jerusalem at the hands of the Babylonian king Nebuchadnezzar (605–567 BCE.), there is a brief excursus on the survival of the Torah thanks to the efforts of Zerubbabel, according to al-Ya'qûbî. He follows this up with an excursus on the laws, the feasts, and the religious practices of the Israelites.[32] In the section that is devoted to the kings after Solomon, as part of the story of King Ahaz of Judah (735–715 BCE), there is a brief excursus on the Samaritans.[33]

Very soon after the publication of the text of al-Ya'qûbî's *Ta'rīkh* in Houtsma's edition (1883), scholars were quick to recognize the debt he owed to the biblical materials preserved in the Syriac *Spelunca Thesaurorum or Cave of Treasures*[34] and other works in the Syriac exegetical tradition. They also noted close parallels between his version of the scriptural passages he quoted and the *textus receptus* of the Syriac Bible, the Peshitta.[35] But the *Cave of Treasures* seems certainly to have been the principal source behind much of what al-Ya'qûbî records about the biblical personae, with the exception

Wickham, "Al–Ya'kûbî's Account of the Israelite Prophets and Kings," *Journal of Near Eastern Studies* 29 (1970), pp. 80–98.

[31] An English translation of the section on Jesus is available in Dwight M. Donaldson, "Al-Ya'qûbî's Chapter about Jesus Christ," in *The Macdonald Presentation Volume* (Princeton, NJ: Princeton University Press, 1933), pp. 88–105. A French translation of the Jesus section is available in André Ferré, "L'historien al-Ya'qûbî et les evangiles," *Islamochristiana* 3 (1977), pp. 61–83, as well as in Ferré, *L'histoire des prophètes*, pp. 90–110, in a somewhat revised version.

[32] See Martin Schreiner, "Al-Jakubî über den Glauben und die Sitten der Juden," *Monatsschrift für Geschichte und Wissenschaft des Judentums* 34 (1885), pp. 135–139. See also Adang, *Muslim Writers on Judaism and the Hebrew Bible*, pp. 71–76, 117–120, 226–227.

[33] Concerning the excurses on the Samaritans and the laws, feasts, and practices of the Israelites, see the translations of selected passages and the discussion in Adang, *Muslim Writers on Judaism and the Hebrew Bible*, pp. 71–76.

[34] See in particular Smit, *"Bijbel en Legende'*, pp. 111–114, 128–134; A. Götze, "Die Nachwirkung der Schatzhöle," *Zeitschrift für Semitistik* 3 (1924), pp. 60–71 (6. Al-Ja'qûbî). There has long been an English translation of the Syriac *Cave of Treasures* available in E. A. Wallis Budge, *The Book of the Cave of Treasures* (London: Religious Tract Society, 1927). The modern edition of the Syriac text, along with a French translation, is by Su-Min Ri, *La caverne des trésors: les deux recensions syriaques* (CSCO vols. 487 and 488; Louvain: Peeters, 1987). See also Su-Min Ri, *Commentaire de La Caverne des Trésors: étude sur l'histoire du texte et de ses sources* (CSCO vol. 581; Louvain: Peeters, 2000).

[35] See the table of equivalencies in Smit, *"Bijbel en Legende'*, pp. 115–127. Smit gives it as his opinion that in the Old Testament narratives al-Ya'qûbî followed a revision of the *Peshitta* text done with an eye to the text of the Greek *Septuagint* by Jacob of Edessa (c. 633–708). *Ibid.*, p. 127.

of Jesus, as a closer examination of his accounts reveals.[36] While he never names the book, he does mention the cave after which it took its title and twice he calls it "the cave of treasure (*maghārat al-kanz*)."[37] He explains that Adam gave this name to the cave in which he took up residence after his expulsion from paradise, and where, as it turns out, he was buried after his death. All of this, as far as it goes, reflects what is said in the *Cave of Treasures* itself. Al-Ya'qûbî omits, of course, the details that made the cave a powerful typological symbol for the Syriac-speaking Christians of his day, but which were of no use for his Islamic purposes.[38]

A curious resonance with the millenarian chronological concerns of the *Cave of Treasures* also somewhat surprisingly appears in al-Ya'qûbî's *Ta'rīkh.* It is surprising because there does not seem to be any immediately available Islamic frame of reference for it, yet al-Ya'qûbî, following the practice of the *Cave of Treasures,* dutifully marks off the periods of the first four of the six millennia usually calculated by the early Christian chronographers.[39] He drops any mention of them after the fourth, consistent with his lack of interest in any aspect of postexilic Israelite history except for the story of Jesus.

[36] For al-Ya'qūbī's presentation of Jesus, see Sidney H. Griffith, "The Gospel, the Qur'ān, and the Presentation of Jesus in al-Ya'qūbī's *Ta'rīkh,*" in John C. Reeves (ed.), *Bible and Qur'ān: Essays in Scriptural Intertextuality* SBL Symposium Series, no. 24; Atlanta: Society of Biblical Literature, 2003), pp. 133–160.

[37] Al-Ya'qūbī, *Ta'rīkh,* vol. 1, pp. 6 and 14; Houtsma, *Historiae,* vol. 1, pp. 3 and 11. The Syriac form of the name is *m'arat gazzê.*

[38] For a discussion of the Christian significance of the cave and its treasures, see Ri, *Commentaire de la Caverne des trésors,* pp. 178–183 *et passim.* For al-Ya'qūbī the treasure seems to have been limited to the body of Adam, which was buried in the cave. Like the *Cave of Treasures,* he tells how successive generations of biblical personae are concerned to carry Adam's remains with them on their migrations and that after the flood it becomes the responsibility of Noah's son Shem to put it "in the middle of the earth, in the holy place (*al-makān al-muqaddas*)," where Melkizedek is to become its attendant. See al-Ya'qūbī, *Ta'rīkh,* vol. 1, pp. 16 and 17; Houtsma, *Historiae,* vol. 1, pp. 13–15.

[39] Al-Ya'qūbī mentions the ends of the first four millennia in his narratives of Yared, Methusaleh, and Reu, and in the time of Ehud in his narrative of "The Prophets and Kings of the Israelites after Moses." In each instance he says that in a certain year of their lives the respective millennium is complete (*tamma/kamala l-alf*). See al-Ya'qūbī, *Ta'rīkh,* vol. 1, pp. 10, 12, 20 and 47; Houtsma, *Historiae,* vol. 1, pp. 7, 9, 18 and 49. However, al-Ya'qūbī's reckoning coincides with that of the *Cave of Treasures* as we now have it in only two instances, those of Yared and Reu! For an explanation of these reckonings, see Ri, *Commentaire de la Caverne des trésors,* pp. 499–520.

For the present purpose, this concern of his once again underlines his debt to the traditions that found their way into the Syriac *Cave of Treasures.*

These observations immediately raise the question of how al-Ya'qūbī used his sources. Did he learn Syriac and consult the *Cave of Treasures* in the original language?[40] Was an early Arabic translation available to him?[41] Did he read the Peshitta in Syriac? Or did he make use of the services of Syriac-speaking Christian informants, who may have translated for him orally directly from the scriptural texts?[42] Al-Ya'qûbî's accounts often stay close to the biblical text, but they just as often paraphrase it. We may gain some general guidance toward an answer to these questions by consulting al-Ya'qûbî's own remarks in other places about how he dealt with his sources.

At the beginning of the second part of the *Ta'rīkh,* the section of the work that deals with Muḥammad and early Islamic history, al-Ya'qûbî makes a few introductory remarks about his methods and sources. He begins by speaking of the just finished first part of the book:

> We have given an abbreviated account of the coming to be of this world and of the reports of the most important ancient peoples, of the various kingdoms and of their manifold affairs. We composed this

[40] It is interesting to read that al-Ya'qûbî says under the entry for Peleg, son of Eber, that Syriac (*Siryânî*) was the language of the Nabateans, and that "it was the language of Adam." Al-Ya'qûbî, *Ta'rîkh,* vol. I, p. 19; Houtsma, *Historiae,* vol. I, p. 17.

[41] André Ferré points out that in his *Annales,* Eutychius of Alexandria (877–940) makes use of many of the same sections of the *Cave of Treasures* for his account of the history of the patriarchs up to Abraham as did al-Ya'qûbî. He says, "la similitude entre les textes des deux auteurs est suffisamment obvie pour qu'on puisse conclure à l'utilisation d'une source commune. On peut même préciser qu'ils ont une affinité évidente avec la version dite 'syriaque orientale'." Ferré, *L'histoire des prophètes,* p. xii. The implication is that there was a common Arabic version available to the two historians. In point of fact there was an early Arabic version, conserved in Sinai Arabic MS 508, dated paleographically to the ninth century. See M. D. Gibson, *Kitāb al-Mājāll, or The Book of the Rolls, Apocrypha Arabica* (Studia Sinaitica, 8; London: J. Clay and Sons, 1901), pp. 1–48 (Arabic); 1–58 (English). See now the edition of A. Battista and B. Bagatti (eds.), *La Caverna dei Tesori; Testo Arabo con Traduzione Italiana e Commento* (Studium Biblicum Franciscanum, Collectio Minor, n. 26; Jerusalem: Franciscan Printing Press, 1979). This version of the *Cave of Treasures* seems to have circulated in Egypt. See Ri, *Commentaire de la Caverne des Trésors,* pp. 63–66. Whether or not al-Ya'qûbî could have had access to it remains an open question. If so, he did not simply copy from it, as a comparison of the two texts shows.

[42] There are some Muslim traditions that speak of such informants. See Hava Lazarus-Yafeh, *Intertwined Worlds: Medieval Islam and Bible Criticism* (Princeton, NJ: Princeton University Press, 1992), pp. 119–120.

> book of ours according to what the ancient authorities have related, the scholars, the transmitters, and the authors of biographies, annals and histories.[43]

In the preface to his *Kitāb al-buldān*, written many years after the *Ta'rīkh* in Egypt, al-Ya'qûbî has more to say about his sources and methods in composing that book:

> I have traveled since I was a youngster. My travels have continued and as long as my foreign sojourns have lasted, I have, whenever I have met anyone from these countries, asked him about his homeland and its metropolis. . . . I would ask about their clothing . . . their religions, and their doctrines. . . . Then I verified everything anyone whose truthfulness I could trust would report to me. I would appeal with questions to more and more people until I had questioned many knowledgeable individuals, in season and out of season, easterners and westerners, and I wrote down their reports, and transmitted their stories. . . . I continued to write down these reports, and to compose this book for a long time. . . . And we made this book an abbreviated account of the reports of the countries.[44]

Unfortunately, there is no surviving preface of this sort for the first part of the *Ta'rīkh*; the beginning of the book has not been preserved. But there is every reason to believe that al-Ya'qûbî in that instance would have followed what was perhaps his accustomed methodology *mutatis mutandis*. In both of the surviving prefaces he speaks of offering "an abbreviated account' (*mukhtasar*) of the material at hand, which is clearly the case in the Bible history section of the work. In the course of the narrative he occasionally speaks of the varying opinions of the 'People of the Book'[45] or, in the case of the Gospels, of 'the evangelists' (*aṣḥāb al-injîl*),[46] whom he quotes by name. At one place he speaks of what the 'Christians' (i.e., *an-naṣārā*) say.[47] Given his attested method of making use of informants and then writing down what they have told him, it makes sense to suppose that al-Ya'qûbî consulted the Peshitta and other Aramaic or Syriac biblical and exegetical

[43] Al-Ya'qûbî, *Ta'rîkh*, vol. 2, p. 5; Houtsma, *Historiae*, vol. 2, p. 2.

[44] Ibn al-Fakih al-Hamadhānī, *Compendium libri: Kitāb al-boldān* (ed. J.J. de Goeje, Bibliotheca Geographorum Arabicorum, 8 vols.; Leiden: E.J. Brill, 1967), vol. 5, pp. 232–233.

[45] See, e.g., al-Ya'qûbî, *Ta'rîkh*, vol. 1, p. 15; Houtsma, *Historiae*, vol. 1, p. 12.

[46] See, e.g., al-Ya'qûbî, *Ta'rîkh*, vol. 1, p. 68; Houtsma, *Historiae*, vol. 1, p. 74.

[47] See, e.g., al-Ya'qûbî, *Ta'rîkh*, vol. 1, p. 78; Houtsma, *Historiae*, vol. 1, p. 87.

texts through the good offices of Christian or Jewish informants. They may well have dictated to him with text in hand. Some of it he seems to have copied almost verbatim; some of it he paraphrased. Of course it is possible that he learned Hebrew, Aramaic, Syriac, or Greek for purposes of consulting the Bible and other Christian or Jewish texts on his own, but that seems unlikely since he gives no hint of it in the text of the *Ta'rīkh*. It seems more likely that he would have used Arabic translations, since he did say in the preface to the second part of the *Ta'rīkh* quoted above that he had consulted "the authors of biographies, annals, and histories."[48] And, as we have seen, it was in the ninth century that Jewish or Christian biblical texts were becoming widely available in Arabic translation, albeit that al-Ya'qûbî makes no explicit mention of them.

It is clear that al-Ya'qûbî approaches Bible history from the perspective of the Qur'ān. He does not name the Islamic scripture often in the first part of the *Ta'rīkh*. Rather, when al-Ya'qūbî quotes from the Qur'ān in the narrative, he usually refers to it by some such phrase as, "God says," or, in reference to a person he names, as one "whom God, exalted be He, has mentioned."[49] He often uses the Qur'ān's names for biblical characters where they exist, as in speaking of Moses as 'son of 'Imrān'.[50] He folds the names and stories of prophets known only from the Qur'ān, such as Hūd and Ṣāliḥ (Q VII:65–72; 73–79), into the course of Bible history in his *Ta'rīkh* by including their names among the Noachites in the story of Nahor, son of Serug.[51] He sometimes corrects what the Bible says or the 'People of the Book' maintain by citing the Qur'ān or Islamic traditions. For example, in the account of Noah's ark, al-Ya'qûbî says that "the vessel traveled over all the earth until it came to Mecca, and it circumambulated the house (*al-bayt*, i.e., the Ka'bah) seven times."[52] As for the ark's final resting place, al-Ya'qûbî, following the Qur'ān, says that "it came to rest on al-Jûdî" (Q XI:44).[53] But he notes that the 'People of the Book' differ with this view. He goes on to mention that they say that al-Jûdî "is a mountain in the neighborhood of Mosul."[54] Similarly, in the matter of the Gospels' reports

[48] See the text cited at n.43 above.

[49] See, e.g., al-Ya'qûbî, *Ta'rīkh*, vol. 1, pp. 79 and 48; Houtsma, *Historiae*, vol. 1, pp. 88 and 50.

[50] See, e.g., al-Ya'qûbî, *Ta'rīkh*, vol. 1, p. 47; Houtsma, *Historiae*, vol. 1, p. 48.

[51] See al-Ya'qûbî, *Ta'rīkh*, vol. 1, p. 22, Houtsma, *Historiae*, vol. 1, pp. 19–20

[52] Al-Ya'qûbî, *Ta'rīkh*, vol. 1, p. 14; Houtsma, *Historiae*, vol. 1, p. 12.

[53] Al-Ya'qûbî, *Ta'rīkh*, vol. 1, pp. 14–15; Houtsma, *Historiae*, vol. 1, p. 12.

[54] Al-Ya'qûbî, *Ta'rīkh*, vol. 1, p. 15; Houtsma, *Historiae*, vol. 1, p. 12.

of Christ's death on the cross, al-Ya'qûbî, quoting the Qur'ān, says, "God, mighty and exalted be He, said, 'They did not kill him, and they did not crucify him, but it seemed so to them'" (Q IV:157).[55]

The Qur'ān's prophetology doubtless played a role in al-Ya'qûbî's decision to present Bible history by way of the sequence of *dramatis personae*, Adam to Jesus, paying close attention to the genealogies of Genesis and the sequence of prophets and kings, up to the Babylonian exile. At that point, as we mentioned above, he gives a quick summary of the laws, the feasts, and the religious practices of the "sons of Israel."[56] But then he turns immediately to the story of Jesus. This is the scheme of the Qur'ān, where there is scant interest in postexilic Israelite history until the time of Jesus. We may highlight al-Ya'qûbî's method by briefly following his presentation of the biblical patriarch, Abraham.

The beginning of Abraham's story in al-Ya'qûbî's *Ta'rīkh* comes in the historian's account of Terah, son of Nahor, who is identified as "the father of Abraham, God's friend (*khalīl Allāhi*)."[57] One readily recognizes here an allusion to the Qur'ān's statement about the patriarch ("God took Abraham as a friend/*khalīlan*," IV *an-Nisā* 125), which is the scriptural basis for the epithet that quickly became common usage in future Islamic references to Abraham. It is also in the account of Terah that al-Ya'qûbî tells the story of Nimrod 'the Hero' (*al-jabbār*),[58] whom he will name as Abraham's first major adversary in the account that follows. As for Terah himself, al-Ya'qûbî has little to say beyond conveying the information that he is also known as 'Āzar, the name he bears in the Qur'ān (VI *al-An'ām* 74), and that he was in the company of Nimrod.[59] It is typical of al-Ya'qûbî 's methodology in presenting the biblical personae that he uses their biblical names, unobtrusively and without comment furnishing their Qur'ānic names where they are different, as in this instance.

[55] Al-Ya'qûbî, *Ta'rîkh,* vol. 1, p. 79; Houtsma, *Historiae,* vol. 1., p. 88.

[56] Al-Ya'qûbî, *Ta'rîkh,* vol. 1, pp. 66–68; Houtsma, *Historiae,* vol. 1, pp. 71–73.

[57] Al-Ya'qûbî, *Ta'rīkh,* vol. 1, p. 23; Houtsma, *Historiae,* vol. 1, p. 20.

[58] In the Syriac tradition of the *Cave of Treasures,* Nimrod is regularly characterized as 'the Hero' (*gabbārâ*). See e.g., Ri, *La caverne des trésors,* XXIV:24.

[59] "Terah, i.e., 'Āzar, the father of Abraham, was with Nimrod, the Hero." Al-Ya'qūbī, *Ta'rīkh,* vol. 1, p. 23; Houtsma, *Historiae,* vol. 1, p. 21. For modern scholarly surmises about the origin of the name 'Āzar, see Roberto Tottoli, *I profeti biblici nella tradizione islamica* (Studi biblici, 121; Brescia: Paideia Editrice, 1999), p. 43, n.17.

Nimrod was the interesting figure for al-Ya'qûbî at the outset of his presentation of Abraham,[60] as he was for other Muslim commentators as well.[61] And here too there are echoes of the traditions that found their way into the *Cave of Treasures,* according to which Nimrod was the first fire worshipper and the first to encourage the development of astrology under the tutelage of one called Yonṭon, whom the Syrian apocalyptic tradition represents as the fourth son of Noah.[62] It seems obvious that this narrative was meant to explain the origin of Zoroaster and Zoroastrianism, 'fire-worshippers' according to both Christians and Muslims, along with the traditional Syrian Christian lore of the Magi and their religion. In the present context of the story of Terah, al-Ya'qûbî makes use of the tradition to furnish a historical background for the Qur'ān's presentation of Abraham's first anti-pagan polemic. For an integral part of the Nimrod story tells how the king, on learning from his astrologers that "in his realm one would be born who would find fault with his religion, who would rebuke him, destroy his idols and scatter his host,"[63] gave orders for the destruction of newborn males. Then, when Terah discovered that his wife was pregnant with Abraham, as al-Ya'qûbî tells it, again following the Jewish and Syrian traditions of the *Cave of Treasures,* "His parents concealed him, hid the very fact of him, and brought him into a cave where no one could know of him."[64] Al-Ya'qûbî then

[60] For the Jewish and Muslim traditions behind the later Islamic accounts of Abraham's origins, see Brian M. Hauglid, "On the Early Life of Abraham: Biblical and Qur'ānic Intertextuality and the Anticipation of Muḥammad," in Reeves, *Bible and Qur'ān,* pp. 87–105.

[61] See Heinrich Schützinger, *Ursprung und Entwicklung der arabischen Abraham-Nimrod Legende* (Bonn: Rheinische Friedrich Wilhelms Universität, 1961).

[62] See Ri, *Commentaire de la Caverne des Trésors,* pp. 341–357. Both modern editors of the *Ta'rīkh,* reflecting what they found in the MSS they used, read the name as Y-n-ṭ-q. This would seem to be a mistake made by scribes who were unaware of the East Syrian tradition of Yonṭon, reflected in the eastern text of the *Cave of Treasures,* which al-Ya'qūbī was actually following; it being an easy mistake to read final *Nūn* for final *Qāf.* Actually, the scribe of the Frankfurt MS left the character unpointed. André Ferré also missed the significance of the name, proposing an otherwise unrecorded Bandâq. See Ferré, *L'histoire des prophètes,* p. 23.

[63] Al-Ya'qūbī, *Ta'rīkh,* vol. 1, p. 23; Houtsma, *Historiae,* vol. 1, p. 21.

[64] Al-Ya'qūbī, *Ta'rīkh,* vol. 1, p. 23; Houtsma, *Historiae,* vol. 1, p. 21. Jewish tradition also records the story of Nimrod, including the episode of hiding the infant Abraham in a cave. See Louis Ginzberg, *The Legends of the Jews* (7 vols.; Philadelphia: The Jewish Publication Society of America, 1946–1969), vol. 1, p. 188. However, al-Ya'qūbī's account follows the narrative line of the *Cave of Treasures,* behind which, no doubt, are the Jewish legends as the ultimate sources.

informs the reader that Abraham's birth was in Kūthā Rabbā,[65] a location also named as Terah/Azar's homeland in Ibn Isḥāq's *Kitāb al-mubtada'*.[66]

At the beginning of the *Ta'rīkh*'s account devoted to Abraham personally, al-Ya'qûbî starts off with the notice: "Abraham arose in the time of the hero Nimrod," and then he picks up where he left off in the previous narrative devoted to Terah with the statement, "When he went out of the cave in which he had been, he directed his gaze to the heavens."[67] Thus al-Ya'qûbî set the scene for the first episode in his account of Abraham, the patriarch's early engagement in the thought-experiment about the worship of the planets, the stars, the moon, and the sun. After surmising that they each in turn might be his Lord, but observing that they rise and vanish in the heavens, Abraham concludes that none of them can in fact be the Lord. As he is made to say, "My Lord will not vanish."[68] Al-Ya'qûbî interweaves words and phrases from *surah* VI *al-An'ām* 75–79 into this account, and at the end, following his usual practice when quoting from the Qur'ān, he says, "So has God narrated his story and his undertaking."[69]

The next episode recounts Abraham's youthful call to his people, challenging their idolatry and his consequent confrontation with Nimrod, ending with the story of his ordeal in the fiery furnace. It is clear that the passage about Abraham in *surah* XXI *al-Anbiyā'* 51–71 lies behind al-Ya'qûbî 's narrative in this episode; at one point he explicitly quotes from verse 69. While the matrix of the story lies deep in Jewish legend,[70] what is now wanting is information about the extra-Qur'ānic sources al-Ya'qûbî actually used for the details of his account that do not appear in the Qur'ān. Perhaps he utilized the services of Jewish informants, as well as accounts by earlier Muslim writers who had themselves made use of Jewish traditions.[71] Curiously, the Syriac exegetical traditions in the *Cave of Treasures* have nothing to say about this episode in the Abraham story, presumably because it does not figure in the typological lore that was the primary preoccupation of the Syrian exegetes who composed the omnibus work. For al-Ya'qûbî the Islamic

[65] Al-Ya'qūbī, *Ta'rīkh*, vol. 1, p. 23; Houtsma, *Historiae*, vol. 1, p. 21. Both MSS seem to have *Kūthā Riyyā*.

[66] See Gordon Darnell Newby, *The Making of the Last Prophet: A Reconstruction of the Earliest Biography of Muhammad* (Columbia, SC: University of South Carolina Press, 1989), p. 67.

[67] Al-Ya'qūbī, *Ta'rīkh*, vol. 1, p. 24; Houtsma, *Historiae*, vol. 1, p. 21.

[68] Al-Ya'qūbī, *Ta'rīkh*, vol. 1, p. 24; Houtsma, *Historiae*, vol. 1, p. 21.

[69] Al-Ya'qūbī, *Ta'rīkh*, vol. 1, p. 24; Houtsma, *Historiae*, vol. 1, p. 21.

[70] See Ginzberg, *Legends of the Jews*, vol. 1, pp. 185–217.

[71] In this connection, see Hauglid, "On the Early Life of Abraham."

message is made clear in the following statement about Abraham: "God sent him as a prophet; He dispatched Gabriel to him and he taught him his religion."[72] And finally, at the conclusion of his account of Abraham's ordeal in Nimrod's fiery furnace, al-Ya'qûbî says, "Lot came to believe along with him; Lot was the son of his brother, Haran, son of Terah."[73]

The next episode in the presentation of Abraham relates God's command to him to emigrate from his homeland into what al-Ya'qûbî calls, "Syria, the Holy Land."[74] A bit further on he adds that Abraham and Sarah, his wife, and his entourage, including Lot, "emigrating (*muhājirīna*) where God commanded them, settled in the land of Palestine."[75] Al-Ya'qûbî is particularly concerned to record Lot's residence "in the twin cities Sodom and Gomorrah, near the place where Abraham was,"[76] and to tell of Abraham's rescue of Lot and his possessions from those who had attacked and despoiled him. From the perspective of the biblical narrative this is straightforward Bible history. Later in the account al-Ya'qûbî will expand on the story of Lot.

Next al-Ya'qûbî turns his attention to the story of Hagar and Ishmael. As he tells it, Abraham was concerned about having so much wealth but no offspring to inherit it, so God sent him a revelation (*awḥī . . . ilayhi*) whereby he understood that his offspring would in fact become as numerous as the stars. Then the narrative abruptly states that Sarah gave Abraham Hagar and that Hagar became pregnant and bore Ishmael when Abraham was eighty-six years old (Gen. 16:16). Subsequently, the text says that Sarah became jealous and ordered the dismissal of Hagar and Ishmael. Thus far al-Ya'qûbî is succinctly and faithfully relating the biblical story, but at this point he introduces elements from Islamic tradition. He tells how Abraham took Hagar and Ishmael to Mecca and settled them in the environs of the

[72] Al-Ya'qūbī, *Ta'rīkh*, vol. 1, p. 24; Houtsma, *Historiae*, vol. 1, p. 22.

[73] Al-Ya'qūbī, *Ta'rīkh*, vol. 1, p. 24; Houtsma, *Historiae*, vol. 1, p. 22.

[74] It is interesting that al-Ya'qūbī uses the expression 'Holy Land' to refer to the larger territory beyond Jerusalem, almost in the Christian sense of *Terra Sancta*, an expression which came into prominence among Christians after the fifth century and was originally used by Christian residents of the locality. See Robert L. Wilken, *The Land Called Holy: Palestine in Christian History and Thought* (New Haven: Yale University Press, 1992), esp. pp. 166 and 249. In Islamic usage the designation *al-Quds* and the epithet 'holy' is usually reserved for Jerusalem proper. See Amikam Elad, *Medieval Jerusalem and Islamic Worship: Holy Places, Ceremonies, Pilgrimage* (Leiden: E. J. Brill, 1995).

[75] Al-Ya'qūbī, *Ta'rīkh*, vol. 1, p. 24; Houtsma, *Historiae*, vol. 1, p. 22.

[76] Al-Ya'qūbī, *Ta'rīkh*, vol. 1, p. 25; Houtsma, *Historiae*, vol. 1, p. 22.

Ka'ba, which he calls simply 'the sacred house' (*al-bayt al-ḥarām*). When Hagar asks into whose care he will leave them, Abraham replies, "With the Lord of this building." And he says in prayer, quoting the words of the Qur'ān (XL *Ibrāhīm* 37), albeit that al-Ya'qûbî does not acknowledge this source, "O God, I have lodged my son in a *wādī* without cultivation, by your sacred house (*'inda baytika l-muḥarram*)."[77] The episode concludes with the story of how Hagar founded the well of Zamzam by watching from the hill of aṣ-Ṣafā (cf. II *al-Baqarah* 158) as a bird was scratching the earth in search of water. When it came out she collected it so that it would not run off and, as al-Ya'qûbî says, "This is the well of Zamzam."[78]

The account of the disobedient sins of 'the people of Lot' (*qawm Lūṭ*, cf., e.g., LIV *al-Qamar* 33) in Sodom and their punishment comes next. Al-Ya'qûbî once more borrows words of the Qur'ān, again without explicitly citing it, to specify the sins of Lot's people. He says, "Of all the people of the worlds, they used to approach males." (XXVI *ash-Shu'arā* 165) And he goes on to say that this came about because Iblīs appeared to them in the form of a beardless boy, bidding them to have intercourse with him. They took to the practice so readily, says al-Ya'qûbî , that they abandoned marriage with women and embarked on marrying males. They would not stop this practice even when Lot forbade it (cf. LIV *al-Qamar* 33). Al-Ya'qûbî comments that the moral outrage at this behavior was so great that it gave rise to an admonitory adage. People would say of a wrong that it was "more outrageous than the case of Sodom."[79] Al-Ya'qûbî also gives the names of two judges in Sodom, Shaqrī and Shaqrūnī, who are said to have aided and abetted the disgraceful behavior of the people. It seems that these names come ultimately from Jewish tradition, perhaps via Syriac intermediaries; however, in the form in which we have them in the Arabic text, they have become garbled.[80]

[77] Al-Ya'qūbī, *Ta'rīkh*, vol. 1, p. 25; Houtsma, *Historiae*, vol. 1, p. 23.

[78] Al-Ya'qūbī, *Ta'rīkh*, vol. 1, p. 25; Houtsma, *Historiae*, vol. 1, p. 23.

[79] Al-Ya'qūbī, *Ta'rīkh*, vol. 1, p. 25; Houtsma, *Historiae*, vol. 1, p. 23.

[80] See Ginzberg, *Legends of the Jews*, vol. 1, pp. 246–247, where a number of names of judges are given for Sodom, Gomorra, and other cities in the same locality. The judge in Sodom is called Shereḳ, while the one in Gomorra is Sharḳar. Ginzberg goes on to say, "Eliezer, the bondman of Abraham, made slight changes in the names of these judges, in accordance with the nature of what they did: the first he called Shaḳḳara, Liar; the second Shaḳrura, Arch-deceiver." *Ibid.* These latter two are perhaps behind the names reported by al-Ya'qūbī, having undergone corruption in the process of transmission.

Al-Ya'qûbî gives a very brief account of Abraham's heavenly visitors, the angels whom God sent to destroy Sodom for the outrages committed there (Gen. XVIII). What interests him most is Abraham's special plea for Lot and the angels' guarantee of his safety in the coming destruction as recorded in the Qur'ān. Al-Ya'qûbî reports that when the angels told Abraham of their mission to Sodom, he said to them, in the very words of the Qur'ān (XXIX *al-'Ankabūt* 32), to which al-Ya'qûbî again does not mention his debt: "Lot is there. They said, 'We well know who is there; we will certainly deliver him and his family, except for his wife'."[81] The final episode in the story of the heavenly visitors to Abraham is their prediction of Sarah's pregnancy with Isaac. Here yet again, after recording Sarah's wonderment at the news, Al-Ya'qûbî quotes her response in the words of the Qur'ān, and yet again he fails to mention that it is a quotation. Presumably the reader is expected to recognize this and other passages from the Qur'ān: "Am I, an old woman, to bear a child, and this husband of mine too is a very old man?" (XI *Hūd* 72, with slight variations). From Genesis 17:17 al-Ya'qûbî records the information that Abraham was one hundred years old at the time and that Sarah was ninety years old.

In the story of the destruction of Sodom, al-Ya'qûbî begins with Lot's wife giving notice to the townspeople of the arrival of the guests, the angels in disguise. He quickly tells of the assault upon the visitors and Lot's defense of them. Echoing the words of the Qur'ān, Lot says, "Do not disgrace me with my guests" (cf. XV *al-Ḥijr* 68). The destruction of the city "in the morning" (cf. LIV *al-Qamar* 34) is foretold by the angels and Lot is advised to escape. When Lot asks why put it off to the morning, Gabriel answers in the words of the Qur'ān: "Is not the morning nigh?" (XI *Hūd* 81). The surprise then is that in the report of Lot's escape with all of his family except his wife, al-Ya'qûbî says that Lot's wife perished with the Sodomites and was turned into salt (cf. Genesis 19:26), as the Bible says, ignoring the Qur'ān's statement seven times that she "was among those lagging behind." (e.g., XXIX *al-'Ankabūt* 32).[82]

Al-Ya'qûbî next lingers over the story of Ishmael's two wives, recorded in both Jewish and Islamic tradition.[83] He recounts Abraham's visit to them incognito and his disapproval of the first one and his esteem for the second,

[81] Al-Ya'qūbī, *Ta'rīkh*, vol. 1, p. 26; Houtsma, *Historiae*, vol. 1, pp. 23–24.

[82] Al-Ya'qūbī, *Ta'rīkh*, vol. 1, p. 26; Houtsma, *Historiae*, vol. 1, p. 24.

[83] See Ginzberg, *Legends of the Jews*, vol. 1, pp. 266–269; Newby, *The Making of the Last Prophet*, pp. 78–79. For the context in the developing Islamic exegetical tradition of al-Ya'qūbī's, account see especially Reuven Firestone, *Journeys in Holy*

whom he names al-Ḥayfā' bint Muḍāḍ; both wives are said to have been of the tribe of Jurhum.[84]

According to Al-Ya'qûbî, "God, exalted be He, ordered Abraham to build the Ka'bah, to raise up its foundations, to issue among the people the call (*yu'adhdhina*) to the pilgrimage (*al-ḥajj*) and to show them their ritual ceremonies (*manāsikahum*)."[85] Having recorded the divine commission, which one notices omits but does not necessarily exclude the traditional idea that Adam was the original builder of the shrine, al-Ya'qûbî then tells how Abraham and Ishmael together raised the walls of the Ka'bah to the place of the stone. At that point, he says, "Abū Qubays called out to Abraham, 'You have a special deposit with me (*inna laka 'indî wadī'atun*).' So he gave him the stone (*al-ḥajar*), and he put it in its place and Abraham issued among the people the call to pilgrimage."[86] Here al-Ya'qûbî records the tradition that at the time of Noah's flood the 'black stone' had been deposited for safekeeping within Mount Abū Qubays; he is probably also reporting a traditional legend that it was the mountain who called out to Abraham at the time of the rebuilding of the Ka'bah, although one has so far not found any other place where it is so recorded.[87]

As for the rites of the pilgrimage, al-Ya'qûbî's brief summary of Abraham's accomplishing them follows the conventional practice of furnishing the folk-etymologies that explain the terms used to name the various stages of the proceedings. At the end, when Abraham sleeps at al-Mash'ar before going to Minā the next day, al-Ya'qûbî tells us: "Then God commanded him to sacrifice (*yadhbaḥa*) his son."[88] Reuben Firestone has shown that in placing Abraham's sacrifice of his son in the context of his completion of the inaugural pilgrimage, al-Ya'qûbî provides the earliest record of the distinctively Shi'ite version of the event.[89]

Lands: The Evolution of the Abraham-Ishmael Legends in Islamic Exegesis (Albany, NY: State University of New York Press, 1990), pp. 72–79

[84] Al-Ya'qūbī, *Ta'rīkh*, vol. 1, pp. 26–27; Houtsma, *Historiae*, vol. 1, pp. 24–25.

[85] Al-Ya'qūbī, *Ta'rīkh*, vol. 1, p. 27; Houtsma, *Historiae*, vol. 1, p. 25.

[86] Al-Ya'qūbī, *Ta'rīkh*, vol. 1, p. 27; Houtsma, *Historiae*, vol. 1, p. 25. Houtsma, *ibid.*, n. a, notes that his MS reads وبا; in the text he corrects it to {ابا, which yields the reading, "Abraham called out to Abū Qubays."

[87] For the context of this episode in the Islamic exegetical tradition, see Firestone, *Journeys in Holy Lands*, esp. pp. 90, 30 and 216, n.50.

[88] Al-Ya'qūbī, *Ta'rīkh*, vol. 1, p. 27; Houtsma, *Historiae*, vol. 1, p. 25. See Firestone, *Journeys in Holy Lands*, pp. 94–103 for further details in the exegetical tradition.

[89] See Firestone, *Journeys in Holy Lands*, pp. 120–121.

Before describing the sacrifice, al-Ya'qûbî notes that the reports (*riwāyāt*) differ on whether it was Ishmael or Isaac who was the intended victim. Some, he says, think it was Ishmael because Isaac was away in Syria. Others think it was Isaac because by that time Ishmael and his mother had been sent away and Ishmael had already fathered children. Without explicitly expressing his opinion on which son it was, al-Ya'qûbî proceeds to describe the sacrifice itself. He says, quoting Abraham:

> He said to his son, "God has commanded me to sacrifice you" (cf. XXXVII *aṣ-Ṣāffāt* 102). And he said, "O father, do what you are commanded" (XXXVII *aṣ-Ṣāffāt* 102). So he took the blade and made him lie down on the firebrands of the high place (*'alā jamrati l-'uqbati*), having spread a donkey blanket under him.[90] Then he put the blade to his throat and turned his face away. Gabriel turned the blade over. Abraham looked, and the blade was turned over. He did that three times. Then there was a shout, "O Abraham, you have believed the vision" (XXXVII *aṣ-Ṣāffāt* 104–105). Gabriel took the boy, and when a ram was brought down from the top of Thabīr, he put it in his place and sacrificed it.[91]

Following this account, al-Ya'qûbî adds, "The people of the books say it was Isaac and that he did this to him in the desert of the Amorites in Syria."[92] This detail shows that he was aware of the Jewish and Christian traditions as they are preserved in the Syriac *Cave of Treasures*, where the text says that the place of the sacrifice was "the mountain of Jebus, which is the mountain of the Amorites, which is the place where the Messiah's cross was set up."[93] But it seems clear that al-Ya'qûbî himself considered Ishmael to be the son of the sacrifice; he was Abraham's companion in rebuilding the Ka'bah, and in the sequel al-Ya'qûbî says:

> When Abraham finished his pilgrimage and he wanted to depart, he gave a commission to his son Ishmael to take charge of the Holy House

[90] Firestone, seemingly following Smit, for reasons not entirely clear to me, reads this passage as follows: "lays his son down on top of a donkey saddle at Jamrat al-'Aqaba." See Firestone, *Journeys in Holy Lands*, p. 120 and Smit, *'Bijbel en Legende'*, p. 34. See also Ferré, *L'histoire des prophètes*, p. 30: "étendit l'enfant sur la pierre de la colline, plaça sous lui le bât d'un âne."

[91] Al-Ya'qūbī, *Ta'rīkh*, vol. 1, pp. 27–28; Houtsma, *Historiae*, vol. 1, pp. 25–26.

[92] Al-Ya'qūbī, *Ta'rīkh*, vol. 1, p. 28; Houtsma, *Historiae*, vol. 1, p. 26.

[93] Ri, *La caverne des trésors*, XXIX:4. See also Ri, *Commentaire de la Caverne des Trésors*, pp. 361–362.

> and to manage their pilgrimage for the people and their rituals. He told him God would multiply his numbers and make his progeny fruitful and among his children He would bring about blessings and well-being.[94]

The last sentence in this paragraph seems to echo the blessings promised to Ishmael and his descendents in such biblical passages as Genesis 16:10–12 and 21:17–18. At this point al-Ya'qûbî brings his story of Abraham to a close with a mention of Sarah's death, his marriage to Ketura, a list of his children with her, and the notice that Abraham died on Tuesday, the tenth of Ab, after a lifetime of one hundred and ninety-five years. In this detail al-Ya'qûbî seems to be following Jewish tradition; the account in one recension of the Syriac *Cave of Treasures* says that Abraham lived for one hundred and fifty, while the other recension gives him one hundred and seventy-five years.[95]

In the Abraham story, al-Ya'qûbî follows his customary practice in the presentation of biblical characters. He follows the guidance of the Qur'ān where it is available, often, as we have seen, citing passages from it or alluding to them, but he supplements the Qur'ān's information with reports from Jewish or Christian sources according to his interests. It is clear that it is the Qur'ān and Islamic tradition that determine the parameters of al-Ya'qûbî's interests rather than the biblical narrative or other non-Islamic sources. In most instances, once he has reached the limits of the Qur'ānic frame of reference, he simply concludes his account without providing further information from biblical or other sources. But it is crystal clear that the Bible in Arabic and the accessibility of Arabic-speaking, Jewish, and Christian informants substantially contributed to al-Ya'qûbî's presentation of Abraham, Jesus, and all the biblical *personae* whose stories he tells in the *Ta'rīkh*. The Qur'ān and Islamic tradition controlled the narrative, but the Bible and the exegetical lore of the Jews and Christians contributed details to the stories, details that al-Ya'qûbî tirelessly sought.

One might say much the same about the use of passages from both the canonical and apocryphal scriptures by the Mu'tazilī *mutakallim* 'Abd al-Jabbār al-Hamdhānī (d.1025), who in his *Tathbīt dalā'il an-nubuwwah* both quotes and alludes to biblical material in some detail in his effort both to show the legitimacy of the prophethood of Muḥammad and to discount the veracity of Christian teachings about Jesus and the claim that Christianity is

[94] Al-Ya'qūbī, *Ta'rīkh,* vol. 1, p. 28; Houtsma, *Historiae,* vol. 1, p. 26.
[95] Ri, *La caverne des trésors,* XXXI:4.

the true religion.[96] Like al-Ya'qûbî, albeit in a different frame of reference, 'Abd al-Jabbār sought out scriptural passages, interpretive traditions, and doctrinal formulae as they circulated in the Christian communities of his day, weaving them into his own Islamic narrative. But it was not long before the general availability of the Jewish and Christian scriptures in Arabic and the concomitant Jewish and Christian scholarship in the Arabic language prompted some Muslim scholars to take a more critical approach to the Bible.

Deconstructing and Reinterpreting the Biblical Text

From the eleventh century onward one can observe a gradual shift in the Muslim view of the text of the Jewish and Christian scriptures. Scholars such as al-Ya'qûbî, 'Abd al-Jabbār, and others consulted the Bible of the Jews and Christians as a source of information for their own Islamic scholarly purposes, not hesitating to put their own Islamic constructions on the texts, or even, as we have seen, emending and 'correcting' them on occasion. Other scholars kept closer to the given scriptures. One such was 'Alī ibn Aḥmad ibn Ḥazm (994–1064 CE), who, among his many other pursuits,[97] paid close attention to the text of the Bible in Arabic in a number of his works, not only in his famous *Al-faṣl fī l-milal wa l-ahwā' wa l-niḥal*,[98] but also in several less-known works, for the polemical purpose of highlighting from a developing Islamic perspective the Bible's inadequacies as a scripture.[99] Ibn Ḥazm was determined to demonstrate the utter unreliability of both the Torah and the Injīl, and to this end he subjected long passages to careful grammatical, historical, and even moral scrutiny with the goal of

[96] See S. Stern, "Quotations from Apocryphal Gospels in 'Abd al-Jabbār," *Journal of Theological Studies* 18 (1967), pp. 34–57; *idem*, "Abd al-Jabbār's Account of How Christ's Religion was Falsified by the Adoption of Roman Customs," *Journal of Theological Studies* 19 (1968), pp. 128–185; S. Pines, "Gospel Quotations and Cognate Topics in 'Abd al-Jabbār's *Tathbīt* in Relation to Early Christian and Judaeo-Christian Readings and Traditions," *Jerusalem Studies in Arabic and Islam* 9 (1987), pp. 195–228. See now Gabriel Said Reynolds, *A Muslim Theologian in the Sectarian Milieu: 'Abd al-Jabbār and the Critique of Christian Origins* (Leiden: E.J. Brill, 2004); Gabriel Said Reynolds and Samir Khalil Samir (ed. and trans.), *'Abd al-Jabbār: Critique of Christian Origins* (Provo, UT: Bringham Young University Press, 2010).

[97] See Anwar G. Chejne, *Ibn Ḥazm* (Chicago: Kazi Publications, 1982).

[98] See 'Alī ibn Aḥmad ibn Ḥazm, *Al-faṣl fī l-milal wa l-ahwā' wa l-miḥal, wa ma'ahu l-milal wa l-niḥal lil-Sharastānī* (5 vols.; Cairo: Muḥammad 'Alī Subayh, 1964).

[99] See Adang, *Muslim Writers on Judaism and the Hebrew Bible*, pp. 59–69.

disclosing their unsuitability as scripture.[100] Most notably, he seems to have been among the first of the Muslim polemicists against the Hebrew Bible to accuse the biblical figure of Ezra of having cobbled together a much distorted Torah after the alleged disappearance of the original during the Babylonian Exile, a polemical trope that would have a long life in later interreligious controversies between Jews, Christians, and Muslims.[101]

While Ibn Ḥazm displays a detailed knowledge of the biblical text, the sources of his extensive quotations are unknown; they do not seem to have come from any translation of the Bible into Arabic that has so far come to the attention of scholars. But in al-Andalus, as in other parts of the Arabic-speaking world, it is clear that by the ninth century Arabic translations of the Bible were commonly available among Jews, Christians, and Muslims alike. And many more of them must have been in circulation than have survived in the available manuscript collections or have so far been discovered by researchers. As for Ibn Ḥazm, some have suggested that he relied on a Christian Bible,[102] indeed the Latin Vulgate, translated into Arabic. This is not impossible. There was a ninth-century Arabic translation of the Vulgate Psalms into Arabic by Ḥafṣ ibn Albar al-Qūṭī (d. 889),[103] and there are reports of even earlier Arabic Bible translations in Spain.[104] But the point not to miss is that whatever the sources available to Ibn Ḥazm might have been, he was in a position to quarrel about even small points of textual detail in the Bible as his exchanges with his Jewish adversaries indicate.[105]

Another Muslim text of the eleventh or twelfth century that quotes extensively from the Gospels and other New Testament texts for polemical purposes (thereby also testifying to the ready availability of the Bible in Arabic at the time) is the work entitled, *Ar-radd al-jamīl li'ilāhiyyati 'Īsā biṣarīḥ al-injīl*, attributed to Abū Ḥāmid Muḥammad al-Ghazālī (1058–1111).[106] Some years ago, Hava Lazarus-Yafeh contested the authenticity of this text as a

[100] See Adang, *Muslim Writers on Judaism and the Hebrew Bible*, pp. 94–109, 133–138, 184–191, 216–222, 237–248. Theodore Pulcini, *Exegesis as Polemical Discourse: Ibn Ḥazm on Jewish and Christian Scriptures* (Atlanta, GA: Scholars Press, 1998).

[101] See Lazarus-Yafeh, *Intertwined Worlds*, pp. 62–67.

[102] See, e.g., Lazarus-Yafeh, *Intertwined Worlds*, p. 123.

[103] See Marie-Thérèse Urvoy (ed.), *Le psautier mozarabe de Hafs le Goth* (Toulouse: Presses Universitaires du Mirail, 1992).

[104] See the summary in Ann Christys, *Christians in al-Andalus (711–1000)* (Richmond, Surrey: Curzon Press, 2002), pp. 154–157.

[105] See Lazarus-Yafeh, *Intertwined Worlds*, pp. 67–71.

[106] See Robert Chidiac, *Al-Ghazali: refutation excellente de la divinité de Jésus-Christ d'après les évangiles; texte établi, traduit et commenté* (Paris: Librairie Ernest Leroux,

work of al-Ghazālī, partly on the grounds that "nowhere in al-Ghazzālī's authentic books is there any exact citation of a verse from the Bible, and no mention of the name of a book in either the Old or the New Testaments, or trace of any Christian terminology."[107] While recently this commonly received opinion has been challenged,[108] further studies of the work have pointed out that the original author's view of the Christian Gospels, whoever he may have been, is evident in his use of the passages he cites. What is wrong with the Christian Gospels on this view, recent scholars contend, is not so much the distortion of the text itself, albeit there are some instances of this, but the faulty interpretations and mistaken meanings the Christians have put on the Gospel passages they customarily cite in defense of the doctrines that Muslims reject. Mark Beaumont argues that the author of *Ar-radd al-jamīl* held the position that many Gospel passages should be understood metaphorically rather than literally, as the Christians have interpreted them.[109] Martin Whittingham proposes that the 'corruption' (*at-taḥrīf*) of the scriptures, and particularly of the Gospels, of which the Christians are guilty according to the author of *Ar-radd al-jamīl*, is not so much a corruption of the biblical text itself but a 'corrupt interpretation' (*taḥrīf ma'nawī*) of their text.[110]

This is a view that finds some support even in the formidable *Al-jawāb aṣ-ṣaḥīḥ li man baddala dīn al-masīḥ* of the Ḥanbalī jurist and anti-Christian polemicist Taqī ad-Dīn Aḥmad ibn Taymiyyah (1263–1328), who addressed the topic in response to Christian claims that the Qur'ān itself affirms the integrity of the Bible text. Ibn Taymiyyah wrote:

> If they mean that the Qur'ān confirms the textual veracity of the scriptural books which they now possess—that is, the Torah and the Gos-

---

1939). See also the extended discussion and commentary in Franz-Elmar Wilms, *Al-Ghazālīs Schrift wider die Gottheit Jesu* (Leiden: E.J. Brill, 1966).

[107] Hava Lazarus-Yafeh, *Studies in al-Ghazzālī* (Jerusalem: The Magnes Press, 1975), appendix A, p. 473. See also the supportive article by Gabriel Said Reynolds, "The Ends of *Al-radd al-jamīl* and its Portrayal of Christian Sects," *Islamochristiana* 25 (1999), pp. 45–65.

[108] See Maha el-Kaisy Friemuth, "*Al-radd al-jamīl*: al-Ghazālī's or Pseudo-Ghazālī's?" in Thomas, *The Bible in Arab Christianity*, pp. 275–294.

[109] See Mark Beaumont, "Appropriating Christian Scriptures in a Muslim Refutation of Christianity: The Case of *A-radd al-jamīl* attributed to al-Ghazālī," *Islam and Christian-Muslim Relations* 22 (2011), pp. 69–84.

[110] See Whittingham, "The Value of *taḥrīf ma'nawī* (Corrupt Interpretation) as a Category for Analysing Muslim Views of the Bible."

> pels—this is something which some Muslims will grant them and which many Muslims will dispute. However, most Muslims will grant them most of that. . . . Concerning the corruption of the meaning of the sacred books by their explanation and interpretation and their replacing its legal judgments with their own, all Muslims, Jews, and Christians witness to this corruption and substitution of theirs.[111]

It was perhaps also in the spirit of this viewpoint that an earlier Ḥanbalī scholar, Najm ad-Dīn Sulaymān ibn ʿAbd al-Qawī aṭ-Ṭūfī (d.1316), wrote a commentary on the four Gospels of the Christians and other biblical books, refuting the doctrines the Christians derived from them. He clearly espoused the view that the extant Gospels are not the Gospel that God gave to Jesus, according to the Qurʾān, but that they may nevertheless preserve some genuine sayings and teachings of Jesus.[112] His commentary therefore was composed very much in the service of his purpose to rebut Christian religious claims and to support Islamic confessional and juridical positions; it was not intended to comment on the Bible as a scripture useful in itself for Muslim scholarship. This in fact is a characteristic feature of almost every work by a Muslim author that pays substantial attention to the Bible.

The late Hava Lazarus-Yafeh wrote that in the Islamic world biblical "exegesis never became a literary genre on its own, nor did it ever play an important role in Muslim medieval theology."[113] Rather, as in the examples we have mentioned, Muslim biblical scholarship in early Islamic times and up into the Middle Ages, as careful as it sometimes was, seems for the most part to have focused almost exclusively on explicating three kinds of passages: those thought to have reference to the coming of Muḥammad; those deemed useful to disprove Jewish or Christian religious claims; and passages indicative of distortion or misinterpretation of the scriptures. For the rest, as we have seen, stories of the prophets and collections of the sayings of Jesus circulated freely, most often with little or no reference to the biblical text. For example, both the historian Abū Jaʿfar Muḥammad aṭ-Tabarī (d.923) and the later historian of Damascus, Ibn ʿAsākir (d.1176), wrote

[111] Thomas F. Michel (trans.), *A Muslim Theologian's Response to Christianity: Ibn Taymiyya's al-Jawāb al-Ṣaḥīḥ* (Delmar, NY: Caravan Books, 1984), p. 213

[112] See Lejla Demiri, "Ḥanbalite Commentary on the Bible: Analysis of Najm al-Dīn al-Ṭūfī's (d.716/1316) *al-Taʿlīq*," in Thomas, *The Bible in Arab Christianity*, pp. 295–313.

[113] Lazarus-Yafeh, *Intertwined Worlds*, p. 110.

biographies of Jesus that have little or no connection at all with the canonical Gospels.[114] But there were exceptions.

In Mamlūk Cairo, the well known Qur'ān commentator Abū l-Ḥasan Ibrāīm ibn ʿAmr ibn Ḥasan al-Biqāʿī (d.1469) not only consulted Arabic translations of the Jewish and Christian scriptures in his interpretations of Qur'ānic passages, but also wrote a separate monograph of considerable erudition in which he made the case that it was not just legitimate, but actually necessary for Muslim scholars to make use of the canonical Hebrew Bible and of the Gospels.[115] While his book was not well received by the Muslim scholars of his day, it nevertheless stands as the exception that proves the rule that from the eleventh century onward, there was scant Muslim interest in consulting the Arabic Bible of the Jews and Christians for purposes other than apologetics or polemics. By contrast, in modern times, in the wake of advances in nineteenth- and twentieth-century biblical scholarship, there has been abundant scholarly interest in the Bible on the part of Muslim scholars.

A Gospel of One's Own

In the early eighteenth century a hitherto unknown *Gospel of Barnabas* was discovered in an Italian manuscript in Amsterdam. The text affirms the unity of God, includes a testimony from Jesus himself that he was only a prophet, foretells the coming of a prophet from among the descendants of Ishmael, and says that Judas Iscariot was crucified instead of Jesus.[116] The text was translated into Arabic from the original Italian (or Spanish?) in the early twentieth century and has been widely acclaimed by some Muslims as a more authentic record of Jesus' life than is offered by the four canonical Gospels or by any other text emanating from Christian scholarly circles. A number of theories have been advanced to account for the *Gospel*

[114] See André Ferré, "La vie de Jésus d'après les *Annales* de Ṭabarī," *Islamochristiana* 5 (1979), pp. 1–29; Suleiman A. Mourad, "A Twelfth-Century Muslim Biography of Jesus," *Islam and Christian-Muslim Relations* 7 (1996), pp. 39–45.

[115] See now Walid A. Saleh (ed.), *In Defense of the Bible: A Critical Edition and an Introduction to al-Biqāʿī's Bible Treatise* (Islamic History and Civilization, vol. 73; Leiden: Brill, 2008). See also Lazarus-Yafeh, *Intertwined Worlds*, pp. 127–129.

[116] See Lonsdale and Laura Ragg, *The Gospel of Barnabas* (Oxford: Oxford University Press, 1907); Luigi Cirillo and M. Frémaux, *Évangile de Barnabé* (Paris: Beauchesne, 1977); David Sox, *The Gospel of Barnabas* (London: Allen and Unwin, 1984); L. F. Bernabé Pons, *El Texto Morisco del Evangelio de San Bernabé* (Granada: Universidad de Granada, 1998).

of Barnabas. Most of them suggest that the text was composed in the western Mediterranean world, perhaps in Italy or in Spain. Proposed dates range from the fourteenth to the sixteenth century, and authorship is variously assigned to the hands of a Morisco, to a Spanish Christian who had converted to Islam, and even to a disenchanted Carmelite in Cyprus who in the fourteenth century had converted to Islam.[117]

Whatever might have been the origins of the *Gospel of Barnabas,* it is clearly not a product of the historical, Islamic biblical scholarship we have been reviewing in this chapter, albeit that some Muslims might subsequently have welcomed it as being closer to the postulated, uncorrupted Gospel of the Qur'ān than to the canonical Gospels that circulate among the Christians. What the history of Islamic biblical scholarship up to the Middle Ages does highlight is the fact that in one form or another the scriptures of the Jews and the Christians were available to Muslim scholars in Arabic translation from at least the early ninth century onward, and that they early on became intertwined with other scriptural and traditional texts as Muslim scholars undertook to express the distinctiveness of Islam's doctrinal and moral posture in the world.

[117] See M. De Epalza, "Le milieu hispano-moresque de l'Évangile islamisant de Barnabe," *Islamochristiana* 8 (1982), pp. 159–183; G. A. Wiegers, "Muḥammad as the Messiah: A Comparison of the Polemical Works of Juan Alonso with the *Gospel of Barnabas,*" *Bibliotheca Orientalis* 52 (1995), pp. 245–292; Jan Slomp, "The 'Gospel of Barnabas' in Recent Research," *Islamochristiana* 23 (1997), pp. 81–109; Theodore Pulcini, "In the Shadow of Mount Carmel: The Collapse of the 'Latin East' and the Origins of the Gospel of Barnabas," *Islam and Christian-Muslim Relations* 12 (2001), pp. 191–209; Jan Joosten, "The *Gospel of Barnabas* and the Diatessaron," *Harvard Theological Review* 95 (2002), pp. 73–96.

✻ CHAPTER VII ✻

Intertwined Scriptures

INTEREST IN THE BIBLE in Arabic outside of the Arabic-speaking world seems first to have arisen in the sixteenth century in Western churches with concerns in the Middle East,[1] and to have culminated in the inclusion of Arabic versions of biblical books in the great polyglot Bibles of the sixteenth century.[2] The first of these to include an Arabic version of the complete Bible, put together from previously printed sources, was the seventeenth-century Paris Polyglot in 1645, a text taken over with some corrections in the London Polyglot of 1655–1657.[3] In the meantime, in Rome in 1651, the Vatican's Sacred Congregation for the Propagation of the Faith published an eclectic edition of the complete Bible in Arabic that eventually, and for a time, gained a wide readership among Arabic-speaking Christians in the Middle East.[4] Thus began the era of the production of printed Bibles in Arabic, projects accomplished largely under the auspices of the Western Christian churches and inspired largely by the principles of Western biblical scholarship. For the most part these translations paid no attention at all to the earlier Arabic translations discussed in the foregoing chapters. The Protestants were first in the field, with the so-called Smith-Van Dyk Version, published in Beirut in 1865. There followed a Catholic translation under the auspices of the Dominicans of Mosul, Iraq, in 1875–1878, a version soon overshadowed in the Arabic-speaking world by the so-called 'Jesuit version', completed in 1880 in Beirut.[5] In subsequent years, and throughout

[1] See the texts listed in T. H. Darlow, H. F. Moule, and A. G. Jayne, *Historical Catalogue of the Printed Editions of Holy Scripture in the Library of the British and Foreign Bible Society* (2 vols. in 4; London: British and Foreign Bible Society, 1903–1911), vol. 2, part 1, pp. 62–84.

[2] See E. Mangenot, "Polyglottes," in F. Vigouroux (ed.), *Dictionnaire de la Bible* (5 vols.; Paris: Letouzey et Ané, 1912–1922), vol. 5, cols. 513–529.

[3] See Darlow, Moule, and Jayne, *Historical Catalogue*, vol. 2, part 1, pp. 65 and 66.

[4] See Darlow, Moule, and Jayne, *Historical Catalogue*, vol. 2, part 1, p. 66.

[5] See the comprehensive study by John A. Thompson, "The Origin and Nature of the Chief Printed Arabic Bibles," *The Bible Translator* 6 (1955), pp. 2–12, 51–55, 98–106, 146–150.

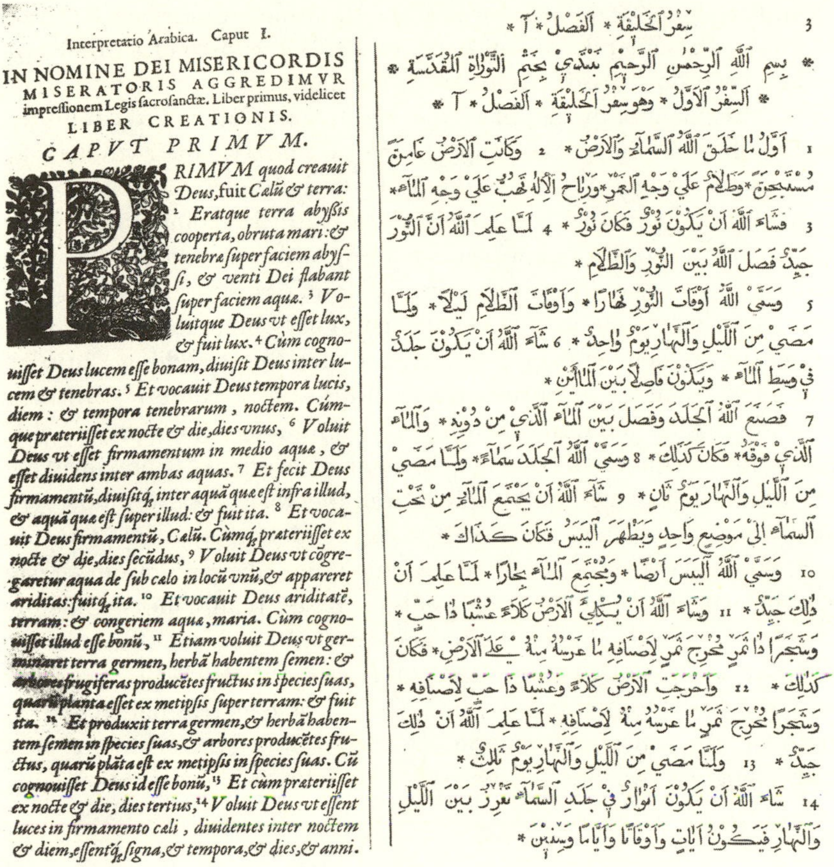
Interpretatio Arabica. Caput I.

IN NOMINE DEI MISERICORDIS MISERATORIS AGGREDIMVR impressionem Legis sacrosanctæ. Liber primus, videlicet LIBER CREATIONIS.

CAPVT PRIMVM.

PRIMVM quod creauit Deus, fuit Cælũ & terra: 2 Eratque terra abyssis cooperta, obruta mari: & tenebræ super faciem abyssi, & venti Dei flabant super faciem aquæ. 3 Voluitque Deus vt esset lux, & fuit lux. 4 Cùm cognouisset Deus lucem esse bonam, diuisit Deus inter lucem & tenebras. 5 Et vocauit Deus tempora lucis, diem: & tempora tenebrarum, noctem. Cúmque præteriisset ex nocte & die, dies vnus, 6 Voluit Deus vt esset firmamentum in medio aquæ, & esset diuidens inter ambas aquas. 7 Et fecit Deus firmamentũ, diuisitq; inter aquã quæ est infra illud, & aquã quæ est super illud: & fuit ita. 8 Et vocauit Deus firmamentũ, Cælũ. Cùmq; præteriisset ex nocte & die, dies secũdus, 9 Voluit Deus vt cõgregaretur aqua de sub cælo in locũ vnũ, & appareret ariditas: fuitq; ita. 10 Et vocauit Deus ariditatẽ, terram: & congeriem aquæ, maria. Cùm cognouisset illud esse bonũ, 11 Etiam voluit Deus vt germinaret terra germen, herbã habentem semen: & arbores frugiferas producẽtes fructus in species suas, quarũ planta esset ex metipsis super terram: & fuit ita. 12 Et produxit terra germen, & herbã habentem semen in species suas, & arbores producẽtes fructus, quarũ plãta est ex metipsis in species suas. Cũ cognouisset Deus id esse bonũ, 13 Et cùm præteriisset ex nocte & die, dies tertius, 14 Voluit Deus vt essent luces in firmamento cæli, diuidentes inter noctem & diem, essentq; signa, & tempora, & dies, & anni.

3 سفر الخليقة * الفصل * آ *
* بسم الله الرحمن الرحيم نبتدي بختم التوراة المقدسة *
* السفر الاول * وهو سفر الخليقة * الفصل * آ *
1 اول ما خلق الله السماء والارض * 2 وكانت الارض غامرة
مستبحرة * وظلام على وجه الغمر * ورياح الله تهب على وجه الماء *
3 فشاء الله ان يكون نور فكان نور * 4 لما علم الله ان النور
جيد فصل الله بين النور والظلام *
5 وسمى الله اوقات النور نهارا * واوقات الظلام ليلا * ولما
مضى من الليل والنهار يوم واحد * 6 شاء الله ان يكون جلد
في وسط الماء * ويكون فاصلا بين المائين *
7 فصنع الله الجلد وفصل بين الماء الذي من دونه * والماء
الذي فوقه * فكان كذلك * 8 وسمى الله الجلد سماء * ولما مضى
من الليل والنهار يوم ثان * 9 شاء الله ان يجمع الماء من تحت
السماء الى موضع واحد ويظهر اليبس فكان كذاك *
10 وسمى الله اليبس ارضا * ومجمع الماء بحارا * لما علم ان
ذلك جيد * 11 وشاء الله ان يكلي الارض كلاء عشبا ذا حب *
وشجرا ذا ثمر يخرج ثمرا لاصنافه ما غرسه منه على الارض * فكان
كذلك * 12 واخرجت الارض كلاء وعشبا ذا حب لاصنافه *
وشجرا يخرج ثمرا ما غرسه منه لاصنافه * لما علم الله ان ذلك
جيد * 13 ولما مضى من الليل والنهار يوم ثالث *
14 شاء الله ان يكون انوار في جلد السماء تفرز بين الليل
والنهار فيكون ايات واوقاتا واياما وسنين *

Fig. 5. Page from the Paris Polyglot, 1645, Genesis chap. I, including Arabic translation by Saʿadyah Ha-Gaon. Courtesy of the Institute of Christian Oriental Research, The Catholic University of America.

the twentieth century, there have been numerous projects undertaken by Christians to translate the Bible into Arabic, and they continue today. But along the way there was a shift in intellectual horizons in both the Arabic-speaking Jewish communities and the Christian churches of the Arab world that changed the fortunes of the Bible in Arabic.

From early in the ninth century up to the fifteenth century, biblical scholarship flourished in the Arabic-speaking Jewish communities, as we have seen. But from that time forward, with the European Christian conquest of al-Andalus in 1492 and the hardening of Muslim attitudes toward non-Islamic religions under the Mamlūks (1254–1517), the torch of Jewish learning was passed northward. While Jewish communities continued to be an important segment of the population in the Islamic world,[6] and continued to esteem the learning and accomplishments of the past, their scholarly attention was no longer focused so intensely on the Bible in Arabic as once was the case. Similarly, in the Arabic-speaking, Christian communities some of these same historical developments, along with other factors—among them a heightened anti-Christian current among Muslims in the wake of the Crusades; an increasing rate of conversion to Islam in the general population, with its demographic consequences for the dwindling Christian communities;[7] and not least the growing intrusion of Western Christians into Arab Christian life from the thirteenth century onward—precipitated a change in the cultural life of Arabic-speaking Christians.[8] Gradually Western thinkers became their philosophical and theological conversation partners, diverting their attention away from Baghdad, Damascus, or Cairo and toward Rome, Paris, or London.[9] A certain cultural alienation from an earlier Islamo-Christian ethos was the result. In these circumstances, while the old translations of the Bible in Arabic continued to be copied and used, particularly in the liturgy, from the Ottoman period (1517–1918) onward Christian projects to translate the Bible into Arabic increasingly relied on the support and active participation of Western Christians. With that shift, the interreligious dynamics of the Bible in Arabic in the Arabic-speaking

[6] See S. D. Goitein, *Jews and Arabs: A Concise History of their Social and Cultural Relations* (3rd rev. ed.; New York: Schocken Books, 1974); Norman A. Stillman, *The Jews of Arab Lands: A History and Source Book* (Philadelphia: Jewish Publication Society of America, 1979); S. D. Goitein, *A Mediterranean Society: The Jewish Communities of the Arab World as Portrayed in the Documents of the Cairo Geniza* (Berkeley, CA: University of California Press, 1967–1993); Mark R. Cohen, *Under Crescent and Cross: The Jews in the Middle Ages* (Princeton, NJ: Princeton University Press, 1994).

[7] See Philip Fargues, "The Arab Christians of the Middle East: A Demographic Perspective," and Bernard Sabella, "The Emigration of Christian Arabs: Dimensions and Causes of the Phenomenon," in Andrea Pacini (ed.), *Christian Communities in the Arab Middle East: The Challenge for the Future* (Oxford: Clarendon Press, 1998), pp. 48–66 and 127–154.

[8] See Jean-Pierre Valognes, *Vie et mort des chrétiens d'orient; des origins à nos jours* (Paris: Fayard, 1994).

[9] See in this connection the remarks of Samir Khalil Samir, "The Christian Communities, Active Members of Arab Society throughout History," in Pacini, *Christian Communities in the Arab Middle East*, pp. 67–91, esp. 83–87.

Fig. 6. Vatican *editio princeps* of Arabic version of the Gospels, Rome 1590/1591, translated from the 'Alexandrian Vulgate', beginning of the Gospel according to Luke. Courtesy of the Institute of Christian Oriental Research, The Catholic University of America.

world of the Jews, Christians, and Muslims changed considerably from the scene we have surveyed in the foregoing chapters.

The Bible in Arabic, from its oral beginnings in pre-Islamic times up to the production and wide circulation of translations from the ninth through the thirteenth centuries, functioned as an important interreligious catalyst in early Islamic times, and this in ways that have gone largely unnoticed due to the general scholarly neglect of the Arabic translations. The focus of even those scholars who have studied the translations has typically been fairly narrow; they have taken account of developments within a single community's frame of reference, without paying much attention to the function of the translated texts within the wider cultural horizon. It is not uncommon even in recent studies of early-Islamic period translations done by Christians for the modern authors to be so focused on the biblical text itself that they systematically leave out of account any other information, liturgical, historical, or editorial, that the manuscripts may also contain. The result is a continued scholarly camouflaging of the role of the Bible in Arabic in the wider religious culture of the Arabic-speaking world in Late Antiquity and the Middle Ages.

The oral Bible in Arabic that circulated among Arabic-speaking Jews and Christians in the first third of the seventh century was the very 'scripture' from which the Qur'ān bade its audience numerous times to recall and recollect the narratives of the patriarchs and prophets, as we have argued in earlier chapters. The range of biblical books the Qur'ān recalls, including Torah, Psalms, Prophets, Wisdom, and Gospel, not to mention numerous echoes of accounts otherwise known only from a range of apocryphal, pseudepigraphical, and other repositories of Late Antique Jewish and Christian lore, suggests that the Arabic-speaking Jews and Christians within the Qur'ān's purview were not the remnants of ancient and isolated sects. Rather, the Qur'ān's echoes of and allusions to this wide range of biblical tradition, not to mention its engagement in doctrinal critiques (especially of Christian teachings), suggests that the 'Scripture People' in its audience, and particularly the Christians among them, were themselves, as numerous studies have shown, *au courant* with the mostly Aramaic/Syriac expressions of the contemporary Melkite, Jacobite, and Nestorian Christian communities.

On this reading, the Bible in Arabic, even prior to its production in writing, had already become intertwined with the nascent Islamic scripture, if not textually in explicit quotations, then in terms of the Qur'ān's retelling, recollecting, and re-presentation of Bible history; the Bible had become in large part the Qur'ān's subtext. But the Qur'ān, as we have argued in an earlier chapter, had in its distinctive prophetology its own criterion of selection for the biblical figures and narratives it recalled. In the Qur'ān, the biblical 'prophets' (*al-anbiyā'*) are evoked along with others called 'God's messengers' (*rusul Allāh*);[10] some biblical prophets also have in the Qur'ān the status of 'messengers' (Noah, Lot, Ishmael, Moses, Jesus, and perhaps

[10] See in particular W. A. Bijlefeld, "A Prophet and More than a Prophet? Some Observations on the Qur'ānic Use of the Terms 'Prophet' and 'Apostle'," *Muslim World* 59 (1969), pp. 1–28.

Elijah and Jonah),[11] suggesting that in the Qur'ān's prophetology the 'messengers' compose the more comprehensive category and provide the hermeneutical horizon within which the role of the biblical prophets is to be interpreted. In other words, the Qur'ān includes the biblical prophets in its antecedent scheme of universal messengers, a more inclusive prophetology than that of the earlier Marcionite-inspired Manicheans, who systematically excluded the biblical prophets between Noah and Jesus from the number of their 'Apostles of Humanity'.[12]

The Qur'ān, as we maintained in an earlier chapter, was compiled and published in the course of the second half of the seventh century CE, becoming the first real Arabic book. This was a momentous event in Late Antique religious and cultural history, coinciding with the Muslim Arab conquest and occupation of the former Roman and Persian territories of the Fertile Crescent. Arguably it was due in no small part to the religious provocation of Islamic scripture and its influence on the linguistic development of Arabic that Arabic emerged as the *lingua franca* of the newly emerging Islamic polity, becoming the public language even of the newly subject Jewish and Christian communities. It followed as a natural development that the Arabic Qur'ān became a stimulus for the first written translations of the Bible into Arabic, first among the Christians from the middle of the eighth century onward, and subsequently among the Arabic-speaking Jews from at least the early ninth century until well into the Middle Ages. It was under the shadow of the Qur'ān and a developing Islamic religious discourse that the language of the early translations of the Bible into Arabic took on the Muslim cast that was, as we have seen, a discernible feature of their diction, especially among the Christians. Some later Christians, seemingly in a bid for more literary grace in the Arabic Bible, made translations of biblical books in the *Saj'*, or 'rhymed prose' style so evident in portions of the Qur'ān.[13] Indeed, the imitation of Qur'ānic diction and literary style

[11] See A. H. Mathias Zahniser, "Messenger," in McAuliffe, *Encyclopaedia of the Qur'ān*, vol. 3, pp. 380–383.

[12] See Nicholas J. Baker–Brian, *Manichaeism: An Ancient Faith Rediscovered* (London: Continuum, 2011), esp. pp. 42–54, 64–66; "Both Marcionite and Manichaean Christians adhered to a model that isolated the memory of Jesus from contact with all classical Jewish laws, prophecies and traditions" (p. 54). See the list of the Manichaean "Prophets or Apostles of Humanity," in Michel Tardieu, *Manichaeism* (trans., M. B. DeBevoise; Urbana and Chicago, IL: University of Illinois Press, 2008), p. 15.

[13] See Devin J. Stewart, "Rhymed Prose," in McAuliffe, *Encyclopaedia of the Qur'ān*, vol. 4, pp. 476–483.

can be seen already in non-biblical Arab Christian compositions of the second third of the eighth century.[14] In this linguistic and literary way, as well as in other more topical areas, the scriptures of the Christians and Muslims inevitably became intertwined with one another in the Arabic language.

The Qurʾān set the tone for scriptural style in Arabic; it became the linguistic standard by which the Bible in Arabic was judged and found wanting. One need only recall in this connection the Muslim polemic against the perceived misuse of Arabic in Jewish and Christian Bible translations of the ninth century to secure this point. We have seen in an earlier chapter that a good case can be made for the suggestion that criticisms of just this sort, as voiced by the famous Muʿtazilī writer and scholar al-Jāḥiẓ, lay in the background of Saʿadyah Gaʾōn's concerns for felicitous and accurate Arabic expression in his *Tafsīr*, in addition to his concern accurately to interpret the original Hebrew text for the benefit of Arabic-speaking Jews. Similarly, the Muslim claim that by way of misleading exegesis Jews effaced the predictions of Muḥammad that occur in the Hebrew Bible, in passages such as Isaiah 21:6–7, have been seen to have elicited responses from Jewish scholars that later influenced Jewish readings of the same passages.[15] Further, the use both Christians and Muslims made of Saʿadyah's *Tafsīr* of the Torah for their own purposes in the Middle Ages testifies to how readily the Bible in Arabic produced in one community could become intertwined with scripture study, interreligious polemic, and even with liturgical use in the other Arabic-speaking communities.

The emergence of the Bible in Arabic facilitated not only intercommunal access to the scriptures of the Jews, Christians, and Muslims, but heightened as well interest in the narratives of the biblical patriarchs and prophets themselves, to the point that their stories often took on a life of their own, well beyond the parameters of the biblical texts. We have taken note of this phenomenon at work in the Islamic communities in the popularity of the 'stories of the prophets' (*qiṣaṣ al-anbiyāʾ*), in the *Israʾīliyyāt*, and in the persistent currency of stories of Jesus, the son of Mary, and collections of sayings attributed to him. But there is one biblical figure in particular whose story has received special attention from Jews, Christians, and Mus-

[14] See, e.g., the study of the prologue of the treatise, *On the Triune Nature of God*, in Mark N. Swanson, "Beyond Prooftexting: Approaches to the Qurʾān in some Early Arabic Christian Apologies," *The Muslim World* 88 (1998), pp. 297–319, esp. 305–308.

[15] See, e.g., John C. Reeves, "The Muslim Appropriation of a Biblical Text: The Messianic Dimensions of Isaiah 21:67," in K. Holum and H. Lapin (eds.), *Shaping the Middle East: Jews, Christians, and Muslims in an Age of Transition 400–800 CE* (Bethesda, MD: University Press of Maryland, 2011), pp. 211–222.

lims alike, each of whom over the centuries have made him into a virtual icon of their own confessional identity. This development began already in second-temple Judaism, continued in the New Testament, and came to a distinctively Islamic expression in the Qur'ān. In modern times, by no small irony from a historical perspective, the biblical figure of Abraham has become a sign not of interreligious self-definition over against others, but a figure in whose name one might enlist Jews, Christians, and Muslims to join together in a sort of monotheistic, interreligious family.

Here is not the place to discuss this prospect in detail. The topic arises, however, in the context of our discussions of the Bible in Arabic and of the intertwined scriptures in the intellectual life of Jews, Christians, and Muslims in Late Antiquity and the Middle Ages, not because it was discussed at the time, but because it looms so large in present-day scholarship and common parlance. Interestingly, all three scriptures speak of Abraham as 'God's friend', a special title for the patriarch that is foreshadowed in Isaiah 41:8 (*'ōhᵃbî*), James 2:23 (*φίλος θεοῦ*), and IV *an-Nisā'* 125 (*khalīl*), but as we shall see, albeit that the epithet bespeaks a common tradition of a special esteem for him, the theological and cultural significance of Abraham is quite different in the three traditions.

In the interreligious and intercultural world of Second Temple Judaism, in non-biblical texts sometimes now described as amounting to a 're-written Bible', in texts such as the *Apocalypse of Abraham* and the *Testament of Abraham*, and later in the Mishnah and subsequent rabbinical texts, Abraham figured in Jewish lore as a resolute opponent of idolatry and sometimes even as a Torah-observant Jew.[16] In other texts, such as the *Book of Jubilees*, Abraham is presented as the archetypal monotheist; in the works of Philo Judaeus (c. 20 BCE–c. 50 CE) the patriarch is a proselyte and philosopher; and in the writings of Flavius Josephus (c. 37–100 CE) he appears in the guise of a Hellenistic philosopher.[17] Interestingly, Josephus seems also to have been the first to have identified the 'Arabs', precisely so called, as

[16] See Jon D. Levenson, "Abraham among Jews, Christians, and Muslims: Monotheism, Exegesis, and Religious Diversity," *ARC, The Journal of the Faculty of Religious Studies, McGill* 26 (1998), pp. 5–29; James L. Kugel, *Traditions of the Bible: A Guide to the Bible as It Was at the Start of the Common Era* (Cambridge, MA: Harvard University Press, 1998), esp. "Abraham Journeys from Chaldea," pp. 243–326; Alon Goshen-Gottstein, "Abraham and 'Abrahamic Religions' in Contemporary Interreligious Discourse: Reflections of an Implicated Jewish Bystander," *Studies in Interreligious Dialogue* 12 (2002), pp. 165–183.

[17] See Nancy Calvert–Koyzis, *Paul, Monotheism and the People of God: The Significance of Abraham Traditions for Early Judaism and Christianity* (Journal for the Study of the New Testament Supplement Series, 273; London and New York: T and T Clar, 2004).

descendants of Abraham and Hagar, thereby introducing a historical surmise that would in Islamic times become an important, interreligious *theologoumenon.*[18] Nevertheless, the common element in all these texts is that Abraham is a veritable paradigm for Jewish life and can be seen to have anticipated if not to have surpassed even the sages of other traditions in erudition and religious stature.[19]

Beginning already in the Epistles of St. Paul, particularly Galatians 3:1–5:12 and Romans 3:27–4:25, Abraham is presented as the "Father of us all," (Romans 4:16) by faith and not by observance of the Law. He thus became a figure both of religious division between Jews and Christians and, in Paul's view, also a common ancestor among whose progeny Christians could count themselves.[20] Here one might see the beginning of Abraham's career as an ambiguous sign of both interreligious kinship and interreligious estrangement. By the fourth Christian century, in Eusebius of Caesarea's (c. 260–c. 340) *Ecclesiastical History*, Abraham, among other biblical figures, could be thought of as a Christian "in fact if not in name." And Eusebius could go on to say, "We must regard the religion proclaimed in recent years to all nations through Christ's teaching as none other than the first, most ancient, and most primitive of all religions, discovered by Abraham and his followers, God's beloved."[21] And so in the Late Antique and medieval Christian view, Abraham became a pre-Jewish harbinger of Christianity, and a proto-Christian.[22]

Given this background, it is perhaps not surprising to find the Qur'ān declaring that "Abraham was neither a Jew nor a Christian, but a *ḥanīf* and a *muslim*. And he was not one of the polytheists" (III *Āl ʿImrān* 67). Further, in the context of controversies with Jews and Christians, the Qur'ān reports:

[18] See Fergus Millar, "Hagar, Ishmael, Josephus and the Origins of Islam," *Journal of Jewish Studies* 44 (1993), pp. 23–45. See also Carol Bakhos, *Ishmael on the Border: Rabbinic Portrayals of the First Arab* (Albany, NY: State University of New York Press, 2006).

[19] It is interesting to note in passing that an early eighteenth century Oxford scholar, Thomas Hyde, an admirer of Zoroastrianism, could even speak of Abraham as "the first Zardusht." See Guy G. Stroumsa, *A New Science: The Discovery of Religion in the Age of Reason* (Cambridge, MA: Harvard University Press, 2010), pp. 106.

[20] See Calvert-Koyzis, *Paul, Monotheism and the People of God.*

[21] G. A. Williamson (trans.), *Eusebius: The History of the Church from Christ to Constantine* (Harmondsworth, Middlesex, UK and New York: Penguin Books, 1965), p. 47.

[22] See J. Siker, *Disinheriting the Jews: Abraham in Early Christian Controversy* (Louisville, KY: Westminster/Knox, 1991).

"They say, 'If you become Jews or Christians, you shall be well guided.' Say, 'Rather, we follow the religion (*millah*) of Abraham, who was upright and not polytheist'" (II *al-Baqarah* 135). And so the phrase 'religion of Abraham' came into use in Arabic as a polemically charged synonym for Islam, in contradistinction to Judaism and Christianity.[23] It is surely a testimony to the phenomenon of the intertwined scriptures. But it is also very much a symptom of a competing exegesis intended to distance the 'Scripture People' from the Muslims rather than to include them in the same faith community. Centuries later, Western scholars would ignore these controversial implications and nuances in the interreligious evocation of the biblical Abraham and find in the common appeal to the scriptural patriarch grounds for classifying Judaism, Christianity, and Islam as 'Abrahamic religions'.

It is not quite clear when in the modern study of religions scholars and others began to speak of the 'Abrahamic religions'; certainly by the 1930's Louis Massignon (1883–1962), a pioneer in the Western study of Sufism and an enthusiastic promoter of Christian/Muslim dialogue, was thinking and writing about Abraham as a patron of rapprochement between Jews, Christians, and Muslims.[24] Subsequently, and especially in the second half of the twentieth century it became commonplace to speak of the 'Abrahamic religions', and some have written enthusiastically about the figure of Abraham as offering a scriptural point of reference for interreligious reconciliation.[25] In some scholarly circles the concept of the 'Abrahamic religions' gave rise to a renewed comparative study of the three Semitic monotheisms.[26] But increasingly it is evident that in spite of good intentions to the contrary and in spite of the handiness of a succinct, scriptural label, the expression 'Abrahamic religions' is in the end something of a misno-

[23] See Shari L. Lowin, *The Making of a Forefather: Abraham in Islamic and Jewish Exegetical Narratives* (Islamic History and Civilization, vol. 65; Leiden: Brill, 2006). See also Uri Rubin, "*Ḥanīfiyya* and Kaʿba: An Inquiry into the Arabian pre-Islamic Background of *dīn Ibrāhīm*," *Jerusalem Studies in Arabic and Islam* 13 (1990), pp. 85–112.

[24] See in particular Louis Massignon, *Les trois prières d'Abraham* (Patrimoines; Paris: Les Éditions du Cerf, 1997), a volume containing essays Massignon wrote in the 1930s. See also Sidney H. Griffith, "Sharing the Faith of Abraham: The 'Credo' of Louis Massignon," *Islam and Christian-Muslim Relations* 8 (1997), pp. 193–210.

[25] See, e.g., Karl-Josef Kuschel, *Abraham: Sign of Hope for Jews, Christians and Muslims* (New York: Continuum, 1995).

[26] As in the pioneering study by F. E. Peters, *Children of Abraham: Judaism. Christianity, Islam* (Princeton, NJ: Princeton University Press, 1982).

mer. It misleadingly suggests a congruence of views about the significance of the biblical patriarch among Jews, Christians, and Muslims that does not in fact exist.[27]

The scriptures of the Jews, Christians, and Muslims are intertwined with one another not so much textually, for there are scarcely any quotations from the Bible in the Qur'ān. Rather, they are intertwined in the recollection of the narratives of the Hebrew Bible in the New Testament, along with some quotations; in the reminiscence of the prophetic and apostolic figures of the Torah, Psalms, and Gospel in the Qur'ān; and in much popular Islamic religious literature. Further, the scriptures became intertwined with one another, often in counterpoint and in struggle with one another, in the exegetical, apologetic, and polemical discourse that continued in the three communities over the centuries. What we see is something on the order of a codependent, interscriptural dialectic that speaks to identity-formation, appeals for legitimacy, and the exercise of interscriptural reasoning.

The Bible in Arabic for a time expedited a lively interreligious conversation between Jews, Christians, and Muslims. But is it important for biblical studies? Modern Bible scholars have typically thought of the Arabic versions of the scriptures as having come too late to be of importance for the textual criticism of the Bible. This is not in fact entirely true because, as we have seen, Arabic versions of a number of biblical books, including especially apocryphal and pseudepigraphical works, have preserved significant passages and indeed whole texts that have disappeared in their original languages or have become fragmentary in what survives of earlier translations. But for all that, the major contribution of the Bible in Arabic to modern biblical studies probably lies in the translations themselves, as the first and most important step in biblical interpretation. Arguably, the requirements of the liturgy and the need for immediately relevant exegesis were among the factors prompting Jews and Christians to make Arabic translations of their scriptures in the first place; the Bible in Arabic in turn became for Muslims an important point of reference both for the interpretation of the Qur'ān and for the articulation of Islamic salvation history. This ever-present interreligious dimension of the Bible in Arabic continues to make its study relevant, not least for the continuing efforts, especially among contemporary Middle Eastern Christians, to carry on with the effort begun

[27] See the remarks of Goschen-Gottstein, "Abraham and 'Abrahamic Religions'," esp. pp. 176–177.

by their forbears to produce Arabic translations of the scriptures suitable for present-day church life. And in the broader context of the ever-more pressing challenges of interreligious dialogue between Jews, Christians, and Muslims in the twenty-first century, the study of the Bible in Arabic becomes an increasingly important component of international biblical scholarship.

* Bibliography *

Abrahamov, Binyamin, "Signs," in McAuliffe, *Encyclopaedia of the Qur'ān* (2001–2006), vol. 5, pp. 2–11.

———, "Some Notes on the Notion of *Naskh* in the *Kalām*," in Anna Akasoy and Wim Raven (eds.), *Islamic Thought in the Middle Ages: Studies in Text, Transmission, and Translation, in Honour of Hans Daiber.* Islamic Philosophy, Theology and Science, Texts and Studies, vol. 75; Leiden: Brill, 2008, pp. 3–19.

Accad, Martin, "Did the Later Syriac Fathers Take into Consideration their Islamic Context When Reinterpreting the New Testament?" *Parole de l'Orient* 23 (1998), pp. 13–32.

———, "The Gospels in the Muslim Discourse of the Ninth to the Fourteenth Centuries: An Exegetical Inventorial Table," *Islam and Christian-Muslim Relations* 41 (2003), pp. 67–91, 205–220, 337–352, 459–479.

Adang, Camilla, *Muslim Writers on Judaism and the Hebrew Bible: From Ibn Rabban to Ibn Ḥazm.* Islamic Philosophy, Theology, and Science, vol. 22; Leiden: E.J. Brill, 1996.

———, "A Rare Case of Biblical 'Testimonies' to the Prophet Muḥammad in Muʿtazilī Literature: Quotations from Ibn Rabban al-Ṭabarī's *Kitāb al-dīn wa-l-dawla* in Abū l-Ḥusayn al-Baṣrī's *Ghurar al-adilla,* as Preserved in a Work by al-Ḥimmaṣī al-Rāzī," in C. Adang et al. (eds.), *A Common Rationality: Mutazilism in Islam and Judaism.* Istanbuler Texte und Studien, 15; Würzburg: Ergon Verlag, 2007, pp. 297–330.

Adang, C. et al. (eds.), *A Common Rationality: Mutazilism in Islam and Judaism,* Istanbuler Texte und Studien 15. Würzburg: Ergon Verlag, 2007.

Adang, Camilla, and Sabine Schmidtke, "Polemics (Muslim-Jewish)," in Stillman, *Encyclopedia of Jews in the Islamic World (2010),* vol. 4, pp. 82–90.

Akasoy, Anna, and Wim Raven (eds.), *Islamic Thought in the Middle Ages: Studies in Text, Transmission, and Translation, in Honour of Hans Daiber;* Islamic Philosophy, Theology and Science, Texts and Studies 75. Leiden: Brill, 2008.

Arbache, Samir, *Une ancienne version arabe des Évangiles: langue, texte et lexique.* Thèse de doctorat de l'Université Michel de Montaigne; Bordeaux, 1994.

Arzhanov, Yury, "Zeugnisse über Kontakte zwischen Juden und Christen im vorislamischen Arabien," *Oriens Christianus* 92 (2008), pp. 79–93.

Astren, Fred, *Karaite Judaism and Historical Understanding.* Columbia, SC: University of South Carolina Press, 2004.

———, "Qirqisānī, Jacob al-," in Stillman, *Encyclopedia of Jews in the Islamic World (2010),* vol. 4, pp. 136–140.

Atiya, A. S., "The Monastery of St. Catherine and the Mount Sinai Expedition," *Proceedings of the American Philosophical Society* 96 (1952), pp. 578–586.

———, "The Arabic Palimpsests of Mount Sinai," in J. Kritzeck and R. B. Winder (eds.), *The World of Islam: Studies in Honor of Philip K. Hitti.* London and New York: Macmillan and St. Martin's Press, 1959, pp. 109–120.

———,"Codex Arabicus (Sinai Arabic MS No. 514)," in H. Lehmann-Haupt (ed.), *Homage to a Bookman: Essays on Manuscripts, Books, and Printing written for Hans P. Kraus on his 60th Birthday, October 12, 1967.* Berlin: Mann, 1967, pp. 75–82.

Avi-Yonah, Michael, *The Jews under Roman and Byzantine Rule: A Political History of Palestine from the Bar Kokhba War to the Arab Conquest.* 2nd ed. ; Jerusalem: Magnes Press, 1984.

Azzi, Joseph, *Le prêtre et le prophète: Aux sources du Coran,* M. S. Garnier (trans.). Paris: Maisonneuve et Larose, 2001.

Baarda, Tjitze, "The Author of the Arabic Diatessaron," in T. Baarda et al. (eds.), *Miscellanea Neotestamentica,* vol. 1, Supplements to Novum Testamentum, vol. 47. Leiden: E.J. Brill, 1978, pp. 61–103.

Bacha, Constantin, *Les oeuvres arabes de Théodore Aboucara, évêque d'Haran.* Beirut: Imp. Alfawïd [du Journal Alawal], 1904.

Bacha, Ḥabīb, *Ḥawāshī (Notes) d'Ibn al-Maḥrūma sur le Tanqīḥ d'ibn Kammūna.* Patrimoine Arabe Chrétien, 6 ; Jounieh, Liban, and Rome: Librairie Saint-Paul and Pontificio Istituto Orientale, 1984.

Baker-Brian, Nicholas J., *Manichaeism: An Ancient Faith Rediscovered.* London: Continuum, 2011.

Bar-Asher, Meir M. et al. (eds.), *A Word Fitly Spoken: Studies in Mediaeval Exegesis of the Hebrew Bible and the Qur'ān, presented to Haggai Ben-Shammai.* Jerusalem: The Ben-Zvi Institute, 2007.

Barsoum, Ignatius Aphram, *History of Syriac Literature and Sciences,* Matti Moosa (ed. and trans.). Pueblo, CO: Passeggiata Press, 2000.

Battista, A., and B. Bagatti (eds.), *La Caverna dei Tesori: Testo Arabo con Traduzione Italiana e Commento.* Studium Biblicum Franciscanum, Collectio Minor, n. 26; Jerusalem: Franciscan Printing Press, 1979.

Bauer, Thomas, "Al-Samaw'al b. 'Ādiyā," in *EI2,* vol. 8, pp. 1041–1042.

———, "The Relevance of Early Arabic Poetry for Qur'ānic Studies, Including Observations on *Kull* and on Q 22:27, 26:225, and 52:31," in Neuwirth, et al., *The Qur'ān in Context (2011),* pp. 699–732.

Baumstark, Anton, "Jüdischer und christlicher Gebetstypus im Koran," *Der Islam* 16 (1927), pp. 229–248.

———, "Die sonntägliche Evangelienlesung im vor-byzantinischen Jerusalem," *Byzantinische Zeitschrift* 30 (1929/1930), pp. 350–359.

———, "Das Problem eines vorislamischen christlich-kirchlichen Schrifttums in arabischer Sprache," *Islamica* 4 (1929/1931), pp. 562–575.

———, "Arabische Übersetzung eines altsyrischen Evangelientextes und die Sure 21–105 zitierte Psalmenübersetzung," *Oriens Christianus* 9 (1931), pp. 164–188.

———, "Der älteste erhaltene Griechisch-Arabische Text von Psalm 110 (109)," *Oriens Christianus* 9 (1934), pp. 55–66.

Beaucamp, Joelle, Françoise Briquel-Chatonnet, and Julien Robin, (eds.), *Juifs et chrétiens en Arabie aux Ve et VIe siècles: Regards croisés sur les sources.* Actes du colloque de novembre 2008, Monographies, 32; Paris: Association des amis du Centre d'histoire et civilization de Byzance, 2010.

Beaumont, Mark, "Muslim Readings of John's Gospel in the 'Abbasid Period," *Islam and Christian-Muslim Relations* 91 (2008), pp. 179–197.

———, "Appropriating Christian Scriptures in a Muslim Refutation of Christianity: The Case of *Al-radd al-jamīl* attributed to al-Ghazālī," *Islam and Christian-Muslim Relations* 22 (2011), pp. 69–84.

Beck, Edmund, "Die Gestalt des Abraham am Wendepunkt der Entwicklung Muhammeds: Analyse von Sure 2, 118 (124)–135 (141)," *Le Muséon* 56 (1952), pp. 73–94.

Becker, Adam H., *Fear of God and the Beginning of Wisdom: The School of Nisibis and Christian Scholastic Culture in Late Antique Mesopotamia.* Philadelphia, PA: University of Pennsylvania Press, 2006.

Bedjan, Paulus, *Homiliae Selectae Mar-Jacobi Sarugensis.* Vol. 4; Paris and Leipzig: Via Dicta and Otto Harrassowitz, 1908.

Bellamy, James A., "More Proposed Emendations to the Text of the Koran," *Journal of the American Oriental Society* 116 (1996), pp. 196–204.

———, "A Further Note on *'Īsā*," *Journal of the American Oriental Society* 122 (2002), pp. 587–588.

Ben Shammai, Haggai, "Qirqisani on the Oneness of God," *Jewish Quarterly Review* 37 (1982), pp. 105–111.

———, "The Karaite Controversy: Scripture and Tradition in Early Karaism," in B. Lewis and F. Niewöhner (eds.), *Religionsgespräche im Mittelalter.* Wiesbaden: Harrassowitz, 1992, pp. 11–26.

———, "Return to Scriptures in Ancient and Medieval Jewish Sectarianism and in Early Islam," in E. Patlagean and A. Le Boulluec (eds.), *Les retours aux écritures: Fondamentalismes presents et passes.* Leuven: Peeters, 1993, pp. 313–339.

———, "Major Trends in Karaite Philosophy and Polemics in the Tenth and Eleventh Centuries," in Polliack, *Karaite Judaism (2003)*, pp. 339–362.

———, "The Tension between Literal Interpretation and Exegetical Freedom: Comparative Observations on Saadia's Method," in J. D. McAuliffe et al. (eds.), *With Reverence for the Word: Medieval Scriptural Exegesis in Judaism, Christianity, and Islam.* Oxford: Oxford University Press, 2003, pp. 33–50.

———, "Sa'adya Gaon," in Stillman, *Encyclopedia of Jews in the Islamic World (2010)*, vol. 4, pp. 197–204.

Bertaina, David, "The Development of Testimony Collections in Early Christian Apologetics with Islam," in Thomas, *The Bible in Arab Christianity (2007)*, pp. 151–173.

Bijlefeld, W. A., "A Prophet and More than a Prophet? Some Observations on the Qur'ānic Use of the Terms 'Prophet' and 'Apostle'," *Muslim World* 95 (1969), pp. 1–28.

Blau, Joshua, *The Emergence and Linguistic Background of Judaeo-Arabic: A Study in the Origins of Middle Arabic.* Oxford: Oxford University Press, 1965.

———, *A Grammar of Christian Arabic, Based Mainly on South-Palestinian Texts from the First Millennium.* CSCO vols. 267, 276, 279; Louvain: Peeters, 1966–1967.

———, "Sind uns Reste arabischer Bibelübersetzungen aus vorislamischer Zeit erhalten geblieben?" *Le Muséon* 86 (1973), pp. 67–72.

———, "On a Fragment of the Oldest Judaeo-Arabic Bible Translation Extant," in Blau and Reif, *Genizah Research after Ninety Years (1992)*, pp. 31–39.

———, *The Emergence and Linguistic Background of Judaeo-Arabic: A Study of the Origins of Neo-Arabic and Middle Arabic.* 3rd rev. ed.; Jerusalem: Ben-Zvi Institute for the Study of Jewish Communities in the East, 1999.

———, *A Handbook of Early Middle Arabic.* Jerusalem: The Max Schloessinger Memorial Foundation, The Hebrew University, 2002.

———, *A Dictionary of Mediaeval Judaeo-Arabic Texts* [Hebrew and English]. Jerusalem: The Israel Academy of Sciences and Humanities, 2006.

Blau, Joshua, and Simon Hopkins, "On Early Judaeo-Arabic Orthography," *Zeitschrift für Arabische Linguistik* 21 (1984), pp. 9–27.

Blau, Joshua, and S. C. Reif (eds.), *Genizah Research after Ninety Years: The Case of Judaeo-Arabic; Papers Read at the Third Congress of the Society for Judaeo-Arabic Studies.* Cambridge: Cambridge University Press, 1992.

Block, C. Jonn, "Philoponian Monophysitism in South Arabia at the Advent of Islam with Implications for the English Translation of '*Thalātha*' in Qur'ān 4.171 and 5.73," *Journal of Islamic Studies* 23 (2012), pp. 50–75.

Blois, François de, "The 'Sabians' (*Ṣābi'ūn*) in Pre-Islamic Arabia," *Acta Orientalia* 56 (1995), pp. 39–61.

———, "Sabians' in McAuliffe, *Encyclopaedia of the Qur'ān (2001–2006)*, vol. 4, pp. 511–513.

———, "*Naṣrānī (Ναζωραιος)* and *Ḥanīf (εθνικος)*: Studies on the Religious Vocabulary of Christianity and of Islam," *Bulletin of the School of Oriental and African Studies* 65 (2002), pp. 1–30.

———, "Elchasai – Manes – Muḥammad: Manichäismus und Islam in religionshistorischen Vergleich," *Der Islam* 81 (2004), pp. 31–48.

Bosworth, C. E., "The Qur'ānic Prophet Shu'aib and Ibn Taimiyya's Epistle Concerning Him," *Le Muséon* 78 (1974), pp. 425–440.

———, "Madyan Shu'ayb in Pre-Islamic and Early Islamic Lore," *Journal of Semitic Studies* 92 (1984), pp. 53–64.

Boud'hors, Anne, "Toujours honneur au grec? À propos d'un papyrus gréco-copte de la region thébaine," in Papaconstantinou, *The Multilingual Experience in Egypt*, pp. 179–188.

Bowman, John, "The Debt of Islam to Monophysite Christianity," in MacLaurin (ed.), *Essays in Honour of Griffithes Wheeler Thatcher*, pp. 191–216; also published in *Nederlands Theologisch Tijdschrift* 19 (1964/1965), pp. 177–201.

———, "Holy Scriptures, Lectionaries and Qur'ān," in A. H. Johns (ed.), *International Congress for the Study of the Qur'ān.* Australian National University, Canberra, 8–13 May 1980; Canberra: Australian National University, 1981, pp. 29–37.

Brashler, James and Roger A. Bullard, "The Apocalypse of Peter," in James M. Robinson, *Nag Hammadi Library*, vii, 3, pp. 372–378.

Brinner, William M., "An Islamic Decalogue," in Brinner and Ricks, *Studies in Islamic and Judaic Traditions (1986)*, pp. 67–84.

———, "Noah," in McAuliffe, *Encyclopaedia of the Qur'ān (2001–2006)*, vol. 3, pp. 540–543.

Brinner, W. M., and S. D. Ricks (eds.), *Studies in Islamic and Judaic Traditions: Papers Presented at the Institute for Islamic-Judaic Studies, Center for Judaic Studies, University of Denver.* Atlanta: Scholars Press, 1986.

Brock, Sebastian, "The 'Nestorian' Church: A Lamentable Misnomer," *Bulletin of the John Rylands University Library of Manchester* 78 (1996), pp. 2–35.

———, "A Neglected Witness to the East Syriac New Testament Commentary Tradition: Sinai Arabic MS 151," in Rifaat Ebied and Herman Teule (eds.), *Studies on the Christian Arabic Heritage.* Eastern Christian Studies, 5; Leuven: Peeters, 2004, pp. 205–215.

Brodersen, Angelika, "Remembrance," in McAuliffe, *Encyclopaedia of the Qur'ān* (2001–2006), vol. 4, pp. 419–424.

Brody, Robert, *The Geonim of Babylonia and the Shaping of Medieval Jewish Culture.* New Haven, CT: Yale University Press, 1998.

Brooks, E. W. (ed. and trans.), *John of Ephesus. Lives of the Eastern Saints* 1. Patrologia Orientalis, 17; Paris: Firmin-Didot, 1923.

Brown, Michelle P., *In the Beginning: Bibles before the Year 1000.* Washington, DC: Smithsonian Institution, 2006.

Budge, E. A. Wallis, *The Book of the Cave of Treasures.* London: Religious Tract Society, 1927.

Buhl, F., and C. E. Bosworth, "Milla," in *EI2,* vol. 7, p. 61.

Burton, John, "Naskh wa 'l-Mansūkh," in *EI2,* vol. 7, pp. 1009–1012.

———, "Abrogation," in Jane Damen McAuliffe, *Encyclopaedia of the Qur'ān (2001–2006),* vol. 1, pp. 11–19.

Busse, Heribert, "Lot," in McAuliffe, *Encyclopaedia of the Qur'ān* (2001–2006), vol. 3, pp. 231–233.

Butbul, Sagit, "Translations in Contact: Early Judeo-Arabic and Syriac Biblical Translations," in Freidenreich and Goldstein, *Beyond Religious Borders,* pp. 57–64.

Canivet, Pierre, and Jean-Paul Rey-Coquais (eds.), *La Syrie de Byzance à l'islam VIIe–VIIIe siècles: Actes du colloque international, Lyon – Maison de l'Orient Méditerranien, Paris – Institut de Monde Arabe, 11–15 Septembre 1990.* Damascus: Institut Français de Damas, 1992.

Carter, Michael G., *Sībawayhi.* New Delhi and New York: Oxford University Press, 2004.

Chabot, J. B. *Anonymi Auctoris Chronicon ad Annum Christi 1234 Pertinens.* CSCO, vol. 81; Paris: J. Gabalda, 1920.

——— (ed. and trans.), *Chronique de Michel le Syrien, patriarche jacobite d'Antioche, 1166–1199.* 4 vols.; Paris: Leroux, 1899–1924.

Chahwan, A., "Le commentaire de Psaumes 33–60 d'Ibn at-Tayib reflet de l'exégèse syriaque orientale." Th.D. Dissertation; Rome: Pontifical Gregorian University, 1997.

Cheikho, Louis (ed.), *Vingt traités théologiques d'auteurs arabes chrétiens (IXe–XIII siècles).* Beirut: Imprimerie Catholique, 1920.

Chejne, Anwar G., *Ibn Ḥazm.* Chicago: Kazi Publications, 1982.

Chidiac, Robert, *Al-Ghazali: refutation excellente de la divinité de Jésus-Christ d'après les évangiles; texte établi, traduit et commenté.* Paris: Librairie Ernest Leroux, 1939.

Chiesa, Bruno, and Wilfrid Lockwood (eds. and trans.), *Ya'qūb al-Qirqisānī on Jewish Sects and Christianity.* Frankfurt: Peter Lang, 1984.

Christys, Ann, *Christians in al-Andalus (711–1000).* Richmond, Surrey: Curzon Press, 2002.

Ciasca, A., *Tatiani Evangeliorum Harmoniae Arabice nunc primum ex duplici codice edidit et translatione Latina donavit p. Augustinus Ciasca.* Rome: Typographia Polyglotta S.C. de Propaganda Fide, 1888, repr. 1914 and 1934.

Cirillo, Luigi, and M. Frémaux, *Évangile de Barnabé.* Paris: Beauchesne, 1977.

Cobb, Paul M., "Hūd," in McAuliffe, *Encyclopaedia of the Qur'ān,* vol. 2, pp. 462–464.

Cohen, Mark R., *Under Crescent and Cross: The Jews in the Middle Ages.* Princeton, NJ: Princeton University Press, 1994.

———, "What Was the Pact of 'Umar? A Literary-Historical Study," *Jerusalem Studies in Arabic and Islam* 32 (1999), pp. 100–157.

Cohen, Mordechai Z., *Three Approaches to Biblical Metaphor: From Abraham ibn Ezra and Maimonides to David Kimhi.* Études sur le Judaïsme Médiéval, vol. 26; Leiden: Brill, 2008.

———, "Bible Exegesis, 1. Rabbanite," in Stillman, *Encyclopedia of Jews in the Islamic World* (2010), vol. 1, pp. 442–457.

Connolly, R. H., *The Liturgical Homilies of Narsai.* Cambridge: Cambridge University Press, 1909.

Cook, Michael, "Anan and Islam: The Origins of Karaite Scripturalism," *Jerusalem Studies in Arabic and Islam* 9 (1987), pp. 161–172.

Cotton, Hannah M. et al. (eds.), *From Hellenism to Islam: Cultural and Linguistic Change in the Roman Near East.* Cambridge: Cambridge University Press, 2009.

Cresswell, K.A.C., *Early Muslim Architecture: Umayyads A.D. 622–750.* 2nd ed. in 2 parts, vol. 1, pt. 2; Oxford: Oxford University Press, 1969.

Croix, Agnès-Mariam de la, and François Zabbal, *Icônes arabes: Art chrétien du Levant.* Méolans-Revel: Éditions Grégoriennes, 2003.

Crone, Patricia, *God's Rule: Government and Islam.* New York: Columbia University Press, 2004.

———, "How Did the Quranic Pagans Make a Living?" *Bulletin of the School of Oriental and African Studies* 68 (2005), pp. 387–399.

———, "What Do We Actually Know about Mohammed?" *OpenDemocracy,* June 10, 2008: http://www/opendemocracy.net.

Cuypers, Michel, *Le Festin: une lecture de la sourate al-Māʾida.* Paris: Lethielleux, 2007. English trans.: *The Banquet: A Reading of the Fifth Sura of the Qurʾān,* Patricia Kelly (trans.); Series Rhetorica Semitica; Miami, FL: Convivium Press, 2009.

Darlow, T. H. et al., *Historical Catalogue of the Printed Editions of Holy Scripture in the Library of the British and Foreign Bible Society.* 2 vols. in 4; London: British and Foreign Bible Society, 1903–1911.

Darrow, William R., "Magians," in McAuliffe, *Encyclopaedia of the Qurʾān* (2001–2006), vol. 3, pp. 244–245.

Davis, Stephen J., *Coptic Christology in Practice: Incarnation and Divine Participation in Late Antique and Medieval Egypt.* Oxford Early Christian Studies; Oxford: Oxford University Press, 2008.

———, "Introducing an Arabic Commentary on the Apocalypse: Ibn Kātib Qayṣar on Revelation," *Harvard Theological Review* 101 (2008), pp. 77–96.

Déclais, Jean-Louis, *David raconté par les musulmans.* Paris: Éditions du Cerf, 1999.

Delgado, Mariano and Sievernich, Michael (eds.), *Un récit musulman sur Isaïe.* Paris: Les Éditions du Cerf, 2001.

———, *Mission und Prophetie in Zeiten der Transkulturalität: Festschrift zum hundertjährigen Bestehen des Internationalen Instituts für missionswissenschaftliche Forschungen 1911–2011.* Sonderband der Zeitschrift für Missionswissenschaft und Religionswissenschaft, 95; St. Ottilien: Eos Verlag, 2011.

Demiri, Lejla, "Ḥanbalite Commentary on the Bible: Analysis of Najm al-Dīn al-Ṭūfī's (d.716/1316) *al-Taʿlīq,*" in Thomas, *The Bible in Arab Christianity,* pp. 295–313.

Derenbourg, Joseph (ed.), *Oeuvres complètes de R. Saadia Ben Josef al-Fayyoûmî.* 5 vols.; Paris: Ernest Leroux, 1893–1899.

Déroche, François, *La transmission écrite du coran dans les débuts de l'islam.* Leiden: Brill, 2009.

De Smet, D. et al. (eds.), *Al-Kitāb: La sacralité du texte dans le monde de l'Islam; Actes du Symposium International tenu à Leuven et Louvain-la-Neuve du 29 mai au 1 juin 2002.* Acta Orientalia Belgica, Subsidia 3; Brussels, Louvain-la-Neuve, Leuven: Société Belge d'Études Orientales, 2004, pp. 185–231.

Di Segni, Leah, "Greek Inscriptions in Transition from the Byzantine to the Early Islamic Period," in Cotton, *From Hellenism to Islam,* pp. 352–373.

Dodge, Bayard (trans.), *The Fihrist of al-Nadīm.* 2 vols.; New York: Columbia University Press, 1970.

Donaldson, Dwight M., "Al-Ya'qûbî's Chapter about Jesus Christ," in *The Macdonald Presentation Volume.* Princeton, NJ: Princeton University Press, 1933, pp. 88–105.

Donner, Fred M., *Narratives of Islamic Origins: The Beginnings of Islamic Historical Writing.* Princeton, NJ: The Darwin Press, 1998.

———, "From Believers to Muslims: Confessional Self-Identity in the Early Islamic Community," *Al-Abḥāth* 50–51 (2002–2003), pp. 9–53.

———, "Quranic *Furqān,*" *Journal of Semitic Studies* 25 (2007), pp. 279–300.

———, *Muḥammad and the Believers: At the Origins of Islam.* Cambridge, MA: Harvard University Press, 2010.

Draguet, René, *Julien d'Halicarnasse et sa controverse avec Sévere d'Antioche sur l'incorruptibilité du corps du Christ: Étude d'histoire littéraire et doctrinale suivie des fragments dogmatiques de Julien; texte syriaque et traduction grecque.* Louvain: P. Smeesters, 1924.

Drint, Adrianna, *The Mount Sinai Arabic Version of IV Ezra.* CSCO, vols. 563 and 564; Lovanii: Peeters, 1997.

Drory, Rina, *Models and Contacts: Arabic Literature and Its Impact on Medieval Jewish Culture.* Leiden: E.J. Brill, 2000.

Dunlop, D. M., "A Letter of Harūn ar-Rashīd to the Emperor Constantine VI," in Matthew Black and Georg Fohrer (eds.), *In Memoriam Paul Kahle.* Beiheft zur ZAW, vol. 103; Berlin: A. Töpelmann, 1968, pp. 106–115.

———, *Arab Civilization to AD 1500.* Arab Background Series; London: Longman; Beirut: Librairie du Liban, 1971.

Duri, A. A., *The Rise of Historical Writing among the Arabs,* L. I. Conrad (ed. and trans). Princeton, NJ: Princeton University Press, 1983.

Dye, Guillaume, and Fabien Nobilio (eds.), *Figures bibliques en Islam.* Fernelmont, Belgium: Éditions Modulaires Européennes, 2011.

Dye, Guillaume, and M. Kropp, "Le nom de Jésus ('Īsā) dans le Coran, et quelques autres noms bibliques: Remarques sur l'onomastique coranique," in Dye and Nobilio, *Figures bibliques,* pp. 171–198.

Ebied, R. Y., and L. R. Wickham, "Al-Ya'kûbî's Account of the Israelite Prophets and Kings," *Journal of Near Eastern Studies* 92 (1970), pp. 80–98.

EI = *Encyclopaedia of Islam,* H.A.R. Gibb et al. (eds.) *The Encyclopaedia of Islam,* new ed., 13 vols. Leiden: Brill, 1960–2004.

Elad, Amikam, *Medieval Jerusalem and Islamic Worship: Holy Places, Ceremonies, Pilgrimage.* Leiden: E.J. Brill, 1995.

Epalza, M. De, "Le milieu hispano-moresque de l'Évangile islamisant de Barnabe," *Islamochristiana* 8 (1982), pp. 159–183.

Ephrem, Saint, *Hymns on Paradise,* Sebastian Brock (trans.). Crestwood, NY: St Vladimir's Seminary Press, 1990.

Fahd, T., "Rapports de la Mekke préislamique avec l'Abyssinie: le cas des *Aḥâbîš,*" in T. Fahd (ed.), *L'Arabie préislamique et son environnement historique et culturel.* Actes du Colloque de Strasbourg, 24–27 juin 1987; Leiden: E.J. Brill, 1987, pp. 537–548.

Fargues, Philip, "The Arab Christians of the Middle East: A Demographic Perspective," in Pacini, *Christian Communities in the Arab Middle East,* pp. 48–66.

Faultless, Julian, "Ibn al-Ṭayyib," in David Thomas and Alex Mallett (eds.), *Christian-Muslim Relations: A Bibliographical History*. Vol. 2 [900–1050]. Leiden: Brill, 2010, pp. 667–697.

Féghali, Paul, "Ibn at-Tayib et son commentaire sur la Genèse," *Parole de l'Orient* 61 (1990–1991), pp. 149–162.

———, "Les Épîtres de Saint Paul dans une des premières Traductions en Arabe," *Parole de l'Orient* 30 (2005), pp. 103–130.

Ferré, André, "L'historien al-Ya'qûbî et les evangiles," *Islamochristiana* 3 (1977), pp. 61–83.

———, "La vie de Jésus d'après les *Annales* de Ṭabarī," *Islamochristiana* 5 (1979), pp. 7–29.

———, *L'histoire des Prophètes d'après al-Ya'qûbî; d'Adam à Jésus*. Rome: Pontificio Istituto di Studi Arabi e d'Islamistica, 2000.

Fiey, J. M., "Tagrît: Esquisse d'histoire chrétienne," *L'Orient Syrien* 8 (1963), pp. 289–342.

Finkel, Joshua (ed. and trans.), *Three Essays of Abu 'Othman 'Amr ibn Baḥr al-Jaḥiẓ*. Cairo: The Salafyah Press, 1926.

Finkelstein, Louis (ed.), *Rab Saadia Gaon: Studies in His Honor*. New York: Jewish Theological Seminary of America, 1944.

Firestone, Reuven, *Journeys in Holy Lands: The Evolution of the Abraham-Ishmael Legends in Islamic Exegesis*. Albany, NY: State University of New York Press, 1990.

———, "Abraham," in McAuliffe, *Encyclopaedia of the Qur'ān* (2001–2006), vol. 1, pp. 5–11.

Fischer, Wolfdietrich, "Classical Arabic," in Versteegh, *Encyclopedia of Arabic Language and Linguistics*, vol. 1, pp. 397–405.

Fowden, Elizabeth Key, *The Barbarian Plain: Saint Sergius between Rome and Iran*. Berkeley, CA: University of California Press, 1999.

Fowden, Garth, *Empire to Commonwealth: Consequences of Monotheism in Late Antiquity*. Princeton, NJ: Princeton University Press, 1993.

Frank, Daniel, "Bible Exegesis, 2. Karaite," in Stillman, *Encyclopedia of Jews in the Islamic World*, vol. 1, pp. 457–461.

Frank, Richard M., "The Jeremias of Pethion ibn Ayyūb al-Sahhār," *The Catholic Biblical Quarterly* 12 (1959), pp. 136–170.

——— (ed. and trans.), *The Wisdom of Jesus Ben Sirach (Sinai ar. 155, IXth/Xth cent.)*. CSCO, vols. 357 and 358; Louvain: Secrétariat du Corpus SCO, 1974.

Freidenreich, David M., and Miriam Goldstein (eds.), *Beyond Religious Borders: Interaction and Intellectual Exchange in the Medieval Islamic World*. Philadelphia, PA: University of Pennsylvania Press, 2012.

Friemuth, Maha el-Kaisy, "*Al-radd al-jamīl*: al-Ghazālī's or Pseudo-Ghazālī's?" in Thomas, *The Bible in Arab Christianity*, pp. 275–294.

Gallez, Edouard M., *Le messie et son prophète: Aux origines de l'islam*, vol. 1: De Qumrân à Muhammad. 2nd ed.; Paris: Éditions de Paris, 2005.

N. Garsoïan et. al. (eds.), *East of Byzantium: Syria and Armenia in the Formative Period*. Washington, DC: Dumbarton Oaks, 1982.

Gaudeul, Jean-Marie, "Textes de la tradition musulmane concernant le *taḥrīf* (falsification) des écritures," *Islamochristiana* 6 (1980), pp. 61–104.

Gaudeul, Jean-Marie and Robert Caspar, "Textes de la tradition musulmane concernant le *taḥrīf* (falsification) des Écritures," *Islamochristiana* 6 (1980), pp. 61–104.

Geiger, Abraham, *Was hat Mohammed aus dem Judenthume aufgenommen?* 1st ed.; Bonn: Baaden, 1833.

Gibson, M. D., *Kitāb al-Mājāll, or The Book of the Rolls, Apocrypha Arabica.* Studia Sinaitica, 8; London: J. Clay and Sons, 1901.

Gignoux, Philippe (ed. and trans.), *Homélies de Narsai sur la création: édition critique du texte syriaque, introduction et traduction française.* Patrologia Orientalis, vol. 34, facls. 3–4; Turnhout: Brepols, 1968.

Gil, Moshe, "The Origin of the Jews of Yathrib," *Jerusalem Studies in Arabic and Islam* 4 (1984), pp. 203–224.

———, "The Creed of Abū ʿĀmir," *Israel Oriental Studies* 12 (1992), pp. 9–47.

Gilliot, Claude, "Muḥammad, le Coran et les 'contraintes de l'histoire'," in Wild, *Qurʾān as Text* (1996), pp. 3–26.

———, "Les 'Informateurs' juifs et chrétiens de Muḥammad: Reprise d'un problème traité par Aloys Sprenger et Theodor Nöldeke," *Jerusalem Studies in Arabic and Islam* 22 (1998), pp. 84–126.

———, "Le Coran, fruit d'un travail collectif?" in De Smet, *Al-Kitāb: La sacralité du texte* (2004), pp. 185–231.

———, "Zur Herkunft der Gewährsmäner des Propheten," in Ohlig and Puin, *Die dunklen Anfänge* (2005), pp. 148–178.

Ginzberg, Louis, *The Legends of the Jews.* 7 vols.; Philadelphia: The Jewish Publication Society of America, 1946–1969.

Gnilka, Joachim, *Die Nazarener und der Koran: Eine Spurensuche.* Freiburg: Herder, 2007.

Goitein, S. D., *Jews and Arabs: A Concise History of their Social and Cultural Relations.* 3rd rev. ed.; New York: Schocken Books, 1974.

———, *A Mediterranean Society: The Jewish Communities of the Arab World as Portrayed in the Documents of the Cairo Geniza.* 6 vols.; Berkeley, CA: University of California Press, 1967–1993.

Goldman, S., "Joseph," in McAuliffe, *Encyclopaedia of the Qurʾān,* vol. 3, pp. 55–57.

Goldstein, Miriam, "Arabic Composition 101 and the Early Development of Judeo-Arabic Bible Exegesis," *Journal of Semitic Studies* 55 (2010), pp. 451–478.

———, "Saadya's *Tafsīr* in Light of Muslim Polemic against Ninth-Century Arabic Bible Translations," *Jerusalem Studies in Arabic and Islam,* forthcoming.

Goodman, Lenn E., *The Book of Theodicy: Translation and Commentary on the Book of Job by Saadiah ben Joseph al-Fayyūmī.* Yale Judaica Series, vol. 25; New Haven, CT: Yale University Press, 1988.

———, "Saadiah Gaon's Interpretive Technique in Translating the Book of Job," in *Translation of Scripture: Proceedings of a Conference at the Annenberg Research Institute, May 15–16, 1989.* A Jewish Quarterly Review Supplement; Philadelphia: Annenberg Research Institute, 1990, pp. 47–75.

Götze, A., "Die Nachwirkung der Schatzhöle," *Zeitschrift für Semitistik* 3 (1924), pp. 60–71.

Grabar, Oleg, *The Shape of the Holy: Early Islamic Jerusalem.* Princeton, NJ: Princeton University Press, 1996.

Graf, Georg, *Geschichte der christlichen arabischen Literatur.* 5 vols.; Città del Vaticano: Biblioteca apostolica vaticana, 1944.

Graham, William A., *Divine Word and Prophetic Word in Early Islam: A Reconsideration of the Sources; with Special Reference to the Divine Saying or Ḥadīth Qudsī.* The Hague: Mouton, 1977.

———, *Beyond the Written Word: Oral Aspects of Scripture in the History of Religion.* Cambridge: Cambridge University Press, 1987.

Grand'Henry, Jacques, "Christian Middle Arabic," in Versteegh, *Encyclopedia of Arabic Language and Linguistics,* vol. 1 pp. 383–387.

Griffith, Sidney H., "Chapter Ten of the Scholion: Theodore bar Kônî's Apology for Christianity," *Orientalia Christiana Periodica* 74 (1981), pp. 158–188.

———, "Theodore bar Kônî's *Scholion*: A Nestorian *Summa contra Gentiles* from the First Abbasid Century," in N. Garsoïan et al. (eds.), *East of Byzantium: Syria and Armenia in the Formative Period.* Washington, DC: Dumbarton Oaks, 1982, pp. 53–72.

———, "The Arabic Account of 'Abd al-Masīḥ an-Nağrānī al-Ghassānī," *Le Muséon* 89 (1985), pp. 331–374.

———, "The Gospel in Arabic: An Inquiry into Its Appearance in the First Abbasid Century," *Oriens Christianus* 69 (1985), pp. 126–167.

———, "Stephen of Ramlah and the Christian Kerygma in Arabic in Ninth-Century Palestine," *Journal of Ecclesiastical History* 63 (1985), pp. 23–45.

———, "A Ninth Century Summa Theologiae Arabica," in Samir, *Actes du deuxième congrès international d'études arabes chrétiennes* (1986), pp. 123–141.

———, "The Monks of Palestine and the Growth of Christian Literature in Arabic," *The Muslim World* 87 (1988), pp. 1–28.

———, "Anthony David of Baghdad, Scribe and Monk of Mar Sabas: Arabic in the Monasteries of Palestine," *Church History* 85 (1989), pp. 7–19.

———, "Images, Islam and Christian Icons: A Moment in the Christian/Muslim Encounter in Early Islamic Times," in Canivet and Rey-Coquais, *La Syrie de Byzance à l'islam VIIe-VIIIe siècles* (1992), pp. 121–138.

———, "Byzantium and the Christians in the World of Islam: Constantinople and the Church in the Holy Land in the Ninth Century," *Medieval Encounters* 3 (1997), pp. 231–265.

———, *"Faith Adoring the Mystery": Reading the Bible with St. Ephraem the Syrian.* The Père Marquette Lecture in Theology, 1997; Milwaukee, WI: Marquette University Press, 1997.

———, "From Aramaic to Arabic: The Languages of the Monasteries of Palestine in the Byzantine and Early Islamic Periods," *Dumbarton Oaks Papers* 51 (1997), pp. 11–31.

———, "What Has Constantinople to Do with Jerusalem? Palestine in the Ninth Century; Byzantine Orthodoxy in the World of Islam," in Leslie Brubaker (ed.), *Byzantium in the Ninth Century: Dead or Alive? Papers from the Thirtieth Spring Symposium of Byzantine Studies, Birmingham, March 1996.* Aldershot, UK and Brookfield, VT: Variorum, 1998, pp. 181–194.

———, "Christians and Christianity," in McAuliffe, *Encyclopaedia of the Qur'ān* (2001–2006), vol. 1, pp. 307–316.

———, "Holy Spirit," in McAuliffe, *Encyclopaedia of the Qur'ān* (2001–2006), vol. 2, pp. 442–444.

———, "The *Life of Theodore of Edessa*: History, Hagiography, and Religious Apologetics in Mar Saba Monastery in Early Abbasid Times," in Patrich, *The Sabaite Heritage (2001),* pp. 147–169.

———, "Melkites, Jacobites and the Christological Controversies in Arabic in

Third/Ninth-Century Syria," in David Thomas (ed.), *Syrian Christians under Islam: The First Thousand Years*. Leiden: Brill, 2001, pp. 9–35.

———, "The Gospel, the Qur'ān, and the Presentation of Jesus in al-Ya'qūbī's *Ta'rīkh*," in John C. Reeves (ed.), *Bible and Qur'ān: Essays in Scriptural Intertextuality*. Symposium Series, 24; Atlanta: Society of Biblical Literature, 2003, pp. 133–160.

———, "Theology and the Arab Christian: The Case of the 'Melkite' Creed," in David Thomas (ed.), *A Faithful Presence: Essays for Kenneth Cragg*. London: Melisende, 2003, pp. 184–200.

———, "Arguing from Scripture: The Bible in the Christian/Muslim Encounter in the Middle Ages," in T. J. Heffernan and T. E. Burman (eds.), *Scripture and Pluralism: Reading the Bible in the Religiously Plural Worlds of the Middle Ages and Renaissance*. Studies in the History of Christian Traditions, vol. 123; Leiden: Brill, 2005, pp. 29–58.

———, "The Church of Jerusalem and the 'Melkites': The Making of an 'Arab Orthodox' Christian Identity in the World of Islam, 750–1050," in Ora Limor and G. G. Stroumsa (eds.), *Christians and Christianity in the Holy Land: From the Origins to the Latin Kingdom*. Turnhout: Brepols, 2006, pp. 173–202.

———, "Syriacisms in the Arabic Qur'ān: Who were 'those who said Allāh is third of three' according to *al-Mā'idah* 73?" in Bar-Asher, *A Word Fitly Spoken* (2007), pp. 83–110.

———, "Christian Lore and the Arabic Qur'ān: the 'Companions of the Cave' in *Sūrat al-Kahf* and in Syriac Christian Tradition," in Reynolds, *The Qur'ān in Its Historical Context* (2008), pp. 109–137.

———, *The Church in the Shadow of the Mosque: Christians and Muslims in the World of Islam*. Princeton, NJ: Princeton University Press, 2008.

———, "Patriarch Timothy I and an Aristotelian at the Caliph's Court," in Erica C. D. Hunter (ed.), *The Christian Heritage of Iraq: Collected Papers from the Christianity of Iraq I—V Seminar Days*. Gorgias Eastern Christian Studies, 13; Piscataway, NJ: Gorgias Press, 2009, pp. 38–53.

———, "*Al-Naṣārā* in the Qur'ān: A Hermeneutical Reflection," in Reynolds, *Reflections on Epigraphy, Language, and Literature* (2011).

———, "Images, Icons and the Public Space in Early Islamic Times: Arab Christians and the Program to Claim the Land for Islam," in Holum and Lapin, *Shaping the Middle East* (2011), pp. 197–210.

Grillmeier, Aloys, and Theresia Hainthaler, *Christ in Christian Tradition*, John Cawte and Pauline Allen (trans.) Vol. 2, part 2; London and Louisville, KY: Mowbray and Westminster John Knox Press, 1995.

Grillmeier, Aloys, with Theresia Hainthaler, *Christ in Christian Tradition* (O. C. Dean, trans.) Vol. 2, part 4; London and Louisville, KY: Mowbray and Westminster John Knox Press, 1996.

Groß, Markus and Ohlig, Karl-Heinz (eds.), *Schlaglichter: Die beiden ersten islamischen Jahrhunderte*. Inârah, vol. 3; Berlin: Hans Schiler, 2008.

Gruendler, Beatrice, "Arabic Script," in McAuliffe, *Encyclopaedia of the Qur'ān*, vol. 1, pp. 135–144.

Grypeou, Emmanouela, "The Re-Written Bible in Arabic: The Paradise Story and Its Exegesis in the Arabic *Apocalypse of Peter*," in Thomas, *The Bible in Arab Christianity*, pp. 113–129.

Guidi, I., *Le Traduzioni degli Evangelii in Arabo e in Etiopico.* Reale Accademia dei Lincei, Anno 285; Rome: Tipografia della R. Accademia dei Lincei, 1888.

Günther, Sebastian, "Muḥammad, the Illiterate Prophet: An Islamic Creed in the Qur'ān and Qur'anic Exegesis," *Journal of Qur'anic Studies* 4 (2002), pp. 1–26.

———, "Illiteracy," in McAuliffe, *Encyclopaedia of the Qur'ān* (2001–2006), vol. 2, pp. 492–500.

———, "Ummī," in McAuliffe, *Encyclopaedia of the Qur'ān* (2001–2006), vol. 5, pp. 399–403.

———, "*O People of the Scripture! Come to a Word Common to You and Us* (Q. 3:64): The Ten Commandments and the Qur'ān," *Journal of Qur'ānic Studies* 9 (2007), pp. 28–58.

Gutas, Dimitri, *Greek Thought, Arabic Culture: The Graeco-Arabic Translation Movement in Baghdad and Early 'Abbasid Society (2nd–4th/8th–10th Centuries).* London: Routledge, 1998.

Haddad, Rachid, "La phonétique de l'arabe chrétien vers 700," in Canivet and Rey-Coquais, *La Syrie de Byzance à l'islam VIIe-VIIIe siècles,* pp. 159–164.

Hadrill, D. S. Wallace, *Christian Antioch: A Study of Early Christian Thought in the East.* Cambridge: Cambridge University Press, 1982.

Hage, Wolfgang, *Das orientalische Christentum.* Die Religionen der Menschheit, vol. 29,2; Stuttgart: Verlag W. Kohlhammer, 2007.

Hainthaler, Theresia, *Christliche Araber vor dem Islam.* Eastern Christian Studies, vol. 7; Leuven: Peeters, 2007.

Haleem, M.A.S. Abdel, "Context and Internal Relationships: Keys to Quranic Exegesis; a Study of *Sūrat al-Raḥmān* (Qur'ān chapter 55)," in G. R. Hawting and Abdul-Kader A. Shareef (eds.), *Approaches to the Qur'ān.* London and New York: Routledge, 1993, pp. 71–98.

Halkin, Abraham Solomon, "Saadia's Exegesis and Polemics," in Louis Finkelstein (ed.), *Rab Saadia Gaon: Studies in His Honor.* New York: Jewish Theological Seminary of America, 1944, pp. 117–141.

Halkin, Abraham Solomon, and Hava Lazarus-Yafeh, "Judeo-Arabic Literature," in M. Berenbaum and F. Skolnik (eds.), *Encyclopaedia Judaica.* 2nd ed.; 22 vols.; Detroit, MI: Macmillan, 2007, vol. 11, pp. 530–545.

Hamadhānī, Ibn al-Fakih al-, *Compendium libri* Kitāb al-boldān (M. J. de Goeje, ed.). Bibliotheca Geographorum Arabicorum, 8 vols.; Leiden: E.J. Brill, 1967), vol. 5.

Harvey, Susan and Hunter, David G. (eds.), *The Oxford Handbook of Early Christian Studies.* Oxford: Oxford University Press, 2008.

Hary, Benjamin, "Judeo-Arabic Shurūḥ (Since the Fourteenth Century)," in Stillman, *Encyclopedia of Jews in the Islamic World* (2010), vol. 1, pp. 469–475.

Hauglid, Brian M., "Al-Tha'labī's *Qiṣṣaṣ al-Anbiyā'*: Analysis of the Text, Jewish and Christian Elements, Islamization, and Prefiguration of the Prophethood of Muḥammad." Ph.D. Dissertation; Salt Lake City, UT: The University of Utah, 1998.

Hauglid, Brian M., "On the Early Life of Abraham: Biblical and Qur'ānic Intertextuality and the Anticipation of Muḥammad," in Reeves, *Bible and Qur'ān,* pp. 87–105.

Hechaïmé, Camille, *Louis Cheikho et son livre: Le Christianisme et la littérature chrétienne en Arabie avant l'islam; étude critique.* Beirut: Dar el-Machreq, 1967.

———, *Bibliographie analytique du père Louis Cheikho.* Beirut: Dar el-Machreq, 1978.

Heffernan, T. J., and T. E. Burman (eds.), *Scripture and Pluralism: Reading the Bible in the Religiously Plural Worlds of the Middle Ages and Renaissance,* Studies in the History of Christian Traditions, vol. 123. Leiden: Brill, 2005.

Heinrichs, Wolfhart, "The Meaning of *Mutanabbī*," in Kugel, *Poetry and Prophecy,* pp. 120–139.

Heyd, Uriel (ed.), *Studies in Islamic History and Civilization;* Scripta Hierosolymitana 9. Jerusalem: The Magnes Press, The Hebrew University, 1961.

Hezser, Catherine, *The Social Structure of the Rabbinic Movement in Roman Palestine.* Tübingen: Mohr Siebeck, 1997.

Hirschfeld, Yizhar, *The Judean Desert Monasteries in the Byzantine Period.* New Haven, CT: Yale University Press, 1992.

———, *The Founding of the New Laura.* New York: Oxford University Press, 1995.

Hoffman, Adina, and Peter Cole, *Sacred Trash: The Lost and Found World of the Cairo Geniza.* Jewish Encounters; New York: Nextbook/Schocken, 2011.

Holum, Kenneth G., and Hayim Lapin (eds.), *Shaping the Middle East: Jews, Christians, and Muslims in an Age of Transition, 400–800 C.E.* Studies and Texts in Jewish History and Culture, 20; Bethesda, MD: University Press of Maryland, 2011.

Hopkins, Simon, *Studies in the Grammar of Early Arabic: Based upon Papyri Datable to before 300 AH/912 AD.* Oxford: Oxford University Press, 1984.

Horn, Cornelia, "Lines of Transmission between Apocryphal Traditions in the Syriac-speaking World: Manichaeism and the Rise of Islam; the Case of the *Acts of John,*" *Parole de l'Orient* 35 (2010), pp. 337–355.

Horner, George W., *The Coptic Version of the New Testament in the Northern Dialect, Otherwise Called Memphitic and Bohairic; with Introduction, Critical Apparatus, and Literal English Translation.* 4 vols.; Oxford: Clarendon Press, 1898–1905, vol. 1, pp. xxxvii–cxxvi.

Horovitz, Josef, *Koranische Untersuchungen.* Berlin: De Gruyter, 1926.

Horovitz, J., and R. Firestone, "Zabūr," in *EI2,* vol. 11, pp. 372–373.

Houtsma, M. Th. (ed.), *Ibn-Wādhih qui dicitur al-Ja'qubî, Historiae.* 2 vols.; Leiden: E.J. Brill, 1883.

Hoyland, Robert, "Language and Identity: The Twin Histories of Arabic and Aramaic (and: Why Did Aramaic Succeed Where Greek Failed?)," *Scripta Classica Israelica* 32 (2004), pp. 183–199.

———, "Epigraphy and the Linguistic Background to the Qur'ān," in Reynolds, *The Qur'ān in Its Historical Context* (2008), pp. 51–69.

———, "Arab Kings, Arab Tribes and the Beginnings of Arab Historical Memory in Late Roman Epigraphy," in Cotton, *From Hellenism to Islam* (2009), pp. 374–400.

———, "Late Roman Provincia Arabia, Monophysite Monks and Arab Tribes: A Problem of Centre and Periphery," *Semitica et Classica* 2 (2009), pp. 117–139.

———, "Mount Nebo, Jabal Ramm, and the Status of Christian Palestinian Aramaic and Old Arabic in Late Roman Palestine and Arabia," in Macdonald, *The Development of Arabic* (2010), pp. 29–46.

Hunt, Lucy-Anne, "Introducing the Catalogue, in Progress, of the Illustrated Manuscripts in the Coptic Museum," *Parole de l'Orient* 91 (1994), pp. 401–413.

———, *Byzantium, Eastern Christendom and Islam: Art at the Crossroads of the Medieval Mediterranean.* London: Pindar Press, 1998.

———, "Cultural Transmission: Illustrated Biblical Manuscripts from the Medieval Eastern Christian and Arab Worlds," in J. L. Sharpe and K. Van Kampen (eds.),

The Bible as Book: The Manuscript Tradition. London: British Library, 1998, pp. 123–136.

———, "Illustrating the Gospels in Arabic: Byzantine and Arab Christian Miniatures in Two Manuscripts of the Early Mamlūk Period in Cambridge," in Thomas, *The Bible in Arab Christianity* (2007), pp. 315–349.

Hunter, Erica C. D. (ed.), *The Christian Heritage of Iraq: Collected Papers from the Christianity of Iraq I–V Seminar Days*, Gorgias Eastern Christian Studies 13. Piscataway, NJ: Gorgias Press, 2009.

Ibn Ḥazm, ʿAlī ibn Aḥmad, *Al-faṣl fī l-milal wa l-ahwāʾ wa l-miḥal, wa maʿahu l-milal wa l-niḥal lil-Sharastānī*. 5 vols.; Cairo: Muḥammad ʿAlī Subayh, 1964.

Ibn Hishām, Abū Muḥammad ʿAbd al-Malik, *Sīrat an-nabī*, (Muḥammad Muḥyī ad-Dīn ʿabd al-Ḥamīd, ed.). 4 vols.; Cairo: Maṭbaʿah Ḥijāzī bil-Qāhirah, 1356.

Ibn Kabar, Shams ar-Riʾāsah Abū l-Barakāt, *Misbāḥ aẓ-Ẓulmah fī Īḍāḥ al-Khidmah*. 2 vols.; Cairo: Maktabat al-Karūz, 1971.

Immerzeel, M., and J. van der Vliet (eds.), *Coptic Studies on the Threshold of a New Millennium: Proceedings of the Seventh International Congress of Coptic Studies*. Leuven: Uitgeverij Peeters en Departement Osterse Studies, 2004.

Jāḥiẓ, Abūʾ Uthmān, al-, "*Min kitābihi fī r-radd ʿalā n-naṣārā*," in ʿAbd as-Salām Muḥammad Hārūn (ed.), *Rasāʾil al-Jāḥiẓ*. 4 parts in 2 vols.; Cairo: Maktabah al-Khābakhī, 1399/1979.

Jeffery, Arthur, *The Foreign Vocabulary of the Qurʾān*. Baroda: Oriental Institute, 1938.

Johns, Jeremy, "The Greek Church and the Conversion of Muslims in Norman Sicily?" *Byzantinische Forschungen* 21 (1995), pp. 133157.

Jones, Alan, "Orality and Writing in Arabia," in McAuliffe, *Encyclopaedia of the Qurʾān*, vol. 3, pp. 587–593.

Joosse, Nanne Pieter George, "The Sermon on the Mount in the Arabic Diatessaron." Ph.D. Dissertation, Free University of Amsterdam; Amsterdam: Centrale Houisdrukkerij, 1997.

Joosten, Jan, "The *Gospel of Barnabas* and the Diatessaron," *Harvard Theological Review* 59 (2002), pp. 73–96.

Kachouh, Hikmat, "The Arabic Versions of the Gospels: A Case Study of John 1:1 and 1:18," in Thomas, *The Bible in Arab Christianity* (2007), pp. 9–36.

Kachouh, Hikmat, "The Arabic Gospel Text of Codex Beirut, Bibliothèque Orientale, 430: Is It Recent or Archaic?" *Parole de l'Orient* 32 (2007), pp. 105—121.

———, *The Arabic Versions of the Gospels and Their Families*. 2 vols.; Ph.D. Thesis; Birmingham, UK: University of Birmingham, 2008.

———, "Sinai Ar. N.F. Parchment 8 and 28: Its Contribution to Textual Criticism of the Gospel of Luke," *Novum Testamentum* 50 (2008), pp. 28–57.

———, *The Arabic Versions of the Gospels: The Manuscripts and Their Families*. Berlin and New York: De Gruyter, 2012.

Kafaḥ, Yosef, *Sefer ha-Nivhar ba-Emunot ufa-deʿot le-Rabenu Seʿadyah ben Yosef Fiumi: Makor ve-targum tirgem le-ʿIvrit*. Jerusalem: Sura; New York: Yeshivah University, 1969/1970.

Karoui, Said, "Die Rezeption der Bibel in der frühislamischen Literatur am Beispiel der Hauptwerke von Ibn Qutayba (gest. 276/889)." Ph.D. Dissertation; Heidelberg: Ruprecht-Karls Universität Heidelberg, 1996.

Kashouh, Hikmat, *see* Kachouh, Hikmat.

Khalidi, Tarif, *Arabic Historical Thought in the Classical Period.* Cambridge Studies in Islamic Civilization; Cambridge: Cambridge University Press, 1994.

———, *The Muslim Jesus: Sayings and Stories in Islamic Literature.* Cambridge, MA: Harvard University Press, 2001.

Khan, Geoffrey, "Al-Qirqisānī's Opinions Concerning the Text of the Bible and Parallel Muslim Attitudes towards the Text of the Qur'ān," *The Jewish Quarterly Review* 18 (1990), pp. 59–73.

———, "Judaeo-Arabic," in Versteegh, *Encyclopedia of Arabic Language and Linguistics* (2005–2009), vol. 2, pp. 526–536.

Khoury, Paul, *Paul d'Antioche, évêque melkite de Sidon (XIIe s.).* Beirut: Imprimerie Catholique, 1964.

Khoury, R. G., "Quelques réflexions sur les citations de la Bible dans les prémieres générations islamiques du premier et du deuxième siècles de l'Hégire," in *Mélanges H. Laoust* in *Bulletin d'Études Orientales* 92 (1977), pp. 269–278.

———, "Quelques réflexions sur la première ou les premières Bibles arabes," in T. Fahd (ed.), *L'Arabie préislamique et son environnement historique et culturel: Actes du colloque de Strasbourg, 24–27 juin 1987.* Travaux du Centre de Recheerche sur le Proche-Orient et la Grèce Antiques, 10; Leiden: E.J. Brill, 1989, pp. 549–561.

Kiraz, George A. (ed.), *Malphono w-Rabo d-Malphone: Studies in Honor of Sebastian P. Brock.* Piscataway, NJ: Gorgias Press, 2008.

Kister, Meir J., "The Campaign of Ḥulubān: A New Light on the Expedition of Abraha," *Le Muséon* 78 (1965), pp. 425–436.

———, "'Ḥaddithū 'an banī Isrā'īla wa-lā ḥaraja'," *Israel Oriental Studies* 2 (1972), pp. 215–239.

Klorman, Bat-Zion Eraqi, "Yemen," in Stillman, *Encyclopedia of Jews in the Islamic World,* vol. 4, pp. 627–639.

Knauf, Ernst Axel, "Arabo-Aramaic and 'Arabiyya: From Ancient Arabic to Early Standard Arabic, 200 CE–600 CE," in Neuwirth et al., *The Qur'ān in Context,* pp. 197–254.

Köbert, R., "Ibn at-Taiyib's Erklärung von Psalm 44," *Biblica* 34 (1962), pp. 338–348.

———, "Die älteste arabische Genesis-Übersetzung," in Franz Altheim and Ruth Stiehl (eds.), *Die Araber in der alten Welt.* 5 vols. in 6; Berlin: Walter De Gruyter, 1965, vol. 2, pp. 333–343.

Koenen, L., "Manichaean Apocalypticism at the Crossroads of Iranian, Egyptian, Jewish and Christian Thought," in Luigi Cirillo (ed.), *Codex Manichaicus Coloniensis: Atti del Simposio Internazionale (Rende-Amantea 3–7 settembre 1984).* Cosenza: Marra Editore, 1986, pp. 285–332.

Körner, Felix, "Das Prophetische am Islam," in Delgado and Sievernich, *Mission und Prophetie in Zeiten der Transkulturalität,* pp. 234–248.

Kollamparampil, Thomas, *Jacob of Serug: Selected Festal Homilies.* Bangalore: Dharmaram Publications and Rome: Center for Indian and Inter-Religious Studies, 1997.

———, *Salvation in Christ according to Jacob of Serug.* Bangalore: Dharmaram Publications, 2001.

Kraemer, Joel L., *Humanism in the Renaissance of Islam: The Cultural Revival during the Buyid Age.* Leiden: Brill, 1986.

Kronholm, Tryggve, "Dependence and Prophetic Originality in the Koran," *Orientalia Suecana* 31–32 (1982–1983), pp. 47–70.

Kropp, Manfred, "Äthiopische Arabischen im Koran: Afroasiatische Perlen auf Band gereiht, einzeln oder zu Paaren, diffuse verteilt oder an Glanzpunkten konzentriert," in Groß and Ohlig, *Schlaglichter*, pp. 384–410.

Kugel, James L., "David the Prophet," in Kugel, *Poetry and Prophecy (1990)*, pp. 45–55.

———, *In Potiphar's House: The Interpretive Life of Biblical Texts*. San Francisco: HarperSanFrancisco, 1990.

——— (ed.), *Poetry and Prophecy: The Beginnings of a Literary Tradition*. Ithaca, NY: Cornell University Press, 1990.

———, *Traditions of the Bible: A Guide to the Bible As It Was at the Start of the Common Era*. Cambridge, MA: Harvard University Press, 1998.

———, *The Bible As It Was*. Cambridge, MA: Harvard University Press, 1999.

———, *How To Read the Bible: A Guide to Scripture Then and Now*. New York: Simon and Schuster, 2008.

Künstlinger, D., "Christliche Herkunft der kurānischen Loṭ-Legende," *Rocznik Orientalistyczny* 7 (1929–1930), pp. 281–295.

Labourt, Jérôme, *Le Christianisme dans l'émpire perse sous la dynastie sassanide (224–632)*. Paris: V. Lecoffre, 1904.

Landauer, S., *Kitāb al-Amânât wa'l-I'tiqâdât von Sa'adja b. Jûsuf al-Fajjûmî*. Leiden: E.J. Brill, 1880.

Lasker, Daniel J., "Rabbinism and Karaism: The Contest for Supremacy," in R. Jospe and S. M. Wagner (eds.), *Great Schisms in Jewish History*. New York: Ktav Publishing House, 1981, pp. 47–72.

———, "*Qiṣṣat Mujādalat al-Usquf* and *Neṣṭor Ha-Komer*. The Earliest Arabic and Hebrew Jewish Anti-Christian Polemics," in Blau and Reif, *Genizah Research after Ninety Years (1992)*, pp. 112–118.

Lassner, Jacob, *Demonizing the Queen of Sheba: Boundaries of Gender and Culture in Postbiblical Judaism and Medieval Islam*. Chicago: University of Chicago Press, 1993.

Lawson, Todd, *The Crucifixion and the Qur'ān: A Study in the History of Muslim Thought*. Oxford: Oneworld, 2009.

Lazarus-Yafeh, Hava, *Studies in al-Ghazzālī*. Jerusalem: The Magnes Press, 1975.

———, *Intertwined Worlds: Medieval Islam and Bible Criticism*. Princeton, NJ: Princeton University Press, 1992.

Lecker, Michael, *Muslims, Jews and Pagans: Studies on Early Islamic Medina*. Leiden: E.J. Brill, 1995.

———, "Zayd B. Thābit, 'A Jew with Two Sidelocks': Judaism and Literacy in Pre-Islamic Medina (Yathrib)," *Journal of Near Eastern Studies* 56 (1997), pp. 259–273.

———, *Jews and Arabs in Pre- and Early Islamic Arabia*. Aldershot, UK: Ashgate, 1998.

———, *The 'Constitution of Medina': Muḥammad's First Legal Document*. Princeton, NJ: Darwin Press, 2004.

———, *People, Tribes, and Society in Arabia around the Time of Muḥammad*. Burlington, VT: Ashgate, 2005.

Lecomte, G., "Les citations de l'Ancien et du Nouveau Testament dans l'oeuvre d'Ibn Qutayba," *Arabica* 5 (1958), pp. 34–46.

Leemhuis, Fred, "The Mount Sinai Arabic Version of the Apocalypse of Baruch," in Samir, *Actes du deuxième congrès international d'études arabes chrétiennes* (1986), pp. 73–79.

———, "The Arabic Version of the Apocalypse of Baruch: A Christian Text?" *Journal for the Study of the Pseudepigraphica* 4 (1989), pp. 19–26.

Leemhuis, F. et al. (eds. and trans.), *The Arabic Text of the Apocalypse of Baruch: Edited and Translated with a Parallel Translation of the Syriac Text.* Leiden: E.J. Brill, 1986.

Lentin, Jérôme, "Middle Arabic," in Versteegh, *Encyclopedia of Arabic Language and Linguistics,* vol. 3, pp. 215–224.

Leroy, Jules, *Les manuscrits coptes et coptes-arabes.* Institut Français d'Archéologie de Beirut, Bibliothèque Archéologique et Historique, vol. 96; Paris: P. Geuthner, 1974.

Lewis, Agnes Smith, and Margaret Dunlop Gibson, *The Palestinian Syriac Lectionary of the Gospels, Re-Edited from Two Sinai MSS. and from P. de Lagarde's Edition of the 'Evangeliarium Hierosolymitanum'.* London: K. Paul, Trench, Trübner and Co., 1899.

Lewis, B., and F. Niewöhner (eds.), *Religionsgespräche im Mittelalter.* Wiesbaden: Harrassowitz, 1992.

Lieu, Samuel N. C., *Manichaeism in Mesopotamia and the Roman East.* Leiden: E.J. Brill, 1994.

———, *Manichaeism in Central Asia and China.* Leiden: Brill, 1998.

Livne-Kafri, Ofer, "A Note on Coptic and Judeo-Arabic on the Basis of Bilingual Manuscript to the Pentateuch," *Massorot* 21 (2002), pp. 97–101 [Hebrew].

———, "Some Notes Concerning the Arabic Version," in A. Shisha-Halevy, *Topics in Coptic Syntax: Structural Studies in the Bohairic Dialect.* Orientalia Lovaniensia Analecta, 160; Leuven: Uitgeverij Peeters en Departement Oosterse Studies, 2007, Appendix 2.

———, "A Note on the Enegeticus in a Coptic-Arabic Translation of the Pentateuch," *Acta Orientalia Academiae Scientiarum Hung.* 26 (2009), pp. 405–411.

———, "Some Notes on the Vocabulary in a Coptic-Arabic Translation of the Pentateuch," *Al-Karmil: Studies in Arabic Language and Literature; University of Haifa* 30 (2009), 17–27.

Lowin, Shari, "Hijaz," in Stillman, *Encyclopedia of Jews in the Islamic World,* vol. 2, pp. 416–417.

Lüling, Günter, *Über den Ur-Qur'ān: Ansätze zur Rekonstruction vorislamischer christlicher Strophenlieder im Qur'ān.* Erlangen: H. Lüling, 1974.

———, *Der christliche Kult an der vorislamischen Kaaba als Problem der Islamwissenschaft und christlichen Theologie.* Erlangen: H. Lüling, 1977.

Luxenberg, Christoph, *Die syro-aramäische Lesart des Koran: Ein Beitrag zur Entschlüsselung der Koransprache.* 2nd rev. ed.; Berlin: Hans Schlier, 2004. English trans., *The Syro-Aramaic Reading of the Koran: A Contribution to the Decoding of the Language of the Koran,* (Tim Müke, ed.); Berlin: Hans Schiler, 2007.

Maccoull, Leslie S. B., "Illustrated Manuscripts in the Coptic Museum: Language and History," *Parole de l'Orient* 91 (1994), pp. 391–399.

Macdonald, M.C.A. "Ancient Arabia and the Written Word," in Macdonald, *The Development of Arabic* (2010), pp. 5–28.

——— (ed.), *The Development of Arabic as a Written Language: Papers from the Special Session of the Seminar for Arabian Studies Held on 24 July 2009.* Supplement to the Proceedings of the Seminar for Arabian Studies, vol. 40; Oxford: Archaeopress, 2010.

MacLaurin, E.C.B. (ed.), *Essays in Honour of Griffithes Wheeler Thatcher 1863–1950.* Sydney: Sydney University Press, 1967.

Madelung, Wilferd, "Al-Qāsim ibn Ibrāhīm," in Thomas and Roggema, *Christian-Muslim Relations: A Bibliographical History,* vol. 1 (600–900), pp. 540–543.

Madigan, Daniel A., *The Qur'ān's Self-Image: Writing and Authority in Islam's Scripture.* Princeton, NJ: Princeton University Press, 2001.

———, "Criterion," in McAuliffe, *Encyclopaedia of the Qur'ān* (2001–2006), vol. 1, pp. 486–487.

Mai, A., *Scriptorum Veterum Nova Collectio e Vaticanis Codicibus Edita.* Vol. 4; Rome: Rypis Vaticanis, 1831.

Malter, Henry, *Saadia Gaon: His Life and Works.* The Morris Loeb Series; Philadelphia: Jewish Publication Society of America, 1921.

Mangenot, E., "Polyglottes," in F. Vigouroux (ed.), *Dictionnaire de la Bible.* 5 vols.; Paris: Letouzey et Ané, 1912–1922, vol. 5, cols. 513–529.

Marazka, Ibrahim et al. (eds.), *Samawʿal al-Maghribī's (d.570–1175) Ifḥām al-Yahūd.* Wiesbaden: Harrassowitz, 2006.

Marmardji, A.-S., *Diatessaron de Tatien: Texte arabe établi, traduit en français, collation avec les anciennes versions syriaques, suivi d'un évangéliaire syriaque.* Beirut: Imprimerie Catholique, 1935.

Marquet, Yves, "Le Shi'isme au IXe siècle à travers l'histoire de Ya'qûbî," *Arabica* 91 (1972), pp. 1–45, 101–138.

Marshall, David, *God, Muhammad and the Unbelievers: A Qur'anic Study.* Richmond, Surrey: Curzon Press, 1999.

———, "Punishment Stories," in McAuliffe, *Encyclopaedia of the Qur'ān* (2001–2006), vol. 4, pp. 318–322.

Marx, Michael, "Glimpses of a Mariology in the Qur'ān: From Hagiography to Theology via Religious Political Debate," in Neuwirth et al., *The Qur'ān in Context,* pp. 533–563.

Massignon, Louis, *Parole donné.* Paris: Firmin-Didot, 1970.

———, *Les trois prières d'Abraham.* Paris: Éditions du Cerf, 1997.

al-Masʿūdī, Abū l-Ḥasan ʿAlī, *Kitāb at-Tanbīh wa l-Ishrāf* (M.J. de Goeje, ed.). Bibliotheca Geographorum Arabicorum, 8 vols.; Leiden: E.J. Brill, 1967), vol. 8.

Mavroudi, Maria, "Arabic Words in Greek Letters: The Violet Fragment and More," in Jérôme Lentin and Jacques Grand'henry (eds.), *Moyen arabe et variétés mixtes de l'arabe à travers l'histoire: Actes dum premier colloque international (Louvain-la-Neuve, 10–14 mai 2004).* Université Catholique de Louvain, Institut Orientaliste; Leuven: Peeters, 2008, pp. 321–354.

———, *Bilingualism in Greek and Arabic in the Middle Ages: Evidence from the Manuscripts,* forthcoming.

McAuliffe, Jane Dammen, *Qur'ānic Christians: An Analysis of Classical and Modern Exegesis.* Cambridge: Cambridge University Press, 1991.

———, "The Qur'ānic Context of Muslim Biblical Scholarship," *Islam and Christian-Muslim Relations* 7 (1996), 141–158.

———, *Encyclopaedia of the Qur'ān.* 6 vols.; Leiden: Brill, 2001–2006.

McAuliffe, Jane Dammen, et. al. (eds.), *With Reverence for the Word: Medieval Scriptural Exegesis in Judaism, Christianity, and Islam.* Oxford: Oxford University Press, 2003.

McLeod, Frederick G., *Narsai's Metrical Homilies on the Nativity, Epiphany, Passion, Resurrection and Ascension.* Patrologia Orientalis, vol. 40, fasc. 1, n. 182; Turnhout: Brepols, 1979.

Μειμαρη, Ιωαννου Εμμ., Καταλογος των Νεων Αραβικων Χειρογραφων της Ιερας Μονης Αγιας Αικατερινης του Ορους Σινα. Αθηναι: Εθνικον Ιδρυμα Ερευνων, 1985.

Metzger, Bruce M., "A Comparison of the Palestinian Syriac Lectionary and the Greek Gospel Lectionary," in E. Earle Ellis and Max Wilcox (eds.), *Neotestamentica et Semitica: Studies in Honour of Matthew Black.* Edinburgh: T and T Clark, 1969, pp. 209–220.

———, *The Early Versions of the New Testament, Their Origin, Transmission and Limitations.* Oxford: Oxford University Press, 1977.

Michel, Thomas F. (trans.), *A Muslim Theologian's Response to Christianity: Ibn Taymiyya's al-Jawāb al-Ṣaḥīḥ.* Delmar, NY: Caravan Books, 1984.

Millar, Fergus, "Christian Monasticism in Roman Arabia at the Birth of Mahomet," *Semitica et Classica* 2 (2009), pp. 97–115.

Miller, Stuart S., *Sages and Commoners in Late Antique Erez Israel: A Philological Inquiry into Local Traditions in Talmud Yerushalmi.* Tübingen: Mohr Siebeck, 2006.

Mingana, A., *Woodbrooke Studies: Christian Douments in Syriac, Arabic and Garshuni,* vol. 2. Cambridge: W. Heffer and Sons, 1931.

———, "Syriac Influence on the Style of the Qur'ān," *Bulletin of the John Rylands Library of Manchester* 11 (1927), pp. 77–98.

Monferrer-Sala, Juan Pedro, "A Nestorian Arabic Pentateuch Used in Western Islamic Lands," in Thomas, *The Bible in Arab Christianity,* pp. 351–368.

Motzki, Harald, "The Collection of the Qur'ān: A Reconsideration of Western Views in Light of Recent Methodological Developments," *Der Islam* 87 (2001), pp. 1–34.

———, "Muṣḥaf," in McAuliffe, *Encyclopaedia of the Qur'ān* (2001–2006), vol. 3, pp. 463–466.

Mourad, Suleiman A., "A Twelfth-Century Muslim Biography of Jesus," *Islam and Christian-Muslim Relations* 7 (1996), pp. 39–45.

———, "On the Qur'ānic Stories about Mary and Jesus," *Bulletin of the Royal Institute for Inter-Faith Studies* 1 (1999), pp. 13–24.

———, "From Hellenism to Christianity and Islam: The Origin of the Palm-Tree Story concerning Mary and Jesus in the Gospel of Pseudo-Matthew and the Qur'ān," *Oriens Christianus* 86 (2002), pp. 206–216.

———, "Mary in the Qur'ān: A Reexamination of Her Presentation," in Reynolds, *The Qur'ān in Its Historical Context* (2008), pp. 163–174.

Nasrallah, Joseph, "Abū l-Farağ al-Yabrūdī: médecin chrétien de Damas (Xe–XIe s.)," *Arabica* 32 (1976), pp. 13–22.

———, "Deux versions Melchites partielles de la Bible du IXe et du Xe siècles," *Oriens Christianus* 46 (1980), pp. 202–215.

Nemoy, Leon, "The Factor of Script in the Textual Criticism of Judeo-Arabic Manuscripts," *Jewish Quarterly Review* 66 (1975–1976), pp. 148–159.

Netton, Ian Richard, "Nature as Signs," in McAuliffe, *Encyclopaedia of the Qur'ān,* vol. 3, pp. 528–536.

Neuwirth, Angelika, "Zur Struktur der Yusuf-Sure," in Werner Diem and Stefan Wild (eds.), *Studien aus Arabistik und Semitistik: Anton Spitaler zum siebzigsten Geburtstag.* Wiesbaden: Harrassowitz, 1980, pp. 123–150.

———, "Erzählen als kanonischer Prozess. Die Mose-Erzälung im Wandel der koranischen Geschichte," in Rainer Brunner et al. (eds.), *Islamstudien ohne Ende.* Würzburg: Ergon, 2000, pp. 322–344.

———, "Mary and Jesus: Counterbalancing the Biblical Patriarchs; A Re-Reading of Sūrat Maryam in Sūrat Āl 'Imrān (Q 3:1–62)," *Parole de l'Orient* 30 (2005), pp. 332–359.

———, *Studien zur Komposition der mekkanischen Suren: die literarische Form des Koran–ein Zeugnis seiner Historizität?* 2nd ed., Studien zur Geschichte und Kultur des islamischen Orients, vol. 10 [NF]; Berlin: De Gruyter, 2007.

———, "Psalmen–im Koran neu gelesen (Ps 104 und 136)," in Dirk Hartwig et al. (eds.), *"Im vollen Licht der Geschichte": Die Wissenschaft des Judentums und die Anfänge der kritischen Koranforschung.* Ex Oriente Lux, vol. 8; Würzburg: Ergon Verlag, 2008, pp. 157–189.

———, Sinai, Nicolai and Marx, Michael (eds.). *The Qur'ān in Context: Historical and Literary Investigations into the Qur'ānic Milieu.* Leiden: Brill, 2011.

Newby, Gordon Darnell, *A History of the Jews of Arabia.* Columbia, SC: University of South Carolina, 1988.

———, *The Making of the Last Prophet: A Reconstruction of the Earliest Biography of Muhammad.* Columbia, SC: University of South Carolina Press, 1989.

Nickel, Gordon, *Narratives of Tampering in the Earliest Commentaries on the Qur'ān.* History of Christian-Muslim Relations, vol. 13; Brill: Leiden, 2011.

Ohlig, Karl-Heinz, and Gerd R. Puin (eds.), *Die dunklen Anfänge: Neue Forschungen zur Entstehung und frühen Geschichte des Islam.* Berlin: Verlag Hans Schiler, 2005.

Olinder, Gunnar, *The Kings of Kinda of the Family of Ākil al-Murār.* Lund: H. Ohlsson, 1927.

Osman, Ghada, "Pre-Islamic Arab Converts to Christianity in Meca and Medina: An Investigation into the Arabic Sources," *The Muslim World* 95 (2005), pp. 67–80.

Pacini, Andrea (ed.), *Christian Communities in the Arab Middle East: The Challenge for the Future.* Oxford: Clarendon Press, 1998.

Papaconstantinou, Arietta (ed.), *The Multilingual Experience in Egypt, from the Ptolemies to the Abbasids.* Farnham, Surrey, UK: Ashgate, 2010.

Paret, Rudi, *Der Koran: Kommentar und Kondordanz.* 2nd ed.; Stuttgart: Verlag W. Kohlhammer, 1977.

Patlagean, E., and A. Le Boulluec (eds.), *Les retours aux écritures: Fondamentalismes presents et passes,* Leuven: Peeters, 1993.

Patrich, Joseph, *Sabas–Leader of Palestinian Monasticism.* Dumbarton Oaks Studies, 32; Washington, DC: Dumbarton Oaks, 1995.

——— (ed.), *The Sabaite Heritage: The Sabaite Factor in the Orthodox Church–Monastic Life, Theology, Liturgy, Literature, Art and Archaeology (5th Century to the Present).* Orientalia Lovaniensia Analecta; P. Peeters: Leuven, 2001.

Payne Smith, R., *Thesaurus Syriacus.* 2 vols.; Oxford: Clarendon Press, 1879–1901: reprint; Hildesheim and New York: Georg Olms, 1981.

Pelikan, Jaroslav, *The Spirit of Eastern Christendom (600–1700).* The Christian Tradition, vol. 2; Chicago: University of Chicago Press, 1974.

Pellat, Charles, *Le milieu basrien et la formation de Gāḥiẓ.* Paris: Librairie d'Amérique et d'Orient Adrien-Maisonneuve, 1953.

Penrice, John, *A Dictionary and Glossary of the Kor-ân.* London: Henry S. King and Co., 1873.

Perlmann, Moshe (ed. and trans.), *Samau'al al-Maghribī, Ifḥām al-Yahūd; Silencing the Jews.* Proceedings of the American Academy for Jewish Research, vol. 32; New York: American Academy for Jewish Research, 1964.

——— (ed.), *Sa'd b. Manṣūr ibn Kammūna's Examination of the Inquiries into the Three Faiths: A Thirteenth-Century Essay in Comparative Religion.* University of California

Publications, Near Eastern Studies, 6; Berkeley and Los Angeles, CA: University of California Press, 1967.

——— (trans.), *Ibn Kammūna's Examination of the Three Faiths: A Thirteenth-Century Essay in the Comparative Study of Religion, Translated from the Arabic, with an Introduction and Notes.* Berkeley and Los Angeles, CA: University of California Press, 1971.

Peterson, William L., *Tatian's Diatessaron: Its Creation, Dissemination, Significance and History in Scholarship.* Supplements to *Vigiliae Christianae*, vol. 25; Leiden: E.J. Brill, 1994.

Pines, Shlomo, "La loi naturelle et la société: La doctrine politico-théologique d'Ibn Zurʿa, philosophe chrétien de Bagdad," in Uriel Heyd (ed.), *Studies in Islamic History and Civilization.* Scripta Hierosolymitana, vol. 9; Jerusalem: The Magnes Press, The Hebrew University, 1961, pp. 154–190.

———, "Gospel Quotations and Cognate Topics in ʿAbd al-Jabbār's *Tathbīt* in Relation to Early Christian and Judaeo-Christian Readings and Traditions," *Jerusalem Studies in Arabic and Islam* 9 (1987), 195–278.Pohlmann, Karl-Friedrich, *Die Entstehung des Korans: Neue Erkenntnisse aus Sicht der historisch-kritischen Bibelwissenschaft.* Darmstadt: Wissenschaftliche Buchgesellschaft, 2012.

Polliack, Meira, *The Karaite Tradition of Arabic Bible Translation: A Linguistic and Exegetical Study of Karaite Translations of the Pentateuch from the Tenth and Eleventh Centuries C.E.* Études sur le Judaïsme Médiéval, vol. 17; Leiden: E.J. Brill, 1997.

———, "Arabic Bible Translations in the Cairo Genizah Collections," in Ulf Haxen et al. (eds.), *Jewish Studies in a New Europe: Proceedings of the Fifth Congress of Jewish Studies in Copenhagen 1994.* Copenhagen: C.A. Reitzel, Det Kongtelge Bibliotek, 1998, pp. 395–620.

———, "Genres in Judaeo-Arabic Literature." The Irene Halmos Chair of Arabic Literature Annual Lecture; Tel Aviv: Tel Aviv University, 1998.

——— (ed.), *Karaite Judaism: A Guide to Its History and Literary Sources.* Handbuch der Orientalistik, vol. 73; Leiden: Brill, 2003.

———, "Rethinking Karaism: Between Judaism and Islam," *AJS Review* 30 (2006), pp. 67–93.

Pons, L. F. Bernabé, *El Texto Morisco del Evangelio de San Bernabé.* Granada: Universidad de Granada, 1998.

Pourjavady, Reza, and Sabine Schmidtke, *A Jewish Philosopher of Baghdad: ʿIzz al-Dawla ibn Kammūna (d.683/1284) and His Writings.* Islamic Philosophy, Theology and Science, vol. 65; Leiden: Brill, 2006.

Pregill, M. E., "*Isrāʾīliyyāt*, Myth, and Pseudepigraphy: Wahb b. Munabbih and the Early Islamic Versions of the Fall of Adam and Eve," *Jerusalem Studies in Arabic and Islam* 43 (2008), pp. 215284.

Prémare, Alfred-Louis de, *Joseph et Muhammad: Le chapitre 12 du Coran; étude textuelle.* Aix-en-Provence: Publications de l'Université de Provence, 1989.

———, *Aux origines du Coran: Questions d'hier, approaches d'aujourd'hui.* L'Islam en débats; Paris: Téraèdre, 2007.

Pulcini, Theodore, *Exegesis as Polemical Discourse: Ibn Ḥazm on Jewish and Christian Scriptures.* Atlanta, GA: Scholars Press, 1998.

———, "In the Shadow of Mount Carmel: The Collapse of the 'Latin East' and the Origins of the Gospel of Barnabas," *Islam and Christian-Muslim Relations* 21 (2001), pp. 191–209.

Raby, Julian, and Jeremy Johns (eds.), *Bayt al-Maqdis: 'Abd al-Malik's Jerusalem.* Part I; Oxford: Oxford University Press, 1992.

Radtke, Bernd, *Weltgeschichte und Weltbeschreibung im mittelalterlichen Islam.* Beiruter Texte und Studien, 51; Beirut and Stuttgart: Franz Steiner Verlag, 1992.

Ragg, Lonsdale and Laura, *The Gospel of Barnabas.* Oxford: Oxford University Press, 1907.

Raven, Wim, "Some Early Islamic Texts on the Negus of Abyssinia," *Journal of Semitic Studies* 33 (1988), pp. 197–218.

Reeves, John C. (ed.), *Bible and Qur'an: Essays in Scriptural Intertextuality.* Atlanta: Sociey of Biblical Literature, 2003.

———, "The Muslim Appropriation of a Biblical Text: The Messianic Dimensions of Isaiah 21:6–7," in Holum and Lapin, *Shaping the Middle East* (2011), pp. 211–222.

———, *Prolegomena to a History of Islamicate Manichaeism.* Sheffield, UK and Oakville, CT: Equinox Publishing, 2011.

Reynolds, Gabriel Said, "The Ends of *Al-radd al-jamīl* and Its Portrayal of Christian Sects," *Islamochristiana* 52 (1999), pp. 45–65.

———, *A Muslim Theologian in the Sectarian Milieu: 'Abd al-Jabbār and the Critique of Christian Origins.* Leiden: E.J. Brill, 2004.

——— (ed.), *The Qur'ān in Its Historical Context.* Routledge Studies in the Qur'ān; London and New York: Routledge, 2008.

———, "The Muslim Jesus: Dead or Alive?" *Bulletin of the School of Oriental and African Studies* 72 (2009), pp. 237–258.

———, "On the Qur'ānic Accusation of Scriptural Falsification (*taḥrīf*) and Christian Anti-Jewish Polemic," *Journal of the American Oriental Society* 130 (2010), pp. 189–202.

———, *The Qur'ān and Its Biblical Subtext.* Routledge Studies in the Qur'ān; London and New York: Routledge, 2010.

——— (ed.), *New Perspectives on the Qur'ān: The Qur'ān in Its Historical Context 2.* Routledge Studies in the Qur'ān; London and New York: Routledge, 2011.

———, "Le problème de la chronologie du Coran," *Arabica* 58 (2011), pp. 477–502.

Reynolds, Gabriel Said and Samir Khalil Samir (eds. and trans.), *'Abd al-Jabbār: Critique of Christian Origins.* Provo, UT: Bringham Young University Press, 2010.

Rhode, Joseph Francis, *The Arabic Versions of the Pentateuch in the Church of Egypt.* Washington, DC: The Catholic University of America, 1921.

Ri, Su-Min, *La caverne des trésors: les deux recensions syriaques.* CSCO vols. 487 and 488; Louvain: Peeters, 1987.

———, *Commentaire de La Caverne des Trésors: étude sur l'histoire du texte et de ses sources.* CSCO vol. 581; Louvain: Peeters, 2000.

Richter, Tonio Sebastian, "Greek, Coptic and the 'Language of the Hijra': The Rise and Decline of the Coptic Language in Late Antique and Medieval Egypt," in Cotton, *From Hellenism to Islam* (2009), pp. 401–446.

———, "Language Choice in the Qurra Dossier," in Papaconstantinou, *The Multilingual Experience in Egypt* (2010), pp. 189–220.

Ricks, Thomas W, "Developing the Doctrine of the Trinity in an Islamic Milieu: Early Arabic Christian Contributions to Trinitarian Theology." Ph.D. Dissertation; Washington, DC: The Catholic University of America, 2012.

Rippin, Andrew, "Saʿadya Gaon and Genesis 22: Aspects of Jewish-Muslim Interaction and Polemic," in Brinner and Ricks, *Studies in Islamic and Judaic Traditions*, pp. 33–46.

Robin, Christian-Julien, "Le judaïsme de Ḥimyar," *Arabia* 1 (2003), pp. 97–172.

———, "Himyar et Israël," *Académie des Inscriptions et Belles-Lettres*, Comptes-Rendus des Séances de l'Année 2004, avril-juin, pp. 831–908.

———, "Joseph, dernier roi de Ḥimyar (de 522 à 525, ou une des années suivantes)," *Jerusalem Studies in Arabic and Islam* 34 (2008), pp. 1–124.

Robinson, Chase F., "Waraḳa b. Nawfal," in *EI2*, vol. 11, pp. 142–143.

———, *ʿAbd al-Malik*. Makers of the Muslim World; Oxford: One World, 2005.

Robinson, James M. (ed.), *The Nag Hammadi Library in English*. 4th rev. ed.; Leiden: E.J. Brill, 1996.

Robinson, Neal, *Christ in Islam and Christianity*. Albany, NY: State University of New York Press, 1991.

———, "Crucifixion," in McAuliffe, *Encyclopaedia of the Qurʾān* (2001–2006), vol. 1, pp. 487–489.

———, "Jesus," in McAuliffe, *Encyclopaedia of the Qurʾān* (2001–2006), vol. 3, pp. 7–21.

Roggema, B., "Ibn al-Layth," in Thomas and Roggema, *Christian-Muslim Relations: A Bibliographical History*, vol. 1 (600-900), pp. 347–353.

———, "Pseudo-'Umar' II's Letter to Leo III," in Thomas and Roggema, *Christian-Muslim Relations: A Bibliographical History*, vol. 1 (600–900), pp. 381–385.

Rosenblatt, Samuel, *Saadia Gaon: The Book of Beliefs and Opinions*. Yale Judaica Series, vol. 1; New Haven, CT: Yale University Press, 1948.

Rosenkranz, Simone, *Die jüdisch-christliche Auseinandersetzung unter islamischer Herrschaft: 7.–10. Jahrhundert*. Judaica et Christiana, vol. 21; Bern, Berlin: Peter Lang, 2004.

Rosenthal, Erwin I. J., *Studia Semitica*. 2 vols.; Cambridge: Cambridge University Press, 1971.

Rosenthal, Franz, *A History of Muslim Historiography*. Leiden: E.J. Brill, 1952.

———, *Knowledge Triumphant: The Concept of Knowledge in Medieval Islam*. Leiden: E.J. Brill, 1970.

———, "Asāṭīr al-awwalīn," in *EI2*, vol. 12, p. 90.

Rousseau, Philip (ed.), *A Companion to Late Antiquity*. Oxford: Wiley-Blackwell, 2009.

Rubenson, Samuel, "The Transition from Coptic to Arabic," *Égypte/Monde Arabe* 27-28 (1996), pp. 77–92.

———, "Translating the Tradition: Some Remarks on the Arabization of the Patristic Heritage in Egypt," *Medieval Encounters* 2 (1996), pp. 4–14.

Rubin, Uri, "Children of Israel," in McAuliffe, *Encyclopaedia of the Qurʾān* (2001–2006), vol. I, pp. 303–307.

———, "Ḥanīf," in McAuliffe, *Encyclopaedia of the Qurʾān* (2001–2006), vol. II, pp. 402–404.

———, "Jews and Judaism," in McAuliffe, *Encyclopaedia of the Qurʾān* (2001–2006), vol. III, pp. 21–34.

———, "Prophets and Prophethood," in McAuliffe, *Encyclopaedia of the Qurʾān* (2001–2006), vol. IV, pp. 289–307.

———, "On the Arabian Origins of the Qurʾān: The Case of *al-Furqān*," *Journal of Semitic Studies* 45 (2009), pp. 421–433.

Rudolph, Wilhelm, *Die Abhängigkeit des Qorans von Judentum und Christentum.* Stuttgart: W. Kohlhammer Verlag, 1922.

Ryding, Karin C. (ed.), *Early Medieval Arabic: Studies on al-Khalīl ibn Aḥmad.* Washington, DC: Georgetown University Press, 1998.

Sabella, Bernard, "The Emigration of Christian Arabs: Dimensions and Causes of the Phenomenon," in Pacini, *Christian Communities in the Arab Middle East,* pp. 127–154.

Sadeghi, Behnam, and Uwe Bergman, "The Codex of a Companion of the Prophet and the Qur'ān of the Prophet," *Arabica* 75 (2010), pp. 343–436.

Sæbø, Magne (ed.), *Hebrew Bible/Old Testament: The History of Its Interpretation.* 3 parts in 2 vols.; Göttingen: Vandenhoeck and Ruprecht, 1996.

Saleh, Walid A. (ed.), *In Defense of the Bible: A Critical Edition and an Introduction to al-Biqāʿī's Bible Treatise.* Islamic History and Civilization, vol. 73; Leiden: Brill, 2008.

Samir Khalil Samir, "Nécessité de l'exégèse scientifique: Texte de ʿAbdallā ibn aṭ-Ṭayyib," *Parole de l'Orient* 5 (1974), pp. 243–279.

———, *Actes du premier congrès international d'études arabes chrétiennes, Goslar, septembre 1980.* Orientalia Christiana Analecta, 218; Rome: Pontifical Institute for Oriental Studies, 1982.

———, "Note sur les citations bibliques chez Abū Qurrah," *Orientalia Christiana Periodica* 94 (1983), pp. 184–191.

——— (ed.), *Actes du deuxième congrès international d'études arabes chrétiennes (Oosterhesselen, septembre 1984).* Orientalia Christiana Analecta, 226; Rome: Pontifical Institute of Oriental Studies, 1986.

———, "La 'Somme des aspects de la foi'," in Samir, *Actes du deuxième congrès international d'études arabes chrétiennes,* (1986), pp. 93–121.

———, "Michel, évêque melkite de Damas au 9e siècle: a propos de Bišr ibn al-Sirrī," *Orientalia Christiana Periodica* 35 (1987), pp. 439–441.

———, "Old Testament, Arabic Versions of the," in Aziz Z. Atiya (ed.), *The Coptic Encyclopedia.* 8 vols.; New York: Macmillan, 1991, vol. 6, pp. 1827–1836.

———, "The Christian Communities, Active Members of Arab Society throughout History," in Pacini, *Christian Communities in the Arab Middle East* (1998), pp. 67–91.

———, "La place d'Ibn aṭ-Ṭayyib dans la pensée arabe," *Journal of Eastern Christian Studies* 85 (2006), pp. 177–193.

Sanders, J.C.J. (ed. and trans.), *Inleiding op het Genesis kommentaar van de Nestoriaan Ibn at-Taiyib.* Proefschrift-Amsterdam; Leiden: E.J. Brill, 1963.

——— (ed. and trans.), *Ibn aṭ-Ṭaiyib, Commentaire sur la Genèse.* CSCO vols. 274 and 275; Louvain: Secrétariat du CorpusSCO, 1967.

Sbath, Paul (ed.), *Vingt traités philosophiques et apologétiques d'auteurs arabes chrétiens du IXe au XIVe siècle.* Cairo: Friedrich and Co., 1929.

Schäfer, Peter, *Jesus in the Talmud.* Princeton, NJ: Princeton University Press, 2007.

Schick, Robert, *The Christian Communities of Palestine from Byzantine to Islamic Rule: A Historical and Archaeological Study.* Princeton, NJ: The Darwin Press, 1996.

Schmidtke, Sabine, "The Muslim Reception of Biblical Materials: Ibn Qutayba and his "*Aʿlām al-nubuwwa,*" *Islam and Christian-Muslim Relations* 22 (2011), pp. 249–274.

Schöck, Cornelia, "Adam and Eve," in McAuliffe, *Encyclopaedia of the Qur'ān,* vol. 1, pp. 22–26.

Schoeler, Gregor, *Écrire et transmettre dans les débuts de l'Islam.* Paris: Presses Universitaires de France, 2002.

———, *The Oral and the Written in Early Islam,* Uwe Vagelpohl (trans.), James E. Montgomery (ed.). London and New York: Routledge, 2006.

Schoeps, Hans Joachim, *Theologie und Geschichte des Judenchristentums.* Tübingen: Mohr, 1949.

Schreiner, Martin, "Al-Jakubî über den Glauben und die Sitten der Juden," *Monatsschrift für Geschichte und Wissenschaft des Judentums* 43 (1885), pp. 135–139.

Schützinger, Heinrich, *Ursprung und Entwicklung der arabischen Abraham-Nimrod Legende.* Bonn: Rheinische Friedrich Wilhelms Universität, 1961.

Sells, Michael A., "Memory," in McAuliffe, *Encyclopaedia of the Qur'ān,* vol. 3, pp. 372–374.

Serjeant, R. B., "Hūd and Other Pre-Islamic Prophets of Ḥadramawt," *Le Muséon* 64 (1954), pp. 121–179.

Shahid, Irfan, "Byzantium and Kinda," *Byzantinische Zeitschrift* 53 (1960), pp. 57–73.

———, "Procopius and Kinda," *Byzantinische Zeitschrift* 53 (1960), pp. 74–78.

———, "A Contribution to Koranic Exegesis," in G. Makdisi (ed.), *Arabic and Islamic Studies in Honor of Hamilton A. R. Gibb.* Leiden: E.J. Brill, 1965, pp. 563–580.

———, *The Martyrs of Najrān: New Documents.* Subsidia Hagiographica, no. 49; Brussels: Société des Bollandistes, 1971.

———, "Byzantium in South Arabia," *Dumbarton Oaks Papers* 33 (1979), pp. 23–94.

———, "Another Contribution to Koranic Exegesis: The *Sūra* of the Poets (XXVI)," *Journal of Arabic Literature* 41 (1983), pp. 1–21.

———, *Byzantium and the Arabs in the Fourth Century.* Washington, DC: Dumbarton Oaks, 1984.

———, *Rome and the Arabs: A Prolegomenon to the Study of Byzantium and the Arabs.* Washington, DC: Dumbarton Oaks, 1984.

———, *Byzantium and the Arabs in the Fifth Century.* Washington, DC: Dumbarton Oaks, 1989.

———, *The Arabs in Late Antiquity: Their Role, Achievement, and Legacy.* The Margaret Weyerhaeuser Jewett Chair of Arabic, Occasional Papers; Beirut: The American University of Beirut, 2008.

———, *Byzantium and the Arabs in the Sixth Century.* 2 vols. in 4; Washington, DC: Dumbarton Oaks, 1995–2009.

———, "Kinda," in *EI2,* vol. V, pp. 118–120.

Sharpe, J. L., and K. Van Kampen (eds.), *The Bible as Book: The Manuscript Tradition.* London: British Library, 1998.

Shboul, Ahmad, and Alan Walmsley, "Identity and Self-Image in Syria-Palestine in the Transition from Byzantine to Early Islamic Rule: Arab Christians and Muslims," *Mediterranean Archaeology* 11 (1998), pp. 255–287.

Shepardson, Christine, "Syria, Syriac, Syrian: Negotiating East and West," in Rousseau, *Companion to Late Antiquity,* pp. 455–466.

Sijistānī, Da'ūd ibn al-Ash'ath, as-, *Kitāb al-Maṣāḥif.* Cairo: al-Maṭba'ah ar Raḥmāniyyah, 1355/1936.

Simon, Róbert, "Mānī and Muḥammad," *Jerusalem Studies in Arabic and Islam* 21 (1997), pp. 118–141.

Slomp, Jan, "The 'Gospel of Barnabas' in Recent Research," *Islamochristiana* 32 (1997), pp. 81–109.

Smit, G., "*Bijbel en Legende'; bij den arabischen Schrijver Ja'qubi; 9th Eeuw na Christus.* Leiden: E.J. Brill, 1907.

Sox, David, *The Gospel of Barnabas*. London: Allen and Unwin, 1984.

Speyer, Heinrich, *Die biblischen Erzählungen im Qoran*. Gräfenhainichen/Breslau: Schulze, 1931. Reprint of 1931 ed.: Hildesheim: G. Olms, 1961.

Staal, H., *Mt. Sinai Arabic Codex 151: I Pauline Epistles*. CSCO, vols. 452 and 453; Louvain: Peeters, 1983.

Steiner, Richard C., "Philology as the Handmaiden of Philosophy in R. Saadia Gaon's Interpretation of Gen 1:1," *Israel Oriental Studies* 91 (1999), pp. 379–389.

———, *A Biblical Translation in the Making: The Evolution and Impact of Saadia Gaon's* Tafsīr. Cambridge, MA: Harvard University Center for Jewish Studies/Harvard University Press, 2010.

Stern, David, "The First Jewish Books and the Early History of Jewish Reading," *The Jewish Quarterly Review* 89 (2008), pp. 163–202.

Stern, M. S., "Muhammad and Joseph: A Study of Koranic Narrative," *Journal of Near Eastern Studies* 44 (1985), pp. 193–204.

Stern, S., "Quotations from Apocryphal Gospels in ʿAbd al-Jabbār," *Journal of Theological Studies* 81 (1967), pp. 34–57.

———, "Abd al-Jabbār's Account of How Christ's Religion was Falsified by the Adoption of Roman Customs," *Journal of Theological Studies* 91 (1968), pp. 128–185.

Stewart, Devin J., "Rhymed Prose," in McAuliffe, *Encyclopaedia of the Qurʾān*, vol. 4, pp. 476–483.

Stillman, Norman A., *The Jews of Arab Lands: A History and Source Book*. Philadelphia: Jewish Publication Society of America, 1979.

——— (ed.), *Encyclopedia of Jews in the Islamic World*. 5 vols.; Leiden and Boston: E.J. Brill, 2010.

———, "Judeo-Arabic: History and Linguistic Description," in *Encyclopedia of Jews in the Islamic World*. Brill Online ed., September 14, 2010, *sub voce*.

Stroumsa, Sarah, "The Impact of Syriac Tradition on Early Judaeo-Arabic Bible Exegesis," *ARAM* 3 (1991), pp. 83–96.

Swanson, Mark N., "Beyond Prooftexting: Approaches to the Qurʾān in Some Early Arabic Christian Apologies," *The Muslim World* 88 (1998), pp. 297–319.

———, "Beyond Prooftexting (2): The Use of the Bible in Some Early Arabic Christian Apologies," in Thomas, *The Bible in Arab Christianity* (2007), pp. 91–112.

Takla, Hanny N., "Copto (Bohairic)-Arabic Manuscripts: Their Role in the Tradition of the Coptic Church," in M. Immerzeel and J. van der Vliet (eds.), *Coptic Studies on the Threshold of a New Millennium: Proceedings of the Seventh International Congress of Coptic Studies*. Leuven: Uitgeverij Peeters en Departement Osterse Studies, 2004, pp. 639–646.

Talia, Shawqi N., "Būlus al-Būshī's Arabic Commentary on the Apocalypse of St. John: An English Translation and Commentary." Ph.D. Dissertation; Washington, DC: The Catholic University of America, 1987.

Talmon, Raphael, *Arabic Grammar in Its Formative Age: Kitāb al-ʿAyn and Its Attribution to Ḳalīl ibn Aḥmad*. Leiden: Brill, 1997.

Tannous, Jack, "Between Christology and Kalām? The Life and Letters of George, Bishop of the Arab Tribes," in Kiraz, *Malphono w-Rabo d-Malphone*, pp. 671–716.

Tardieu, Michel, "L'arrivée des manichéens à al-Ḥīra," in Canivet and Rey-Coquais, *La Syrie de Byzance à l'Islam VIIe–VIIIe siècles* (1992), pp. 15–24.

———, *Manichaeism*, M. B. DeBevoise (trans.). Urbana and Chicago : University of Illinois Press, 2008.

Tardy, René, *Najrân: Chrétiens d'Arabie avant l'Islam.* Recherches, 8; Beirut: Dar el-Machreq, 1999.

Thackston, W. M. (trans.), *The Tales of the Prophets of al-Kisaʾī.* Boston: Twayne Publishers, 1978.

Thomas, David, "Tabari's Book of Religion and Empire," *Bulletin of the John Rylands University Library of Manchester* 96 (1986), pp. 1–7.

———, "The Bible in Early Muslim Anti-Christian Polemic," *Islam and Christian-Muslim Relations* 7 (1996), pp. 29–38.

——— (ed.), *The Bible in Arab Christianity.* The History of Christian-Muslim Relations, vol. 6; Leiden: Brill, 2007.

———, "ʿAlī l-Ṭabarī," in Thomas and Roggema, *Christian-Muslim Relations: A Bibliographical History* (2009), vol. 1 (600–900), pp. 669–674.

———, "Ibn Qutayba," in Thomas and Roggema, *Christian-Muslim Relations: A Bibliographical History* (2009), vol. 1 (600–900), pp. 816–818.

Thomas, David and Alex Mallett (eds.), *Christian-Muslim Relations: A Bibliographical History,* vol. 2, 900–1050. Leiden: Brill, 2010.

Thomas, David, and Barbara Roggema (eds.), *Christian-Muslim Relations: A Bibliographical History.* History of Christian-Muslim Relations, vol. 11; Leiden: Brill, 2009, vol. 1 (600–900).

Thompson, John A., "The Origin and Nature of the Chief Printed Arabic Bibles," *The Bible Translator* 6 (1955), pp. 2–12, 51–55, 98–106, 146–150.

Tobi, Yosef, "On the Antiquity of the Judeo-Arabic Biblical Translations and a New Piece of an Ancient Judeo-Arabic Translation of the Pentateuch," in Tobi and Avishur, *Ben 'Ever la-'Arav,* pp. 17–60 [Hebrew].

Tobi, Yosef, and Y. Avishur (eds.), *Ben 'Ever la-'Arav: Contacts between Arabic Literature and Jewish Literature in the Middle Ages and Modern Times.* Vol. 2; Tel Aviv: Afikim Publishers, 2001 [Hebrew].

Tottoli, Roberto, *Vita di Mosè secondo le tradizioni islamiche.* Palermo: Sellerio, 1992.

———, "Origin and Use of the Term *Isrāʾīliyyāt* in Muslim Literature," *Arabica* 64 (1999), pp. 193–210.

———, *Biblical Prophets in the Qurʾān and Muslim Literature.* Richmond, Surrey: Curzon, 2002.

———, "Ṣāliḥ," in McAuliffe, *Encyclopaedia of the Qurʾān,* vol. 4, pp. 521–522.

———, "Shuʿayb," in McAuliffe, *Encyclopaedia of the Qurʾān,* vol. 4, pp. 605–606.

Trimingham, J. Spencer, *Christianity among the Arabs in Pre-Islamic Times.* London and New York: Longman, 1979.

Tritton, A. S., *The Caliphs and their Non-Muslim Subjects: A Critical Study of the Covenant of ʿUmar.* London: Frank Cass, 1930/1970.

Urvoy, Marie Thérèse (ed.), *Le psautier mozarabe de Hafs le Goth.* Toulouse: Presses Universitaires du Mirail, 1992.

Vajda, G., "Judaeo-Arabica: Observations sur quelques citations bibliques chez Ibn Qotayba," *Revue des Études Juives* 99 (1935), pp. 68–80.

———, "Judaeo-Arabic Literature," in *EI2,* vol. 4, pp. 303–307.

Valentin, Jean, "Les Évangéliaires arabes de la bibliothèque du monastère ste. Catherine (Mont Sinaï): Essai de classification d'après l'étude d'un chapitre (*Matth.* 28); traducteurs, réviseurs, types textuels," *Le Muséon* 116 (2003), pp. 415–477.

Valognes, Jean-Pierre, *Vie et mort des chrétiens d'orient; des origins à nos jours.* Paris: Fayard, 1994.

Van Bladel, Kevin, "Heavenly Cords and Prophetic Authority in the Quran and Its Late Antique Context," *Bulletin of the School of Oriental and African Studies* 70 (2007), pp. 223–246.

———, "The *Alexander Legend* in the Qur'ān 18:83–102," in Reynolds, *The Qur'ān in Its Historical Context* (2008), 175–203.

Van der Velden, Frank, "Konvergenztexte syrischer und arabischer Christologie: Stufen der Textentwicklung von Sure 3, 33–64," *Oriens Christianus* 91 (2007), pp. 164–203.

———, "Kontexte im Konvergenztrang–die Bedeutung textkritischer Varianten und christlicher Bezugstexte für die Redaktion von Sure 61 und Sure 5, 110–119," *Oriens Christianus* 92 (2008), pp. 130–173.

Van Esbroeck, Michel, "Les versions orientales de la Bible: Une orientation bibliographique," in Margaret Davis et al. (eds.), *Interpretation of the Bible.* Ljubljana: Slovenska Academija Znanosti in Umetnosti; Sheffield, UK: Sheffield Academic Press, 1998, pp. 399–415.

Van Reeth, J.M.F., "Le prophète musulman en tant que Nâsir Allâh et ses antécédents: Le 'Nazôraios' évangélique et le livre des Jubilés," *Orientalia Lovaniensia Periodica* 23 (1992), pp. 251–274.

———, "L'Évangile du Prophète," in De Smet, *Al-Kitāb: La sacralité du texte* (2004), pp. 155–184.

———, "La typologie du prophète selon le Coran: Le cas de Jésus," in Dye and Nobilio, *Figures bibliques* (2011), pp. 81–105.

Van Rompay, Lucas, "The Christian Syriac Tradition of Interpretation," in Sæbø, *Hebrew Bible/Old Testament,* vol. 1, part 1, pp. 612–641.

———, "Development of Biblical Interpretation in the Syrian Churches of the Middle Ages," in Sæbø, *Hebrew Bible/Old Testament* (1996), vol. 1, part 2, pp. 559–577.

Versteegh, Kees et al. (eds.), *Encyclopedia of Arabic Language and Linguistics.* 5 vols.; Leiden: Brill, 2005–2009.

Vida, G. Levi della, "Salmān al-Fārisī," in *EI2,* Supplement, pp. 701–702.

Violet, Bruno, "Ein zweisprachiges Psalmfragment aus Damaskus," *Berichtigter Sonderabzug aus der Orientalistischen Literatur-Zeitung.* Berlin: Akademie-Verlag, 1902.

Vollandt, Ronny, message posted on the list-serve of the North American Society for Christian Arabic Studies, March 8, 2010.

———, "Christian-Arabic Translations of the Pentateuch from the 9th to the 13th Centuries: A Comparative Study of Manuscripts and Translation Techniques." Ph.D. Thesis; Cambridge: St. John's College University of Cambridge, 2011.

Wansbrough, J., *Quranic Studies: Sources and Methods of Scriptural Interpretation.* London Oriental Series, vol. 31; Oxford: Oxford University Press, 1977.

———, *The Sectarian Milieu: Content and Composition of Islamic Salvation History.* London Oriental Series, vol. 34; Oxford: Oxford University Press, 1978.

Wasserstein, David J., "Why Did Arabic Succeed Where Greek Failed? Language Change in the Near East after Muḥammad," *Scripta Classica Israelica* 22 (2003), pp. 257–272.

Wasserstrom, Steven M., *Between Muslim and Jew: The Problem of Symbiosis under Early Islam.* Princeton, NJ: Princeton University Press, 1995.

Watt, William Montgomery, *Muhammad at Mecca.* Oxford: Clarendon Press, 1953.

———, "The Christianity Criticized in the Qur'ān," *The Muslim World* 57 (1967), pp. 197–201.

Wechsler, Michael G., "Japheth (Abū ʿAlī Ḥasan) ben Eli," in Stillman, *Encyclopedia of Jews in the Islamic World*, vol. 3, pp. 11–13.

Weil, G., *The Bible, the Koran, and the Talmud, or, Biblical Legends of the Musselmans.* New York: Harper, 1846.

Weitzmann, Michael, *The Syriac Version of the Old Testament: An Introduction.* University of Cambridge Oriental Publications, vol. 56; Cambridge: Cambridge University Press, 1990.

Wellhausen, Julius, *Reste arabischen Heldentumes.* Berlin: G. Reimer, 1897.

Wensinck, A. J. and C. E. Bosworth, "Al-masīḥ," in *EI 2*, vol. 6, p. 726.

Wheeler, Brannon M., *Moses in the Quran and Islamic Exegesis.* London and New York: Routledge/Curzon, 2002.

———, *Prophets in the Qurʾān: An Introduction to the Qurʾān and Muslim Exegesis.* London and New York: Continuum, 2002.

Wherry, E. M., *A Comprehensive Commentary on the Qurʾān.* 4 vols.; London: K. Paul, Trench, Trübner and Co., 1896.

Whittingham, Martin, "The value of *taḥrīf maʿnawī* (Corrupt Interpretation) as a Category for Analysing Muslim Views of the Bible: Evidence from *Al-radd al-jamīl* and Ibn Khaldūn," *Islam and Christian-Muslim Relations* 22 (2011), pp. 209–222.

Wiegers, G.A., "Muḥammad as the Messiah: A Comparison of the Polemical Works of Juan Alonso with the *Gospel of Barnabas*," *Bibliotheca Orientalis* 25 (1995), pp. 245–292.

Wild, Stefan, *Das Kitāb al-ʿAyn und die arabische Lexikographie.* Wiesbaden: Harrassowitz, 1965.

——— (ed.), *The Qurʾān as Text.* Islamic Philosophy, Theology, and Science, Texts and Studies, vol. 27; Leiden: E.J. Brill, 1996.

Wilken, Robert L., *The Land Called Holy: Palestine in Christian History and Thought.* New Haven: Yale University Press, 1992.

Wilkinson, John (trans.), *Egeria's Travels to the Holy Land: Newly Translated, with Supporting Documents and Notes.* Jerusalem: Ariel Publishing House and Warminster, UK: Aris and Phillips, 1981.

Wilms, Franz-Elmar, *Al-Ghazālīs Schrift wider die Gottheit Jesu.* Leiden: E.J. Brill, 1966.

Witztum, Joseph, "Joseph among the Ishmaelites: Q 12 in Light of Syriac Sources," in Reynolds, *New Perspectives on the Qurʾān*, pp. 425–448.

Yaʿqûbî, Aḥmad, al-, *Taʾrīkh al-Yaʿqûbî.* 2 vols.; Beirut: Dar Sadir and Dar Bayrut, 1379/1960.

Young, M.J.L. et al. (eds.), *Religion, Learning and Science in the ʿAbbasid Period.* Cambridge: Cambridge University Press, 1990.

Zaehner, R. C., *At Sundry Times: An Essay in the Comparison of Religions.* London: Faber and Faber, 1958.

Zahniser, A. H. Mathias, "Messenger," in McAuliffe, *Encyclopaedia of the Qurʾān*, vol. 3, pp. 380–383.

Zebiri, Kate, "Polemic and Polemical Language," in McAuliffe, *Encyclopaedia of the Qurʾān*, vol. 4, pp. 114–125.

Zinner, Samuel, *The Abrahamic Archetype: Conceptual and Historical Relationships between Judaism, Christianity and Islam.* London: Archetype Publishers, 2012.

Zwettler, Michael, "A Mantic Manifesto: The Sūra of 'The Poets' and the Qurʾānic Foundations of Prophetic Authority," in Kugel, *Poetry and Prophecy*, pp. 75–119, 205–231.

⁎ Index ⁎

Jews, Christians, and Muslims from the Ancient to the Modern World

Imperialism And Jewish Society, 200 B.C.E. To 640 C.E. by Seth Schwartz

A Shared World: Christians and Muslims in the Early Modern Mediterranean by Molly Greene

Beautiful Death: Jewish Poetry and Martyrdom in Medieval France by Susan L. Einbinder

Power in the Portrayal: Representations of Jews and Muslims in Eleventh- and Twelfth-Century Islamic Spain by Ross Brann

Mirror of His Beauty: Feminine Images of God from the Bible to the Early Kabbalah by Peter Schäfer

In the Shadow of the Virgin: Inquisitors, Friars, and Conversos *in Guadalupe, Spain* by Gretchen D. Starr-LeBeau

The Curse of Ham: Race and Slavery in Early Judaism, Christianity, and Islam by David M. Goldenberg

Resisting History: Historicism and Its Discontents in German-Jewish Thought by David N. Myers

Mothers and Children: Jewish Family Life in Medieval Europe by Elisheva Baumgarten

A Jewish Renaissance in Fifteenth-Century Spain by Mark D. Meyerson

The Handless Maiden: Moriscos and the Politics of Religion in Early Modern Spain by Mary Elizabeth Perry

Poverty and Charity in the Jewish Community of Medieval Egypt by Mark R. Cohen

Reckless Rites: Purim and the Legacy of Jewish Violence by Elliott Horowitz

Living Together, Living Apart: Rethinking Jewish-Christian Relations in the Middle Ages by Jonathan Elukin

The Church in the Shadow of the Mosque: Christians and Muslims in the World of Islam by Sidney H. Griffith

The Religious Enlightenment: Protestants, Catholics, and Jews from London to Vienna by David Sorkin

American Evangelicals in Egypt: Missionary Encounters in an Age of Empire by Heather J. Sharkey

Maimonides in His World: Portrait of a Mediterranean Thinker by Sarah Stroumsa

The Scandal of Kabbalah: Leon Modena, Jewish Mysticism, Early Modern Venice by Yaacob Dweck

Artists and Craftsmen: Jewish and Christian Cultural Exchange in the Medieval Marketplace by Jacob Shatzmiller

The Bible in Arabic: The Scriptures of the "People of the Book" in the Language of Islam by Sidney H. Griffith